ROTH FAMILY FOUNDATION

Music in America Imprint

Michael P. Roth

and Sukey Garcetti

have endowed this

imprint to honor the

memory of their parents,

Julia and Harry Roth,

whose deep love of music

they wish to share

with others.

The publisher and the University of California Press Foundation gratefully acknowledge the generous support of the Roth Family Foundation Imprint in Music, established by a major gift from Sukey and Gil Garcetti and Michael P. Roth.

The Jazz Bubble

The Jazz Bubble

Neoclassical Jazz in Neoliberal Culture

Dale Chapman

UNIVERSITY OF CALIFORNIA PRESS

University of California Press, one of the most
distinguished university presses in the United States,
enriches lives around the world by advancing scholarship
in the humanities, social sciences, and natural sciences. Its
activities are supported by the UC Press Foundation and
by philanthropic contributions from individuals and
institutions. For more information, visit www.ucpress.edu.

University of California Press
Oakland, California

Library of Congress Cataloging-in-Publication Data

Names: Chapman, Dale, author.
Title: The jazz bubble : neoclassical jazz in neoliberal
    culture / Dale Chapman.
Description: Oakland, California : University of
    California Press, [2018] | Includes bibliographical
    references and index. |
Identifiers: LCCN 2017043467 (print) | LCCN 2017048225
    (ebook) | ISBN 9780520968219 () | ISBN
    9780520279377 (cloth : alk. paper) | ISBN
    9780520279384 (pbk. : alk. paper)
Subjects: LCSH: Jazz—Economic aspects. | Jazz—History
    and criticism—20th century. | Jazz—Social aspects. |
    Sound recording industry—Economic aspects. |
    Music-halls (Variety-theaters, cabarets, etc.)—
    California—History. | Gordon, Dexter, 1923–1990. |
    Verve Records (Firm)—History. | Verve Music
    Group—History.
Classification: LCC ML3508 (ebook) | LCC ML3508 .C47
    2018 (print) | DDC 306.4/84250973—dc23
LC record available at https://lccn.loc.gov/2017043467

Manufactured in the United States of America

25 24 23 22 21 20 19 18
10 9 8 7 6 5 4 3 2 1

For my mother and father,
Elizabeth and Douglas Chapman,
with love and gratitude

Contents

Acknowledgments

One of the ironies inherent in writing a book about neoliberalism—about an ideology premised upon a culture of rugged individualism and ruthless atomization, in which we are all ostensibly to be left to our own devices—is that the process of writing a book demonstrates something like its opposite. The work that I've done here has come to fruition in large part owing to the vibrancy, creativity, and support provided by a community of scholarship and practice to which I feel honored to belong.

First, I am very fortunate to benefit from the support and generosity of my home institution of Bates College. Research for this book was completed under the auspices of the Whiting Teaching Fellowship at Bates College, funded by the Whiting Foundation, and through a Phillips Faculty Fellowship, made possible through the generosity of the Evelyn and Charles Phillips endowment. I am also grateful to staff in the Dean of Faculty's office at Bates, the Bates Academic Affairs Council, and to the assistance of Joseph Tomaras with external grant applications.

Research for this work would not have been possible without the thoughtful assistance of staff at numerous archives, libraries, and research institutions. I would like to express my appreciation to Edward Berger, Tad Hershorn, and Vincent Pelote at the Institute of Jazz Studies at Rutgers University Newark; to Sarah Moazeni at the Robert Wagner Labor Archives at NYU; to Mark Ekman at the Paley Center for Media; and to the archival and library staffs at the Schomburg Center for Research in Black Culture, the Performing Arts Library in the New

York Public Library system, the Center for Black Music Research at Columbia College, the Huntington Library, the Werner Josten Performing Arts Library at Smith College, and the Special Collections of the Charles E. Young Research Library at UCLA.

I am grateful to all those who assisted with copyright permissions for the book's images. I would like to thank jazz critic John McDonough for pointing me in the direction of useful resources. I am also immeasurably grateful to my Bates colleague and friend Christopher Schiff for his time and assistance, and for our conversations on matters extending from the jazz avant-garde to Montreal-style bagels.

Early versions of material from *The Jazz Bubble* have been presented at the Mediating Jazz Conference in Salford, England, in 2009, the annual meeting of the American Studies Association in 2010, and the annual meeting of the Society for American Music in 2013; my appreciation goes out to those who offered comments and suggestions on these presentations. I also owe a debt of gratitude to Eric Lott and to fellow participants of a workshop at the Futures of American Studies Institute at Dartmouth College in 2009, where my colleagues offered thoughtful criticism of early work for the project. I'm also grateful to Olufemi Vaughan and Tracy McMullen at Bowdoin College, who invited me to campus to present work from *The Jazz Bubble,* and I'm grateful to the students in Olufemi's seminar History of African and African Diaspora Political Thought for their singular engagement. Moreover, I'm thankful to Gail Woldu, Krin Gabbard, Richard Leppert, and the late Adam Krims, who took the time to read my work in their capacity as an external evaluation committee.

I am tremendously excited, and humbled, to be working with formidably talented scholars at the leading edge of jazz studies, musicology, and American studies. My sincere thanks go out to Scott DeVeaux, Dana Gooley, Travis Jackson, Aaron Johnson, Mark Laver, George Lewis, Paul Machlin, Tracy McMullen, Ben Piekut, Heather Pinson, Jason Robinson, Charles Sharp, Jeff Schwartz, Yoko Suzuki, Chris Wells, Tony Whyton, Pete Williams, and the many others who have provoked me to think about jazz and improvised music from new and engaging perspectives. I am also exceedingly fortunate to have had the opportunity to converse, commiserate, and collaborate with such compelling interlocutors as Byron Adams, Tim Anderson, Paul Attinello, Jacky Avila, Christina Baade, David Brackett, Seth Brodsky, Mark Burford, Charles Carson, Theo Cateforis, William Cheng, Richard Crawford, James Deaville, Will Fulton, Michael Gillespie, Mary Hunter,

Stephanie Jensen-Moulton, Charles Kronengold, Kendra Leonard, Richard Leppert, Kristin Lieb, Renee Lysloff, Fred Maus, Andrea Moore, John Pippen, Ivan Raykoff, Marianna Ritchey, Steve Swayne, Carol Vernallis, and Deborah Wong.

At Bates, I am extraordinarily fortunate to have colleagues of singular dedication and creativity, and I have benefited from our countless discussions and collaborations over the past decade and a half. Gina Fatone, Bill Matthews, James Parakilas, Laurie O'Higgins, Kirk Read, Charles Nero, and Val Carnegie read early versions of this work, and I am considerably indebted to their considered and attentive feedback. Particular thanks go to my colleagues in the interdisciplinary programs in African American Studies and American Cultural Studies, including Myron Beasley, Val Carnegie, Margaret Creighton, Hilmar Jensen, Baltasar Fra-Molinero, Sue Houchins, Eden Osucha, Therí Pickens, Mary Rice-DeFosse, and Josh Rubin, and to my co-conspirators in the Department of Music, including John Corrie, Gina Fatone, Bill Matthews, Hiroya Miura, and Tom Snow; I am very lucky to get to work with each of you. I am exceptionally grateful to Jim Parakilas for those many times when the two of us set aside course prep, paperwork, and the administrative minutiae of daily life to get into the weeds in a conversation about politics, music, or academia, and for his thoughtful, patient, and unstinting support throughout my early years at Bates. Finally, I am exceedingly indebted to my students at Bates College, who keep me curious, creatively galvanized, and productively provoked.

Our graduate cohorts in the Musicology program at UCLA benefited from extraordinary mentorship with an inimitably brilliant group of advisors, and I'm grateful to have been able to spend a few years in an environment whose intellectual vibrancy has left what continues to be an indelible imprint on my work as a scholar and teacher. I'm grateful to Raymond Knapp, Elizabeth LeGuin, Tamara Levitz, Mitchell Morris, and Elizabeth Upton, and to Roger Savage and Timothy Rice in the Department of Ethnomusicology, for your warmth, your intellectual generosity, and your unwavering support. My work over the years can in some sense be understood as the upshot of countless procrastinatory conversations in the office of Robert Fink; I am also indebted to Susan McClary's rigorous, elegant, and humane approach to musical scholarship, and to her generous advice and support. All these years later, I remain particularly indebted to my dissertation advisor Robert Walser: few scholars can explicate as lucidly as he does the sense that when we engage in deliberations over music, we are debating things that matter.

For these things, and for his patience and untiring advocacy, I am grateful beyond what words can say.

My intellectual community at UCLA was also the one that we students cultivated beyond the seminar room. For your feedback in our dissertation seminar, for our spirited arguments over pints, for your support at conferences throughout the years, and for your friendship, I will always be grateful to Cristian Amigo, David Ake, Kate Bartel, Steve Baur, Andrew Berish, David Borgo, Durrell Bowman, Olivia Carter Mather, Maria Cizmic, Andy Connell, Martin Daughtry, Kevin Delgado, Francesca Draughon, Lester Feder, Amy Frishkey, Charles Garrett, Daniel Goldmark, Jonathan Greenberg, Sara Gross Ceballos, Gordon Haramaki, Joseph Jenkins, Loren Kajikawa, James Kennaway, Erik Leidal, Neal Matherne, Christian Molstrom, Lisa Musca, Louis Niebur, Caroline O'Meara, Stephan Pennington, Glenn Pillsbury, Jonathan Ritter, Rossella Santagata, Erica Scheinberg, Charles Sharp, Cecilia Sun, Eric Usner, Stephanie Vander Wel, Jacqueline Warwick, and Larry Wayte.

I am especially grateful to the editorial staff of the University of California Press for providing a platform for me to tell this story, and to the anonymous readers whose critical engagement with my work has been galvanizing and inspiring, and has helped me to improve my project considerably. I am tremendously indebted to Mary Francis, who listened to a great many dubious ideas of mine over coffee at the conference book exhibits, and whose thoughtful and patient oversight of the project in its early stages was crucial in enabling me to arrive at a more compelling framing of the book's argument. I am also immensely thankful for the professionalism and support of Raina Polivka and Zuha Khan, who have assumed oversight of the project during its latter stages and whose lucid and thoughtful guidance have been invaluable as I set about completing the work.

I've dedicated this book to my mother and father, Elizabeth and Douglas Chapman, simply because their love and encouragement has made all else possible. They have heard repeatedly over the years that the book was nearing completion, and I'm so glad for them to see that this is finally true. It is hard to know how to thank them for the countless ways that their support has allowed me to flourish. Finally, I wish to thank my beloved partner Nancy for pretty much everything; her intelligence and sardonic wit are the indispensable counterpoint to my days.

Introduction

Banks, Bonds, and Blues

The Jazz Bubble proceeds from the idea that there is a story to be told about the relationship between jazz, culture, and contemporary financial capitalism. I argue that jazz may provide us with an unexpected avenue of approach as we seek to understand the cultural dynamics of neoliberal ideologies and institutions, in an era in which the volatility of the financial markets has come to inform the texture of everyday life. As a window onto the complex issues I aim to tackle here, I would like to begin here with a case study that in my view shows us, rather than telling us, why this line of inquiry is an important one.

On April 2, 2015, the New Orleans Jazz Orchestra, along with renowned jazz vocalist Dee Dee Bridgewater, performed on the opening night program for a new, jazz-specific concert venue, a gleaming minimalist facility located on the site of a former discount store in New Orleans's Central City. The People's Health New Orleans Jazz Market would serve as the new permanent home for NOJO, a group founded in 2002 by trumpeter Irvin Mayfield as an institutional base for the city's jazz community. NOJO received considerable attention in November 2005, when, at an emotional concert performed at Christ Church Cathedral, Mayfield and his group presided over the first high-profile cultural event held in New Orleans since the catastrophic events of Hurricane Katrina.[1] A little more than a decade following the calamity, the grand opening of the New Orleans Jazz Market put jazz to work as a powerful vector of social renewal in the same moment that it reaffirmed the city's symbolic place in the national imaginary.

However, viewed with a mind to the details, the context of the Jazz Market's establishment can tell us about those things that tend to elude the national imaginary in our cultural moment, about those invisible structural considerations that often reside just outside of our line of sight. The circumstances of the Jazz Market's creation can be understood as deriving from subtly pervasive tendencies in our contemporary alignments of culture and political economy. The funding portfolio that enabled the venue's development, for instance, indexes the increasingly prominent role that global finance capital is asked to play in the promotion of local cultural vibrancy: while the project benefits from a semipublic loan provided by the New Orleans Redevelopment Authority, in the amount of $800,000, the key line item in the project's realization was an infusion of $10 million in capital made available by the Urban Investment Group of Goldman Sachs.[2]

The participation of Goldman Sachs's Urban Investment Group in the development of the Jazz Market was made possible by way of a new financial instrument known as a "social impact bond." Social impact bonds enlist the private sector to bridge a gap between diminished local, state, and federal budgets on the one hand, and public policy challenges identified by state actors on the other: once a service provider identifies a tangible solution to a specific government priority, "impact investors" are brought on board to finance the costs of the project's realization.[3] The program relies upon a "pay-for-success" model, in which the achievement of agreed-upon metrics of "success," as assessed by an outside evaluator, determines whether or not impact investors see a return on their investment.[4]

In its public relations campaign for the Jazz Market initiative, Goldman Sachs has worked assiduously to ensure that the abstract mechanism of the social bond is translated into terms that are readily identifiable to audiences beyond the financial sector. In particular, a promotional video produced by the Urban Investment Group holds out the promise that the use of the mechanism to finance the new venue will facilitate the emergence of a formidable vector of cultural renewal in postmillenial New Orleans: As the camera settles on the Jazz Market's sleek façade, Irvin Mayfield, buttressed by Ronald Markham's rollicking gospel-inflected comping on the piano, settles into a simple, riff-based blues melody (see fig. 1). Their jam continues in the background as Mayfield describes the mission of the NOJO organization, delineating its com-

FIGURE 1. Exterior of the People's Health New Orleans Jazz Market, New Orleans. Photo by Infrogmation of New Orleans, Creative Commons Attribution 2.0 Generic License.

mitment to "enhance life, transform place, and elevate spirit." Following on from Mayfield's disquisition, Urban Investment Group managing director Margaret Anadu outlines the careful orchestration of municipal, state, and private-sector resources necessary for the realization of the Jazz Market project. Taken together, the video's sophisticated editing, elegant rhetoric, and ebullient musical supplement amount to a compelling celebration of the Jazz Market's transmutation of private capital into public space, its capacity for enacting Mayfield's notion that "great ideas can come from anywhere."[5]

Of course the story of the Jazz Market is more complex than Goldman Sachs's glowing promotional video profile might indicate. Among other things, local observers have raised concerns about the physical and economic footprint of the Jazz Market development within the Central City neighborhood of New Orleans, its potential to serve as a beachhead for unwanted gentrification. The New Orleans journalist Owen Courrèges has argued that the arrival of the Jazz Market in Central City should be understood against the backdrop of its predecessor on the same lot: Gator's Discount Store, founded in 1989 by the Cuban immigrant Gotardo Ortiz, had served as an "inexpensive source of general merchandise" in the context of a low-income neighborhood largely dependent upon such stores. For Courrèges, the replacement of the discount store by the more high-profile Jazz Market complex reflected an unfortunate shift in priorities for the city and its nonprofit sector, a sign of their unwillingness to privilege the needs of the area's existing residents over those of an anticipated constituency of affluent tourists.[6]

Perhaps most saliently for our purposes here, though, the significant role played by a leading investment bank in the financing of the Jazz Market project must be understood in terms of the distinctive structural and ideological contradictions that are potentially at work in any Wall Street cultivation of jazz communities. For one thing, the socially engaged, intensively *localized* posture assumed here by Goldman Sachs stands in marked contrast to the bank's documented role as a powerful agent of financial *deterritorialization,* singularly epitomizing the Marxian adage that "all that is solid melts into air." In the years leading up to the 2008 financial crisis, Goldman Sachs was one of the key intermediaries in the market in collateralized debt obligations (or CDOs). With CDOs, banks took thousands of mortgages initiated by commercial lenders and repackaged the debt in rated "tranches" of asset-backed securities, which were in turn sold on to pension funds and other institutional investors as revenue-generating instruments.[7] From the standpoint of its social impact, the key structural innovation of the collateralized debt obligation was the means through which it took the highly concrete, illiquid, and above all, *local* asset of the stand-alone single-family dwelling, and translated it into terms that could be trafficked within the highly delocalized and abstract confines of the global financial markets. One of the most disturbing ramifications of the crisis was the extent to which the lives of vulnerable individual borrowers were affected by large, impersonal market actors, operating at a distant remove from the "facts on the ground."

Seen against this backdrop, Goldman Sachs's new interest in the concrete particulars of built environments, and in the communities that inhabit them, is a striking development, one that some market observers have received with a degree of skepticism. In part, their skepticism derives from an analysis of the structural assumptions latent within the design of social impact bonds: as one nonprofit executive has argued, the widespread advocacy of this financial instrument "trains the capital markets and social investors to expect maximum, easily measureable financial return on efforts to solve all social problems," applying excessively neat metrics of success to the messy arena of social policy.[8] It trains us, in essence, to believe that philanthropy is ultimately inseparable from the domain of profit seeking.[9] Speaking about his institution's involvement in social impact investing, Lloyd Blankfein, CEO of Goldman Sachs, does attribute an element of altruism to the initiative, but he ultimately frames it less as an expression of "pure" philanthropy than as an unorthodox site of "value creation" for investors.[10]

An important part of the context here is the fact that such projects as the Jazz Market initiative, or the introduction of "social bonds" in general, are frequently seen as efforts on the part of the investment banks to ameliorate the optics of their hegemonic position within the global economy, particularly in the wake of the 2008 financial crisis.[11] Consequently, Goldman Sachs's effort to harness jazz as a powerful conduit of community building may strike us as a particularly sophisticated attempt, on the part of the bank, to reposition itself as *grounded,* as tangibly invested in the fates of ordinary urbanites: faced with an narrative that paints Wall Street's major investment banks as vehicles of rapacious wealth extraction—deracinated entities wholly unrestrained by conceptions of place, belonging, and social responsibility—Goldman Sachs has turned its attention to what is arguably that most "rooted" of American musical legacies, harnessing the blues collectivity of the "second line" as a resonant tool of public relations.

NEOCLASSICAL JAZZ IN THE ERA OF NEOLIBERAL IDEOLOGIES

The prominent role played by finance capital in the establishment of the People's Health New Orleans Jazz Market provides us with an intriguing perspective upon the political economy of jazz in the early twenty-first century. Moreover, the various attributes of the deal, its complicated distillation of a range of themes—the urban dynamics of corporate-driven gentrification; the unexpected role of financial securitization in the financing of a local jazz venue; the reflexive invocation of jazz as a catalyst for economic growth; the contradictory role of profit seeking in twenty-first-century philanthropy—suggest that the political economy of jazz has a great deal to tell us about the interconnections between culture, ideology, and socioeconomic conditions in an era of ascendant finance capital. It is these ideas that I take up in *The Jazz Bubble,* where I look to demonstrate that jazz can serve as a powerful interpretive lens for our understanding of trends in late twentieth- and early twenty-first-century capitalism.

In approaching this topic, my focus is a cluster of stylistic trends in the postmodern jazz world that goes by the name of *neoclassicism*.[12] The term neoclassicism has in large part come to refer to a musically conservative, stylistically traditionalist revival in the jazz world, with its most vocal advocates celebrating a very specific range of aesthetic choices in the music. Both on and off the bandstand, the neoclassicists promote a music that emphasizes "straightahead" swing feel, adherence to conventional blues-based and popular song forms, the use of primarily acoustic instrumentation, and the privileging of a stylistic vocabulary that extends (roughly) from New Orleans polyphony through to 1960s postbop.[13]

Postbop in particular serves as a crucial antecedent for the stylistic approach of the neoclassicists, with the renowned 1960s Miles Davis Quintet laying out an aesthetic template of "controlled freedom" that would be emulated by such later artists as Wynton Marsalis, Kenny Kirkland, Terence Blanchard, and Jeff "Tain" Watts. The neoclassicist sensibility is also heavily indebted to a blues-inflected hard-bop sound associated with the Blue Note label during the 1950s and 1960s: in the 1990s recordings of Roy Hargrove, the Harper Brothers, or Benny Green, we hear echoes of the midcentury Blue Note roster, as reflected in the music of Lee Morgan, Art Blakey's Jazz Messengers, and others. Historically, the neotraditionalist moment is often seen as beginning in earnest in the late 1970s, when one of those classic Blue Note artists, the expatriate tenorist Dexter Gordon (then residing in Copenhagen) returned to New York for a crucial series of engagements at the Storyville club and the Village Vanguard. Gordon's stateside return took place in the middle of a minor boom in bebop and straightahead jazz in New York, with artists such as Barry Harris, Woody Shaw, and the band VSOP (made up of the legendary rhythm section from Miles Davis's mid-1960s quintet) building a groundswell of interest for bebop, hard bop, and postbop sensibilities. In the early 1980s, jazz A&R executive George Butler signed Wynton Marsalis, Branford Marsalis, Terence Blanchard, and Donald Harrison to Columbia Records: all four artists were dynamic, very young musicians from New Orleans, many of them having studied at the prestigious New Orleans Center for the Creative Arts. Wynton Marsalis, in particular, became the spokesman for a conception of jazz culture that jealously guarded the boundaries of its stylistic legacy and musical canon.[14]

In *The Jazz Bubble,* I look to situate this neoclassicist jazz movement in relation to the socioeconomic moment that it inhabits in American culture. For some time, jazz scholars have been attentive to the relationship between music and political economy: in contexts ranging from Scott DeVeaux's study of bebop as a niche-market response to the swing industry, to Aaron Johnson's groundbreaking work on the institutional history of jazz radio, jazz scholars have engaged in work that recognizes the intimate relationship between jazz practices and the socioeconomic conditions that they inhabit.[15] This intimate relation extends beyond the strictly material circumstances of market exchange, encompassing the field of representations and cultural meanings as well: in album cover art, in car commercials, and in the performative dimensions of the music itself, jazz has long been intertwined with the libidinal economies of consumer culture, and this interrelation has been the subject of a vital range of scholarship.[16]

At the same time, jazz studies inhabits a larger interdisciplinary context in which musicologists, ethnomusicologists, and scholars in cognate fields have sought to develop new lines of inquiry regarding the relationship between musical practices on the one hand, and the ideological and structural dimensions of market economies on the other. In this connection, we could look to Adam Krims's groundbreaking work on the cultural geography of popular music, with its nuanced account of music's relation to post-Fordism (in which new technologies and social practices have reshaped the rigid, hierarchical structures of mass production), or Timothy Taylor's account of the operation of contemporary music industries within the cultural logic of neoliberal capitalism.[17]

Scholarly investigation of the relationship between music and political economy takes on a new urgency in the early decades of the twenty-first century, as we confront the ongoing turbulence of quotidian life under the neoliberal regime of accumulation. Neoliberalism, depending upon the context, can either be used to designate a prescriptive theory of political economy, or a descriptive account of the ideological, socio-cultural, and material transformations that have governed life in the globalized economy since the late 1970s.[18] In the first instance, it may be defined as a theory of political economy in which the state is enjoined to maximize individual freedom, by cultivating an environment in which the market is cut loose from government restrictions or impediments to growth. In David Harvey's critical formulation, neoliberal theory holds that "human well-being can best be advanced by liberating individual entrepreneurial freedoms and skills within an institutional framework characterized by strong private property rights, free markets, and free trade. The role of the state is to create and preserve an institutional framework appropriate to such practices."[19]

From this perspective, the theories of neoliberalism advocated by such figures as Friedrich Hayek outline a set of radical policy measures to be implemented by the state. In this respect, the rise of Margaret Thatcher and Ronald Reagan at the close of the 1970s figures as a defining moment in the history of neoliberalism, with the two leaders moving quickly to establish conditions congenial to Hayek's social vision. By the mid-1980s, Reagan and Thatcher had moved to implement tight controls on monetary policy (initially begun under Jimmy Carter's watch), to take aggressive new measures against organized labor, to roll back tax rates on the wealthy, and to loosen regulatory control in a number of industries.[20]

These overarching structural interventions by the state work in tandem with a more ideological set of interventions, inculcated at the level of ideas, sensibilities, and subjective experience.[21] The individual subject of neoliberal theory conceives of herself as an *enterprise of one,* an autonomous actor who deploys her "human capital" to the best advantage in a competitive marketplace made up of many other individual "entrepreneurs": each such atomized subject is enjoined to maneuver, with nimble virtuosity, through the volatile environment of a market-centered culture. Within this ideological framework, every decision undertaken at the most intimate level of social experience becomes bound up within a market logic, as each "*homo economicus*" maximizes her value in relation to other atomized actors.[22] The culture of neoliberalism is one whose every gesture is potentially subject to the mechanisms of exchange and ultimately held up to metrics of performance.

Indeed, to return for a moment to our opening example, the pervasiveness of market-centered ideologies in contemporary American culture, with their celebration of heroic individualism, their privileging of dexterous risk taking in turbulent environs, and their insistence on a ubiquitous and absolute contractual logic at the core of all social relations, may help us to make sense of such developments as the Goldman Sachs partnership with the New Orleans Jazz Market, through the questions they raise about the strange bedfellows whom the project brings together. For instance: Why jazz? Why are state and corporate actors in the postmillenial era particularly attached to jazz as a site of urban philanthropy, as evidenced by the development of lavishly financed jazz performing arts centers in New Orleans, San Francisco, Los Angeles, and New York?[23] Why, decades after the peak of the music's commercial heyday, do market actors continue to bullishly embrace an idea of jazz that is in some sense difficult to square with the genre's own well-established market underperformance?[24]

NEOCLASSICISM IN JAZZ

Straightforward answers to such questions are not readily available, of course, but one potential springboard for our inquiries is to consider the *kind* of jazz that has proven to be so resonant to the music's boosters in corporate, nonprofit, educational, and governmental institutions since the 1980s. I provide here a brief genealogy of neoclassicism as a term of art in jazz critical discourses, in order to understand the shifting valence of the genre's identity and its changing signification for institutional observers.

Despite the common usage of "neoclassicism" as a shorthand for the stylistic orientation of Marsalis, Blanchard, Marcus Roberts, and many of the early 1990s "young lions" (alongside the programming orientation of Jazz at Lincoln Center), it is important to note that discourses of neo-classicist jazz used to encompass a more stylistically catholic range of musics. In the early 1980s, as often as not, the term was used to describe a crucial subset of the jazz avant-garde that had integrated a posture of robust engagement with earlier stylistic moments (New Orleans polyphony, swing, bebop, hard bop) into its vision of experimental improvisation. Shortly after joining the vibrant SoHo "loft jazz" scene in New York in the mid-1970s, Arthur Blythe, an alto saxophonist from Los Angeles, began to establish himself with powerful interpretations of jazz standards viewed through the lens of free improvisation. His Columbia Records albums from the late 1970s, *Lenox Avenue Breakdown* and *In the Tradition,* made him the first loft artist to obtain a major-label contract.[25] Tenor saxophonist David Murray, who had also been active in the improvised music avant-garde in Los Angeles, moved to New York around the same time; his decision to reject his contemporaries' preoccupation with John Coltrane, and to integrate the warm ebullience of such swing tenorists as Ben Webster and Coleman Hawkins into his playing, garnered the praise of the jazz critical establishment.[26] In the wake of Wynton Marsalis's subsequent musical prominence, and in light of his movement's general hostility toward the avant-garde tradition from whence Murray and Blythe derived, we need to remind ourselves that, in 1985, an article by Larry Kart could refer to Marsalis, Blythe, and Murray in the same breath, positioning this more capacious vision of "neoclassicism" (which also could be said to describe such artists as Henry Threadgill, Muhal Richard Abrams, or Lester Bowie) as the emerging future of the music.[27]

It is noteworthy that the career of Stanley Crouch, a onetime black nationalist who rose to become a key interlocutor in the more conservative musical vision of Jazz at Lincoln Center, bridges the two musical moments invoked by the term neoclassicism. In the 1970s, Crouch's vision sought to reconcile aspects of black vernacular traditions with the politics and aesthetics of the post-1960s avant-garde. When Crouch arrived in New York, following years of affiliation with UGMAA and other facets of the Los Angeles improvised music scene, the writer became an advocate of fellow new arrivals Murray and Blythe (both of whom were close friends of Crouch on the West Coast, and musical collaborators), celebrating their tendency to embrace what he saw as the structural discipline of conventional jazz forms, as opposed to the more free-form textures of New York "energy music" in the post-Coltrane, post–Albert Ayler vein.[28]

By the close of the 1970s, Crouch had moved on from this largely latent strain of aesthetic conservatism to a more overt political *and* aesthetic conservatism, as was dramatized through a raucous and bitter debate between Crouch and his onetime mentor Amiri Baraka in the *Village Voice* in 1979.[29] For his part, Crouch attributes his sudden break with the black musical and intellectual avant-garde to his friendship with Albert Murray, whose book *The Omni-Americans: Black Experience and American Life* challenged a variety of 1960s-era orthodoxies, from the negative post-Moynihan social scientific discourses about black life to the devaluation of black middle-class experience in black Marxist and black nationalist analyses.[30] What Crouch embraced in Murray's work was its tendency, following Ralph Ellison, to understand black vernacular expression as central to the promise of American exceptionalism: jazz is to be understood as a black tradition bound up in a fundamentally *American* tradition of cultural ferment, rather than as a counterhegemonic site of resistance to Americanism itself. With respect to musical style, this approach saw Crouch and Murray hewing to an increasingly traditionalist conception of the jazz tradition, understood now *as* a single tradition bound to a narrowly linear trajectory of development. This conception of jazz and African-American culture would become a key point of reference for Wynton Marsalis's discursive interventions as a public advocate for jazz from the 1990s onward.[31]

This period in Stanley Crouch's intellectual life serves as a useful window through which to approach the variegated meanings of "neoclassicism" in the 1980s and 1990s. Initially, for many artists and critics in this period, the retrospective gaze of jazz in the 1970s and early 1980s could encompass an expansive palette of stylistic gestures, from New Orleans polyphony and big band swing on the one hand, to the timbral densities and rhythmic complexities of the "New Thing" on the other. For writers such as Gary Giddins and Joachim Berendt, this historical inclusivity was at the core of what it meant to refer to neoclassical jazz. By the early 1990s, though, references to neoclassical, "neobop," or even "neo-con" jazz (in which a political implication is more than latent) tended to refer to a much more tightly circumscribed range of musics, with such potential stylistic points of reference as jazz-rock fusion, the post-1960s jazz avant-garde, or contemporary No Wave kept meticulously away from the music's studied historicism.[32]

What accounts for this shift in the basic contours of "neoclassicism" as a jazz movement? There is unquestionably a political analogy here: the broader cultural moment that attended the emergence and growth of jazz neoclassicism was one of increasing political polarization, as Ronald Reagan and his allies in the conservative movement sought to channel the polyglot ecumenicalism of American public discourse into a set of reductive moral binaries, positioning women, people of color, and LGBTQ people as adversaries in their efforts to remake the social compact.[33] This Manichean dimension of conservatism, its pitting of a valorized identity or tradition against encroachment from without, serves as a suggestive template for certain aspects of the neoclassicist project. I will return to this point later on; for the moment, it is perhaps sufficient to point out the ways in which the Marsalis-Crouch conception of neoclassicism, more than the more pluralistic, hybrid, and eclectic understanding of neoclassical jazz attributed to figures such as Arthur Blythe and David Murray, resonates with the rigid binaries of the conservative worldview in certain carefully limited respects.

At the same time, we should recognize that the recalibration of the jazz aesthetics of young performers during this period was, as often as not, informed by the attractive pull of market trends, as institutional and commercial pressures steered them in the direction of prevailing stylistic sensibilities. In the context of the neoclassical revival, one factor, unquestionably, was the emergence and popularity of CD reissues of older jazz recordings in the late 1980s and early 1990s, a trend which provided a new space for emerging artists to emulate the repertory and stylistic gestures of classic midcentury releases from Verve or Blue Note.[34] What was as important here, though, as any specific music that young artists sought to emulate was the *mode of interpretation* they brought to the task. For Ronald Radano, observing the emerging neoclassicist trend on the cusp of the 1990s, a key feature of neoclassicism was its valorization of a highly simplified template for cultural interpretation: "Where the neoclassical model goes wrong, however, is in its presumption of telling the whole story of jazz. No need for charting the complexities of the past, it would seem, for neoclassicism, recast as a mode of interpretation, now supplies all the answers. Important countermovements fall by the wayside; notable challenges recede into a clutter of ancillary diversions."[35] From a market-oriented perspective, of course, what Radano describes as the place where "the neoclassical model goes wrong" is perhaps also the place where the music, together with its metanarrative, accomplishes precisely what it sets out to do. What the stripped-down, reductionist historicism of neoclassicism achieves is to render itself *legible,* to bracket those components that might inhibit the intelligibility of its brand; it is to make the music market-worthy by, in Tracy McMullen's words, "presenting jazz in easily digestible consumables."[36] Speaking of the Jazz at Lincoln Center program, Farah Jasmine Griffin makes the point that, "had Marsalis not struck such a conservative stance, whereby some of the most innovative practitioners are left out of the jazz canon, it is highly unlikely he would have been able to acquire the resources necessary to do the kind of work on behalf of the music that he has done."[37] For Griffin, the aesthetic conservatism of Marsalis's vision of jazz has made it legible to those individuals and institutions who might otherwise have been skeptical about reviving such a transgressive musical legacy, originating from such a culturally charged site of identity.

THE JAZZ METAPHOR

In the late 1990s, Matthew Shipp, a groundbreaking pianist affiliated with a sphere of "out" jazz operating at a remove from neoclassicist ideals, identified what he saw as the problem with the interpretive lens put forth by Wynton Marsalis and Jazz at Lincoln Center:

> I'm not into the Jazz at Lincoln Center scene at all. They're trying to make jazz legitimate, and I think the good thing about anything good is that it's *illegitimate.* Charlie Parker and Thelonious Monk were illegitimate when they came along. If somebody's going to come up with an idea like Monk's— "I've got a way of playing the piano that's *new*"—that can't be dressed up in a way that's going to be good for people with funding to get immediately; it's going take years. That's instantly a problem for Lincoln Center. But you can't make creativity legitimate. You just can't do it.[38]

For Shipp, the institutional heft of Jazz at Lincoln Center renders it a kind of philanthropic oil tanker, unable to respond to the innovations of the music as they unfold in the immediacy of cultural ferment. A key irony here is that, even as the conservatism of neoclassicism has rendered jazz palatable for the consumption of large institutional actors by putting a brake on innovation, what these actors see reflected in jazz neoclassicism is precisely a quality of nimble, dynamic, and democratic innovation that they would like to see in themselves.

What institutions might be particularly receptive to the vision outlined by Marsalis, and what would they wind up doing with it? Contemporary jazz scholars have offered particularly interesting answers to this latter question, highlighting discourses that foreground the frequently contradictory fascination of the private sector with a certain idea of jazz. Mark Laver and Ken Prouty have drawn attention to the peculiar circulation of jazz metaphors in the field of management theory, where the music is called upon to model a disposition of extemporaneous, quicksilver mobility that individuals, business units, and corporate organizations might seek to emulate in the face of market uncertainty. Laver rightly goes on to note that this trend amounts to nothing less than an enlistment of jazz performance as a flattering analogy for the strategic and interpersonal dynamics of corporations under the neoliberal regime of accumulation.[39]

All analogies are only partial, though, and some analogies are more partial than others, more susceptible to distortion. It is crucial to note that, with rare exceptions, the "jazz metaphor" in management consulting rarely extends further than the edge of the bandstand: if organizational theorists and management theorists are endlessly fascinated with the playful, volatile interactions of musicians in the act of performing, they almost never consider the jazz musician as an economic actor in his or her own right, an "enterprise of one" whose steady pursuit of piecemeal, contingent labor resembles nothing so much as the independent contractor of the contemporary "gig economy."[40] The problem for corporate celebrants of the "jazz metaphor" is that such an interpretive move shifts jazz from the field of exuberant play to the much more concrete domain of material consequences: to consider the economic agency of the freelance musician as a component of their jazz metaphor is, perhaps, to scrutinize too closely the ways in which economic precariousness figures into the experience of the neoliberal subject.

That jazz should be interpreted as a metaphor for business is perhaps not surprising, given that the music has frequently been positioned as a powerful microcosm of American exceptionalism. In a tradition dating back to the State Department tours of the early Cold War, which prominently featured such musicians as Dizzy Gillespie and Duke Ellington as "jazz ambassadors," the music has been deployed as a performative embodiment of an American "freedom" that ostensibly transcended social and racial boundaries.[41] More recently, the neoclassicist rhetoric of Crouch, Murray, and Marsalis teaches us about how the music exemplifies the productive tension between the individual and the collective in democratic societies; about the ways in which American culture, following Ralph Ellison, may be conceived of as uniquely "jazz-shaped"; about how jazz, in an intriguing sleight of hand, may be seen simultaneously as distinctively American and culturally universal.[42] It is not difficult to find fault with this line of argument, to problematize the easy collapsing of jazz values with those of the American nation-state: after all, African-American jazz artists have often defined themselves in opposition to the more self-congratulatory accounts of American democracy, and have themselves often been subjected to its least democratic impulses. Moreover, numerous observers have argued that the very same nation-state that is celebrated for its "jazz-shaped" dynamism and inclusivity has engaged in practices (racist, patriarchal, neo-imperialist) that belie its claims to democratic virtue.[43] Nevertheless, the efficacy of this jazz-centered narrative of American exceptionalism has been remarkably difficult to dislodge.

Given that state and private-sector actors have long encouraged a kind of ideological slippage between the celebration of democratic values and the promotion of market logics, it was perhaps inevitable that the well-established trope of a "jazz-shaped" democracy would be repurposed as a straightforward account of the music's metaphorical resemblance to the dynamics of late capitalism itself. Indeed, Laver's recent work on JALC's efforts to establish an institutional beachhead in Doha, Qatar, highlights the elegant fluidity with which the organization's rhetoric collapses distinctions between American democratic governance and free-market economics.[44] A side effect of these collapsed distinctions is an oft-noted *rebranding* of jazz, a reinvention of its imagery that aligns the music with the priorities of an upper-middle class (and usually male) subjectivity: in print ads and television spots that sell Movado watches and Infiniti sedans to affluent professionals, a taste for jazz is frequently, if tacitly, linked to the privileged upmarket subjectivities of the neoliberal workforce.[45]

THE FINANCIALIZATION OF AMERICAN CULTURE

These analyses, alongside the aforementioned scholarly treatments of "the jazz metaphor" in business consulting and management theory, attend to the ways in which the music can be brought to bear in our understanding of neoliberal ideology. Important as it is, though, this *ideological* component of neoliberalism, as I noted earlier, must be understood in terms of the ways that it supplements a broader set of *structural* considerations, those elements of the infrastructure and phenomenology of contemporary global markets that characterize the neoliberal regime of accumulation. What is indispensable in discussions of the efficacy of neoliberal modalities of thought is the sense in which it has mobilized a set of market structures that we can call *financialization.*

In a working paper from 2001, Gerald Epstein defined financialization as a term that helps to illuminate "the increasing importance of financial markets, financial motives, financial institutions, and financial elites in the operation of the economy and its governing institutions, both at the national and international level."[46] We may locate the effects of financialization throughout the entirety of the contemporary economy: at the level of the financial sector itself, financialization manifests in contexts as divergent as the trade in financial derivatives (instruments that speculate on the anticipated price movement of an underlying asset); asset securitization (the repackaging of interest-bearing loans as securities tradable on the financial markets); corporate restructuring (in which companies are reorganized to precipitate increases in "shareholder value"); and leveraged buyouts (in which private-equity firms harness the "leverage" of debt to acquire and restructure companies, also in the pursuit of improved pricing of shares).[47] At the same time, the financialization of the consumer economy has inscribed the mechanisms of credit, debt, and financial risk at the core of everyday social practice. One index of these changes can be found in the financial services units of conventional manufacturing firms such as General Electric, whose profitability as lenders made them increasingly central to the business models of their parent companies.[48] We might also look here to the aggressive marketing of payday loans, subprime mortgages, and other such high-risk financial products to low-income consumers.[49] All of these developments are underwritten by a set of recently established cultural proclivities that Randy Martin has identified as the "financialization of daily life," the sense in which habits of "risk management" now extend beyond the confines of the executive boardroom to encompass the intimate domain of the nuclear family.[50]

The rise of financialization has precipitated fundamental changes in the structural dynamics of American institutions. For instance, the resurgence of the financial markets in the 1980s was an important factor in the ascendency of *shareholder value* as the overriding priority of public corporations: if midcentury American companies had sought to address a range of stakeholders, establishing strong relationships between management and labor, these same companies came to adopt a remarkably different strategic orientation in the closing decades of the twentieth century, as market observers came to position stock valuation as the lone metric of financial performance. In this new environment, cost cutting at major corporations, accomplished by way of labor downsizing and corporate restructuring, became a kind of performative measure, executed for the benefit of the investor class.

The logic of financialization has also manifested itself in more immediately tangible ways, as for example with its dramatic impact upon the physical topography of American cities. David Harvey has noted that the social transformations wrought under the contemporary dynamics of capitalism derive much of their impact from what he calls *uneven geographical development,* the asymmetrical spatial distribution of power and resources across disparate communities, states, and regions.[51] In our present moment, financial capital must be seen as a key protagonist in that process of unequal dissemination. For instance, the new centrality of the so-called FIRE sector (that is, its finance, insurance, and real estate) in New York since the 1960s was a development that benefited from the restructuring of economies at both the local and global levels, and that had important ramifications for those economies in turn. New "global cities" such as New York, London, and Tokyo emerged to serve as command centers for a global economy that required the easy circulation of flows of global capital on the one hand, and the coordination of distantly located industrial centers on the other.[52]

At the local level, these changes precipitated the emergence of property, taxation, and development regimes that would cater more exclusively to the outsized economic growth of the FIRE sector in New York.[53] Within the boundaries of New York City, this meant the city would see the relative devaluation of its manufacturing sector and a concomitant rise in a low-wage consumer-service sector, even as skyrocketing property values would make the city unaffordable to the majority of its inhabitants.[54] Beyond the confines of the five boroughs, the implications of these changes were more dramatic still, as speculative re-allocations of capital in New York came to undermine the economic viability of erstwhile manufacturing centers such as Buffalo, Youngstown, Pittsburgh, and Detroit.[55]

The deindustrialization of Rust Belt cities foregrounds the ways in which race factors into the contemporary political economy of "creative destruction." At a fundamental level, uneven geographical development in the United States is informed by legacies of white supremacy and structural racism, legacies that were themselves bound up in a long-standing logic of "accumulation by dispossession." Ta-Nehisi Coates has argued that "the heritage of white supremacy was not so much birthed by hate as by the *impulse towards plunder*."[56] This impulse toward plunder underwrites the emergence and formalization of racialized practices at the heart of the transatlantic slave trade; it informs the complex legal and economic mechanisms of dispossession that shaped African-American experiences in the decades between the end of Reconstruction and the passage of the Civil Rights and Voting Rights Acts; it tacitly informs, too, the ostensibly race-neutral procedures that shape differential access to support networks and upward mobility in our present era. The impulse toward plunder is an old one: it derives from a logic at the core of settler colonialism and its confrontation with indigenous and enslaved peoples, the sense in which, according to Patrick Wolfe, "settler colonialism *destroys to replace*." This logic informs many of the episodes that will be taken up in the pages that follow: in contexts ranging from the utility of a municipal fiscal crisis as a pretext for altering the compact between capital and labor, or the use of eminent domain to flatten an existing community and make room for developers, the long shadow of earlier regimes of accumulation are at work.[57]

The emergence and consolidation of neoliberalism takes place in the decades immediately following the passage of the Civil Rights and Voting Rights Acts, and the demise of more explicit forms of race-based discrimination; the moment when the market becomes the measure of all things coincides with the rise of a new language of race-neutral meritocracy. This fact may lead us to believe that a more judicious socioeconomic dispensation has taken hold, that the value of our entrepreneurial selves is judged according to scrupulously fair-minded metrics of performance. However, what has in fact occurred, in this era of "racism without racists," is that the application of racist discrimination has simply shifted to other, less visible registers of social interaction. In housing, education, finances, health care, and the law, discriminatory bias continues to operate by covert means, perpetuating inequities that took root under earlier and less circumspect systems of racialized oppression. In such contexts as the criminal justice system, new legal mechanisms, alongside the uneven application of old ones, have become vehicles for the continuation of long-standing practices of exclusion: felony convictions, disproportionately applied to young men of color, provide public and private institutions with a legal pretext for denial of housing, political disenfranchisement, and employment discrimination.[58] In many instances, these new mechanisms of discrimination receive assistance from contemporary market logics. Aggressive law-enforcement postures in predominantly African-American communities often turn out to be driven by revenue models dependent upon frequent traffic citations, the liberal application of fee assessments, and the use of bench warrants to enforce these financial measures through the threat of incarceration.[59] Even while such market-informed practices continue to reinforce structures of racial inequality established under earlier social conditions, though, it is important to note that the installation of neoliberal modes of governmentality has in some sense also "democratized" the exposure of ordinary Americans to economic precarity, with declining wages, increased personal debt loads, and other sources of economic insecurity becoming facts of life for an ever-increasing number of Americans.[60]

NEOCLASSICAL JAZZ, THE CULTURE WARS, AND FANTASIES OF LIQUIDITY

And so it becomes clear that the contextual framework of neoliberal ideology, brought together with the emergent structural logics of financialization, provides us with a useful point of departure for our understanding of numerous aspects of contemporary American culture. But at this point it would be helpful, for our purposes, to return to the same question that I asked earlier regarding the Goldman Sachs involvement in the New Orleans Jazz Market: Why jazz? Why does this book seek to hold up jazz for special scrutiny as an interlocutor in our examination of the structural and cultural dimensions of twenty-first-century capitalism?

In my view, one of the most compelling reasons to pursue this line of inquiry resides in the profound contradictions that characterize American culture's current relationship with jazz. Many decades after the peak of the music's popularity, as the music's streaming figures and chart performance linger near the bottom of industry statistical rankings, official culture has belatedly repurposed jazz as an emblem of populist dynamism. Perhaps more importantly, even though the music's claims to moral transgression or political subversiveness have generally lost their purchase in mainstream American culture in recent decades, the nation's most powerful institutions claim to recognize themselves in the music's playful boldness, its performative realization of risk, its willingness to mobilize practices of "disruptive innovation." This latter trope circulates well beyond the perimeter of the jazz world proper, its numerous variants articulated at roundtables convened with ex-presidents; among thought leaders at TED talks; before global dignitaries at the Davos World Economic Forum.[61]

The ease with which such "thought leaders" have appropriated jazz as a metaphor for institutional risk taking may be attributed in part to the utility of certain *kinds* of jazz in making this point. Both the renewed interest in jazz as a metaphor for democracy as well as the emergent interest in jazz as a private-sector organizational metaphor coincide with the rise of neoclassical jazz in the late 1980s and early 1990s. To understand the potential appeal of neoclassicism as a point of departure for jazz-centered organizational analogies, we might begin with the terms of the structural analogy itself. In particular, it is noteworthy that, particularly in the first decade of its emergence, artists devoted to neoclassicism have often proceeded from a set of stylistic approaches that Herbie Hancock refers to as *controlled freedom*. What is at stake in controlled freedom is the allowance for wide harmonic and rhythmic latitude within a framework that still insists, however loosely, upon bop-derived metrical and formal structures. Such an approach is particularly appealing for theorists who wish to describe organizational practices that are themselves held in tension between nimble maneuverability on the one hand, and clear organizational constraints on the other. Along the same lines, the jazz pedagogies that have emerged in the wake of the neoclassical revival are often (though by no means always) invested in a largely rule-bound and technically prescriptive understanding of jazz practices, one in keeping with the movement's privileging of bebop-centered stylistic conventions. This sense in which jazz neoclassicism understands itself as a freedom shaped by rules has frequently been seen as attractive for those looking to translate contemporary jazz into the terms of business-centered analogies, given that it suggests the ways that modern corporations always walk the line between strategic flexibility and rigorous standards of performance.[62]

For the private sector in the 1980s and 1990s, the utility of jazz neoclassicism as a point of departure for thinking through the strategic dynamics of market procedures was also supplemented by its utility as a touchstone for certain kinds of social values. The success of market financialization since the 1980s has at least tacitly relied upon a theory of the subject that seeks to retroactively explain, in essence, the distinguishing characteristics of the market's "winners" and "losers." Randy Martin accounts for this approach in terms of what he sees as an institutionally sanctioned distinction between *at-risk* and *risk-capable* subjectivities: borrowing their logic from processes of securitization in the financial sector, school systems, credit-reporting bureaus, health care providers, and government agencies all increasingly define citizens in terms of their risk exposure, as well as their potential to perform or underperform. Even while such metrics reveal factors that may be largely outside of their subjects' hands (belonging to a "high risk" group vulnerable to specific maladies, or living in a neighborhood where hazards are unusually common), the designation of "at risk" nevertheless becomes a kind of stigma, retroactively applied, a judgment that is read back onto the individual whose vulnerabilities it purports to identify:

> Risk is not unilateral but operates as a kind of moral binary, sorting out the good from the bad on the basis of capacities to contribute. . . . Those who cannot manage themselves, those unable to live by risk, are considered "at risk." . . . Those who are subject to risk, as opposed to those who can make of it a subjectivity, are treated to various modes of domestic violence or wars. Unlike the War on Poverty (1964–68) during the Great Society years, which aimed to assimilate the poor to middle American affluence on the model of new immigrants, the risk wars have turned pathology into social partition.[63]

It is here that the cost/benefit discourses of the financial markets dovetail with the moral binaries of social conservatism. A distinction between at-risk and risk-capable subjects tacitly informs the moral binaries that gathered steam in the 1980s during the Reagan administration: on the one side, the ambitious upper-middle-class avatars of personal responsibility, those for whom the decade indeed constituted a "morning in America"; on the other, the specter of the "welfare queen," the object of countless moral panics, from the AIDS crisis to the drug war.[64]

Jazz neoclassicism has found itself enlisted in debates over precisely these kinds of binary oppositions, and in this way, it has also become ensnared in rhetoric that conflates social vulnerability with social pathology. The neoclassicist aesthetic defines itself as much by what it excludes as by what it includes: many of its protagonists have professed disinterest in the legacy of avant-garde improvised music since the 1960s, as well as any hybrid musics (rock-, funk-, and rap-based collaborative fusions) that might undermine the integrity of the music's boundaries. Of course, as numerous jazz scholars have argued, this highly prescriptive aesthetic program easily spills over into a broader cultural or *moral* argument about the desirable character of music at the turn of the millennium. At its height, neoclassical jazz was supported by an unusually prominent strain of intellectual advocacy, as figures such as Wynton Marsalis, Stanley Crouch, Albert Murray, and others sought to position the music within the context of broader debates about race, personal responsibility, and cultural morality. In his 1995 essay "Blues to Be Constitutional: A Long Look at the Wild Wherefores of Our Democratic Lives as Symbolized in the Making of Rhythm and Tune," Stanley Crouch positions the neoclassicist jazz movement at the front lines of the culture wars, its resilient work ethic placed in opposition to what he viewed to be the cynicism and irresponsibility of contemporary black popular culture.[65] Here, Crouch reinforces what Eric Porter has described as an element of "cultural Moynihanism" in neotraditional jazz discourses, a tendency to rely upon arguments that echo the so-called "Moynihan report" of 1965 in their identification of black culture with criminal pathology.[66] What is held up for criticism here is a specter of pathological working-class blackness in which impulsive material desire is tied to moral lassitude; the remedy resides in the aspirational figure of a motivated, disciplined, and clean-cut black middle-class professionalism. This idealized subject, made manifest in the person of the young, committed straightahead jazz musician, simultaneously embodies two sets of conservative virtue: he is, on the one hand, heroically resistant to youthful vice, and is at the same time the avatar of something close to entrepreneurial selfhood, with the ambition and virtuosic self-discipline to "*be adult,* [and] not just shriek for adult privileges."[67] Crouch's young musical professional is at once fortified with an appreciation of timeless values, and perfectly calibrated to flourish in the ruthlessly atomized environment of the free market. He (and it is almost invariably a "he" that is hailed in Crouch's critical celebrations of jazz) is adamantly positioned as the agent, and not the object, of risk management.

The institutions of political and musical officialdom belatedly celebrate jazz as democratically populist, at the very nadir of its commercial popularity; corporations, management consultants, and thought leaders seize upon a music with long dormant intimations of subversive provocation, precisely to serve as a model for the provocative innovation of their own postmodern institutions. As I noted above, though, this celebration of jazz practices as a set of usefully maverick dispositions, as ways to think "outside the box," only becomes possible in an environment where multinational corporations feel that an affiliation with this music gives them no cause for concern.

These contradictions tell us an enormous amount about the self-understanding of public- and private-sector actors in the age of resurgent finance capital. We need to recall here that the flexible, nimble disposition of the postmodern corporation derives from its broader structural response to the new mobility of capital since the 1970s: with the advent of floating exchange rates, far-flung industrial sites, and the new financial networks and communication technologies necessary to manage these developments, the corporate imaginary has sought to divest itself of its earlier investment in the stable, bureaucratic organizations of the postwar era, with their long-standing commitments to multiple types of stakeholders and their valorization of long-term stability. The new corporate institution of the late twentieth century, newly subject to the demands of a mercurial investor class, has an abiding interest in quick-witted responsiveness, in an ability to divest itself of redundant workers or underperforming units; in other words, it seeks *liquidity*. What improvised aesthetics offers to corporate thought leaders is precisely a *fantasy of liquidity,* a means of realizing the disruptive turbulence of contemporary market dynamics as something playfully ebullient and eminently positive.

At the same time, beyond what it offers to thought leaders in the private sector, the improvised aesthetics of neoclassicism in particular must also offer something to the community that produces it. Eric Porter, in his critique of the discourses surrounding jazz neoclassicism, has argued that the ideas put forward by Wynton Marsalis, Stanley Crouch, and others must be seen as "a strategic response—both to the state of jazz and to the state of African American society" in the era of neoliberalism.[68] Such a strategic response is made manifest, not only in the playfulness of the music's fantasies of liquidity (an aspect of the music that recommends it to the agents of capitalism's creative destruction), but also to the discursive and aesthetic explanations it offers for those who seek to navigate and survive socioeconomic turbulence on the other end: for instance, neoclassicism's particular responses to post-Moynihan social assertions about black pathology, however problematic they may be, often come from a place of good faith, outlining an avenue of response for African Americans that celebrates "risk-capable" subjectivities and the politics of respectability.

In this way, the music is put to work in a manner analogous to what Clyde Woods, commenting upon an earlier moment of black socioeconomic disruption during the Jim Crow era, has referred to as a *blues epistemology,* a comprehensive cultural "system of explanation" that helps people to make sense of systemic disruption.[69] It is true that in our moment hip hop, which addresses its critique of the neoliberal carceral state from within those communities most subject to it, manifests itself as a more obvious analogue to Woods' concept.[70] But in its own way, from its own place in the cultural fabric, the neoclassical impulse also serves as a blues epistemology for the late twentieth and early twenty-first centuries, providing its own distinctive soundtrack for contemporary black negotiations of wealth polarization, economic precariousness, and other forms of structural violence. Even as we look to critique the particulars of its approach, this other dimension of the music's fantasy of liquidity should be taken into account.

THE JAZZ BUBBLE

So, what would it be like for jazz scholarship to take this fantasy seriously? In what sense might the contradictory reception of jazz in our contemporary market and government institutions provide us with a point of departure for understanding aspects of neoliberal culture? What the present study seeks to do is to foreground four points of convergence between jazz culture since the late 1970s, on the one hand, and the reshaping of contemporary political economy by finance capital, on the other. These points of convergence illuminate the various ways in which wholly disparate elements of American life (the culture industry, the built environment, our political consensus, our intimate self-understanding) have been altered through our exposure to an increasingly pervasive cultural logic of financialization.

To my mind, this convergence manifests itself most powerfully in those areas where we can locate a shared phenomenology of *risk,* and it is there that my discussion begins. Musical improvisation, of course, is bound up in the dynamics of risk, as its entire procedural approach, its departure from preordered composition and established musical conventions, entails a risky leap into the aesthetic unknown. At the same time, the culture of financialization has in large part been shaped by an ethos in which risk taking is seen as normative and pleasurable: in the United States, as new mechanisms of retirement savings have galvanized public interest in stock-picking and investment strategy, corporate CEOs, hedge fund managers, and angel investors, from Peter Thiel to Richard Branson, have become the swashbuckling antiheroes of neoliberal culture, their exploits held up as models of entrepreneurial adventure. At the same time, American culture has seen a concomitant rise in the public fascination with gambling as a once-maligned, newly "respectable" modality of pleasure-in-speculation.[71]

In chapter 1, I use managerial theory discourses about jazz as an entry point for a broader discussion of this relationship between jazz and risk. If a recent spate of TED talks, management seminars, and entries in the popular business literature have looked to jazz performance to provide us with an elegant and tidy analogy for risk taking in contemporary business strategy, the jazz legacy in fact affords us with a powerful window onto an altogether more complex and ambivalent narrative of risk in American life. While the "jazz metaphor" in business tends to plug a largely sanitized, abstract, and ahistorical understanding of jazz practices into its idealized market framework, jazz historiography teaches us that political volatility and the violence of racist expropriation must figure into any accurate account of the music's embodiment of risk, its aesthetic response to a cultural environment of social antagonism. Here, I proceed from a distinction between risk and uncertainty initially crafted by economic theorist Frank Knight, where uncertainty implies a conception of risk in which the very parameters of risk are immeasurable and impossible to quantify. In this context, we may read jazz as a cultural trace of the manifold uncertainties in the economic lives of African Americans, uncertainties forged by way of the structural violence of chattel slavery, of debt peonage, of systemic disenfranchisement from economic and social institutions. Chapter 1 culminates with an examination of the musical and social dynamics surrounding the celebrated Miles Davis Quintet of the mid-1960s, which served as a crucial model for those "young lions" who sought to revive the group's postbop musical style during the first wave of jazz neoclassicism in the 1980s. Davis's group provides us with an especially appealing interpretive lens, as its approach to "controlled freedom" brought an unprecedented level of virtuosity to bear upon improvisatory risk taking.

Chapter 2 devotes its attention to a specific moment in the biography of celebrated tenorman Dexter Gordon, where it coincides with an important episode in the broader cultural history of New York City. Dexter Gordon's engagements at Storyville and the Village Vanguard in summer of 1976, which marked the beginning of a more permanent "homecoming" for the artist after an extended period in Europe, fell in the midst of a period of profound uncertainty for the city of New York, as it confronted one of the worst fiscal crises in its 350-year history. The ecstatic public reception that greeted the artist upon his return to New York stood in contrast to the broader air of pessimism that befell the city as it confronted the implications of the crisis. Many of the city's social problems derived from a systemic disinvestment in those communities made most vulnerable by deindustrialization, white flight, and the collapse of social services precipitated by the specter of municipal default. The city's resolution of New York's fiscal crisis prioritized bondholders in the private sector over the city's public sector workers and its most vulnerable residents, intensifying patterns of systemic disinvestment and contributing to the decline of the city's civic life.

However, none of these factors, which emerged from structural contradictions at the core of the city's political economy, prevented New Yorkers from viewing their city's failings largely through the lens of *cultural* crisis. Observers of New Yorkers' woes laid the city's problems at the feet of its African-American, Latino/a, and LGBTQ residents, with each of these communities blamed for what was perceived as an era of decadence and moral decay. Within the jazz community itself, this general atmosphere of cultural alarmism made its presence felt in contemporaneous debates over the genre boundaries of jazz. In the minds of conservative listeners, Dexter Gordon's place in the nascent bebop revival of the mid-1970s positioned him as an appealing alternative to the period's rock, funk, and disco fusion projects: disco, in particular, provoked consternation among those invested in conventional norms of gender and sexuality, and those who sought to protect jazz from the perceived taint of commercialism.

The arrival of Dexter Gordon on American shores, on the cusp of New York's fiscal crisis, provides us with a useful case study for understanding how cultural and economic conservatisms become conflated, and how arguments waged on the terrain of culture provide cover for strategies of fiscal austerity. In particular, Gordon's laudatory reception in the press, much like the city's assertive I♥NY public relations campaign of the era, occurs in the broader context of a nation increasingly looking to culture as a salve for material and structural problems.

In chapters 3 and 4, I turn to an examination of the corporate history of Verve Records, the erstwhile independent label founded by Norman Granz, and subsequently acquired by PolyGram. The label's fate under PolyGram illuminates the ways in which the implications of neoliberal financialization were translated into the conditions of possibility for jazz recording on the major labels between 1980 and the turn of the millennium. The revitalization of the Verve legacy under the stewardship of PolyGram A&R executive Richard Seidel, beginning in the early 1980s, provides us with an intriguing window onto corporate strategy in the music industry at the height of the neoclassical jazz "boomlet":

what began as the jazz division's effort to take advantage of PolyGram's strengths in the marketing of classical records and back catalog soon expanded into a more ambitious strategy of new artist development, as Seidel sought to cultivate what Verve saw as the commercial viability of the "young lions" movement.

In 1998 Edgar Bronfman Jr., the CEO of the prominent Canadian distillery Seagram and head of what would become the Universal Music Group, set about engineering a new merger of unprecedented scope, acquiring PolyGram from Philips and merging the record company with Universal's music division. It was a deal that reflected the changing orientation of the music business, where the cultural logic of Wall Street came to inform the new firm's strategic priorities. Bronfman Jr. foregrounded what he saw as the ability of the merger to generate significant value for shareholders. The massive debt burden incurred by the new company as a corollary of the merger would require dramatic cuts to the company's artist roster and workforce, and as such, it telegraphed Bronfman's privileging of the company's publicly traded stock over existing stakeholders in the company.

The "jazz as business" metaphor that we encountered earlier in this discussion holds up the small jazz combo as a model for a certain kind of fleet-footed and extemporaneous corporate organization in the twenty-first century. It is clear that Bronfman has thought of the strategic benefits of the Universal-PolyGram merger in very similar terms: from the standpoint of the twenty-first-century financial sector, the structural upheaval created by mergers becomes a way of forcibly enjoining corporate organizations to take on the aspect of a combo maneuvering swiftly through the risky, turbulent "changes" demanded under contemporary economic conditions. However, in order to achieve this flexibility on behalf of its corporate parent, and thus to respond to the demands of "shareholder value," a musical *subsidiary* like Verve (the very subsidiaries that may be acquiring, developing, and promoting jazz talent) must often become risk-averse in the extreme, abandoning those projects that cannot immediately demonstrate their own viability in the commercial marketplace. In the case of Verve, this dynamic resulted in the downsizing and eventual abandonment of the label's assertively cultivated development of straightahead instrumental jazz in the neoclassical vein. Crucial here is the relationship between the Verve subsidiary and its multinational parent company, as the structural turbulence of the Universal-PolyGram merger made its presence felt at the granular level of artist and repertory decisions. Moreover, if the logic of financialization ultimately established the conditions in which neoclassical jazz was purged from the label, it was also a kind of financial-sector logic that may have initially created the conditions for neoclassicism's ascent at Verve. Looking back on the jazz "boomlet" in 2004, *Chicago Tribune* jazz critic Howard Reich once compared the intensity of major-label support for neoclassicism in the early 1990s to the "dot-com" bubble from later in that same decade, what he called a "jazz bubble" that, much like its stock market counterpart, reflected an unsustainable over-investment in the single, stylistically homogenous niche market of neo-classical jazz.[72]

Finally, in chapters 5 and 6, I turn to the relationship between jazz, urban redevelopment, and the neoliberal city. My discussion here takes up the case of the San Francisco Redevelopment Agency, one of many such units created as conduits for urban renewal in the decades follow-ing the Second World War. California's Community Redevelopment Agencies, much like their counterparts in other municipal jurisdictions across the country, provided city boosters in urban governments with a means of galvanizing significant changes in the built environment of the postwar city, putting public resources at the disposal of private real estate interests as a catalyst for urban transformation. Communities targeted for redevelopment had to be demonstrably affected by urban "blight," and in the context of postwar cultural politics, the attribution of "blight" was, more often than not, a euphemistic means of marking racial and class "others" as undesirable. In the case of San Francisco, the most notorious effort to target and redevelop urban blight took place in the city's Fillmore district, a largely African-American and Asian-American community that was then home to one of the most vibrant jazz scenes on the West Coast. In the late 1950s, under the pre-text of urban amelioration, the city's redevelopment agency embarked upon a hugely destructive three-decade initiative that displaced tens of thousands of local residents, decimated the area's small businesses, and dismantled the neighborhood's lively cultural ecology.

In a bid to atone for its actions in the 1950s and 1960s, the SFRA, beginning in the early 1980s, set about planning a "jazz preservation district" to be located in the heart of the Lower Fillmore neighborhood. In addition to targeting promising small businesses for loans, the SFRA program also envisioned the development of a more ambitious mixed-use project. This latter initiative originally took the form of a combined multiplex and jazz venue, pairing AMC Theaters with a franchise of the well-known New York-based Blue Note club. While this first proposal was never realized, the SFRA did succeed in launching a different mixed-use project in the early millennium, a complex that mixed affordable and market-rate housing with a branch of the prominent Oakland-based Yoshi's Jazz Club.

While the San Francisco Redevelopment Agency's jazz preservation district was launched with the best of intentions, it was also launched in a social and political climate that has been fundamentally reshaped by a set of assumptions and practices that social theorists refer to in terms of *speculative urbanism*. Speculative urbanism characterizes a context for urban development that has emerged over the last thirty years, as federal block grants and other sources of public funding have been scaled back, and as municipal governments have looked to the global bond market as a source of financing for localized urban revitalization projects. Currently, proposals slated for redevelopment via these contemporary finance mechanisms (including what is called tax increment financing) tend to favor bold, high-profile initiatives with major anchor tenants, many of them functioning as entertainment destinations for constituencies well outside of the project area itself. As I argue in this chapter, this was a strategy, in the case of the Fillmore Jazz District, that proved to be ill suited to the needs of the community's own residents. The SFRA's attempts to harness speculative urbanism to create a jazz-themed business district in the Fillmore provides us with a case study that illuminates the gap separating a top-down vision of urbanism championed by finance capital, on the one hand, and a grassroots one advocated by local residents and community activists, on the other.

Here, I want to touch upon a couple of points that, while they are not taken up in the present discussion to any large extent, are nevertheless salient as we consider the relationship between jazz, finance capital, and neoliberalism. One area in which the rise of neoclassical jazz has been particularly important has been in its role in cultivating a strong institutional base for jazz education in the United States. The neoclassicist "young lions" belonged to one of the first generations of jazz musicians to benefit from the introduction of jazz studies as a formal area of academic study.[73] The expansion of interest in jazz pedagogy has made its presence felt through the growth of the International Association of Jazz Educators (or IAJE), and of what has amounted to its successor organization, the Jazz Education Network (or JEN), both of whom have organized massive annual conventions, bringing together jazz educators in secondary and post-secondary education, retailers of resources for jazz pedagogy, music industry executives, and practicing musicians.[74] The IAJE and JEN conferences are only the most visible manifestation of a broader explosion of formal jazz education in postsecondary institutions. Indeed, as David Ake has noted, one area where jazz historians have not quite kept pace with the realities of the contemporary jazz scene is in their recognition of the extent to which the university music department has superseded the urban nightclub venue as the employer of choice for many emerging jazz musicians.[75]

The rise of formalized jazz education coincides with important structural shifts in the development of educational institutions themselves. At the level of primary and secondary education, the passage of the No Child Left Behind Act has created significant pressures for art and music instruction, as its prioritization of reading and mathematics in its standardized testing has moved numerous schools to re-allocate resources away from the arts or extracurricular activities.[76] At the same time, the university is itself quickly becoming an institution remolded in the image of neoliberalism: both its structural exigencies (including the move toward a precariously employed workforce of adjunct professors) and its intellectual commitments (with strategic decisions driven by concerns over student readiness for the workforce) bespeak a widespread effort, on the part of twenty-first-century postsecondary institutions, to conform to prevailing market logics.[77] The study of how these developments implicate musical studies in general, and jazz studies in particular, constitutes an important field of inquiry in its own right, one that is beyond the scope of the present book. In this connection, we might look to Eiten Wilf's 2014 book *School for Cool: The Academic Jazz Program and the Paradox of Institutionalized Creativity,* in addition to many of the essays in a 2016 collection entitled *Improvisation and Music Education: Beyond the Classroom,* edited by Ajay Heble and Mark Laver, where much of the discourse centers around this question of the function and survival of jazz and improvisational music in the university classroom under present market conditions.[78]

A second area that the present study touches upon, without developing extensively, is the question of how feminist critique and queer theory might be brought to bear in our understanding of the dynamics of jazz in the age of neoliberalism, particularly with respect to the neoclassicist movement. It is safe to say that the heteronormative masculinist sensibility and male-dominated creative sphere of neoclassicist instrumental jazz in the 1980s and 1990s bear more than a passing resemblance to the social dynamics of the financial sector during this period, in an era which saw the Wall Street values of heroic individualism and intense competition permeate so many disparate aspects of American culture.[79] An atmosphere of moral panic surrounding women and LGBTQ people is a crucial ingredient in the rise of cultural conservatism beginning in the 1970s (itself a crucial determinant of the broader cultural embrace of neoliberal logics), and we can see the resonances of this panic in various aspects of the neoclassicist revival: chapter 2, for example, outlines the ways in which homophobic and heteronormative conceptions of masculinity inform the ways that both Dexter Gordon's critical reception and the antidisco backlash manifest themselves in the jazz press during the late 1970s. However, one area that remains for future scholars to develop is the broader question of how the gender dynamics of neoliberal culture might relate to our understanding of the gender dynamics of contemporary jazz culture, and it is my hope that the present book serves as a useful point of departure for those discussions.

CONCLUSION

What is at stake in an investigation of the relationship between contemporary jazz cultures and contemporary political economy? As I noted above, one answer that might be given here is to note that jazz, as a cultural point of departure for this investigation, has the advantage of being relatively old, its emergence antedating the advent of neoliberal culture by something on the order of seventy years. It is this very longevity of the jazz legacy that allows us to understand the profundity of the social, economic, and cultural changes that have been precipitated under the neoliberal "turn." We hold up the century-old constellation of practices called "jazz" as a kind of critical barometer, and in this way, we can come to learn manifold things about our broader cultural moment: we come to see cities with formerly vibrant jazz ecologies, dense networks of local venues, give themselves over to jazz monocultures based upon a small handful of upmarket jazz institutions, each of these bankrolled through the "speculative urbanism" of redevelopment agencies and public-private partnerships. We come to see storied jazz subsidiaries at the major labels, having historically demonstrated a willingness to subsidize jazz as a prestigious and galvanizing site of aesthetic disruption, suddenly curtailing their efforts in the face of *market* disruption, the volatility inherent in a financial culture of persistent restructuring, mergers, and buyouts. We come to see an African diasporic cluster of traditions, forged in the face of racial terror and existential risk, being repurposed as a metaphor for a much more *play-*

ful ideal of market risk, a spirit of high-stakes speculative adventure embraced by celebrants of neoliberal capitalism.

The stakes of this line of inquiry extend well beyond the boundaries of the jazz world itself. Music renders audible the effects of our institutional, ideological, and ethical transformations; as such, it serves as a channel through which the dispositions of a time can come within earshot. The contradictions inherent in our contemporary jazz ideologies map out along a broader cultural topography in which wealth polarization, racial inequality, and economic precarity have become characteristic features of our present moment. What I seek to present here is an analysis of the economy of financialization that attends to the particulars of its cultural implications, to its resonances within the confines of a beloved and longstanding cultural legacy. This more intimate analysis of a localized culture becomes, in turn, a means of accessing the lived texture of the present, of what it means to *inhabit* an economy that is more often rendered in the abstract. It is through observing this relationship between the general and the particular, between an idiosyncratic subculture and the distinctive market dynamics within which it is embedded, that we can come to a unique understanding of the peculiarities of the early twenty-first century.

CHAPTER I

"Controlled Freedom"

Jazz, Risk, and Political Economy

In spite of everything, there was in the life I fled a zest and a joy and a capacity for facing and surviving disaster that are very moving and very rare. Perhaps we were, all of us . . . bound together by the nature of our oppression, the specific and peculiar complex of risks we had to run; if so, within these limits we sometimes achieved with each other a freedom that was close to love.

—James Baldwin, *The Fire Next Time*

Every time I go on stage to play, I'm risking. . . . I recently got into the stock market and it's a hobby now. The stocks that I'm most interested [in] are the riskier ones, the growth stocks. I told the stockbroker, "Yo! I'm used to risk. I do it every night."

—Tony Williams, in Don Snowden, "A Lifetime of Risky Riffs," *Los Angeles Times*

I begin here with a brief account of a "TED Talk" presented by jazz vibraphonist Stefon Harris and his quartet, entitled "There are no mistakes on the bandstand."[1] Harris' 2011 "TED Talk" outlines the oft-noted insight that jazz musicians can take ostensible "mistakes" and turn them to their advantage: the initial appearance of a jarring dissonance can, with the right touch, be integrated into the sonic palate of the performance in the immediacy of the moment. Harris's argument about navigating "mistakes" in jazz would be relatively unremarkable if he were presenting it to an audience of music educators, who have

encountered this argument numerous times over the past several decades.[2] However, in the context of this particular TEDSalon presentation, the argument took on a more intriguing application: Ten minutes
into the thirteen-minute talk, having elaborately demonstrated the jazz
musician's capacity for adapting to musical "mistakes" on the fly, Harris turns to his audience and asks, "So how does all this relate to behavioral finance?" The casual viewer of Harris' video could be forgiven for
overlooking the fact that the occasion for the talk, the TEDSalon New
York 2011, was in fact a conference devoted to the field of behavioral
finance, which TED produced in concert with Allianz Global Investors,
a subsidiary of the Munich-based multinational financial services corporation.[3]

Behavioral finance is an emerging field that harnesses behavioral psychology as a tool for understanding investor decisions, particularly insofar as they deviate from the rational market behaviors postulated by
traditional economics.[4] At the TEDSalon conference, behavioral finance
was put to work in a variety of contexts, including Shlomo Benartzi's
talk on the psychological impediments to saving for retirement, or Daniel Goldstein's lecture on the usefulness of "commitment devices" in
binding us to presently unpalatable investing decisions. For its part, Harris's workshop on mistakes in jazz improvisation enjoins the investor to
embrace those opportunities denied to the financially risk-averse. Here,
Harris's lesson in performative flexibility is deployed as a broader analogy for the idealized subject of the financial markets: nimble and
dynamic, the contemporary investor-subject is hailed as uniquely alive to
the potentiality of the moment, seizing its possibilities in the manner of
the jazz soloist navigating a set of turbulent harmonic changes.

Jazz has recently been taken up as a metaphorical point of departure
for a variety of sites in contemporary business practice. As Mark Laver
and others have noted in a recent special issue of *Critical Studies in
Improvisation*, the small jazz combo has served as a leitmotiv in jazz-
themed management theory, serving as a metaphor for corporate strategy and organization.[5] Scholars in the field of organization studies have
deployed this business-centered jazz analogy in a variety of divergent
contexts, addressing such topics as the question of "strategic fit" (the
effort to coordinate an organization's internal dynamics and its external
environment), or the issue of how to develop new practices of product
development.[6] Moreover, management consultants have put these theo-
retical approaches to work in practical environments: Michael Gold
weaves live jazz into his Jazz Impact leadership workshops for Credit

Suisse employees and the faculty of Ivy League business schools, while Chris Washburne and John Kao have each riffed on jazz as a metaphor for business innovation before the assembled dignitaries at the World Economic Forum in Davos.[7] These ventures in jazz-centered management theory and practice almost invariably point to the jazz musician's proclivity for *taking risks*.

If the jazz musician's willingness to take chances has been understood as a powerful analogy for behavioral finance, or as a useful metaphor for the post-Fordist corporation, it likely derives from the alignment of risk taking with the prevailing ideologies of neoliberal capitalism. The individual "entrepreneurial self" of the neoliberal imaginary, set loose within the volatile conditions of the free market, is ultimately responsible for finding their own way within this shifting terrain.[8] Without recourse to state institutions or collective solidarities, the isolated market actor is forced to rely upon a quicksilver intuition, a heightened attunedness to the possibilities latent within rapid economic change. Consequently, as Philip Mirowski has noted, risk has been moved to the center of postmodern life, and it has assumed an emboldened form: we no longer strictly adhere to a prudent, *actuarial* sense of risk, in which the designation of "risky" is assigned only to rainy-day contingencies. Rather, the "risk profile" of the neoliberal, entrepreneurial self is given over to "irrational leap[s] of faith," to a "bald impetuous abandon in the face of an intrinsically unknowable future."[9] The same quality of disinhibition that allows Stefon Harris to embrace musical mistakes is promoted elsewhere as a necessary condition of advancement in the contemporary private sector.

Our contemporary language of risk presents the concept as a neutral abstraction. In a context shaped by the dehistoricizing impulses of neoclassical economics, we have learned to understand risk as pure potentiality, severed from its origins in the messier terrain of social disparities and structural inequality. Risk has a history, a traceable legacy of shifting cultural meanings. If it is usually understood as abstract and disembodied, it can take on tactile and audible forms. As Randy Martin has suggested, modernist and postmodern aesthetic practices of chance, improvisation, and indeterminacy are shot through with the sensibility of risk, and their appearance across the gamut of twentieth century expressive forms indexes the wax and wane of risk as a resonant category of experience.[10] These sensibilities are particularly relevant to our understanding of jazz and African diasporic musical forms, as numerous observers have marshaled rhetorics of risk as a way of explaining the music's aesthetic and social dynamism, in contexts ranging from the so-called "moldy fig" debates of the 1930s through to the "jazz wars" of the 1990s.[11]

The present chapter takes up the music of postbop, a jazz legacy extending from the 1960s Miles Davis Quintet through to the "young lions" of the 1980s, as a focal point for a historically situated genealogy of risk. Throughout my analysis, I maintain a focus on varieties of *financial* risk, in order to accentuate the indebtedness of our broader risk vocabularies to questions of political economy. At the same time, I hope to demonstrate that prevailing discourses of financial risk operate without recourse to a sufficiently capacious conceptualization of their historical resonances and social consequences: in contrast to the abstract conceptions of risk associated with our present culture of financialization, I propose to trace an alternative lineage of risk that attends to its historical particularities in midcentury and late twentieth-century American life. In particular, I'm interested in the ways that the exclusion of African Americans from the trappings of postwar middle-class prosperity anticipates certain aspects of the more generalized precariousness of economic life under neoliberalism.

An attention to a properly historicized account of risk will offer a useful point of entry as we consider the aesthetic, political, and socioeconomic discourses that accompany the emergence of neoclassicist jazz as a historical phenomenon. Attending to dynamics of risk provokes us to consider a variety of interesting questions: In what sense does neoclassicist jazz serve as a trace of broader tensions in the relationship between class dynamics, race thinking, and political economy? How might the analysis of political economy be harnessed as a properly *hermeneutic* tool, a way into our understanding of "the music itself?"

RISK, UNCERTAINTY, AND NEOLIBERAL IDEOLOGIES

American economic life in the early twenty-first century operates under the weight of a century-old legacy in which risk is understood as potentially quantifiable, knowable, and *manageable*. The models of probabilistic calculation embraced by lenders, merchants, insurance companies, and financial speculators during the nineteenth century anticipate the rise of a neoclassical model of economics in which the tumultuous vagaries of market dynamics are made manageable through their reduction to quantitative inputs.[12] In its most simplistic form, neoclassical economics holds that market actors have complete and transparent access to information, distilled within the quantitative abstraction of the commodity's *price,* and maximize their individual self-interest by acting upon this information in a rational manner.[13] The availability of probabilistic modeling lent a numerically rigorous imprimatur to economic thought, during the period in which "political economy" underwent its transition to the modern discipline of "economics": under the new rubric, economists were increasingly beholden to a set of abstract metrics that they kept meticulously separate from any qualitative approach to social thought.[14] With new modes of probabilistic calculation and neoclassical methodologies at hand, capital and its academic tributaries increasingly held out the possibility of a world in which risk could be completely domesticated.

However, some economic observers have expressed skepticism about the degree to which probabilistic models can outline a clear topography of risk. One of the most well-known formulations of this argument was articulated by Frank Knight, whose 1921 work *Risk, Uncertainty, and Profit* challenged the field's prevailing assumptions about the calculability of probable outcomes in the analysis of market dynamics.[15] Crucial here is his distinction between *risk* and *uncertainty:* a situation of "risk" involves an unknown future in which a statistical distribution of possible outcomes is known, while in situations of "uncertainty," statistical probabilities are more difficult to calculate, owing to a fundamental uncertainty about the appropriate categories of analysis. Situations of "uncertainty" require the analyst to engage in a qualitative and *intuitive* judgment about the range of possible outcomes, before a probability can be calculated for each one.[16] For example, a situation of Knightian risk may involve something along the lines of insurance for fire hazard, in an environment where reliable actuarial data is obtainable about the availability of fire hydrants, density of housing, building materials, and so forth: probabilities can be generated for a narrow range of outcomes ("house burns down" or "house doesn't burn down") based upon a known set of categories. By contrast, a situation of uncertainty, as one might encounter in attempting to determine the performance of economic indices in emerging markets, may confront the market analyst with an inordinately complex range of possible categories of analysis, not all of which may be readily obvious: the observer must factor in the impact of environmental conditions, labor conditions, political unrest, and a host of other factors elusive to probabilistic analysis.[17] Situations of uncertainty entail a dimension of volatility: there is a sense in which the market actor grappling with a situation of uncertainty must ultimately abandon any uncritical faith in actuarial prediction, and give himself or herself over to a radical *extemporaneity* of decision making.

Since the early 1970s, our contemporary market dynamics have become caught up in a set of contradictory tensions between prevailing assumptions about the sound efficiencies of quantitative, "data-driven" methodologies of Knightian *risk*, on the one hand, and the market's de facto exploitation of volatile Knightian *uncertainty*, on the other. We can look to the collapse of the Bretton Woods agreement as one likely point of departure for many of these tensions. During the Nixon administration, the long-standing stability of the postwar Bretton Woods agreement, which pegged the value of international currencies to a U.S. dollar valued at $35 per ounce of gold, came under mounting pressure overseas as the U.S. government took on an expanding trade deficit and accumulated significant war debt from its intervention in Vietnam. Concerns over the continued viability of the gold-backed dollar led foreign nations to drain U.S. gold reserves, and so, on August 13, 1971, the Nixon administration announced that it was closing the "gold window," effectively decoupling the value of the U.S. dollar from the gold standard and negating the Bretton Woods consensus.[18]

The collapse of the Bretton Woods system and the resultant regime of floating international currency rates have had a variety of important ramifications. The deregulation of currency ratios catalyzed the rollback of numerous other regulatory mechanisms, as commercial banks sought to elude domestic restrictions by pursuing offshore financial transactions. The ability of states to maintain domestic policy priorities became undermined as financial markets sought, and acquired, new autonomy from government oversight. The trade in financial derivatives took on new, unforeseen volatilities as currency swaps and other financial instruments became the principal means through which market actors hedged against uncertainty.[19] The "liberation" of exchange rates from the fixity of the Bretton Woods consensus, coupled with the ensuing turbulence of newly deregulated financial markets, has magnified the potential for genuinely unpredictable conditions of Knightian uncertainty.

Contemporary economic conditions have often tended to reward those adept in an extemporaneous, *improvised* response to market unknowns. As Arjun Appadurai has noted, the reliably successful protagonist of contemporary market volatility adheres to a set of "swashbuckling" and heroically contrarian dispositions, ultimately siding with the qualitative, intuitive strategies appropriate to Knightian uncertainty over prevailing quantitative methodologies of risk management. According to Appadurai, "it is not hard to see, especially in the past year or two . . . that we are in the presence not of sober risk managers but of individuals who have chosen to define—without any models, methods, or measurements to guide them—the space of financial uncertainty as such."[20] As Mirowski has suggested, this "swashbuckler" has become a central protagonist in the historical circumstances leading up to the global financial crisis of 2008. The rhetoric of the free market frequently celebrates the agent of reckless abandon, given over to an unshakeable faith in the trajectory of future events: if the midcentury image of the corporate CEO was that of the gray-flannel bean-counter, bringing a Calvinist risk aversion to the most minor business decision, our present notion of the chief executive has come to resemble something closer to the adrenaline-fueled publicity stunts staged by Virgin's Richard Branson, who has rappelled down the sides of his own buildings in a bid to tie his adventurous corporate brand to his own outsized personality.[21]

RISK, JAZZ, AND MANAGEMENT CONSULTING

Something like this valorization of Knightian uncertainty over Knightian risk likely informs the recent interest in jazz among contemporary managerial theorists. For the impulse to look to a jazz combo performance as a kind of corporate tutorial in creative improvisation is not so far removed from the conversations that must have been taking place at countless firms over the past couple of decades: old logics of adherence to fiscal prudence have been deemed inadequate in the face of contemporary market volatility, and emboldened CEOs have called upon their employees to throw themselves into an embrace of something closer to Knightian uncertainty. Organization theorist Frank Barrett, in his book *Yes to the Mess: Surprising Leadership Lessons for Jazz*, makes explicit this analogy between jazz improvisation and the recent corporate celebration of creative "disruption": "Jazz improvisers focus on discovery in times of stress. They know how to ensure that they don't get stuck in old habits even when reliable routines might seem like the quickest way to relieve anxiety. . . . While there are no guarantees of outcomes, they realize the benefit of a mind-set that maximizes opportunities, understands the importance of intelligent risk taking, and most important, learns by saying yes and leaping in."[22] Elsewhere, as Laver has noted, Michael Gold's Jazz Impact consultancy incorporates Risk as one of five organizing principles for his application of the business-centered jazz metaphor, grouped together by way of the acronym APRIL (Autonomy, Passion, Risk, Innovation, and Listening).[23] For Gold, jazz musicians' cultivation of a "zone of improvisational freedom" provides a space in which risk taking can generate new and innovative ideas.[24]

Some consultants see fit to emphasize a more ruthlessly competitive strain of jazz practices in their presentations of the jazz-as-business analogy. In such instances, jazz is held up as embodying a model of social interaction commensurate with the more pitiless dimensions of free-market ideology. The leadership consultant John Kao, who has parlayed his version of the jazz metaphor into broader recommendations about global innovation strategies, sees the competitive rituals of the bandstand as "almost eerily metaphorical of the macroeconomic processes of capitalism," with the jazz jam session offering nothing less than a synecdoche for Joseph Schumpeter's notion of "creative destruction": " 'Next, please!' That's what life is always saying in a creativity-driven market. That's the wordless imperative in a jam session as well. The faint-hearted, the security-minded, the easily contented, the slacker need not apply. Everyone else will do so with high spirits and nimble imaginations. Businesses, however, have no choice in the matter. They adopt a cultural and organizational framework of 'Next, please!' or, quite simply, they go out of business. Jam or die—the issue is that stark."[25] Kao envisions the contemporary postindustrial economy as a site of dynamic uncertainty, in which each subsequent innovation radically displaces what has come before. The hero of Kao's "creative-driven market" is a subject who is equal to this relentless onslaught of the new. In his dismissal of "the faint-hearted, the security-minded, the easily contented, the slacker," Kao makes no allowances for either financial precariousness or its collective remedies: the subject who hesitates before this social Darwinist environment is simply seen as not pulling her weight.

In Kao's formulation, risk and uncertainty are positioned as politically neutral and socially universal, a ubiquitously shared logic of chance in which divergent threats and potentialities manifest themselves as abstract price points. As Edward LiPuma and Benjamin Lee have argued, these assumptions about risk reflect the ways in which techniques of risk management in the broader corporate world have been reshaped to better reflect the demands of the financial marketplace: faced with the increased need to hedge against such uncertainties as social and political upheaval or environmental change, investment banks and hedge funds have sought to develop new financial instruments that reduce the complexities of concrete social risk to an abstract set of quantitative values.

The pricing formula for a financial derivative (such as a currency swap) will attempt to account for concrete social risks by expressing each one as a numerical value: it converts the myriad unpredictable factors attending social change in a specific market (labor unrest, political repression, or disease, for instance) into a series of inputs that, taken together, yield a specific price point, a quantitative distillation of the potential for risk in a certain set of social conditions. The end result is a conception of risk that collapses myriad layers of social turbulence into an ostensibly neutral and transhistorical abstraction.[26]

The social values articulated in the business-centered "jazz metaphor" literature reflect this investment in an ahistorical and abstract conception of risk.[27] The environment of risk cited in each of these disparate business-centered jazz analogies is one in which other, mitigating considerations are bracketed. Social justice and asymmetrical relations of power are not factored into these accountings, and no allowances are to be made for the structural disparities that may serve to explain the radically different outcomes experienced by diverse market actors. As Kao bluntly states, the choice here is simply whether to "jam or die": to give oneself over to virtuosic extemporaneity, or to succumb to the summary judgment of the market.

If jazz has become repurposed as an unwitting metaphor for the market's invisible hand, this is perhaps because of the uncompromising terms set by many of the music's champions since the beginning of the 1980s. Many advocates of jazz neoclassicism have contended that the music is based upon a nonnegotiable set of musical fundamentals (swing feeling, functional harmony, and a well-defined set of rhythmic, formal, and melodic procedures). The responsibility for navigating these fundamentals lies with the individual musician, whose years of diligent practice, study, and performance instill in him or her a virtuosic agency adequate to the music's exacting demands. Many scholars have noted the myriad contexts in which Wynton Marsalis, Stanley Crouch, and some of their contemporaries, playing changes on the "politics of respectability," have refashioned this aesthetic vision as a tool of conservative *cultural* critique, denouncing musics as varied as jazz-rock fusion, the 1960 avant-garde "New Thing," and hip hop for failing to measure up to a set of rigidly defined cultural standards.[28] However, I would note that this development is also legible in relation to the 1980s expansion of the financial sector, a moment in which such developments as the expansion of trade in over-the-counter financial derivatives, or the increasing normalization of a rhetoric of "shareholder value," begin to transform the normative understanding of *risk:* in the new dispensation, risk becomes an abstract object of privatized accountability, rather than a historically embedded object of collective responsibility.[29] Whether on the bandstand or on the trading floor, the individual subject of contemporary risk is celebrated to the degree that he or she rises to this exacting standard of performance.

However, the standards to which individuals are held in both of these environments, whether with respect to music or market "fundamentals," do not reflect the wildly variegated world of social reality. The contemporary financial sector has failed to reckon with the cultural constructedness of its own abstracted and transhistorical conception of risk.[30] For that matter, this perspective also invites us to see risk in *other* times and places as historically and culturally dynamic: in this way, we become open to an understanding of risk that attends to its historical and cultural particularities.

The emergence of neoclassicist jazz sensibilities and the subsequent rise of jazz metaphors in business practice both serve as useful windows onto broader social conceptions of risk contemporaneous with their production. Insofar as both of these discourses explicitly celebrate the adherence of individual virtuosi to a set of ostensibly timeless and universal technical standards, they reproduce the logic of abstract risk that LiPuma and Lee locate within the ideologies and procedures of the financial markets. However, as I hope to demonstrate, the histories of jazz and African-American cultural production in reality bear witness to a far more complex, turbulent, and expansive understanding of risk, one perhaps more characteristic of *Knightian uncertainty* than of Knightian risk.

HISTORICIZING RISK

To investigate the history of risk sensibilities in post–Civil War America is to examine a turbulent period in which the absence of legal protections for a class of citizen-subjects rendered them vulnerable to a situation of radical uncertainty. An examination of the social dynamics of risk in the context of midcentury American life will necessarily foreground the complexities that separate risk (as a known distribution of probabilities) from the more expansive and less quantifiable category of uncertainty.

As it happens, our modern understanding of risk can be traced to a relatively specific set of historical coordinates: as Jonathan Levy has noted, in the early nineteenth century a "risk" referred very specifically to an instrument of marine insurance, designed to protect sea merchants' property in the event of its exposure to "perils of the sea." On land, the significance of "risk" did not yet extend past this relatively obscure technical context: unforeseen "acts of God" continued to be understood as the inscrutable workings of fate, and best addressed through the support networks of family and community. However, with the advent of the industrial revolution, the exposure of business enterprises to unforeseen calamities, commonly referred to as "freaks of fortune," led entrepreneurs to seek financial mechanisms for hedging against the uncertainties of the market economy.[31]

The racial determinants of power in nineteenth-century America reside at the core of this early history of postmaritime "risk." Levy notes that the ascendency of risk in nineteenth-century American culture is closely bound up with broader struggles over the institution of slavery. Indeed, owing to the close interweaving of the slave trade with the maritime merchant trade, the ability of an individual to purchase "risks" on enslaved property antedated the ability to invest in "risks" on one's own free self: risk applied to slave ownership before it applied to "self-ownership" (in the form of insurance policies or other financial protections of the self).[32]

While enslaved people were radically subject to the commodification of the "chattel principle," they frequently sought to act in ways that would affect the terms of their sale, engaging in a risky performativity designed to showcase (or undercut) their value to prospective buyers. Even as financial risk was understood to reside entirely with the owner of the chattel slave, the enslaved person herself took risks calculated to affect his or her own status as a commodified human.[33] This performative self-risk of the chattel slave is part of a broader dynamic of coerced performance outlined by Saidiya Hartman in her analysis of slavery's "scenes of subjection": enslaved people's command performances for slave owners, whether in the context of coffles bound for the slave market, or in the privacy of the masters' homes, were ultimately inseparable from the political economy of slavery itself.[34] This distinctive structure of slavery, in which the object of risk is *herself* capable of performative risk, manifested itself as a complex locus of uncertainty, where the agency of the commodified human potentially complicated questions of exchange value. However, the degree to which this performative agency exposed the slaveowner to uncertainty was scarcely comparable to the near-constant uncertainty faced by the enslaved person herself: the prospect of being brought to market, of being involuntarily uprooted from home and family and put down in entirely new and hostile conditions, manifested itself as a constant and existential exposure to radical risk.[35] In this context, the enslaved person's performative intervention in her own valuation served as a means of managing uncertainty, of attempting to forestall the radical unpredictability of the open market.

With abolition, African-American freedmen had in principle secured the prerogative of "self-ownership," the right to assume the risks of self-care and of the support of family and relatives. However, in practice, African Americans in the postbellum period faced considerable barriers to full participation in the American life of risk. The practice of sharecropping, for example, allowed black tenants a share of the proceeds from the annual crop, though this advantage was frequently complicated by the control that landlords exerted over the relationship: landlords extracted value from their tenants in the form of crop liens (tenants borrowed against the expected value of the forthcoming crop), deducted expenses against the sharecropper's share, and frequently paid the tenant in scrip, redeemable only through the landowner's store, where prices for everyday necessities were drastically inflated. Such arrangements amounted to a classic debt trap: the exorbitant expenses prevented freedmen from saving toward the prospective goal of independent land ownership, thereby ensuring their continued reliance upon the landlord's credit.[36] African-American farmers who did succeed in purchasing land independently usually had access only to the least fertile land, and where they sought loans, they often faced usurious interest rates from racist lenders.[37] Even as the possibility of homesteading was legally extended to freedmen through the Southern Homestead Act in 1866, black applicants faced patently discriminatory court challenges and decisions, illegal discriminatory fees, and other barriers to participation in the act's provisions. If the decades following the end of the Civil War presented an opportunity for African Americans to partake of the privileges and responsibilities of "self-ownership" in a risk-based society, the legal, institutional, and social instruments of white supremacy conspired to deny black freedmen full access to this mechanism of wealth accumulation. This failure of postbellum policymakers and market institutions to furnish freedmen with the necessary bases for full economic participation in American life must be understood as a crucial factor underlying our contemporary racial disparities in socioeconomic status.[38]

Here, a quality of radical indeterminacy, of Knightian risk, characterizes the legal and socioeconomic environment faced by African Americans in the era extending from the end of Reconstruction through to the middle decades of the twentieth century: it resides in the absence of basic financial protections, in the subjection of African-American families to discriminatory lending practices, in the exposure of African Americans to conditions of economic precariousness deriving from the absence of saved assets, income, or both, with all of these structural disparities underwritten by the regime of terror implicit within the Jim Crow order.[39] As I noted earlier, one of the sets of conditions that scholars identify as constitutive of Knightian uncertainty is one in which corruption and political instability undermine the capacity for observers to arrive at meaningful statistical projections of probable events. Those who find themselves operating in such a socially complex and volatile environment must rely upon their intuitive *estimates* of potential outcomes.[40] By this reckoning, an element of Knightian uncertainty inhabits the core of black American modernity.

These conditions of structural, racialized disparities of risk persisted well into the middle decades of the twentieth century, even as white Americans became the beneficiaries of new, collective mechanisms of state intervention in the management of risk. As Ira Katznelson has argued, African Americans entered the decades of the postwar boom without complete access to the same New Deal programs that subsidized the entry of millions of white Americans into the middle class. Southern conservative legislators ensured that domestic and agricultural workers would be excluded from the provisions of the Social Security Act, thereby effectively disqualifying the vast majority of African Americans for benefits.[41] If the G.I. Bill provided benefits and loan guarantees to millions of returning veterans after the Second World War, allowing them to attend college or to buy homes, it was also set up in such a way so as to privilege local control, enabling the private banks that oversaw disbursement of loans to discriminate against African-American applicants.[42] This latter practice was buttressed by the widespread practice of "redlining," in which private lenders, under the acquiescent guidance of the Federal Housing Administration, designated majority-black or low-income neighborhoods as "high risk" for mortgages.[43] Moreover, as consumers, African-American urban residents remained largely shut out of the flexible revolving credit system available to white, affluent consumers in suburban department stores and retail institutions, and were thus reliant upon the usurious interest rates and inflexible installment plans available at neighborhood stores.[44]

The period extending from the 1930s to the 1960s is generally understood (and frequently romanticized) as a time of broadly shared middle-class prosperity, buttressed by a shared social investment in the common good. However, as we have seen, this is only partially true: in contrast to white Americans, who enjoyed a period of comparative economic security, the conditions facing African Americans in midcentury perhaps more closely resembled the less egalitarian economic dispensation that would follow in subsequent decades. These various structural impediments to full participation in economic life exposed midcentury African Americans to conditions of precariousness that anticipate the broad contours, if not the mechanisms, of economic exclusion under neoliberalism. Much like the early twenty-first-century subject, navigating a market environment of radical, Knightian uncertainty, African Americans in the postwar period found that they could not count on access to certain state-regulated procedures that ensured a modicum of predictability for the white, middle-class beneficiaries of the New Deal legacy.

"TIGHTROPE"

Scott DeVeaux, documenting the emergence of bebop during the Second World War, noted that African-American musicians, faced with systematic marginalization within the wartime institutions of the music industry, looked for ways to "take advantage of the disadvantages." Faced with the exclusionary pressures that reserved prestigious radio gigs and extended hotel engagements for white big bands, bebop artists located opportunities at the interstices of the culture industry, harnessing the late-night jam session, the small-club venue, and the independent record label as improvised sites of economic potential.[45] Similarly, the midcentury economic environment facing African Americans nationwide precluded reliance upon the prevailing institutions of the postwar boom: here, the situation of radical indeterminacy, the sense that full citizenship and legal rights are not even in place to stabilize the conditions in which risks might be taken, speaks to the distinction between Knightian risk and Knightian uncertainty. In these conditions, a posture of radical extemporaneity becomes necessary.[46]

So, what would this posture sound like, in the event that we could hear it? How might midcentury jazz musicians realize this set of tensions and dispositions as a structure of feeling? In my view, the aesthetic strategies taken up by the members of the 1960s Miles Davis Quintet can collectively be understood as a useful window onto the negotiation of risk in this period. Miles Davis's quintet, from the years 1964 through to

1968, often referred to as the "second great quintet" (in relation to the renowned 1950s unit comprising "Philly Joe" Jones, John Coltrane, Red Garland, and Paul Chambers), developed a highly idiosyncratic musical vocabulary at the interstices of conventional post-bebop and avant-garde practices. The band's musical style would become inordinately influential in late twentieth-century jazz, as it became a key point of departure for the neoclassicist revival. By the end of 1963, Davis had put together a band consisting of saxophonist George Coleman, bassist Ron Carter, drummer Tony Williams, and pianist Herbie Hancock, with Wayne Shorter replacing Coleman on saxophone in September 1964.[47] Once established, the band enjoyed a longevity that saw them through the release of an extraordinary corpus of studio work, including *E.S.P.*, *Miles Smiles*, *Sorcerer*, and *Nefertiti*, along with *Miles in the Sky* and *Filles de Kilimanjaro*.[48] This longevity established conditions of trust and mutual support for the group's members, which allowed them to cultivate an environment in which musical turbulence, instability, and openness to risk served as the baseline assumptions of the band's work.

How might we read the aesthetics of the Davis quintet in terms of Knightian risk and Knightian uncertainty? One suggestive point of departure here is the Davis quintet's performance at New York's Philharmonic Hall on February 12, 1964, a benefit concert in support of the joint fundraising efforts of SNCC, CORE, and the NAACP Legal Defense Fund. This performance by an early incarnation of the 1960s quintet (with George Coleman on saxophone, rather than Wayne Shorter) was noteworthy both for its superlative musical achievement, and for the circumstances that surrounded the band's participation in the event: famously, Davis did not tell his bandmates until the night of the concert that they would be forgoing their standard performance fee, in deference to the concert's cause. While Davis's generous earnings were sufficient to allow him to waive compensation without a thought, his younger emerging sidemen faced different financial circumstances, and they were annoyed that Davis would make this decision without their input.[49] It is likely that the night's amazing performance, which yielded two groundbreaking live albums for Columbia (*My Funny Valentine* was made up of the set's ballads, while *Four + More* was devoted to its uptempo tunes), succeeded not *despite* these backstage tensions but *because* of them. As Davis would later recall, Carter and the others failed to convince him to release the quintet from its shared financial commitment, and consequently, they went onstage simmering with resentment: "There was a lot of creative tension happening that night that the people out front didn't know about. . . . When we came out to play, everybody was madder than a motherfucker with each other and so I think that anger created a fire, a tension that got into everybody's playing, and maybe that's one of the reasons everybody played with such intensity."[50]

Davis's insight into the aesthetic "fire" galvanized by the band's financial disagreement suggests that we should read this incident within the context of Davis's propensity to take interpersonal risks in the pursuit of his goals. In a different context, such an incident might have come off as a simple manifestation of clumsy mismanagement, but what we know about Davis's working methods suggest that there might have been an intentionality at work here. As Christopher Banks has argued, Davis consciously worked to cultivate an ambiguous social dynamic in which information was supplied, withheld, and manipulated in such a way as to derive a certain "quality of attention" from them.[51] Davis sought to forge a creative ecology in which risk taking was made normative by a shared sense of heightened mutual attunedness: "See, if you put a musician in a place where he has to do something different from what he does all the time, then he can do that—but he's got to think differently in order to do it. He has to use his imagination, be more creative, more innovative; he's got to take more risks."[52] Read in this context, Davis's belated revelations to his sidemen about pay for the Philharmonic Hall event seems to have been effective (whether intentionally so or not) in creating a space of productive antagonism. Davis was acutely aware that the bandstand was a social arena in which these tensions could be amplified, harnessed, and redirected.

In his reading of Davis's well-known interpretation of "My Funny Valentine," one of the signature tracks from Columbia's live recordings of the concert, Robert Walser reveals a performative approach saturated with risk, with the trumpeter willfully creating situations in which he constantly brings himself up to the threshold of failure. Davis bends a long tone almost a semitone downward without changing valves, taking a risk that the note would crack. He half-valves certain notes, setting up the possibility that the unfocused airstream would break abruptly to one side or the other of his fuzzy pitches. At a broader level, Davis risks the very possibility of losing his audience, as his reading of the song departs radically from any literal interpretation: dramatic interruptions, deliberately ugly phrasing, and uncomfortably long silences thwart all expectations of formal and melodic continuity.[53]

If Davis's interpretation of "My Funny Valentine" is one manifestation of aesthetic risk from the Philharmonic Hall date, the incendiary tempos and bold temporal manipulations of his rhythm section on such tunes as "Four," "Walkin'," and "Seven Steps to Heaven" are something else yet again. As many critics and scholars have noted, the aesthetic cultivated by Williams, Hancock, and Carter radically extends the supportive roles conventionally attributed to the rhythm section, reconfiguring harmonic support and timekeeping as explosive *melodic* interventions in their own right.[54] Their performances here and on subsequent recordings would not only provide the contexts for Davis's own risky performances, but would also enact an ethic of collective risk taking that Hancock later referred to as "controlled freedom": "When people were hearing us, they were hearing the avant-garde on the one hand, and they were hearing the history of jazz that led up to it on the other hand— because Miles was that history. . . . We were sort of walking a tightrope with the kind of experimenting we were doing in music, not total experimentation, but we used to call it 'controlled freedom.'"[55] A close reading of the quintet's music demonstrates how its aesthetic of controlled freedom operates at a level extending beyond its immediate sonic impact. As an aesthetic logic, controlled freedom entails the cultivation of a tension between individual risk taking and an unplanned, decentralized group coordination: while players are given extended latitude within a radically expansive constellation of metric, harmonic, and formal possibilities, these conventional points of departure never entirely lose their basic *regulatory* function. As such, performers navigating a space of controlled freedom construct a social dynamic in which freedom and responsibility are held in tension through the shared currency of risk.

How is this delicate balance achieved? The key stylistic elements of the quintet's music are consistently multivalent, always pointing outward, beyond themselves. This is readily apparent in the band's harmonic procedures, outlined in Wayne Shorter's compositions and elaborated via the rhythm section's interpretations. Ambiguity, of course, is built into the accumulated historical vocabularies of jazz harmony. In the canonical styles of swing and bebop, sevenths, ninths, and upper extensions always threaten to undermine the stability of root triads, and blues sonorities teeter ambivalently between competing modal orientations. However, in both Shorter's compositions and Hancock's chord voicings, this quality of ambiguity is pushed to extremes: Hancock's reliance upon dense harmonic clusters and polychordal or quartal constructions sets up internal dissonances that shimmer with tension, gesturing toward potential resolutions that never arrive. Describing the groundbreaking live set that was later documented on the recording *Live at the Plugged Nickel,* Hancock recalls the degree to which this sense of perpetually unresolved suspension inflected all dimensions of the group's sound: "In music, if you're going up a ski slope, you usually slide down on the other side . . . [but in the Plugged Nickel sessions,] you'd go up the ski slope and all of a sudden there'd be nothing there. Tony would make a crash and it would just be with the cymbal, without the bass drum as usual. Or I would build up to a big chord and Ron would do nothing. Everything we did was the opposite of what everyone expected us to do."[56] Part of what Davis's group does to destabilize bebop conventions is to move away from improvisations based upon rapid arpeggiation of the underlying chord structures. Instead, the fragmented melodic and harmonic environment of the quintet's music adheres more toward what Bob Gluck has termed a language of physical *gesture,* in which "melodic fragments, intervallic relationships, rhythmic cells, chromatic elements, repetition of rhythmic elements, or newly invented musical motifs" all point in open-ended trajectories toward a momentum outside of musical resolution.[57]

At the level of the underlying composition, the quintet's orientation is also toward chord sequences and melodic constructions that postpone or foreclose the arrival of harmonic stability. Shorter's compositions frequently hew to the periphery of functional harmony: at the local level, nonfunctional chords interrupt the flow of conventional progressions, and unusual harmonizations complicate bass lines that are otherwise legible as stable and straightforward, thwarting conventions of goal-directed motion.[58] This instability is intensified at the broader structural level of form: Shorter's compositions often tend to establish multiple tonal centers, which are rarely reinforced by ii-V-I progressions or any of the strong cadential sequences found in conventional bebop changes.[59] Thus, even within the framework of a conventionally repeating form, with the quintet cycling through thirty-two-bar choruses, the consequence of this absent or subterranean functionality is to generate a sphere of tonal uncertainty. In practice, of course, many of the quintet's performative realizations of Shorter's compositions would replace functional with nonfunctional harmonic substitutions, or would dispense with the stated chord changes altogether, moving into undefined harmonic territory negotiated on a moment-to-moment basis. This oft-cited "time, no changes" procedure would become tremendously influential for later generations of jazz performers.[60]

The "time" of "time, no changes" was itself a radically multilayered and unstable thing. Here, Tony Williams's approach to the drums would set the template for the rest of the group, with a roiling, unpredictable turbulence that jettisoned conventional understandings of the drummer as timekeeper. In playing the ride cymbal, Williams would sit slightly on top of the beat, a fraction of a second ahead, and his own ride cymbal patterns fragmented and rearranged the metrically stable patterns used by other players, intensifying the displacement of the beat implicit in conventional post-bebop drumming.[61] In many contexts, Williams would often establish a secondary time-feel working within and against the dominant timeline, a procedure that Keith Waters has referred to in terms of "metrical conflict."[62] Such polymetric frameworks would often set up the group for metric modulations, recentering the predominant swing feel around a new pulse, but as often as not Williams would hold the polymeter in place, sustaining both times at once. These constructions enabled his colleagues to approach a song's rhythmic terrain as an expansive temporal field, open to a variety of interpretive strategies and creative directions.

Williams's capacity for producing such radically open, multivalent metric frameworks derives in part from a cultural openness, a voracious catholicity of musical interests. Alongside his interest in rock, and in western classical music, which he was exposed to growing up in Boston, Williams had studied Indian classical music in the early 1960s, several years before the Beatles' travels to the subcontinent led to the wide-spread popularization of Hindustani music.[63] As Herbie Hancock would later attest, Williams's familiarity with this tradition made its presence felt in his jazz drumming, where it could often be discerned in his use of particular technical devices:

> There were no drummers out there doing any of the stuff that Tony was doing. The closest one I would say was Elvin Jones; he was playing with counter rhythms but musically most of what I heard from Elvin involved triplets. Tony was playing with much more complex things that involved phrases ending in five and seven and eleven, and looping those phrases, almost like in Indian music. He would start at the end of a chorus, he would play this thing in some other kind of meter, and always wind up landing on [his] feet. Since then jazz musicians have done that kind of thing a lot but it really started with Tony.[64]

What Hancock is describing here is quite similar to the North Indian rhythmic process called the *tihai*, a thrice-repeated structure in which complex additive rhythmic patterns would be played in groupings seemingly independent from the underlying meter.[65] As with Williams's tendency to land "on his feet" in his performance of these "phrases . . . ending in five and seven and eleven," the goal with a *tihai* is to arrange the repetitive groupings in such a way that the last beat of the final grouping falls on the downbeat of the next rhythmic cycle. Owing to both its internal complexities and its complex relation to the underlying meter, the *tihai* is something of a technical feat, and in attempting to emulate Williams's jazz adaptation of the pattern, Hancock experienced his eventual success in resolving the pattern with something close to euphoria:

> I said, "I want to be able to do that with notes." . . . I was fascinated by what was coming out of [Williams] musically and I wanted to translate that into what I could do on the piano. I remember playing a concert in Europe somewhere, and I was soloing. At the end of the choruses I played some figure that had one of these magical, non-triplet, non-duple phrases that came out . . . bam . . . right on the one, where I was hoping it would come out. I was stunned I actually did that and I looked up at Tony and Tony just had a little smile on his face. He nodded his head, like a sign of approval—that I had gotten an A.[66]

What is noteworthy in both the *tihai* and the embedded polyrhythmic phrasing that Hancock describes here is that their establishment of a loose, seemingly unconnected relation to the underlying meter creates a feeling of suspension whose resolution only becomes clear at the point of articulation between underlying and superimposed meters. It establishes a musical risk—the risk of continued disarticulation, of a rhythmic imprecision heard as failure—that demands of its performer both the proper advance calculation of the point of arrival and the virtuosic command of the instrument necessary to carry it out. Here, the ostensibly free-floating phrases are grounded in points of rhythmic synchrony that function as sites of tacit mutual accountability for the quintet's performers.

Video footage of the quintet's performance of "Agitation" before a live audience in Stockholm in 1967 provides a striking example of how the band negotiates these situations of metrical conflict in practice.[67] Shortly after Davis's opening melodic phrase establishes the tempo at around 320 to the quarter note in common 4/4 time, Ron Carter begins a slow walking bass line that tacitly suggests a secondary meter of 3/4, overlapping with the initial tempo and maintaining the original quarter-note pulse as a common ictus between the two conflicting meters. Even as Carter reverts to the prevailing 4/4 meter, Williams's ride cymbal pattern preserves something of the conflicting 3/4 grouping, subtly accentuating the alternate meter through the strategic emphasis and omission of certain beats. Periodically, he interrupts the flow of the underlying swing feel with explosive snare drum fills that temporarily establish a third countervailing meter.

The turbulent, multivalent, and highly ambiguous temporal framework that the quintet establishes here can be understood as radically *uncertain,* in the specific sense outlined earlier in this chapter. Its internal tensions can be resolved in multiple unpredictable ways, and yet the individual rigidities of each competing metrical timeline also suggest multiple avenues for failure: a band member could fail to keep up with the tempo of the prevailing meter; he could fail to hear the establishment of a secondary meter in the regrouping of beats and their subdivisions; he could also miss the decisive resolution of one or several of these competing tempi. Each of these sites of potential rhythmic error are magnified by the harmonic context of "Agitation" as a composition that occupies a midpoint between the fixed harmonic rhythm of conventional post-bebop forms and the radically undefined harmonies of "time, no changes": the elastic lengths of its fungible formal sections demand a rigorous attentiveness from all players. For these reasons, the band's rapid, elegant, and decisive transition to a new, medium-tempo swing one minute into the performance is a mark of its collective virtuosity: following quickly upon Davis's new melodic cue, Williams suddenly cuts to a pace of approximately 216 to the quarter note, at around two-thirds of the initial prevailing tempo (and doubling the pace of the dotted half-figures accentuated by Ron Carter and Tony Williams in the opening section of the performance). Unlike half-time or double-time transitions in conventional post-bebop performance, this one falls at a more complex mathematical remove from the song's original time-feel, and highlights the ways in which the quintet's musical idiom demands an acutely intense awareness of musical risk from its performers.

The Davis Quintet's explosive, ambivalent, and yet still pulsatile approach to rhythm and meter highlights the way that it locates risk in the space between post-bebop and avant-garde musical sensibilities. If bebop drumming remains largely isometric, grounded in the regular grouping of pulses into hierarchies of emphasis, a key innovation of "new thing" drummers such as Rashied Ali and Sunny Murray is to dismantle isometer as an implicit temporal anchor, thereby allowing multiple registers of rhythmic organization to be heard simultaneously.[68] By contrast, one dimension of Williams's playing that was noted by contemporary observers was that he never entirely abandons the metrically grouped pulse as a point of reference, even as his surface cross-rhythms alternately undermine, deemphasize, and temporarily suspend its efficacy.[69] Both Ali's and Williams's drumming styles are the product of virtuosities, but one virtuosity is more easily *quantifiable*, more easily subject to logics of enumeration. No matter what liberties may be permitted through the open ambiguities of polymetric combinations, pulse functions as a tacit common denominator in the Davis quintet's works. Such is the "tightrope" implied in Hancock's account of controlled freedom: a quicksilver negotiation of the space between expansive potentiality and a tacit, underlying accountability.

What is at stake in the Davis quintet's aesthetic of controlled freedom is an intricate set of tensions between individual and collective responsibility, a complex dialectical space that is held open, refusing resolution. In the same way that the band's membership walked what Hancock referred to as a "tightrope" between straightahead and avant-garde sensibilities, its daunting polyrhythmic energy called upon its members to take up strategies of improvisation that demanded considerable individual virtuosity, in the same moment that they helped to affirm and magnify the contributions of others. As such, the quintet's music embodies an ambiguous social model of risk that resonates with its environment in a complicated, irresolvable way, gesturing toward a variety of overlapping and contradictory cultural dynamics. Read in relation to the turbulent and rapidly shifting topography of race in late 1960s America, it suggests a manifestly flexible model for confronting *uncertainty*, for gracefully negotiating the accelerated temporalities of a historical moment in which the center did not hold. For African Americans facing the manifold social, political, and economic obstacles of the period, extending from housing discrimination, underemployment, and economic precariousness to the continued intransigence of white-dominated institutions, this period embodied the manifestly unpredictable dynamics of Knightian uncertainty. We find ourselves here in the domain of what Clyde Woods has called a *blues epistemology*, a cluster of gestures and dispositions that helped people to make sense of structural upheaval as it was unfolding.[70] The quintet's music did not offer a concrete, easily legible set of solutions to this context, so much as it proposed a way of being that was equal to it: alert to the individual's creative responsibilities, and yet committed to navigating cultural terrain in concert with others, in a mutually supportive network of collective realization.

DOING THE MATH: THE NEOCLASSICISTS
TAKE ON POSTBOP

The "second" Miles Davis Quintet has long been understood as one of the most influential jazz groups of the last fifty years. The impact of the quintet's compositions, technical procedures, and rhythm-section performance is apparent across the breadth of late twentieth-century jazz. In particular, the quintet's work was one of the key points of reference for the first wave of neoclassicist "young lions" during the 1980s, establishing postbop as a template for a generation of musicians looking to reconcile musical innovation with a particular conception of the jazz canon. In some respects, this influence was direct: Davis's Hancock-Williams-Carter rhythm section reformed as the group V.S.O.P. in the late 1970s along with trumpeter Freddie Hubbard, and helped to precipitate a new interest in acoustic, straightahead jazz during that period.[71] Following Wynton Marsalis's recruitment to CBS records, Herbie Hancock served as producer on Marsalis's eponymous debut record for the label in 1982, and the V.S.O.P. rhythm section played behind Marsalis on several of the album's tracks (including Wayne Shorter's composition "RJ," taken from *E.S.P.*, the inaugural studio album of the Davis quintet).[72] Terence Blanchard also looked to the Davis quintet as a site of inspiration, and his debt to the Davis group's style is particularly evident in some of his collaborations with saxophonist Donald Harrison during the 1980s.[73] Whether through direct collaboration or indirect emulation, the subsequent generation of jazz artists (many of whom were alumni from the later iterations of Art Blakey's Jazz Messengers) would look to the legacy of the second Davis quintet as a key point of stylistic departure, as is evidenced in the work of such figures as Bobby Watson, Mulgrew Miller, Wallace Roney, Jeff Watts, and Kenny Kirkland, among others.[74]

Given the long shadow cast by the postbop innovations of the Davis quintet, how might we go about interpreting the changing significance of postbop as it found its way into the late twentieth century? One way to answer this question is to look at the discursive logic that Marsalis brings to bear in explicating his own band's approach to technical procedures originally explored by the Williams-Carter-Hancock rhythm section. In 2010, Ethan Iverson, the former pianist for the trio known as the Bad Plus, conducted an interview with Wynton Marsalis for his blog, *Do the Math*, in which he presented the trumpeter with a kind of "blindfold test" of notable jazz trumpet tracks. One of Iverson's selections was "Knozz-Moe-King," a fiercely polyrhythmic track from one of Marsalis's most acclaimed early albums, *Live at Blues Alley*, featuring Marcus Roberts on piano, Jeff "Tain" Watts on drums, and Robert Hurst on bass. Marsalis's reflections on his band's *Blues Alley* set give us some insight into the demanding musical devices that his early working bands put into play on albums such as *Think of One*, *Black Codes (From the Underground)*, and *Marsalis Standard Time Vol. 1*. Marsalis describes a procedure of "rhythmic stretto," in which one or several players would set up countervailing rhythmic patterns that worked in dissonance with the underlying metrical structure. Once these patterns were established, creating a feeling of musical tension, Marsalis would give a thematic cue to let everyone know to "come out of that rhythm [they're] playing," resolving the metrical ambiguity and reestablishing the prevailing time.[75] Elsewhere, he has described this procedure in terms of "call-and-response rhythms," temporal procedures governed by what Marsalis attributes to a West African conception of rhythmic overlay:

> Mainly we were trying to create drama in the music. We had a rhythmic conception, and it was an African conception that we actually got from listening to [John Coltrane's] band. . . . But, as an example, Kenny [Kirkland, his then-pianist] would play a rhythm and set up a repetition. Then Jeff [Watts, drummer] would play something against that rhythm. The bass would keep a constant part, and the piano would play a rhythm against that. We would have a three-way rhythm that would develop against an underlying form. The bass would keep that form, sort of like the main drum in an African drum ensemble around which everything else revolves. Then at the apex of the rhythm, we would resolve, and it was just like a little explosion almost.[76]

If Marsalis cites Coltrane as a key point of reference here, the rhythmic procedure he describes is also clearly indebted to the metric superimpositions employed by the 1960s Miles Davis Quintet: as with the "phrases . . . ending in five and seven and eleven" that Herbie Hancock emulated in his interactions with Tony Williams, Marsalis and his rhythm section had developed a sophisticated series of procedures that set up elaborate rhythmic groupings, positioned at a remove from the prevailing meter, but also grounded in the common denominator of an underlying rhythmic subdivision.[77]

However, if the technical devices used by the Davis quintet and the early Marsalis group are clearly similar at the level of their sonic traces, the language that the two bands use to account for their respective applications of these devices reveals a difference of emphasis. For example, the sense we get of the Davis rhythm section's resolutions of metrical ambiguity was that his players felt their way tentatively through procedures whose internal logic was negotiated on the fly: the cues that the quintet used to shift rhythmic emphasis were often subtle, and only identifiable *as* cues in retrospect. Hancock, for example, recalls that "no matter how much we as a rhythm section may have been struggling to stretch, but keep the groove happening—you know if it was kind of falling apart, as it did from time to time—Miles, with his playing, would *center* it, kind of tie it all together, as though he *sensed* what the link was."[78] By contrast, Marsalis's account of the similar polyrhythmic devices employed by his band tends to imply that their logic, if not their precise timing, was meticulously rehearsed: once Marsalis, Watts, and Kirkland (or Roberts) had settled upon a mutually agreeable rhythmic pattern, the unambiguous trajectory of the band's interactions was directed toward the telos of its resolution, signaled through the performance of a prearranged thematic cue. In Marsalis's description of the technique, these cues serve a role analogous to the cadential fills employed by master drummers in the context of West African music, which cue the ensemble to move on to the next ostinato in the musical process. What is implied here is a clear hierarchy, with one player (Marsalis himself, according to one of the above accounts) responsible for indicating the precise moment in which the band would emerge from the metric overlay, realized in a decisively cumulative "explosion." Moreover, in valuing the decisive execution of these "rhythmic stretti," Marsalis also stresses that there are clear criteria by which to evaluate failures in their "proper" execution. Reviewing "Knozz-Moe-King" some twenty-four years later, Marsalis (much to Iverson's surprise) dismisses the performance as "sad," ruefully noting that Jeff Watts had failed to meet the trumpeter's cues, the thematic signals that indicate when they are to break out of the repeated cross-rhythms.[79] The polymetric constructions and their resolutions are here framed as a musical problem for which there could be "right" and "wrong" answers.

In the decade that saw the emergence of neoclassicism in jazz, one criticism that was leveled at the "young lions" generation was that they had taken a stylistic and procedural vocabulary that midcentury musicians had worked out in an ad hoc, extemporaneous fashion, and *codified* it, subjected it to a rule-based logic well removed from its earlier 1960s resonances. One instance of this criticism can be found in a 1986 article by critic Larry Kart, in which he takes issue with the music of the band OTB (Out of the Blue), a quintet of emerging artists that the revived Blue Note label assembled through a nationwide audition process in the mid-1980s. Comparing OTB's self-titled debut album to what he describes as a stylistically very similar recording, Tyrone Washington's *Natural Essence* (featuring Woody Shaw and Kenny Barron, among others), Kart argues that the difference between the approaches of the two bands lies in the fact that OTB treats postbop as a stylistic moment to be emulated as an end in itself, rather than a point of departure to be radically exceeded:

> But the emotional tone of the two albums is quite different. While most of the members of Out of the Blue sound as though they thought of their music as a style (i.e. as a series of rules one must adopt and accept), the music of Washington and his partners is fundamentally explosive, a discontented elegance that keeps zooming off in search of extreme emotional states. . . . The strains of transition that supposedly were confined to the [1960s] jazz avantgarde may have been even more violently felt in the music that lay just to the "right" of it.[80]

Kart's analysis gets at a dimension of 1980s neoclassicism that helps to explain its perspective on 1960s postbop: in many instances, musical procedures forged in the heat of an extraordinarily turbulent cultural moment would subsequently be reinterpreted as a formalized musical language. What may initially have been conceived as a *descriptive* grammar, a means of pinpointing the internal dynamics of individual performances, becomes repurposed as a *prescriptive* grammar, imposing a rigid code of conduct upon its adherents. For Kart and others, this move effects a collapse in tension, an erasure of the world-historical turbulence that informs the singular intensity of the 1960s postbop aesthetic.

Wynton Marsalis's early 1980s work is often highlighted as one of the high points of this postbop codification, but the significance of his band's aesthetic extends beyond any "purely musical" realization. Marsalis's comments in Stanley Crouch's liner notes for *Marsalis Standard Time Vol. 1* interprets his band's polymetric language as the site of a musical parable, outlining a broader message about the relationship between freedom and individual responsibility. "Every instrument," says Marsalis,

> is allowed the freedom to interpret the form from a different metric vantage point. This frees Marcus [Roberts], Bob [Hurst], and Jeff [Watts] from having to keep a strict basic time, but gives them the responsibility of resolving superimposed meters correctly in the original form. . . . Though we are approaching the form with rhythmic and metric freedom, everyone has to work within the flow of the improvisation. The last thing I'm interested in is

freedom that can only justify itself by its existence. I'm interested in freedom that encompasses the fundamentals of music, allowing for inspiration rather than desperation.[81]

Marsalis's comments provide a new interpretive framework for understanding the rhythmic vocabularies they derived from the Davis quintet's "controlled freedom." In contrast to the collaborative ambiguities at work in the interactions of the Davis quintet's rhythm section, Marsalis's conception highlights the stakes that they raise for the individual performer, as well as the criteria that establish whether or not the performer has risen to the challenge. In doing so, he establishes extremely clear guidelines for the kind of virtuosity that he deems to be nonnegotiable for jazz musicians. At the same time, his comments contain a moral edge: by his reckoning, a bright line exists between success and failure, in music and in life, and the individual must learn to respect it.

CONCLUSION: "AT-RISK" AND "RISK-CAPABLE" SUBJECTIVITIES

In cultivating musical environments of intensive risk, both the 1960s Davis band and the 1980s Marsalis units model new and powerful modalities of virtuosity. However, their deployment of risk also manifests itself as a phenomenological, tactile embodiment of an idea that over the last half-century has increasingly come to occupy the center of contemporary social and economic life. In our present moment, risk has become the site of an elegant ideological suturing of social morality and market values. Contemporary valorizations of the "free market" would locate morality at the core of our culture of risk, driving it from within. However, in our social construction of financial risk, moral values tend to be imposed upon market dynamics after the fact, as a retrospective explication of their logic. In the context of our present culture of financialization, what serves as a universal bedrock for the operation of the markets is not so much a constellation of moral values (thrift, moral discipline, and the work ethic made corporeal through the workings of the "invisible hand"), but rather, an abstract series of metrics largely stripped of accountability to the social world that they inhabit.[82]

This shift to abstract risk, implemented in the name of increased rationality, has in fact had a hand in intensifying the more irrational twists and turns of the market. To invest in a financial *derivative* is, as its name implies, to invest in something one step removed from an underlying asset that it "bets" upon: one is no longer invested in the physical plant, the labor force, or the stakeholders bound up in that asset, but rather, in a derivative linked only to the price movements of that asset. By effacing the connection of financial instruments to any underlying social turbulence, market actors alter the dynamics of trade, redefining financial assets as objects of play. Indeed, as Jean Comaroff and John Comaroff have suggested, these developments collapse the moral space separating the stock markets from conventional gambling, and it is perhaps not coincidental that the market's regular abandonment to fits of "irrational exuberance" has coincided with a rise in the status and respectability of the casino as an institution.[83]

However, it is one thing to embrace risk and quite another to manage risk successfully. If the gleeful assumption of high-stakes risk has become a prerequisite of contemporary "entrepreneurial selfhood," as self-described "futurists" enjoin us to throw ourselves into an unknowable tomorrow, we are nevertheless still subject to a kind of actuarial accounting, in which our ability to deal with risk becomes a metric of stature and moral worth. It is in this context that we begin to see risk retroactively commandeered as a moral tool of explanation for chronic social problems. As Randy Martin has noted, responsibility for socioeconomic disparities, which was at one time attributed to the broader shortcomings of market processes and institutions, now falls decisively on the individual:

> The term "at risk" . . . came into common parlance in the early 1980s to designate those who are objects of structural inequalities. Instead of talking about economic exploitation, racial domination, or sexual oppression, the attribution of risk shifted the burdens of these exclusionary social effects to the groups themselves. Poverty and race could then become risk factors for failure . . . . By describing negative outcomes of social life in terms of risk, unpredictabilities of the market like layoffs through downsizing could become integrated into the experience of the employed as an ongoing uncertainty that all would have to live with.[84]

In the emergent social environment described by Martin, life takes the form of a performance review in which the isolated market actor is held up to particular standards of financial acumen, assessed without regard for historical circumstances or structural inequities. The "at-risk" individual, her economic deficiencies attributed to a host of personal, individual failings, is excluded from society's circle of care.

The subject of "at-risk" behavior, much like the hedge fund swashbuckler cited by Appadurai and Mirowski, is a figure specific to our own historical moment. Like its parent concept of "risk," the concept of being "at-risk" has a genealogy, a history traceable to emergent practices in the insurance industry, the health sciences, and education. Beginning in the early twentieth century, life insurance companies, who already employed mortality tables to set premiums for their clients, extended their probabilistic analyses to other so-called "risk factors," statistically tabulated categories ranging from workplace occupation to blood pressure. In their effort to combat the increasing prevalence of certain types of chronic disease, physicians increasingly sought to integrate the risk factor approach into their own diagnoses, and by the early 1960s, the statistical methodologies of risk-factor analysis had become widely accepted as a means of intervening in public health debates.[85] Throughout the 1970s and 1980s, the tendency to assess certain lifestyle proclivities or social trends as "at risk" was extended to other domains, particularly the field of education. One of the most dramatic invocations of "at-risk" status was in the very title of a prominent 1983 white paper commissioned by the Reagan administration: *A Nation at Risk: The Imperative for Educational Reform* sounded an alarm about what its authors saw as a "rising tide of mediocrity" in American education, a miasma of soaring illiteracy rates and plunging test scores that its authors saw as placing the country "at risk" of falling behind its industrialized western competitors.[86] The attribution of "at-risk" status to specific demographics during the AIDS crisis dovetailed with a toxic political environment in which marginalized groups were increasingly "held to account" as the ostensible sources of social pathology.[87]

The active period of the "second" Davis quintet coincides with the cultural moment in which some of the underlying assumptions behind the "at-risk" concept are first articulated. An emergent social-scientific discourse about the black "underclass" begins to establish the notion, popular to this day in conservative circles, that disparities in economic opportunity between whites and African Americans can be attributed to a putative "culture of poverty." One of the formative texts in this literature was an internal policy document penned by then-Undersecretary of Labor Daniel Patrick Moynihan, entitled *The Negro Family: The Case for National Action*. Though it was not initially intended for widespread dissemination, the paper, which would soon achieve notoriety as the "Moynihan report," was released to the public by the Lyndon Johnson administration in its effort to respond to political fallout in the wake of the 1965 Watts uprisings.[88] In many ways, this controversial analysis stood at the interstices of what we would recognize as fiscally liberal and socially conservative worldviews. Even as it highlighted the importance of the legacies of slavery, systemic disinvestment, and employment discrimination in explaining ongoing structural disparities in African-American communities, it attributed the *persistence* of these disparities to a putative "tangle of pathology" at the core of the African-American family structure. It is important to reiterate here the degree to which Moynihan's analysis proceeded from a *liberal* point of departure: Moynihan was driven to author the report out of a conviction that African-American economic inequality was at the root of the problems he was seeking to address. Moreover, for Moynihan, the solution to these problems was seen to be a liberal one, in which wealth redistribution would play a key part.[89] Nevertheless, his argument, shorn of its liberal features, would later be taken up by conservatives as the basis of a purely *cultural* explanation for persistent racial inequality.[90]

The language of the Moynihan report anticipates the emergence of an analytical consensus in which "risk factors" and "at-risk behaviors" stand in for structural inequality as a proximate cause of racial disparities. The report insists that black youth raised in fatherless households are "in danger" of being drawn into socially deviant behavior, giving themselves over to "instant gratification" and falling short in measures of educational attainment. Moreover, even as he recognizes the important recent economic gains made by middle-class African Americans in the postwar period, Moynihan argues that this group, kept in proximity to lower-income neighborhoods via the realities of housing discrimination, were "therefore constantly exposed to the pathology of the disturbed group and constantly in danger of being drawn into it."[91] Moynihan's rhetoric of black middle-class "exposure" to "danger" closely resembles the tone and terminology of later "at-risk" discourses, their insinuation that African Americans stand in precarious relation to prevailing metrics of social and economic performance.

However, as I have argued throughout this discussion, the situation facing African Americans "on the ground" in the mid-1960s, its resonances felt in the turbulence of the decade's music, was in fact always much closer to a condition of *Knightian uncertainty* than of ordinary risk. The radical indeterminacy of the socioeconomic conditions facing African Americans effectively suspended the predictable logic through which African Americans might have approached the social metrics cited in the Moynihan report: the unknowable vicissitudes of employment, home ownership, or consumer loans for African-American families destabilize efforts to place this situation in any straightforward relation to prevailing narratives of white upward class mobility. In the context of the underlying volatility of American culture in the 1960s, this situation makes plain its resistance to the ordinary tools of risk management.

In part, the Great Society programs introduced under Lyndon Johnson were implemented with the intention of addressing some of the profound uncertainties of black economic life in midcentury America. However, even as a context was created for socioeconomic stability, new sources of instability emerged in the 1970s and 1980s, as the institutions of our present regime of flexible accumulation began to take shape. Liberalized trade, deindustrialization, the deregulation of the private sector, and the dismantling of long-standing labor protections and forms of social assistance—all of these developments worked to inscribe new sites of precariousness in lower-income communities, even as the old, explicitly discriminatory practices were swept aside. Social and economic risk were now regulated via new, ostensibly race-neutral mechanisms of discrimination, which enabled state and market institutions to separate the "at-risk" from the "risk-capable," in contexts ranging from the prosecution of the War on Drugs to the marketing of subprime mortgages.[92]

This realignment of American economic and social life since the midtwentieth century, in which individual performance is increasingly understood as falling along an axis separating "at-risk" from "risk-capable" subjects, may help to provide a context for the subtle yet important differences between the stylistic vocabularies of 1960s and 1980s postbop, and the rhetorics deployed to explain them by their respective protagonists. In the densely polyrhythmic intensities of the Davis quintet's work, in its privileging of a radical *attunedness,* we hear one potential response to a chaotic moment of social possibility, one in which the radical unpredictability of American social life was taken as given. The cultural moment of the 1980s, by contrast, was no less given over to uncertainty, but its ideological, social, and economic terrain were increasingly shaped by a polarized language in which uncertainty and ambiguity were no longer welcome. In contexts ranging from the emergent faith in "shareholder value" as the lone arbiter of market performance, to the resuscitated Manichean oppositions of the Cold War, the virtuosic subject of the new era increasingly saw Knightian uncertainty as merely another variety of risk to be mastered. Here, in and alongside its old meanings, its multivalent, unresolvable complexity, the postbop of the 1980s takes on a new layer of resonances, as it assumes the contours of the hypercompetitive decade in which its performers live and work.

As I have argued above, in their effects, if not in their particulars, the postwar conditions of economic precariousness facing African-American communities anticipate the structural disparities endemic to our era of deindustrialization and financialization. Both the social upheaval of the 1960s and the economic volatility of our present age of financialization are saturated by an ontology of turbulence, in which ordinary people are exposed to radical uncertainty. In this context, improvisation, as a cultural technique for responding to risk, becomes an indispensable structure of feeling. Our present culture embraces a pointedly abstracted understanding of risk, uprooted from the specific conditions that give rise to it. But we should remember that such risk taking always bears the traces of social struggle and antagonism, that uncertainty is always shot through with historical intensities and unfinished business.

CHAPTER 2

"Homecoming"

*Dexter Gordon and the 1970s Fiscal
Crisis in New York City*

In 1976, the legendary saxophonist Dexter Gordon, who had been living in Europe for fifteen years, returned to New York for a series of
engagements at George Wein's Storyville jazz club and the Village Vanguard. Gordon had made other visits to the United States during his
years abroad, including a well-received appearance at the Newport Jazz
Festival in 1972 that saw him participating in an all-star midnight jam
session at Radio City Music Hall.[1] However, the ecstatic reception Gordon received during his 1976 tour was something altogether different,
an outpouring of adulation from critics and fans that led, in short order,
to Bruce Lundvall's signing of Gordon to the Columbia jazz roster, and
to Gordon's permanent relocation to the United States in 1977.[2] The
impact of Gordon's visit was such that later historical accounts, including Ken Burns's popular *Jazz* documentary, would pinpoint the moment
as a pivotal event in the public's renewed interest in acoustic, straightahead jazz in the late 1970s, culminating in the emergence of the first
generation of young neoclassicists during the subsequent decade.

Gordon's triumphant return to the United States is often portrayed as
an event whose implications are wholly internal to the jazz world.[3] His
position as a key figure in the bebop movement, a style seen as embat-
tled in the context of 1970s fusion and avant-garde sensibilities, helps
to frame his return as a long-awaited vindication of a putative "jazz
mainstream," centered around the acoustic, swing-driven interpretation
of compositions based upon the blues or Tin Pan Alley forms. Gordon's

New York engagements were among the most visible events in a nascent traditionalist trend that was already in progress in the mid-1970s, ranging from the neo-swing of Scott Hamilton to the intricate postbop of Woody Shaw, and as such, they constitute an important, if neglected, early chapter in the history of the neoclassicist movement. At the same time, the "hero's welcome" given to Gordon also has the potential to tell us something about events beyond the Village Vanguard's fabled awning, providing us with a window onto the social tensions enveloping the city of New York at the time of the saxman's visit.

Gordon's visit in 1976 coincides with a particularly challenging moment in the history of New York City, with the metropolis reeling from the impact of a recent fiscal crisis. The New York of the 1970s, portrayed in numerous historical and fictional representations as a site of lawlessness and moral decay, had become a key object of critical invective during a decade of conservative retrenchment. Events such as the uprisings that attended the notorious power outage of July 1977, or the citywide manhunt for a serial killer throughout that same "Summer of Sam," had crystallized in the public mind as evidence that New York had simply ceased to function as a normal city.

Gordon's return stands out in sharp relief against the apocalyptic imagery of these events, hailed as a redemptive trace of the past made manifest in the compromised New York of the present. In liner notes, interviews, and letters to publications such as *Down Beat,* critics, fans, and artists attribute to Gordon an integrity that they hold up as an implicit repudiation of the era's less defensible trends. This nostalgic enthusiasm for Gordon participates, however indirectly, in a larger climate of cultural conservatism in the late 1970s, a pervasive sense that the well-meaning liberal reforms of the previous two decades had resulted in grave consequences for Americans. Nowhere was this conservative critique more pointed than in contemporaneous denunciations of New York City. In their narrative, the city's failings during the 1970s had less to do with wealth polarization, unemployment, or the city's systemic underfunding of social programs than with cultural problems. New York's malaise, its image as a site of cultural degeneracy, was increasingly laid at the feet of African Americans, Latino/Latina residents, immigrants, and the LGBTQ community. However, as Miriam Greenberg has pointed out, this influential narrative ignores the larger structural crises underlying New York's fall from grace, crises precipitated by the unsustainable actions of the city's political and corporate elites.

New York City's experience of fiscal crisis and cultural polarization during the 1970s anticipates key dimensions of the culture of neoliberalism in subsequent decades. The city's massive debt, accrued in large part through its underwriting of a massive real estate expansion in the late 1960s, had brought the city to the brink of default. Its solution entailed severe cuts to social services, and the appropriation of union pension funds to pay off the city's municipal bonds. These draconian measures were coupled with an aggressive wooing of financial capital, with the city using marketing campaigns, real estate rezoning, and financial incentives to reframe New York's tarnished image and make the city appealing to investors and the middle class. As David Harvey has noted, this response to the crisis can best be understood as a trial run for the measures undertaken by Reagan and Thatcher at the close of the decade. The city's actions in the 1970s established a precedent for the structural transformations enacted by the Reagan administration, whose policies initiated a redistribution of wealth from middle- and working-class Americans to the country's financial elite. At the same time, the country's vehement denunciations of New York's most marginalized communities is itself an anticipation of another aspect of neoliberalism: the deflection of blame for structural or material failures onto the domain of culture.

My discussion here situates Dexter Gordon's "Homecoming" against the socioeconomic backdrop of mid-1970s New York, in order to identify the ways in which these two stories, that of New York culture and of its political economy, both inform and in turn are informed by the contested place of acoustic jazz in this time and place. Proceeding from an account of the city's volatile cultural climate in the years following the fiscal crisis, I will approach the moment of Gordon's return as an event that concretizes the link between New York's emergent neotraditional jazz scene and the public's ambivalence about New York during this period. Alongside my analysis of music from *Homecoming,* a recording that coincides with the moment of Gordon's return, I devote particular attention to the perspectives of jazz critics and fans, who frequently position their advocacy of acoustic jazz as a response to the changing landscape of contemporary popular music in this period, a bulwark against the encroachment of punk's nihilism or disco's artifice. Finally, I argue that these discourses, with their rhetorics of nostalgia and their suspicion of social change, participate in a larger trend of cultural conservatism that would serve to legitimize the neoliberal transformations of New York and the United States in the coming decades.

THE BLACKOUT AND THE FISCAL CRISIS

In the mid-1970s, New York was undergoing a period of turmoil infamous in its social history. One noteworthy episode in the city's ongoing crisis of that period serves as an especially resonant visual shorthand for the city's troubles. Within a year of Dexter Gordon's New York engagements at Storyville and the Village Vanguard, New York City would suffer the blackout of July 13, 1977, when key power stations and transmission lines north of the city were struck by lightning, and the readership of the local and national media would be treated to images presenting a singularly ominous take on the Manhattan skyline. One such image, which centers around the World Trade Center towers, depicts the financial district shrouded in darkness, the mute twin towers eerily backlit by light emanating from somewhere on the Jersey shore. Another photograph surveys the dim, indistinct blur of the skyline as seen from Windows on the World, the World Trade Center restaurant opened the previous year to foreground the spectacularity of the new towers.[4] Such allusions to the "darkened" skyline served as a kind of establishing shot for the representation of events on the ground, as coverage of the blackout implicated racial and ethnic minorities in the breakdown of social order that ensued.

As Miriam Greenberg notes in her account of this period, the panicky, apocalyptic media accounts of the blackout, with their verbal and visual representations of looting and violence in the most economically disadvantaged sections of the city, served to reinforce a pervasive attitude of reactionary intolerance that had increasingly come to characterize the public understanding of New York City in the mid-1970s. The coverage of the event was suffused with classic racist imagery, as journalists applied animal metaphors and implications of disease to looters' behavior, and used references to "darkness" and "blackness" to signify on the long-standing negative implications of these words in Eurocentric discourse: dirtiness, fear, primitivism, and racial inferiority.[5]

In this context, it becomes useful for us to situate the picture of mid-1970s New York we derive from these conservative discourses in relation to contemporaneous narratives of Dexter Gordon's New York return in the jazz media. There is a tendency, in some later jazz narratives, to meticulously separate the whole question of Gordon's contributions to the jazz revival from the broader social history of New York in this period: Gordon's return is often discussed largely as a response to other strictly musical developments in the jazz world, as a return to form for mainstream jazz in the face of what were often depicted as encroaching threats from jazz-rock hybrids and the jazz avant-garde.[6] However, if we attend to the tenor of these debates over jazz as they unfolded in mid-1970s jazz publications, it becomes clear that Gordon's "homecoming" was hugely resonant for the very reason that his return was implicitly understood as a tacit commentary on decline and renewal in late-1970s American culture in general, and that of New York City in particular.

The 1977 blackout brought out into the open a latent racist sentiment of anti-urbanism bound up in the rightward shift of American politics throughout the decade.[7] This sentiment was shaped by a number of factors, from the demographic changes in inner urban cores precipitated by midcentury white suburban flight, to the increasing unease of exurban whites with the cultural and political upheavals of the late 1960s, which were often centered in urban enclaves such as Haight-Ashbury, Berkeley, or Greenwich Village. However, each of these shifts circulated around the central ordering fact of the civil rights movement, which had utterly destabilized the predictable contours of postwar American society. Above all, the movement sought to install the visibility of black life at the core of American consciousness, and outside the South, the major cities were the primary locus of this new visibility. With the radicalization of the civil rights movement in the late 1960s, and the explosive unrest in black working-class communities in sites such as Watts, Newark, and Detroit, the public image of the inner city in white suburban communities became increasingly wedded to their anxieties about the political demands of African Americans.[8]

However, white fear about black political mobilization soon gave way to fears generated by a new social scientific discourse of black social pathology. In the wake of the publication of the "Moynihan report," which attributed social problems in black communities to the "deterioration of the black family," political conservatives, with an assist from academic sociologists, began to promulgate the notion that African-American communities were caught up in a "culture of poverty."[9] In opposition to previous analyses, which emphasized material inequality as a key factor in the emergence of social problems among inner-city residents, the culture of poverty theorists outlined an intractable legacy of social pathology responsible for everything from welfare dependency to elevated crime rates in black communities. It was this latter discourse of black social pathology that fueled the backlash against New York's poorest residents in the wake of the 1977 blackout, framing the reports of looting in neighborhoods such as the South Bronx or Flatbush in Brooklyn as evidence of cultural, rather than material, deprivation.[10]

This privileging of cultural over socioeconomic explanations for endemic crime, poverty, and social disorder in mid-1970s New York was reinforced by depictions of the city in the movies and the mass media. In Martin Scorcese's *Taxi Driver,* the peep shows and prostitution of "pre-Disney" Times Square are presented as the source, and not the symptom, of New York's social tensions.[11] A similar tone of street menace runs through a variety of films from the mid-1970s, ranging from edgy "Asphalt Jungle" movies such as *Mean Streets* or *Midnight Cowboy* to vigilante thrillers such as *Death Wish.*[12] At the same time, the nightly news offered Americans an ongoing spectacle of urban jeopardy, with New York crime subject to the increased sensationalism of local news coverage during the 1970s. The shift to profitable "eyewitness" formats among local affiliates, with their heavy use of video and live on-site coverage, placed particular emphasis upon violent crime.[13]

The panorama of crime and social decay emanating from American movies and nightly news coverage traced a specific geography of fallen New York, devoting its attention to the most spectacular sites of failure. The burned-out tenements of the South Bronx, Harlem, and the Lower East Side offered readily visible evidence of the bleak social conditions facing residents of particular communities throughout New York.[14] However, what is effaced in these visceral images is the constellation of forces linking these tangible signs of "blight" to less tangible factors, to the effects of local policymaking, real estate development, and global market forces.[15] A more accurate conceptual geography of New York's mid-1970s predicament would account for the network of freeways and urban development projects initiated in the 1950s and 1960s, as well as the looming office spires at the southernmost tip of Manhattan. Viewed from this perspective, the spectacularity of New York's urban blight becomes merely one part of a larger story, caught up in structural pressures that are abstract in character yet systemic in scope.

Many commentators have noted the devastating impact of the large-scale infrastructural projects initiated in New York from the 1940s to the 1960s, initiated by city planners working under Robert Moses.[16] Moses's investment in the freeway as an emblem of progress, coupled with his indifference to the impact of urban planning on working-class and African-American residents, resulted in development projects that wrought extensive structural violence within the urban topography of

New York. The most notorious of these projects, chronicled in the anguished prose of Marshall Berman's *All That Is Solid Melts into Air,* was the Cross-Bronx Expressway, which cut a destructive path through the densely populated surface streets of the South Bronx, on the pretext of facilitating traffic between Long Island, Manhattan, and New Jersey. More than 170,000 residents, many of whom were nonwhite, were displaced from properties condemned through the specious application of the Title I Slum Clearance program. The disruption caused by the project led to plummeting property values, in turn precipitating widespread vandalism as landlords torched their own properties to collect insurance money. The borough's poorest African-American residents, many of whom had relocated to the South Bronx after they were displaced by an earlier wave of slum clearance in Manhattan, suffered the brunt of this planned catastrophe, their neighborhood reduced to a desolate moonscape accompanied only by the unceasing din of freeway traffic.[17] The marginalized residents of the South Bronx paid the social cost of a project directed squarely at affluent and middle-class commuters, who used the Expressway as a means of bypassing the borough's urban blight on their way to jobs in Manhattan.

If the Cross-Bronx Expressway emerged from a planning process remote from the quotidian scrutiny of New Yorkers, its physical impact upon the built environment of New York City is nevertheless easy to grasp. By contrast, the fiscal crisis of 1975 occupies that ethereal space reserved for finance in the public consciousness, its implications obscure and difficult to keep in view. However, the crisis would have tangible and profound consequences for New York, every bit as calamitous as the "urban renewal" initiatives of Moses and his planners.

In the popular imagination, the fiscal crisis of 1975 has frequently been seen through the same lens of conservative backlash that has shaped the discourse of popular anti-urbanism discussed earlier in this chapter. As Greenberg has noted, the conventional narrative about the fiscal crisis is that it was an unfortunate outgrowth of good intentions, the consequence of excessive spending in support of liberal social polices enacted by the city during the 1960s. According to its critics, the city's maintenance of welfare programs, subsidized housing, and generous pensions for city workers was unsustainable during a period of dwindling tax revenues and diminished federal and state support.[18] This view was especially popular among the city's public officials and business leaders, as it legitimated cuts to social spending, even as it deflected blame for the crisis onto those constituencies most vulnerable to cuts in spending.

However, several commentators argue that this explanation for the fiscal crisis, which justifies the subsequent period of fiscal austerity as a necessary correction to liberal excesses, fails to account adequately for the financial pressures faced by the city of New York during the early 1970s.[19] Indeed, according to this perspective, much of the blame for the crisis can be attributed to the city's aggressive expenditures in support of powerful moneyed interests, including real estate developers, private corporations, and financial institutions affiliated with the FIRE sector (Finance, Insurance, and Real Estate).[20] In a pattern that should be familiar to contemporary observers, the city would pull itself out of insolvency by catering to the very institutions that hastened the onset of the crisis, and it would do so at the expense of unionized workers, low-income residents, and communities of color.

In the late 1960s, New York faced the prospect of a large-scale corporate exodus from New York, precipitated in large part by suburbanization, deindustrialization of the major cities, and the comparatively favorable business climate of the Sunbelt economies.[21] In its effort to woo back these corporations, the city borrowed billions of dollars in order to finance a program of office-tower development unprecedented in the city's history. At the same time, New York had also lowered its property-tax assessments on commercial properties as another means of placating these businesses, despite its increasing budget shortfall. Moreover, a major consortium of investors, responding to the city's diminished bond rating, sold off all of New York City's municipal bonds in early 1975.

This constellation of events brought the city to the brink of default in the summer of 1975, and New York governor Hugh Carey moved to intervene. Carey set up a temporary institution called the Municipal Assistance Corporation (the "Big MAC") that would sell bonds to retire outstanding debts and cover city operating expenses, on the condition that the city impose draconian austerity measures, including deep cuts to municipal worker's wages and social services. Even these measures were insufficient to close the budget gap, and after a failed delegation to the White House in September 1975, the city took the radical step of appropriating the retirement savings of its own workers, buying up $2.5 billion worth of unsellable bonds with the pension funds of the city's public-sector unions. In this way, the city undermined its unionized and working-class constituencies, even as it provided some of the world's most powerful financial institutions with carte blanche to divest themselves of all fiscal responsibility for New York's economic welfare.[22]

Alongside the problems associated with the fiscal crisis itself, New York's political and corporate leadership had to contend with a crisis of faith in the continued viability of the city. The social and economic crises of mid-1970s New York forced the city's political and financial establishments to experiment with new approaches in order to restore the city's prosperity and reputation. This period saw the city redirect its financial resources toward a new strategy of aggressively courting businesses in the FIRE sector and developing New York as a *brand*. Instead of materially investing in communities that suffered from New York's decline, the city chose to combat the *imagery* of decline, promoting a counterimagery of tourist-friendly attractions and business-friendly environments. As New York's working-class, Latino/a, and African-American communities languished in the wake of transit fare hikes, limits on rent control, and cuts to law enforcement and welfare support, New York spent $4.3 million on a new tourist campaign entitled "I♥NY."[23]

As David Harvey has argued, the municipal, state, and federal response to the New York fiscal crisis provided future governments with a strategic model for introducing, securing, and maintaining the emerging "flexible accumulation" model of neoliberalism.[24] These dramatic changes to the structure of the global economy could not be simply imposed from above by fiat, especially where the consequences of introducing neoliberal relations of production could be shown to negatively affect the quality of life for average citizens. Instead, a kind of consent was required from those about to become subject to the new strictures.[25]

The consent obtained for these drastic transformations was often indirect and elliptical, derived from people's responses to social antagonisms that were strategically disarticulated from public awareness of the effects of capitalism itself. In late 1970s New York, the new politics of conservative backlash served as a mechanism through which the consequences of fiscal crisis could be reconfigured as outcomes of cultural change alone. Moreover, the city's strategy for addressing these problems conditioned the public to seek solutions within the domain of culture. The "I♥NY" campaign, with its upbeat gloss on the existing city, was one such example, but one could cite other such efforts. For example, Leslie Savan, writing in 1976, noted that the city's sanitation department commissioned Walter Kacik to redesign its fleet of garbage trucks, placing the single word "Sanitation," rendered in the minimalist Helvetica typeface, against an all-white backdrop that wordlessly suggested the cleanliness the trucks were deployed to promote. The font, which was also adopted as part of the visual iconography of the Metropolitan

Transportation Authority, helped to sanitize the city's image, even as it aligned New York with the sleek visual style of its multinational corporations, many of whom were also adopting the typeface.[26] The so-called "broken windows" strategy of crime enforcement, introduced in the early 1980s, was another crucial manifestation of this impulse to cultural amelioration. Claiming that minor "lifestyle crimes" (loitering, panhandling, or vandalism of property) were directly emblematic of a larger decline in New Yorkers' quality of life, the city of New York began to enforce a systematic crackdown on such misdemeanor offenses, based on the theory that each such infraction constituted a kind of "gateway offense" that would lead inexorably to more severe crimes down the road. As Greenberg has noted, such mechanisms redirected public attention from the structural inequities underlying New York's elevated crime rates toward the surface image of public disorder.[27]

It is here that New York's cultural institutions, including its jazz scene, take on a key role in mediating New Yorkers' (and Americans') emotional response to the complex social forces shaping the city during this turbulent decade. New York culture during this period is caught between antagonistic social tendencies, between the lure of the new and the promise of the old. New musical scenes, such as punk or disco, offer younger New Yorkers exciting alternatives to the cultural orthodoxies of an earlier era, with punk repudiating the reflexive optimism of the postwar years, and disco upending an entire constellation of attitudes about sexuality, stylistic "authenticity," and social interaction. Against this backdrop, the renewed interest in acoustic, straightahead jazz can be read as a straightforward expression of nostalgia, but it can also be interpreted as reflecting pervasive anxieties about the direction of contemporary culture in the era of New York's putative "social decline." In this way, the contrast between elements of New York culture, between the Dionysian excesses of punk or disco and the virtuous nostalgia of the acoustic jazz resurgence, could be marshaled as evidence in support of a vision for the city that advocated for moral renewal in the same moment that it carefully obscured questions of material change.

If the *cultural* optics of Dexter Gordon's return to New York serves as a key object of consideration here, my goal in what follows is to use it as a site for addressing larger questions about the relationship between cultural practices and political economy during this initial period of neoliberal policymaking: what role does the jazz revival's stylistic nostalgia play in the inscription of culturally conservative attitudes in late-1970s New York? Does this nostalgia help to reinforce or to resist the explanations given for the crisis by those invested in neoliberal strategies of governance?

"RETURN OF THE CONQUERING HERO"

While Gordon receives the lion's share of attention in later historical accounts of the return to traditionalism in 1970s jazz, it is important to note his position within a vibrant community of acoustic jazz performers in late 1970s New York. Artists such as Woody Shaw, Freddie Hubbard, and Herbie Hancock (the latter two members of the "V.S.O.P." band) were receiving accolades for their promulgation of an intense postbop sound based upon the stylistic innovations of Miles Davis's mid-1960s acoustic quintet. Alongside Gordon himself, other veterans of the jazz scene had returned to prominence. Percy, Jimmy, and Albert Heath, musicians active since the 1950s, had come together as the Heath Brothers, a quartet playing bop-derived acoustic jazz, and Johnny Griffin, a virtuosic bebop contemporary of Gordon's, had followed the tenorist home from Europe in 1978. Concord Jazz, a record label founded in 1972 by the former car dealer and jazz enthusiast Carl Jefferson, was promoting a popular traditionalist sound. The Concord stable of artists during this period ranges from the exuberant, post–Cannonball Adderley bebop of Phil Woods to the music of tenor saxophonist Scott Hamilton, whose meticulous re-creations of Basie-era swing anticipate the jazz repertory movement of the 1980s and 1990s.[28]

Jazz media coverage contemporaneous with Gordon's stateside return also tends to affirm this vibrant image of late 1970s acoustic jazz, in marked contrast to the melancholy depiction of the period outlined elsewhere in jazz historiography.[29] As early as 1970, the *New York Times* noted with cautious optimism that younger listeners might be returning to the music, frequenting clubs such as the Village Vanguard, which had faced declining attendance throughout most of the 1960s.[30] Throughout the decade, a series of new venues were opening up to accommodate a revival in interest in mainstream acoustic jazz. These include Storyville, which the eminent concert promoter George Wein had opened in 1976, and which became the site of Gordon's initial New York appearances later that same year; a successful new jazz series at the Church of the Heavenly Rest, initiated in the same year by printing executive and jazz enthusiast Paul Weinstein; Fat Tuesday's, a basement jazz bar alluding both to "Mardi Gras" and to the adjacent restaurant Tuesday's; and Sweet Basil, a former health food restaurant that maintained a redoubtable lineup of straightahead artists into the first years of the new millennium.[31] The success of these and other similar venues contradicts the pervasive narrative of the 1970s as a putative "dark age" for mainstream acoustic jazz.

All this being said, Dexter Gordon's return to New York in 1976 was treated as an event of singular importance in the jazz community. Gordon was a key participant in the Billy Eckstine orchestra of the mid-1940s, with its decisive role in the development of bebop, and had also figured as a key influence in the tenor saxophone styles of Sonny Rollins and John Coltrane. Moreover, his Blue Note records of the early 1960s (Dexter Calling, One Flight Up, or Go!, among others) remain classics in the label's catalog, his robust, laid-back sound ideally suited to the hard-bop aesthetic.[32] All of these factors help to explain the enthusiastic reception given to Gordon's Storyville and Village Vanguard engagements in the fall of 1976, when the artist returned to New York for what was by all accounts another brief, temporary stateside visit.

However, by themselves, these factors are of limited help in explaining why Dexter Gordon stayed, why a U.S.-based career had become sufficiently attractive to him by 1977 that he would decide to return permanently to the United States and to make New York City his home. Despite its romanticized portrayal as a "homecoming," this eventuality could just as easily have not happened. As late as the winter of 1976, an interview with Leonard Feather depicts Gordon as content with his European residency, citing Copenhagen as an ideal location for the steady international work he was enjoying during that period.[33] Since Gordon's relocation to Europe in 1962, Copenhagen had built up a thriving expatriate core of American jazz musicians, many of them African American, who appreciated the city's tolerant atmosphere and the depth of knowledge about jazz exhibited by its residents. The Monmartre Jazzhus had become one of the key sites on the European jazz circuit, and the city had become a home away from home for such figures as Stan Getz, Ben Webster, Kenny Drew, Don Cherry, and Ed Thigpen.[34] Copenhagen's expatriate jazz community counted as one part of the postwar generation of black artists and intellectuals who relocated to Europe, in search of better living and working conditions than were available to them back home. In many instances, these transplants were attracted to the image of European countries as oases of racial tolerance, though the realities often belied this utopian conception of Europe.[35]

Dexter Gordon was both a catalyst for and a beneficiary of this jazz exodus to Europe. His presence in Copenhagen helped to promote the city as a viable site for African-American artists living and working in Europe, and Gordon himself noted in a 1972 *Down Beat* interview that his whole lifestyle had become "much calmer, much more relaxed," removed as it was from the "scuffle" of the New York jazz world.[36] He enjoyed considerable loyalty among Danish fans: public clamor on his behalf pressured the Danish government to overturn its decision preventing Gordon from reentering the country, following his detention on drug charges in Paris.[37] Moreover, in describing his years spent in Denmark, Gordon invoked the same sense of comparative racial tolerance cited by previous African-American expatriates: "I was having a ball. Musically it wasn't much, but it was so much freer socially. There was no discrimination or prejudice. . . . After I'd been there about a month or six weeks, all of a sudden I realized how good I felt, as a human being, without all that weight on my shoulders."[38]

Despite this affirming experience in Europe, Gordon's stateside reception during his 1976 return to New York was affirmation of a different order. The visit was the product of extensive preparation by Maxine Gregg (later Gordon), Dexter Gordon's manager and eventual spouse, who had to overcome considerable reluctance from New York club owners, many of whom felt that Gordon had lost touch with the American market in his years abroad.[39] In this, Gregg was vindicated beyond anyone's expectations. Even prior to his legendary club engagements, Gordon's visit was the subject of considerable buzz. At a recording date for the Xanadu label, the sound booth was packed with industry insiders, who had all come to hear the tenorist lay down some tracks with Blue Mitchell, Al Cohn, Barry Harris, and others.[40] From the first night of his New York engagements, Gordon was playing for standing-room-only crowds. At Storyville, Gordon was supported by trumpeter Woody Shaw and his current rhythm section, comprising Stafford James on bass, Louis Hayes on drums, and Ronnie Matthews on piano.[41] Robert Palmer, covering Gordon's opening night set for the *New York Times,* noted the "almost aggressively adoring" audience that packed the club to hear Gordon play: "After his rehearsal, Mr. Gordon reflected on the ovation he received during his first evening at Storyville. The audience included a remarkable array of jazz writers, numerous musicians and executives from at least one major record company, and when Mr. Gordon had finished playing there was much cheering and table-pounding. The saxophonist had to plead exhaustion and the hour—it was almost 3 A.M.—to avoid the vociferous requests for encores."[42] Elsewhere, Gordon offered further reflections on his own incredulity at the intensity of the audience reception at Storyville: "It happened so rapidly, you know, so spontaneously. There was no big publicity campaign. Just a few people who knew: Dex was comin' back. So I went up to Storyville that night and the joint was packed!—In the rain, man! I didn't even play a note, I just walked towards the scene, the stage and . . . it was *already* an ovation."[43] This warm reception from fans, critics, and record executives was itself a preview of the ecstatic welcome that Gordon would receive the following week, during his residency at the Village Vanguard. Every night, the line of fans waiting to hear the veteran saxophonist would jam the narrow staircase and extend out onto Seventh Avenue.[44] Every song would finish to thunderous applause, with Gordon smiling and holding his Selmer saxophone aloft to the crowd in tribute. As with the Storyville gig, each night at the Vanguard ended with exquisite reluctance, the audience staying seated until the last possible moment. This reaction prompted Gordon himself to note the messianic ardor of his reception, in an interview with Ira Gitler:

> "There was so much love and elation," [Gordon] mused.
> "Can you handle all that love?" I asked.
> "Sometimes it's a little eerie," he replied. "At the Vanguard after the last set they'd turn on the lights and nobody moved."
> "What does it do to you to turn everyone on that way? How does it make you feel?"
> "A little like Jesus," he said, and laughed his broad, held-not laugh [*sic*], definitely one of the apostles.[45]

This messianic intensity that Gordon located in the crowd response at the Vanguard would become a pervasive point of reference in critical accounts of Gordon's multiple visits to the United States throughout 1976 and 1977. This intensity also made its presence felt in the celebratory coverage of his return, with Gordon receiving high-profile treatment in the *New York Times,* the *Village Voice,* the *New York Post,* and television interviews.[46] As one fan was overheard saying at one of Gordon's Storyville appearances, "It's almost as though we were in Europe and *he* was visiting *them*."[47]

Alongside the powerful impression Gordon's tour made on the New York public, his visit would have tangible economic repercussions in the jazz corner of the music industry. If nothing else, the visit constituted the starting point of Columbia Records' assertive role in the promotion of a revitalized acoustic jazz sensibility over the next decade and a half. On the second night of the phenomenal Storyville gig, label president Bruce Lundvall approached Gordon after the show and immediately proposed that Gordon sign on with Columbia. Gordon, who was mired in difficult negotiations with SteepleChase records (then his current label in Denmark), met with Lundvall the following morning and accepted his offer.[48] By spring of the following year, Columbia had released *Homecoming: Live At The Village Vanguard,* a double LP featuring material from three nights of live sets at the fabled club in December 1976.[49]

To be sure, Lundvall's own personal enthusiasm for bebop in general, and Gordon's music in particular, must factor into any account of his decision to sign the artist.[50] However, Lundvall's commitment to acoustic jazz extended well beyond his personal admiration of Dexter Gordon. Gordon was to become the first of a series of high-profile acoustic jazz artists recruited by Lundvall for Columbia after his 1976 appointment, as he and Columbia vice president George Butler sought what they envisioned as an expanding, college-age market for traditional jazz.[51] The list of luminaries signed to Columbia during this period included McCoy Tyner, Woody Shaw, V.S.O.P., Freddie Hubbard, and the Heath Brothers.[52] These signings anticipated the direction the label would take during the 1980s, when George Butler would add such key neoclassicist "young lions" as Branford and Wynton Marsalis, Terence Blanchard, Donald Harrison, and others to Columbia's jazz roster.[53] Moreover, they established a precedent for other major labels, who would expand their jazz offerings over the next two decades: MCA, Atlantic, RCA, Capitol-EMI, and Polygram would all follow Columbia's lead, by establishing new jazz divisions, reanimating old ones, or intensifying their recruitment of individual jazz artists.[54]

The fervor with which critics and fans responded to Gordon's performances; the volume of newsprint devoted to Gordon's return; the sense in which Gordon's signing to Columbia initiated an era of major-label support for jazz—all of these developments emphasize the singularity of Gordon's return as an event. If Gordon's return had such an explosive impact within the jazz world, though, this is because it resonated with a broader constellation of social developments in its period. As I have noted above, the New York contemporaneous with Gordon's 1976 visit was bound up in a tumultuous discourse about social pathology, cultural change, and moral decay. For this reason, the intensity with which Gordon's return was heralded by New Yorkers cannot be separated from the complex feeling that New Yorkers had for their city, and for the culture that formed the immediate backdrop to Gordon's visit. As I hope to demonstrate, Gordon's return would take on a near-messianic cast, precisely because it seemed to offer a salve to these tensions, a means of addressing at the level of culture the nebulous and frightening structural transformations that were then shaping city life in New York.

BARBARIANS AT THE VILLAGE GATE

If *Down Beat*'s "beat," so to speak, has almost invariably been limited to the jazz world, there have occasionally been moments where the magazine has cast its gaze beyond this circumscribed bubble, to take in events in the outside world. One such event was the infamous blackout of July 1977, discussed earlier in this chapter, which *Down Beat* covered in a brief eyewitness report that captured something of the ill temper of New York's jazz enthusiasts at that time. The article, which focused on the situation in the city's jazz clubs the night of the blackout, noted that some clubs with upright pianos fared all right when the power went out, with patrons of the Village Gate treated to a candelit piano-vocal duet with Ernie Soskin and Elaine Caswell. Elsewhere, however, the mood was more desultory, with McCoy Tyner thwarted at his gig in the downstairs section of the Gate, and Cedar Walton unable to "do much more than plunk a little" as his All Stars faced the blackout at Boomer's on Bleecker Street. Conversation among jazz club patrons turned swiftly towards hostile condemnation of the city and of Con Edison, the city's power utility:

> That was the mood around the city. The attitude of the public was quite different from the folklore-laden '65 failure. "We are angry as hell this time," one patron said. "Why did we have a power failure when we were promised it would never happen again? As usual, we were lied to by Con Ed." The frustration grew to anger. "I'm grounded and I don't like it," was the way one jazz clubhopper put it. He was referring to the fact that expatriate fluegelhornist Art Farmer was at the Village Vanguard with pianist Jimmy Rowles. The Vanguard was shuttered. There wasn't even a crowd around it, like there were around the other clubs.[55]

The reference to a shuttered Vanguard, and to its interference with Art Farmer's stateside return engagement, provides us a visual analog for the jazz world's conception of itself during this period as a community forgotten, neglected, and threatened by external forces. This point is reinforced by a second article that *Down Beat* chose to run immediately beneath its account of the blackout: in "Punk Comes to Village Gate," *Down Beat* reports that Gate owner Art D'Lugoff has decided to supplement its existing jazz offerings with a lineup of punk bands. The article, nominally addressing the practical issue of noise pollution in the immediate vicinity of the Gate's Greenwich Village location, also seems to betray a host of larger anxieties about the implications of the club's embrace of punk:

> The "straight" Gate gives credence to a music that might be a put on, a stepping stone for some of the lesser talents to gain a foothold on bigger things. . . . While D'Lugoff is claiming altruism towards jazz, he is also taking a major step in becoming a progenitor of the punk scene, something that his Greenwich Village neighbors might rebel against. . . . D'Lugoff has had trouble with tenants complaining about the loudness of such acts as Larry Coryell and Lonnie Liston Smith. What happens when the punks amp up?[56]

If the author's immediate concern is about sound levels, they nevertheless position the "noise" of punk as a threat to several more intangible values. The first of these is the concept of musical professionalism, which will take a hit, by the author's reckoning, if this "put on" genre enables "lesser talents to gain a foothold on bigger things." Punk, commonly understood as having challenged standards of virtuosity in the rock world, is here denounced as a potential threat to the virtuosic practices embodied in bebop and other subgenres of jazz. At the same time, punk is positioned on a sonic continuum with jazz-rock artists such as organist Lonnie Liston Smith or guitarist Larry Coryell, undercutting aesthetic distinctions between punk and fusion and reducing both genres to their potentiality for violating noise ordinances. Taken together, these complaints betray *Down Beat*'s unease about the physical and psychic impact of punk on the jazz scene. Moreover, *Down Beat*'s decision to place the Village Gate article right below the blackout report (which also addresses the Village Gate) ensures that it reads like an addendum to the apocalyptic events of July 13, 1977, further evidence for panicked jazz enthusiasts of the imminence of the city's demise.

Down Beat's portraits of a Village Gate besieged by punks and power failures gives us the sense that the New York jazz scene, much like the city surrounding it, was suffused with a feeling of dread during this period. For all the excitement surrounding the acoustic jazz resurgence of the late 1970s, the public conversations about jazz during this period often conveyed the sense that the music's place in contemporary society was besieged from without by forces that threatened to overwhelm it. In prominent jazz periodicals, both musicians and fans, in interviews and fan mail, decried what they saw as the destructive impact of commercialism, displacing "authentic" jazz in favor of more profitably hybridized strains of the music. Such newly emergent genres as punk, funk, or disco were seen as palpable threats to jazz, embodying new sensibilities that seemed antithetical to what readers valued in their music.

For the most part, these discussions focused narrowly upon the contested place of jazz in the musical world of the mid-to-late 1970s. However, in a number of instances, the comments betrayed artists' and listeners' anxieties about issues that seemed to extend beyond the purview of *Down Beat,* issues that resonated with the broader emotional topography of late 1970s American culture. In the vehemence with which these voices debated the finer points of jazz aesthetics, authenticity, and musical technology, we can locate a charged rhetoric that overlaps with the pervasive anxieties and moral panics of post-bicentennial American "malaise."[57]

Punk, which was emerging from a vibrant subculture affiliated with clubs such as CBGB's and Max's Kansas City in New York, and the Roxy in London, faced a critical reception in jazz circles that was in some ways distinct from that accorded to other popular genres of the time. In the late 1970s, no one at *Down Beat* seemed particularly worried about punk as a site of jazz crossover, though punk and its generic progeny would certainly become formative impulses in the "downtown" avant-garde aesthetic associated with the Knitting Factory during the 1980s. Instead, late 1970s jazz supporters, echoing *Down Beat*'s reservations about punk at the Village Gate, seemed to perceive this loud new genre as a more generalized, existential threat to jazz culture, an inchoate wall of amplified distortion that would simply blanket out the nuanced intricacies of jazz and other acoustic genres. For this reason, many *Down Beat* readers were adamant that punk had no place in its critic or reader polls, its feature articles, or its record reviews.

In one letter to the editor, *Down Beat* reader Bruno Strapko takes the journal's critics to task for their inclusion of such bands as the Ramones and the Sex Pistols in the August 1978 critics' poll, where they appear under the category of "Vocal Group, established": "[The poll] shows that *all* good musicians in all fields of contemporary music are appreciated. Unfortunately, I don't understand how the Ramones, The Sex Pistols and Bootsy's Rubber Band got any votes. Although their 'music' spans two very distinct styles, I have to agree with the saying that there are only two kinds of music—good and bad. The 'music' of the three bands mentioned is definitely bad."[58] If Strapko invokes a common "saying" that privileges artistic quality over snobbery about genre distinctions, there can be little question that the letter reads like a warning to *Down Beat* that it has overstepped crucial genre boundaries in its efforts to cover a more inclusive range of contemporary music. In a similar fashion, Max Gordon, the proprietor of the Village Vanguard, protests the magazine's recent (and positive) review of punk band Television in this acerbic letter: "What are you guys trying to do? On one hand, there are articles on people like Carla Bley, Don Cherry and Egberto Gismonti. Then in the same pages, there will be coverage of utter junk like Television and Elvis Costello. Somewhere along the line, confusion reigns in your editorial offices. When quality gives way to quackery, the result is cancelled subscriptions."[59] Gordon's "quackery" is another reader's quality, of course, and in a subsequent issue, two readers would rush to the defense of Television and Elvis Costello, while chastising Gordon for narrow-mindedness.[60] Both readers invoke *Down Beat*'s description of itself as the "contemporary music magazine," and it is a measure of *Down Beat*'s ambivalent and unstable role as a custodian of jazz culture that these readers could feel fully justified in citing this open-ended self-definition. Alongside recordings by Woody Shaw, Dexter Gordon, Joe Pass, and other jazz artists, *Down Beat* back issues from the late 1970s continue to include reviews or feature articles devoted to more unequivocally pop or rock artists, including Tom Waits, Frank Zappa, David Bowie, Pink Floyd, and even the Village People.[61] Inclusive readers' tastes notwithstanding, though, there was an increasingly insistent pressure in this period from *Down Beat* subscribers demanding that the magazine do more to police what they saw as meaningful distinctions between popular music and jazz culture "proper."

From the artists' perspective, two of the more passionate critics of the relationship between jazz, popular music, and commercialism in this period are Jimmy and Percy Heath, who (as I noted above) had formed an acoustic hard-bop quartet with their brother Albert "Tootie" Heath during the same decade. In many ways, the tenor of their statements anticipates the strong rhetoric advanced by Wynton Marsalis and Stanley Crouch in the following decade, rhetoric that sought to police the boundaries separating a putative unitary "jazz tradition" from such genres as rock, R&B, and rap. In a searing *Down Beat* interview from 1979, two of the Heath siblings set up an opposition between bebop, which they situate as a key aesthetic moment in the emergence of civil rights–era black pride, and popular musics, which they excoriate as the latter-day echoes of nineteenth-century blackface minstrelsy:

> *Jimmy:* I think the presentation of the music has gone back to minstrel show time. During the bebop era the guys had pride in what they were doing . . .

> *Jimmy:* The minstrel thing is all the pop tunes, and the thing they're going through now is a kind of return back to giving up that evolutionary black pride that we had a few years ago, giving up and saying, "Well, we might as well show our teeth and buckdance and sing, 'cause that's all we're going to do anyhow; we're just minstrels."

> *Percy:* They're only imitating the white minstrels that did it and made it, so they're come-lately minstrels, white minstrels on down to the ridiculous: Kiss and miss and punk and funk and junk. Not only the black, it's the whole world that's gone for bullshit and flamboyance. I am the greatest. If everybody says "I am the greatest," somebody's lying.[62]

Jimmy and Percy Heath's statements about jazz, popular music, and minstrelsy straddle two divergent discourses about the relationship of jazz to commerce. On the one hand, they invoke bebop as a crucial precursor to the period of intensified black consciousness that emerged in the wake of the civil rights movement. In this way, bebop becomes linked to the same social conditions that many affiliate with the 1960s jazz avant-garde, including its repudiation of commercial exploitation by the recording industry. On the other hand, the way in which they dismiss contemporary pop as self-obsessed showmanship bordering upon minstrelsy, sets up themes that would become central to a more conservative, neoclassicist critique of popular music in the years to come.

The Heath siblings' adamant criticism of what they saw as the corrupting effects of popular music would come to the fore in a semipublic context in 1978, when Percy Heath engaged in a heated exchange with the successful crossover artist Grover Washington Jr. during a panel on "The State of Jazz Records Today." The panel, which took place as part of the annual meeting for the National Academy of Recording Arts and Sciences, featured Washington alongside a broad range of artists from disparate areas of the jazz scene, including Randy Brecker, Stan Getz, Bob James, and Muhal Richard Abrams. However, it was Washington alone who would become the focal point of the panel, as Percy Heath rose to chastise him and other crossover artists from his seat in the audience. In Washington's recollection, Heath said that "all the stuff you hear on the radio today isn't jazz, that us young people are bastardizing the music. He was really ranting and raving. Suddenly, the whole thing focused on me. I was doing this to jazz and I was doing that to jazz—I couldn't believe it."[63]

As Charles Carson has noted, the vehement denunciation of Washington's crossover aesthetic, as evidenced in Heath's comments at the NARAS jazz panel, reflects a pervasive anxiety in the jazz community during this period about the cultural politics of race, commerce, and musical hybridity. Crossover jazz, as Carson has compellingly argued, may have been a crucial site of identification for an emergent black middle class during the late 1970s. The music touches upon familiar elements of the African-American legacy of popular music in the same moment that its smooth production values made the music "'genteel' enough to distance [African Americans] from those ever-present reminders of just how tenuous their own position within mainstream society truly was."[64] Nevertheless, critics of the music, both black and white, have continued to frame crossover and smooth jazz as having *betrayed* African-American culture, by ostensibly "whitewashing" those elements of the music that might make it unsalable to white middle-class listeners. Despite its resonances with the experiences of many upwardly mobile African-American listeners, crossover becomes reduced to an artificial and corrupted musical style, a repudiation of authentic blackness.

This anxiety about commercialism, hybridity, and jazz purism has been outlined in numerous discussions of fusion, crossover, and smooth jazz.[65] When understood purely as an expression of concern over the direction of musical styles, the intensity of this discourse may be difficult to understand. However, framed within a specific historical context, this discourse may take on a range of additional meanings. In particular, the impetus to defend some core of authentic black experience against encroaching market forces or cultural amalgamation may have seemed especially urgent within the New York–centered jazz community of the late 1970s. As I have noted earlier in this discussion, black culture in New York had become increasingly subject to vilification during this period, as an increasingly conservative discourse of urban decline took hold in the public imagination, affiliating crime and social disorder with black pathology.[66] Against this backdrop, Percy and Jimmy Heath's arguments about crossover and black popular music reveal an intense concern about the cultural values adopted by young black musicians, those who would become the public face of black culture during this period of increasingly reactionary attitudes *toward* that culture.

DISCO DISCONTENT AT *DOWN BEAT*

In this respect, it is significant that Bret Primack's interview with the Heath Brothers leads off with his own critical denunciation of disco, a genre that was coming in for considerable public criticism as it reached a place of prominence in American culture: "I'm sick of reading about Studio 54. So what if people dance naked? So what if they snort cocaine to a disco beat? I'm not impressed; disco decadence is not for me. What really bothers me is that millions seek escape via disco. Why can't they listen to bebop?"[67] Primack's rhetoric sets his readers up for an exploration of the Heath siblings' own forthright opinions about disco, the interview section of the article leading off with their criticism of repetition and funk vamps in contemporary popular music:

> *Percy:* I vamped in '47, but we didn't lay on it too much. With Joe Morris, we vamped while Johnny Griffin was marching up and down the aisles and playing. But now they got this hypnotic disco thing. If people sit down and listen to that music for listening pleasure, there's something wrong with them . . .

> *Jimmy:* To me, they are repeating the same licks we played in the bebop era but now they play them over and over and over again. . . . Meanwhile, that march beat is going on under it. Now it's all about parading and looking at yourself in the mirror at a disco. But, we're trying to turn that around so people go to a concert and listen again.[68]

Here, while Percy and Jimmy Heath cite the practice of bar-walking saxophonists in early jump blues as a precedent for disco spectacularity, they hold up bebop itself as evidence that a more listener-centered, aesthetically thoughtful practice predominated among their generation of musicians. Further on, Percy Heath further develops this argument about the distinction between jazz as a "listening" music and disco as mindless hypnosis, advancing an almost Adornian thesis about the role of disco in securing a complacent, productive workforce: "Maybe that's why they don't foster [jazz] so much because all the workers can turn on the disco station and work vigorously and produce, but if they turned it to a jazz thing, they might want to sit down and listen and relax, because that's what it does to me."[69] In citing what they see as disco's celebration of mindless repetition, narcissistic self-indulgence, decadent artifice, and machinelike rigidity, the Heath siblings and Bret Primack revisit what were then becoming pervasive criticisms of this genre.

Recent scholars have emphasized the legacy of critical invective about disco in rock and R&B circles since its late 1970s heyday.[70]

However, we need to remember that this genre faced a similarly harsh reception among jazz enthusiasts in this period. In more recent accounts of jazz during the 1970s, we are accustomed to seeing descriptions of the period's musical hybridity centering around rock or funk: the centrality of figures such as Miles Davis, John McLaughlin, and Weather Report to the fusion repertory have conditioned us to thinking of "fusion" as synonymous with "jazz-rock fusion." However, during the late 1970s, it is the genre of disco that appears in *Down Beat*'s reviews, feature articles, and reader mail with obsessive regularity. In these conversations, disco often functions as shorthand for the entire range of nonjazz popular music, and for the ominous cultural ramifications that this music seems to portend. Nevertheless, jazz fans' disco discontents also reveal anxieties that are specific to this genre, and to the time and places that it has come to represent.

In light of the persisting public image of disco as a genre manufactured by major record labels and imposed upon consumers from above, it is important to emphasize the vibrant underground context of the music's emergence. These institutions include the Loft, David Mancuso's weekly, all-night Friday gathering in his SoHo loft apartment, in which his exquisite sound system served as a point of departure for intimate, spiritual communion among like-minded dancers and audiophiles. They also include the warehouse club known as the Paradise Garage, where DJ Larry Levan spun epic, wildly eclectic sets for an audience largely made up of gay African-American and Latino men. The spirit of community that defined these scenes stands in contrast to the images of exclusivity, escapism, and narcissistic individualism that would become associated with disco as it came into mainstream popularity.[71] All of this will be important to bear in mind as we confront the tremendously hostile reception of disco articulated by contemporaneous jazz musicians and audiences.

In the late 1970s, negative images of disco would become an important part of the discursive background at *Down Beat*. Fierce controversies surrounded *Down Beat*'s reviews of records such as Maynard Fergusson's *Carnival,* or *Mr. Gone* by Weather Report, as these artists ventured into stylistic and production techniques associated with disco.[72] As jazz groups incorporated studio overdubbing, lavish orchestration, or other stylistic nuances of disco into their music, the question of the genre's encroachment on jazz norms would become a hot topic in the "Chords and Discords" section (the letters to the editor section) of *Down Beat*. A typical letter in this regard, submitted by reader Neil

Lusby and printed in the December 21, 1978, issue of *Down Beat*, implores the jazz publication to restrict itself to a putative "real jazz," or to at least clearly define the boundaries between the various genres that it covers: "I hope that others feel as I do—that [*Down Beat*] should confine its coverage to jazz. I am not opposed to advances of technique or ability, but don't confuse rock or disco music with the real thing. Perhaps you should define what is—and what is not—jazz!"[73] *Down Beat*, having approached Lusby to clarify aspects of his letter, came away incredulous that the latter would willfully omit such artists as Freddie Hubbard, Chick Corea, Weather Report, or Stanley Turrentine from any hypothetical list of "authentic" jazz artists.[74] However, the types of projects pursued by many of these artists at that time, from the fusion of Weather Report to Freddie Hubbard's mid-1970s flirtations with "quiet storm" soul, would indeed place many of these artists in an unstable relation to the jazz canon in subsequent years, as neoclassicist assumptions about jazz became influential.[75]

One especially pointed letter, which also touches upon disco, cites the music in passing as one offending element in the greater breakdown of musical civilization represented by contemporary pop:

> In these unfortunate musical times of disco, punk rock, crossover, fusion and other ear-offending trash, when small-timers like Bruce Stringbead, Chuck Mangyonly, Barbra Strident and Elton Yawn [*sic*] are worshipped by an American public consisting of musically comatose hedonists, it is a genuine pleasure to see [*Down Beat*] space devoted to the real father of modern American music, John Cage. . . . I hope that [*Down Beat*] plans to devote more space to *real* music and less to immature rockers, paunchy sell-out jazzers in their silly effeminate outfits, and all other identical non-conformists.
>
> Also, let's have fewer letters from readers who are negative and sarcastic.[76]

Estes' self-deprecating humor notwithstanding, the letter provides a relatively cogent summary of a pervasive stance toward late 1970s musical culture, a kind of siege mentality in which Sid Vicious, Donna Summer, and Peter Frampton are pigeonholed as "barbarians at the gate." In particular, Estes's denunciation of "musically comatose hedonists" and "sell-out jazzers in their silly effeminate outfits" invokes a conservative panic over gender norms, sexuality, and the politics of pleasure that aims its moral opprobrium at a range of post-1960s cultural transformations.

The Lusby and Estes letters, which both target disco in passing, cite the music primarily as an example of the kind of genre that *Down Beat* should not be covering. In numerous other letters, though, the complaints about disco enumerate a more specific list of grievances. In *Down Beat,* as in much of late 1970s popular culture, disco would come in for particular criticism as a genre whose glossy production, mediated presentation, and repetitive "four-on-the-floor" rhythmic structure produce a sound associated with sterility, artifice, and hypnotic mindlessness.[77] In readers' responses to an issue that featured hard-bop trumpeter Ted Curson alongside disco and funk musicians the Brothers Johnson, several letters set up an opposition between jazz, understood as an organic, creative "roots music," and disco, understood as the insipid antithesis to these qualities: "The Brothers Johnson—the place for star-spangled glitter dancing machines is in the discotheque, not the pages of [*Down Beat*]! One chord funk . . . is the big thing today, but people need to hear more about the [Ted] Cursons, the Ira Sullivans, etc. . . . Let's get back to the roots; I think they still call it jazz."[78]

John Yarling's barb about "one chord funk" alludes to the repetitive dimension of disco which, as with other vamp or loop-based dance musics, is often understood by detractors as a site of sonic and cultural regression, owing to its close affiliation with the body.[79] However, in *Down Beat*'s disco letters, concern about riffs, vamps, and repetition ultimately takes a back seat to anxieties about the sexual identities with which disco was associated. Rarely stated overtly, these anxieties are more often sublimated within specific keywords or indirect references, as in the following letter, submitted by Peter Fallico: "I feel that if today's jazz did return to hard bop, as Ted [Curson] suggests it might, another renaissance of the roots would take form. Disco alone is impotent; it denies us the delineation of commercialism and music. It would contribute to a rebirth in jazz if more musicians were as concerned. Go ahead on, Ted."[80] Fallico's letter rehearses a pervasive trope in antidisco discourse, framing commercialization and technological mediation as impediments to full masculine subjectivity. Fallico's thoughts on disco's "impotence," which resonate with fan comments published elsewhere (including the aforementioned "paunchy sellout jazzers in their silly effeminate outfits"), reinscribe a vocabulary that implicitly attacks the queer dimensions of disco culture, positioning the music's artifice as a locus where cultural authenticity, artistic integrity, and masculine virility are all fatally compromised.

The negative and implicitly homophobic treatment of disco in *Down Beat*'s late 1970s critical and fan discourse helps to emphasize how widespread these ideas were at the time, cutting across distinctions of race, class, or musical preference. What lingers on as the definitive embodiment of the "Disco sucks" sentiment are the images of disco records burned by angry white rock fans in Comiskey Park during a baseball doubleheader on July 12, 1979, at the behest of local Chicago DJ Steve Dahl.[81] However, as the *Down Beat* letters make clear, many divergent communities were preoccupied with what they saw as the morally and economically corrupting influence of disco. For example, the genre was the subject of bitter debate among African-American listeners, radio DJs, and music industry figures.

The African-American music critic Nelson George famously attributed responsibility for what he called the "death of rhythm and blues" to disco culture, reserving his most bitter criticism for white "Eurodisco" projects by the likes of Giorgio Moroder, and for the gay subculture at the core of disco's audience: "At least the Philly [Philadelphia International] records sounded like they were made by humans. Soon, Eurodisco invaded America. . . . It was music with a metronomelike beat—perfect for folks with no sense of rhythm—almost inflectionless vocals, and metallic sexuality that matched the high-tech, high-sex, and low passion atmosphere of the glamorous discos that appeared in every major American city."[82] Noteworthy here is George's indictment of a "metallic sexuality" associated with "high-tech, high-sex," and "low passion" discotheques. The opposition of "high sex" to "low passion" invokes a logic cited by Lee Edelman in his account of what he calls an ideology of *reproductive futurism:* if only procreative, heteronormative sex is productive of meaning (meaning embodied in the act of reproduction), then other acts of desire are incapable of buttressing the social fabric that guarantees the possibility of futurity.[83] If disco is implicated in the "death of rhythm and blues," this commercial death, for George, is tacitly linked to the theme of sterility that conservative voices have so often linked with queer sexualities.

George's patronizing commentary on the "singular attitude" of gay club DJs, coupled with his uncharitable barbs directed at European clubgoers, might initially seem to position the respected R&B critic as an unlikely ally of the angry white suburbanites that stormed Comiskey field during Dahl's Disco Demolition Night. However, the factor of race complicates this comparison. Disco, perceived as "too black" by white rock enthusiasts, is nevertheless seen by George as *insufficiently* black, a machinelike oversimplification of the rhythmic suppleness of funk. This aesthetic response to disco resonates with a broader contemporaneous anxiety among African-American artists, producers, and label executives about the commercial effects of disco. During this period, the Black Music

Association, a group of African-American music industry figures, had cited disco as a problem for black musicians, who were often expected to tailor their recordings for disco audiences, and yet were increasingly shut out of disco-centered media markets.[84] Against this backdrop, George's comments can be seen as reflecting legitimate anxieties about the white appropriation of black music, even as they couch these anxieties within the language of homophobia. Indeed, such anxieties likely inform the denunciations of disco among *Down Beat*'s jazz readers, who lament what they see as the capitulation of black jazz artists such as Donald Byrd or Freddie Hubbard to the market imperatives of disco.

Ultimately, however, such economic concerns about disco can never be entirely separated from the larger atmosphere of moral panic that surrounds its emergence into the commercial mainstream. For both Nelson George and the Comiskey Park disco rioters, disco functions as a site where fear and disgust about broader social developments are concentrated. Upending the idea of the autonomous subject, as well as received notions about the "natural" or the "organic," disco's technological mediation and queer aesthetic instead offer powerful alternatives to these reified categories. In this respect, disco threatens assumptions about autonomy, authenticity, and masculine self-control that are key to the self-understanding of rock, jazz, and R&B fans alike.[85]

If conventional explanations of jazz-rock fusion's controversial place in jazz history typically stress issues of commercial exploitation, or the ostensibly corrupting role of overdubbing or amplification, the anti-*disco* rhetoric articulated by the *Down Beat* readers cited here modifies our understanding of this discourse by underscoring its links to a broader set of cultural antagonisms. Debates about the hybrid character of fusion or crossover projects in jazz gain an additional layer of complexity from their proximity to debates over disco: the gendered rhetoric of moral panic that permeates conservative denunciations of disco throughout the late 1970s must be understood as a potential subtext in the contemporaneous backlash against fusion.

Another thing to note here is the way in which this gendered and often latently homophobic discourse about disco among jazz, rock, and R&B enthusiasts subtly inflects their legitimate concerns about the political economy of music during this period. Crucial here is the charge of commercialism: the charge that disco is a cynical commercial strategy to displace other more "genuine" musical practices makes it a powerful target for listeners who may be otherwise indifferent to, or perplexed by, the more amorphous large-scale transformations that were shaping the global economy at this time. Complaints about the vanity and exclusivity of the Studio 54 door policy, for example, become a way of talking about the rise of economic inequality in late 1970s New York, with gaudy celebrities on the club scene receiving criticism that might otherwise have been directed at the faceless moguls of the real estate or financial industries, those who were the principal agents and beneficiaries of inequality. Nevertheless, the terms of the debate, where the excesses of Studio 54 become attributed to a narcissistic "Me Generation" (rather than to the structural conditions that enable such excesses), ensure that crucial material determinants get left out of what becomes largely a struggle over culture. Moreover, this shift also ensures that the constituencies most closely affiliated with and empowered by disco (women, gay men, African Americans, and Latino/a people) are also those most likely to be vilified for problems that originate elsewhere.

DEXTER'S GOTHAM, GOTHAM'S DEXTER

The *Down Beat* controversies over punk, crossover, and disco provide us with a useful means of evaluating the overlap between late 1970s jazz culture and the broader turbulence of late 1970s American culture. As I noted earlier, the conservative bromides directed at New York City in the late 1970s may play themselves out on a cultural terrain, even as the situations they address derive in large part from structural, socioeconomic factors. Shaped by the conditions of New York's fiscal crisis, and by the decade's global recessions, they nevertheless present themselves as unrelated to policymaking decisions or realignments of capital. Culture becomes bracketed as an airtight loop of cause and effect, in which the groups most violently disrupted by the effects of budget cuts, housing shortages, infrastructure problems, or deindustrialization find themselves facing the exclusive blame for declining conditions. Moreover, according to the circular logic of this closed loop, problems of culture can only be ameliorated through cultural solutions. It was in this latter sphere that the media and cultural commentators would look for evidence of New York's potential for recovery or redemption.

Gordon's return to New York, and the triumphant reception that accompanied it, constitute a small but instructive element in this narrative of New York's cultural redemption. Indeed, in the years following Gordon's stateside return, representations of the artist in jazz criticism, album covers, and other promotional material sought to present Gordon as an embodied realization of a different New York, an icon of nostalgic possibility removed from the turbulent New York of daily experience. These representations can help us to understand the intricate web of relations binding the bebop renaissance of the late 1970s to the cultural context of New York City at that time.

A key aspect of contemporaneous representations of Gordon is their fixation on Gordon's appearance and physicality. From the moment of Gordon's initial visit to New York City in October of 1976, critics, photographers, and filmmakers would locate the tenorist's magnetic appeal in terms of a visual language as lovingly rendered as accounts of his musical style. In many instances, profiles of the artist placed overwhelming emphasis upon his physical presence, leading off their discussions with detailed descriptions of Gordon's considerable height, his large hands, his beaming smile, or his deep voice. A number of these descriptions move beyond the laudable impulse to sketch a three-dimensional representation of the artist, verging over into a kind of fetishization of his black masculinity. For example, in his profile of Gordon for the *New York Daily News,* Pete Hamill begins with a long paragraph of staccato sentences, each one lingering on some detail of the artist's embodied presence:

> The dude is tall. Real tall. Six foot five inches of tall. He sits on the edge of the bed in a high room of the Southgate Towers, down near the Garden. The legs shoot out at hard right angles. A telephone is cradled between his jaw and left shoulder. His hair is gray, the mustache, too. He is talking in a deep voice. "Yeah, babe. Okay. Yeah. Tha's cool. Right. Yeah, yeah." Smiling. Only the hands, with the cigaret [sic] dancing gingerly in the long tapered fingers, might tell you that this is the greatest tenor saxophone player of his time. This tall dude isn't some basketball player in for a reunion. This is Dexter Gordon.[86]

In similar fashion, Bob Blumenthal's portrait of the artist in the *Boston Phoenix* places considerable weight on the extramusical nuances of Gordon's performance, devoting the first third of his article to his audience banter, bodily expressivity, and personal charisma. He argues that Gordon's performance style, which he compares to the showboating of stride pianists in 1920s cutting contests, evinces a visual and verbal theatricality that eclipses the tenorist's musical style, a theatricality which he can convey "without blowing a note." Blumenthal's comments on Gordon are worth quoting at length:

> At age 53 he remains aristocratically handsome, with a face that would be striking enough on a man of average height. But Gordon is six-feet- five—Long Tall Dexter, in the words of one of his compositions—and all other

physical details are secondary to his frame's size and power. One need only look at him to recognize a hard blower, a *boss* tenor; even the saxophone appears to take on new dimensions in his hands.

The voice which emerges from that towering body is predictably deep and resonant. It says its piece slowly, laconically, with more than a tinge of put-on. . . .

Body language is more Gordon's style. When the spirit moves him, his knees flap like the wings of some great bird and his right shoulder begins crawling toward his ear. . . . What's reliable is the pose Gordon strikes in acknowledgement of applause: body erect, head lowered, he holds his tenor before his chest with both hands in a horizontal, "present arms" position, as if to divert all credit to the horn from the horn's manipulator.[87]

In this painstaking depiction of Gordon's verbal and visual performativity, Blumenthal takes extended pleasure in Gordon's body, locating in its movements something greater than the mere visual complement to his musical style. Moreover, the critic devotes a solid paragraph to Gordon's speech acts in front of the audience. The overall picture one is left with is a sense that the critic is utterly besotted with Gordon's charisma, to a degree that exceeds conventional appreciation of a musician's presence.

The question of sexuality is always latent within such critical meditations, with their extended account of Gordon's physique, but on occasion it can be more overt, as we might deduce from the following passage, drawn from Ira Gitler's profile entitled "Dexter Gordon Loves In":

If I called Dexter Gordon "The Love Machine" I would be copping a little from Hollywood . . . but my meaning isn't quite like theirs. Of course there is sexuality involved because all you have to do is look at the handsome giant and listen to his sexophone [*sic*] and his appeal in that department is immediately evident. But the kind of love I'm talking about is just that good feeling, person to person, which suffuses all the rooms where he plays. Dexter has filled people with the cream of human kindness wherever he has appeared on his most recent trip to the United States. It is hard to have enmity for the people at the next table when your best instincts have been aroused.[88]

Here, Gitler's language consistently interweaves the sexual and the utopian registers of the word *love*. Moreover, in a remarkable passage, Gitler goes on to explicitly connect this erotic subtext of Gordon's presence to a language of potency and fertility. When Gordon states that, "Many [older fans] kind of identify with me. I'm 53 and still popping," Gitler goes on to note that, "Gordon was talking of his music but his remark could have also referred to the fact he has two grown daughters by his first wife living in California and a robust toddler named Benjamin Dexter Gordon with his Danish wife Fenja."[89] The fetish made of Gordon's black physicality by other critics is here intensified through a rhetoric of heteronormative virility, one that explicitly links musical and sexual registers of production.[90] I noted in an earlier section that readers of *Down Beat* used words such as *impotence* and *sterile* to describe disco; set against this backdrop, the critical encomiums to Gordon, which privilege his height, charisma, and physical magnetism, inscribe the artist within the logic of "reproductive futurism," the promise that Gordon's bebop constitutes a vital cultural lineage that will persevere in the face of the dissipated, infecund environment that surrounds it.[91] For Gordon's critical admirers, his return holds out the hope that the bebop revival of the late 1970s will not only survive amid the perceived onslaught of punk, disco, or R&B, but that in doing so, it will serve as the implicit guarantor of a future grounded in heteronormative masculinity.[92]

However, if the critical establishment of the late 1970s affirms Gordon as an avatar of masculine virility, some critics situate their validation of Gordon's masculinity within the constraints imposed by contemporaneous fears about blackness. In at least one instance, critical infatuation with Gordon manifests itself as an expression of palpable relief, as the white critic, intimidated by what he sees as the irrational "anger" of younger black avant-garde artists, takes comfort in Gordon's warmth and accessibility as a black male performer. Richard Sudhalter is an observer of the jazz scene who would go on to write *Lost Chords: White Musicians and Their Contributions to Jazz, 1915–1945,* a text that decries the focus on African-American musicians in jazz historiography as a kind of "reverse racism."[93] In a 1978 profile of Gordon, Sudhalter cites the tenorist appreciably as a jauntily "mature" counterweight to the "anger" of younger African-American performers: "Remarkable in one so forceful is the total absence of the hate and anger which mar the work of many younger players. Dexter, for all his past hardships, projects a musical self which is rather jaunty and good-humored, even in its most serious moments. A hallmark, perhaps, of his maturity."[94] For Sudhalter, Gordon's beaming visage offers the critic a reassuring salve to white anxieties about the political militancy or social menace of black culture during the 1970s. For Sudhalter and like-minded observers, it is only Gordon's "mature," properly constrained manifestation of black masculinity that could serve as an adequate guarantee of the jazz future.

For whose future does Gordon's image hold out hope of redemption? In visual representations, album titles, and critical descriptions throughout the late 1970s and early 1980s, the artist's image is closely linked to the fate of New York City. Indeed, there are numerous situations in which Gordon's image is called upon to embody New York City in corporeal form: the tenorist's considerable height, referenced as a kind of visual pun in the album cover photo for the classic Blue Note release *One Flight Up,* lends him a compelling iconicity that photographers connect metonymically to the vertical spires of the New York skyline. One image situates Gordon in proximity to the World Trade Center, whose twin towers served as a powerful visual trope in the city's promotional campaigns in the decade following its construction. In the cover photo for Gordon's 1983 album *American Classic,* released on the Elektra label, the artist appears alongside the Trade Center towers, shot from a vantage point on the Brooklyn shoreline overlooking the Manhattan financial district. Gordon and the towers bookend the photo, as the center of the image is taken up by a gleaming 1937 Cord Phaeton in immaculate condition.[95] The car model in the *American Classic* image, built in the bittersweet final year of the Phaeton's production, delicately mediates the tension between the gleaming modernity of the then-new World Trade Center, on the one hand, and the "classic" timelessness of Dexter Gordon on the other. The picture's affiliation of Gordon with the classic car and the city's corporate architecture conveys the optimistic promise of a modern future built in tradition's image.

The pairing of Dexter Gordon with images of New York would become a pervasive trope in the late 1970s and early 1980s.[96] In many instances, the visual iconography or written descriptions would pinpoint Gordon as a source of salvation for the city's woes. The cover art for the summer 1977 issue of *Jazz* magazine, in which Peter Keepnews profiles Gordon in the wake of his stateside return, depicts the artist ascending the subway staircase, tenor sax in hand, as a radiant light illuminates him from behind. The cover lead for the Gordon article, "Dexter Gordon: Back from Underground," alludes to Gordon's many years recording for small, independent labels (SteepleChase, Cobblestone, Arco, but also the better-known Prestige label) during the interregnum between his Blue Note and Columbia output. "Underground" here is also clearly meant to reference Gordon's long residency in Copenhagen and Paris, a sojourn that the New York–centric jazz world might interpret as a retreat from the limelight. However, the illustration of Gordon ascending the subway staircase goes beyond a visual pun on these implications of "underground": the "halo" lighting up Gordon's ascent from the subway also subtly imparts an element of redemptive

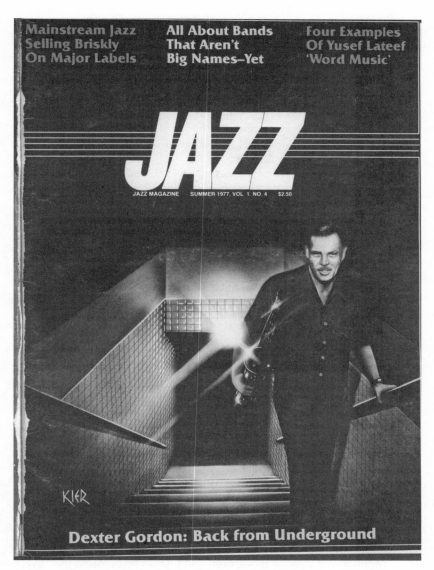

FIGURE 2. Dexter Gordon ascending subway staircase. Cover image, *Jazz* magazine, summer 1977. ©1977, Stites-Oakey Inc.

promise to Gordon's return, a sense that the city itself is on the threshold of better things (fig. 2).[97]

If the promise of revitalization is largely implicit in the previous representations of Gordon's return, Ira Gitler's liner notes for *Sophisticated Giant,* which recount Gordon's whereabouts during the night of the July 1977 blackout, put a finer point on this narrative of redemption. In Gitler's account, Gordon occupies the lone point of light in a city shrouded in darkness and wracked with chaotic upheaval:

> When the Big Blackout of 1977 hit New York, Dexter Gordon, his wife, and friends of theirs were on their way to meet some other friends at Nirvana, the Indian restaurant on Central Park South. As their car made its way uptown from 31st Street, lights—including traffic signals—were disappearing *en bloc,* almost as if their vehicle were a portable power snuffer. But when they arrived near their destination, a single beacon shone in the gloom, lighting a path directly to the entrance of the building on whose 21st floor waited Nirvana.
>
> Because the building houses medical facilities it has its own generator, even the elevator was working and the Gordon party was able to ascend and enjoy until 1 a.m. while the turmoil, anxiety and confusion went on below in the mean streets. The next day Dexter called one of his companions of the previous night and summed up, "It was magic."[98]

The block-by-block outages synchronized with the passage of Gordon's car; the fortuitously lit Indian restaurant, fortuitously named "Nirvana"; the "magical" tableau of Gordon and his companions gazing out on the mean streets from their brightly lit redoubt on Central Park South—all of these elements attribute to Gordon a supernatural, almost messianic presence, a lone beacon of hope in the fallen city.

How might bebop in general, or Gordon's bebop in particular, be seen as sites of renewal for New York, according to this cultural logic? Genres such as disco and punk, in which musical creation is heavily mediated, or in which individual virtuosity is muted or eradicated, offer challenges to individual subjective autonomy that seem threatening to many fans of "straightahead," acoustic jazz. To the degree that bebop performers efface the effects of musical mediation, and instead foreground the "live," real-time, and spontaneous dimensions of music making, they model an assertive, virtuosic individual agency in the process of creation.[99]

Dexter Gordon's musical style constitutes a particularly effective manifestation of this capacity for bebop to model autonomous agency. On tenor sax, Gordon uses a harsh attack and broad, massive tone, with each phrase slightly modulated at its end with a slight vibrato. In his music (as in his offstage witticisms), he is given over to a wry, sardonic humor in which musical quotation figures prominently, every musical gesture pointing playfully outward to the world outside the song. He phrases well "behind the beat," pulling back from the timeline established by the rhythm section, and this approach infuses his playing with a laconic, self-assured quality, a sense of relaxed confidence. (Gordon's preference for "behind the beat" phrasing apparently informed the direction he gave to his rhythm section. In Paul Berliner's *Thinking Jazz*, Rufus Reid recounts a story told to him by one of Gordon's bassists, in which the bassist struggled to find his way in Gordon's more relaxed time feel. The bassist decided one night to push the "behind the beat" sensibility to the point of absurdity, only to be told, "That's it!" by an elated Gordon.)[100]

We can see some of these ideas at work in one of his interpretations of "Body and Soul," found on a previously unissued track from the live Village Vanguard sets documented on *Homecoming*, where Gordon appropriates the so-called "Coltrane changes" for the standard in a way that makes them recognizably his own.[101] The opening vamp for the Coltrane arrangement of "Body and Soul" entails a series of unison hits, played together by the rhythm section, and Gordon's recording has all three rhythm players (Ronnie Matthews on piano, Stafford James on bass, and Louis Hayes on drums) conspicuously dragging out these hits, even as the overall tempo of the piece sits at a languorous quarter note = 50. Gordon, entering with the melody, sits even further behind the beat, re-articulating the key pitches, so as to lend them an even greater weight. Haynes, on drum kit, supports Gordon with a cacophonous triplet figure, alternating between snare hits and ride and crash cymbals. The texture emulates the driven intensity of Coltrane's original version of the arrangement, recorded with Elvin Jones and McCoy Tyner, but something in the swelling attack and delayed placement of Gordon's phrasing transforms the sensibility of the ballad. Far from being overly severe, Gordon's rendition evokes a weighty exuberance, investing the song with a relaxed feeling absent in Coltrane's interpretation. Gordon, who is seen as having both contributed to and borrowed from the Coltrane sonic legacy at different moments in his career, here enacts a performance that uses Coltrane's materials in the same moment that it preserves what is distinctive in Gordon's voice.

Gordon's robust tone, his playfully sardonic demeanor, his penchant for quotation, his use of microrhythmic displacement—all of these elements of Gordon's performativity seem to resonate with the portraits of the African-American sonic legacy outlined by scholars such as Samuel

Floyd or Olly Wilson, who argue that these gestures reinscribe key tropes or stylistic elements that embody meaning for successive generations of African diasporic musicians.[102] In particular, Wilson's conception of the "heterogeneous sound ideal" in African diasporic music, where contrast and idiosyncratic voices are privileged over sonic homogeneity, provides a particularly inviting context for our understanding of Gordon's style: his sound, indebted to practices ranging from Ben Webster's swing to Coltrane's "New Thing," nevertheless remains entirely his own.

In this way, Gordon's style seems to offer observers a powerful affirmation of a putative authenticity of African-American expression: the individual voice within an overarching tradition, the performer who sonically affirms the past by playing with it, "signifyin'" upon it, in a distinctive way.[103] However, beyond functioning in a general way as a signifier of authenticity, Gordon's musical voice presents itself to his contemporaries as an intervention in a specific historical moment, a remedy for what ails urban culture in the waning years of the 1970s. Where Gordon's style is seen as affirming tropes about the vital, spontaneous, and embodied dimensions of bebop, it seems to offer jazz enthusiasts an authentic response to what cultural conservatives were increasingly seeing as a troubling artifice and antimusicality in contemporary forms of popular music. We can in no way neglect the importance of the era's turbulent discourses about masculinity as a key factor shaping this response to Gordon. Every resonant, low-register long tone, every delayed beat placement, every sardonic witticism becomes interpreted through the prism afforded by Gordon's myriad visual and critical representations at this time, which present him as the visceral embodiment of a charismatic black heteronormative masculinity. At the same time, his affiliation with a musical style from an earlier moment in New York history, a moment that contemporary observers dissociate from the charged racial context of New York's ostensible mid-1970s decline, reassures white listeners unsettled by the innovative practices forged by younger musicians of color.

What is also crucial here—crucial to the subsequent efflorescence of jazz neoclassicism—is a pairing of this robust black heteronormative masculinity with ideas of creative *potency*. Discursive representations of Gordon's personality and music (so often rendered as barely distinguishable from one another) tacitly link a vibrant, culturally creative production to the latent promise of heterosexual *re*production, to a masculine virility encoded in aesthetic output. In this, the widespread fetishization of Dexter Gordon anticipates the saleable black masculinities at the core of the "young lions" phenomenon in the 1980s and 1990s.[104] But we should also note that a similar pairing of creative accomplishment with masculine prowess was also beginning to establish itself in the FIRE sector office towers discussed earlier in this chapter, less than three miles from the club where Gordon made his triumphant stateside return.[105] These parallel constructions of creative masculinity help to explain how a certain idea of jazz could come to resonate as a symbol for capitalism itself: perhaps the celebration of jazz as a distillation of competitive virtuosity by management consultants or corporate leadership gurus of the kind discussed in chapter 1 is a celebration tacitly underwritten by a mutual investment in constructions of virtuosic masculine creation.

It is these aspects of Gordon's visual presence and musical style that would have served as a site of immense catharsis for those troubled by the cultural transformations shaping daily life for New Yorkers during the 1970s. In later chapters, I will be outlining the emergence of something that could be called a "jazz bubble" associated with neoclassical jazz in the 1980s and 1990s: corporate and institutional actors, invested in the promise of neoclassicism as an alluring brand, concentrate their resources in the monoculture of a narrowly cast "jazz tradition." As I hoped to have demonstrated here, the emotional resonance of this future trend has at least some of its roots in the atmosphere of catharsis surrounding the moment of Gordon's "homecoming."

CONCLUSION

Faced with the numerous assessments of late 1970s New York that I have outlined in this chapter, where the metropolis has been excoriated as a site of cultural decline, we must be sure to note that this narrative has been complicated by more recent, and more recuperative, stories of 1970s New York. With hindsight, we can now look back on the late 1970s as a period of unprecedented artistic ferment and cultural vibrancy for the city, as the decade that witnessed the emergence of the CBGBs scene, the Paradise Garage, Jean-Michel Basquiat, Grandmaster Flash.[106] In many of these cases, we can see the way that the cultural vibrancy of the period happened not merely in spite of the city's socioeconomic upheaval but in some ways because of it. However, recognition of the social worth of this era of mid-1970s New York cultural radicalism has been very late in coming. At the time of their initial emergence, public reactions to these cultural transformations were fraught with moral panic: graffiti understood as the visual signifier of criminality, punk seen as a will to chaotic destruction, disco understood as the embodiment of deviant sexual license. In this context, it becomes possible to understand the comparative appeal that an all-acoustic jazz resurgence could offer to those unsettled by disco, punk, and hip hop. Late 1970s observers could easily hail the stateside return of expatriate bebop veterans as a wholly positive development, the artists' return providing onlookers with a pretext for a nostalgic idealization of the past.

The cultural faultlines inscribed within these debates betray the traces of a deeper, materialist history. The tenor of latent unease that underlies even the most benign critical writings from this period hints at a world that is undergoing a transformation both invisible and far-reaching, a sea change that resists conventional modes of explication. The nascent rise of financial capital in 1970s New York City, which inscribes itself as a force at once elusively abstract and manifestly consequential, nevertheless fails to register in residents' minds as the proximate cause of New York's difficulties. What asserts itself in the register of political economy can often only be rendered legible in the register of culture, and in the context of this period's emergent conservatism, we see a body politic increasingly disposed toward social explanations that begin and end on the terrain of culture.

The densely woven texture of economic upheaval and cultural ferment that characterizes the New York fiscal crisis serves as singular point from which to examine the oft-celebrated "jazz renaissance" that Gordon and others helped to bring about. The challenge for contemporary musicology is to outline a program of sociocultural analysis that attends to all sides of such events, acknowledging both the immediate cultural tensions that animate them, as well as the larger structural antagonisms that so often constitute the secret, implicit histories of cultural developments.

CHAPTER 3

Selling the Songbook

The Political Economy of Verve
Records (1956–1990)

The major record labels have long been an important, if unstable, site of cultural production for jazz musicians. The history of jazz can in some sense be told as a story about the vacillating fortunes of small, independent imprints, on the one hand, and major labels and their jazz subsidiaries, on the other: for example, Scott DeVeaux has documented the role that fly-by-night labels such as Dial, Savoy, and Guild played in locating "incipient cracks in the monolith," exploiting niche markets for small-group music ignored by the era's majors.[1] By the same token, the major labels have served as powerful, if fickle, advocates for recorded jazz, their outsized economies of scale placed at the service of the scene's most prominent artists.[2]

More recently, though, the music majors have become a less hospitable site for jazz production, owing to their increasingly complicated position within the global economy. In an environment in which entertainment conglomerates angle for market "synergies" or increases in market share, the day-to-day operations of major record labels are increasingly affected by the strategic maneuvers of their parent companies, expansive multinational corporations that see record sales as just one of innumerable revenue streams. (Presently, *record* sales, whether understood as physical commodities or digital sound files, no longer remain the principal revenue stream for even the *musical* subsidiaries of the entertainment multinationals.)[3] In response, as Keith Negus and others have noted, many of these companies have altered their posture

toward jazz and similar genres, moving from a paternalistic management of jazz subsidiaries as prestigious loss-leaders to a more hard-
nosed expectation that they, too, will perform as profit centers for the
company.[4]

Moreover, both the major labels and their parent companies find
themselves increasingly subject to a logic of financialization that over-
rides other considerations. By recalibrating corporate priorities in relation to a privileged emphasis on "shareholder value," record companies
alter the very temporal horizon of the music business, forging a corporate culture in which the trajectories of artist development and marketing strategies inside the company are closely aligned with the volatility
of market processes outside the company. As entertainment conglomerates have entered into a period of rapid consolidation and restructuring,
corporate mergers and leveraged buyouts have become as important to
understanding the fortunes of jazz artists on the major labels as decisions within the units themselves.

The endeavors of Seagram magnate Edgar Bronfman Jr. are particularly noteworthy in this connection. Since the mid-1990s, Bronfman Jr.
has helped to catalyze at least three seismic transformations in the structure of the recording industry. Having overseen the creation of the Universal Music Group in 1995, Bronfman orchestrated the 1998 merger
of UMG and PolyGram, creating what was then one of the largest music
conglomerates in the world. In 2000, Bronfman oversaw the sale of
Seagram and its Universal film and music holdings to Vivendi, a French
waste-management and telecommunications corporation, and its affiliated French pay-TV unit Canal+, helping to create the world's preemi-
nent media and entertainment giant. However, under the reckless management of Jean-Marie Messier, the newly created Vivendi Universal
experienced a collapse in its stock price, and the Bronfman family saw
the value of its stake in the company drop precipitously. Bronfman initially maintained a low profile in the wake of the Vivendi Universal
crash, but before long, he was once again trying his hand at the music
business: with a team of private-equity investors, Bronfman oversaw
the use of a leveraged buyout to acquire the music holdings of the Time-
Warner conglomerate, reforming Warner Music Group as a stand-alone
music "super-independent."[5]

In the late 1990s and early 2000s, these and similar structural
changes implemented at the entertainment multinationals had the effect
of reversing the gains made by jazz artists at the major labels during the
1980s and 1990s. The financial pressures of consolidation forced sev-

eral labels to either trim their rosters or dissolve their jazz divisions entirely. This in turn led a considerable number of contemporary jazz artists to look for alternatives to the major-label model. Independent labels have presented themselves as an attractive place of refuge for those displaced by market trends, but both independents and majors have been faced with the realities of the digital music economy, in which market actors are pressed to find alternatives to the "object-based" market in tangible music commodities.[6]

This latter point is important: since the early 2000s, artists and labels in all domains have had to reckon with a transformed business landscape, in which file sharing and streaming platforms have effectively "liberated" the recorded sonic trace from its inscription in the physical artifact. As Tim Anderson has argued, record companies are still in the process of figuring out what revenue models are potentially viable in this climate.[7] However, the post-Napster implosion of the record industry cannot by itself explain its rapid downsizing of its jazz artist rosters. Given that the economic resuscitation of jazz in the 1990s depended in large part on a wave of CD reissue programs, we might expect jazz to have been especially exposed to the disruptive effects of the emergent digital music business environment. However, for all of its other commercial vulnerabilities, jazz is a genre that has historically been marketed to an upscale, middle-aged "adult" clientele, and might quite possibly have been able to find a comfortable home within the major labels' early millennial strategies.[8] At the height of the post-Napster fallout, the thirty-to-sixty demographic demonstrated comparatively little interest in downloading music, and had the highest disposable income of all listening demographics. As such, this affluent middle-aged demographic was actually a *growth* market for CD consumption during this period.[9] If jazz lost its standing at the major-label jazz subsidiaries in spite of continued robust CD sales to the adult market, this would suggest that other important forces were in play, beyond the impact of the "invisible jukebox." It is in this connection that I believe we need to situate the *financialization* of the music industry at the center of discussions about jazz's waning fortunes at the major imprints: the pressures that subsidiaries have faced at the retail point of sale are magnified by the pressures imposed upon them from above, a volatility written into the very terms of corporate restructuring.

My discussion in chapters 3 and 4 will proceed from an overview of market dynamics in the age of financialization to a more detailed accounting of how one storied major-label jazz subsidiary has been affected by these developments. I devote the present chapter to a historical account of Verve records in its successive manifestations as a privately-owned independent, a vertically-integrated component of MGM Records, and a subsidiary of the Philips/PolyGram corporate umbrella. In the next chapter, following an account of the neoclassical "boomlet" of the early 1990s, I will turn my attention to the fallout from the PolyGram/Universal merger of 1998, identifying the means through which changes at the upper echelons of the label's corporate parent would shape aspects of the label's staffing, artist roster, and marketing decisions. Verve's wholesale corporate transformation in the late 1990s and early 2000s would see the label relinquish its commitment to the music with which it has long been closely identified: by the turn of the millennium, Verve would oversee a historical catalog of jazz recordings released under the Verve, Impulse!, and GRP imprints, while its active artist roster prioritized vocal music in a generalized "adult contemporary" vein.[10] The label's cuts to its instrumental jazz roster allowed it to respond to the aggressive cost-cutting measures taken by its parent company in the wake of the PolyGram merger.

I am interested in the ways that changes at the highest levels of corporate hierarchies articulate with developments within labels and their subsidiary units: to what degree, for example, does the logic of "shareholder value," which shapes the broader context of corporate mergers, consolidation, and downsizing, serve to explain the vicissitudes of daily life within the jazz divisions of major labels? Here, my intention is to illuminate the ways that market volatility shapes the environment in which musicians record and perform. It is worth noting that from the perspective of actors in the financial sector, volatility is often seen as a good thing: the business model celebrated by the financial sector and the shareholder class is predicated upon rapid and unpredictable changes in the market, and upon the embrace of dramatic financial risk. However, as one might imagine, this has deleterious effects for musicians who are subject to this structure of risk at a different level within the corporate hierarchy.

"SHAREHOLDER VALUE" AND CONTEMPORARY FINANCIAL CAPITALISM

With the ascendency of the financial sector since the late 1970s, businesses have reoriented themselves toward a prioritization of the concept of *shareholder value*. The value system of shareholder value has become so deeply inscribed in our contemporary economic worldview that we have come to see it as a kind of underlying common sense. As Karen Ho has argued, we frequently take as given the notion that a company's lone fiduciary accountability is to its owners, and that this duty's practical realization manifests itself through increases in stock price. Shareholder value subsumes the complexity of a corporation's institutional voices and multivalent priorities to the singular telos of the quarterly report. At the same time, despite its preoccupation with short-term temporalities, the effect of shareholder value ideology has been to project a contemporary idyll back across historical capitalisms and past regimes of accumulation.[11] However, the primacy of shareholder value in contemporary political economy is a thoroughly modern cultural construction, sustained via a mutually reinforcing network of political rhetorics, managerial discourses, and institutional practices.

Prior to the mid-1970s, large corporations frequently oriented themselves around a form of corporate organization that Ho refers to in terms of *managerial capitalism.* The primacy of managerial capitalism reflects the relatively marginal position of financial capital in the decades extending from the introduction of the New Deal in the 1930s to the collapse of the Bretton Woods consensus in the early 1970s. After the destabilizing shocks of the 1930s, new regulatory measures were implemented to put restrictions on financial sector transactions, including the Glass-Steagall Act and the Securities and Exchange Acts. The stock market was delegitimized as a center of economic activity, and shareholders with nominal control over corporations increasingly took a back seat to the oversight of corporate management.[12] Under this new rubric, the health of the corporation was understood as a function of the health of its various *stakeholders,* as well as its shareholders.

By contrast, the economic consensus that has increasingly held sway in recent decades recognizes no other legitimate priorities for corporations outside of the key measure of shareholder value. The concept of shareholder value emergences from an attempt to reconcile the profit-driven, entrepreneurial model of the nineteenth-century corporation with the complex, bureaucratic magnitude of the midcentury firm. Drawing upon the classic economic assumptions established by figures such as Adam Smith, neoclassical economics reduces the firm's fiduciary structure to two inputs: the owner (a position that, for their purposes, is conflated with the shareholder), and private property, treated as an undifferentiated monad. This model effectively repudiates the notion of the modern corporation as a *social* entity with responsibility to multiple claimants.[13]

In the wake of economic crises during the 1970s, neoclassical arguments about the sanctity of shareholder value increasingly held sway, as business leaders increasingly blamed the faltering economy on what they saw as the bloated workforce and sluggish managerial style of the postwar firm. It is not a coincidence that the return to rhetorics of shareholder value coincides with the period which saw the financial sector return to the center of economic life. It was the re-allocations of capital made possible by a reinvigorated financial sector that facilitated the process by which large American firms could shift from a Fordist model of production, in which large-scale manufacturing is located domestically and managed in-house, to a post-Fordist model in which corporations could outsource manufacturing capacity in order to cut costs.[14] Ideologies of shareholder value seemed to offer a means of recalibrating the overextended postwar corporation, allowing it to pare itself down to its core functions and to concentrate on profit maximization in an uncertain world.[15]

The realignment of the corporation around the principle of shareholder value had the effect of dramatically truncating the temporal horizon of business, as management increasingly privileged short-term elevation of stock price over the long-term footing of the corporation as an employer. Moreover, with respect to mergers and acquisitions, the priorities of management shifted here, too. The regulatory and strategic orientation of the postwar corporation favored *conglomeration,* which entailed the expansion of an existing company through the simple addition of a noncompeting firm in a different business sector. During this era, the primary motivation for conglomeration was to pursue expansion without falling afoul of antitrust restrictions. By contrast, the mergers and acquisitions movement of the 1980s and 1990s was in large part predicated upon achieving dramatic improvements in stock price: following a merger of two extant firms in *similar* markets, corporate leadership in the era of financialization would pursue the selloff of inefficient divisions, the liquidation of assets, and the downsizing of the newly combined workforce, all in the service of maximizing the position of shareholders. The leverage required to undertake mergers and acquisitions also ensures that a considerable debt burden is imposed upon the new corporate entity, introducing costs that are passed on in the form of downsizing and budget cuts.[16] In the context of the music industry, this latter point becomes especially relevant to our understanding of the wave of mergers in the entertainment sector since the 1990s. Increasingly, such mergers have been accompanied by a rhetoric of "shareholder value" that is somewhat new to the music industry: a quick search for the phrase "shareholder value" appearing in *Billboard* magazine shows no mention of the phrase prior to 1994, but subsequent years have brought numerous citations of shareholder value, in contexts ranging from discussion of Clear Channel's role in media consolidation in the late 1990s, to speculation about a Warner Music Group initial public stock offering in 2005.[17]

The accelerated pace of corporate restructuring in the entertainment industry, from the acquisition of Columbia Records by Sony in 1987 to the Universal Music Group acquisition of EMI in 2012, takes place in an economic environment fundamentally shaped by the emergent primacy of shareholder value as a strategic point of departure. An action such as the announcement of a major corporate merger, or the Initial Public [stock] Offering (IPO) of a company that has been taken private and returned to marketworthiness, is often less about establishing a new trajectory for long-term internal growth than it is about orchestrating a dramatic, punctuating event for the benefit of the financial markets. A corporation may make a bold acquisition in order to demonstrate a dramatic increase in market share (as with the Universal Music Group acquisition of PolyGram), or in order to showcase their creation of market "synergies" (as with Sony's acquisition of Columbia Pictures/Columbia Records, which complemented its "hardware" consumer electronics with "software" film and music titles).[18] To the extent that these maneuvers are predicated upon the creation of "shareholder value," their generation of profit or long-term growth matters less in and of itself than their *performative staging* of 'shareholder value,'" presented for an audience of market analysts and potential investors.[19]

The potential relevance of shareholder value sensibilities needs to be kept in view as we consider the market environment traversed by major-label jazz divisions in the late 1990s and early 2000s. While the impact of media consolidation upon the global circulation of music is an important subject in its own right, it must be considered in tandem with the broader question of how the music industry has weathered the era of financialization: how do the contemporary dynamics of financial capital figure in to our understanding of the waning fortunes of jazz at the major labels?

THE VERVE MUSIC GROUP AND THE STATE OF POSTMILLENNIAL JAZZ

In December of 2011, Lucian Grainge, chairman and CEO of Universal Music, announced that the renowned Canadian producer David Foster would become chairman of the Verve Music Group, where he would be tasked with leading its creative operations and developing its roster of adult contemporary artists.[20] Foster, the erstwhile composer of the "Love Theme" from *St. Elmo's Fire* (1985), has had an illustrious career as a producer and composer, with production credits on Barbra Streisand's "Somewhere," Natalie Cole's "Unforgettable," and Whitney Houston's hugely popular cover of Dolly Parton's "I Will Always Love You."[21] The press release announcing Foster's appointment to Verve stressed his position at the core of mainstream pop hitmaking and his special aptitude for developing singer-songwriter artists, claiming that "under his leadership, Mr. Foster will build upon Verve's legacy of nurturing great talent at a time when music lovers are now re-embracing the singer-songwriter artistry of the genre."[22] In line with this vision, David Foster has signed artists such as Smokey Robinson and Sarah McLachlan to Verve, as the label continues to oversee a roster comprising such figures as classical crossover artist Andrea Bocelli and *American Idol* finalist Ruben Studdard.[23]

David Foster's arrival at VMG indexes an important moment in the development of Verve as a *brand*. For most of its nearly seventy-year history, Verve Records had been indelibly associated with jazz as a musical genre, boasting a roster of names extending from Ella Fitzgerald to Stan Getz. As recently as the mid-1990s, Verve was developing a slate of emerging and veteran jazz artists schooled in the post-bebop jazz legacy, including figures such as Christian McBride, Roy Hargrove, Nicholas Payton, and most notably, Joe Henderson. Much like Blue Note, another crucial imprint that established its brand in the postwar era, Verve was for all intents and purposes seen as synonymous with jazz: the title page for the label's 1994 commemorative publicity brochure could lead off with the straightforward claim that "for fifty years, the best jazz has been played with Verve."[24]

Over the last fifteen years, Verve has taken on a radically different identity, showcasing a roster of wide-ranging eclecticism: among the work released by currently signed artists, the retro-1980s power funk of Dirty Loops jostles with the French-language songs of Italian-born chanteuse and former first lady of France Carla Bruni.[25] Presently, jazz is not so much absent at Verve as it is secondary to other parameters of the Verve brand. The label is still home to jazz pianist and vocalist Diana Krall, and the jazz-inflected New Orleans funk hybrid of Trombone Shorty was recently released on Verve Forecast (Verve's former folk label, revived by then-VMG president Ron Goldstein in the mid-

2000s).[26] However, in both instances, their recent presence on the label had less to do with their genre identity than with their appeal to a specific market demographic: a 2005 article about Ron Goldstein's reintroduction of the Verve Forecast label identifies this group as an educated, "Starbucks-sipping," "college-age-plus" market with a highly eclectic range of musical tastes. From the perspective of the label, jazz was increasingly seen as just one element of this mix: Goldstein cited the continued presence of Krall at Verve less in terms of her appeal to jazz enthusiasts than as a jazz artist with crossover appeal *beyond* a specific jazz listenership. By that time, jazz had long since ceased to be the overriding sensibility of the Verve brand, and Verve Forecast, with its mandate of exploring a vibrant "nonjazz" component of the adult contemporary market, can in retrospect be seen as part of an "exit strategy" for the label, justifying its eventual abandonment of jazz as fundamental to the label's identity.[27]

By 2005, the diminished position of jazz at the major labels had long been firmly established: industry pessimism was made manifest in the elimination of the jazz division at Columbia, downsizing of the RCA/Victor jazz roster, significant cuts at the Verve Music Group, and later on, the shutdown of Warner Jazz and the folding of its remaining artists into Elektra/Nonesuch.[28] Even Blue Note, partially protected by virtue of its careful stewardship under jazz enthusiast Bruce Lundvall, had made a strategic diversification into other aspects of the adult contemporary market. However, these closures and downsizings at the jazz majors cannot be attributed solely to the question of the music's modest profitability: this had long been a reality of the music's position in the recording industry, where even "Gold"-selling records have historically been the exceptions to the rule. So the question becomes: what is distinctive about the specific moment of the late 1990s and early 2000s that accounts for the radical downsizing of jazz rosters at the major labels?

In their respective accounts of the state of jazz at the turn of the millennium, Stuart Nicholson and Travis Jackson have enumerated many of the most important factors at work in the demise of instrumental jazz at the major labels. Nicholson cites the overinvestment of imprints such as Verve, Columbia Jazz, and other jazz divisions in the neoclassicist "young lions" phenomenon in the late 1980s and early 1990s, and the parallel boom of CD-reissue programs at these labels. Young artists were placed in the awkward situation of competing against the back catalog of classic recordings released by the same artists whose styles they were emulating. A CD release of a remastered classic hard-bop recording from the 1960s is a much less expensive proposition than the development and promotion of a new set of recordings by emerging artists. At the point of sale, conventional music retailers in the late 1990s provided ever-diminishing shelf space to jazz recordings, as they faced competition from much larger retailers such as Wal-Mart (whose shelves contained few jazz recordings). In the early 2000s, as the emergence of Napster and other file-sharing platforms increasingly threatened the viability of the youth market in CD sales, major labels increasingly sought to target the same adult contemporary market cited in *Billboard*'s profile of the Verve Forecast rollout: in this context, vocalists such as Diana Krall or Jamie Callum were seen as offering considerable appeal to an affluent "thirty-plus" demography, for whom music (in Nicholson's estimation) served primarily as a tasteful, complementary backdrop to conspicuous consumption.[29] As Jackson has argued, these considerations at the majors were frequently driven by a logic of *portfolio management,* the sense that all artists within a subsidiary label's portfolio needed to demonstrate profitability to the parent company: the new corporate sensibility no longer allowed for artists who were prestigious loss leaders, but instead required that all inhabitants of the roster demonstrate a trajectory of rapid and immediate sales.[30] The cumulative external pressures of CD-catalog reissues, declining retail space, and the prioritization of crossover jazz vocalists under portfolio management ensured that by the early 2000s, very few of the artists who enjoyed major-label support during the 1990s were still signed to those subsidiaries.

Taken together, the various factors enumerated by Jackson and Nicholson lay out a compelling narrative of the major labels' divestment from jazz at the turn of the millennium. In particular, the global downturn in CD sales since the late 1990s, in and alongside the cumulative effects of the digitization of music (its circulation via the conduits made available by peer-to-peer networks, iTunes, YouTube, and Spotify and other streaming platforms) certainly forms an important part of the context for the strategic reprioritization of the majors. However, I would argue that, as an explanation for the precise timing of roster cuts at VMG, RCA/Victor, and other jazz subsidiaries, the drive toward "portfolio management" and other approaches to "rationalization" at label subsidiaries in the late 1990s was driven as much by a logic of maximizing shareholder value as by any specific pessimism about the future viability of record sales. Many of the most high-profile roster cuts at the labels coincide with mergers or periods of significant reorganization: for instance, the dissolution of the RCA/Victor, BMG Classics, and Windham Hill imprints in 2000, which saw the departure of D.D. Jackson and Ravi Coltrane from the BMG/RCA stable and the elimination of more than a hundred jobs, was part of a broader cost-cutting initiative pursued by BMG Entertainment as it sought to position itself for subsequent label acquisitions.[31]

These restructuring initiatives need to be part of any historical account of the major labels and their systemic disinvestment in jazz. The acquisition of PolyGram/Verve by Universal Music Group provides us with a window onto the relationship between strategic and aesthetic decisions under the present conditions of financialization. In order to contextualize what is at stake in our contemporary moment, I will now turn my attention to Verve's shifting position within the constellation of entertainment conglomerates since its formation under Norman Granz in the 1950s.

THE VERVE LEGACY

Beyond the depth of its catalog, which comprises such jazz luminaries as Ella Fitzgerald, Dizzy Gillespie, Oscar Peterson, Blossom Dearie, Stan Getz, and Jimmy Smith, two elements of the midcentury Verve label are particularly important for understanding its later identity as a PolyGram subsidiary, and as an expanded label "group" under the Vivendi/Universal corporate umbrella. First, the Artists and Repertory (A&R) strategies pursued at the label in the 1950s and 1960s, under the supervision of its initial owner Norman Granz, and its subsequent A&R chief, Creed Taylor, have set important templates that contextualize the label strategy over the course of the 1990s and early 2000s. Recent decision making about content, about artist rosters, and about the "sound" of Verve can be traced to a legacy that dates back to the midcentury practices of the label. Second, the structure of the contemporary Verve Music Group is informed by the origins of the imprint as an independent label, shaped by the idiosyncratic vision of Norman Granz and by its subsequent acquisition by the MGM Records label, through which the label became tied to its parent company through the dynamics of vertical integration. This carefully forged label identity may help to explain something of its efficacy as a subsidiary of PolyGram in the context of the latter's loosely federated structure: through various upheavals and transformations, the depth of the Verve catalog, and the distinctive shape of its development under its midcentury A&R managers, would instill in the label a sense of its potentiality as an autonomous, highly specialized arm within a larger multidivisional corporation.

We can locate the origins of the current Verve legacy in Norman Granz's fundamentally populist orientation as a concert impresario, producer, and agent, and in his efforts to harness his jazz entrepreneurship as a vehicle for social and economic justice. In his excellent study of Granz's life and career, Tad Hershorn documents his efforts to introduce jazz to a mass audience, and to provide the jazz world's most prominent musicians with a degree of remuneration and respect worthy of their accomplishments. In negotiating on behalf of his artists, many of whom were subject to the brutally discriminatory institutions of the contemporaneous music industry, he sought to ensure top-shelf compensation, travel, accommodation, and working conditions, and beginning in the mid-1940s introduced antisegregation clauses into his contractual agreements with performance venues. Granz's progressive social values also shaped his attitudes about the proper context of jazz performance: in Hershorn's formulation, "Granz's philosophy of jazz rested on his belief in a race-blind democracy of talent as vetted by the jam session."[32] The Jazz at the Philharmonic series, whose inaugural concert was held on July 2, 1944, at the Philharmonic Auditorium in Los Angeles, served as the concrete realization of this philosophy: centering upon the extended improvisations of the jam session format, and often given over to a bluesy, riff-based aesthetic, the concert series redefined the rarified concert hall as a performance site for the era's most exuberantly populist jazz sensibilities. Granz's recordings of the JATP concerts, distributed via an agreement with Mercury Records beginning in 1945, demonstrated to the music industry that live concert recording was not only technically viable but potentially extremely lucrative.[33]

The circumstances surrounding the establishment of the Verve label proper are also important for our understanding of the label's later approach to artist development. Granz's signing of Ella Fitzgerald to the new label, following her departure from Decca in 1956, was a catalyzing moment in the foundation of Verve: if the nominal occasion of Verve's founding was Granz's decision to amalgamate his Clef, Norgran, and Down Home imprints, it was Fitzgerald's inaugural series of *Song Book* recordings (beginning with the release of *Ella Fitzgerald Sings the Cole Porter Song Book* in May of 1956) that served to put the nascent label on a solid financial footing and to signal its intention to target a pop audience for its jazz recordings. Backed by lavish orchestration, the *Song Book* records established a new context for Fitzgerald, previously understood as a quintessential bebop artist. Her warm interpretations of show tunes and standards introduced her work to a new audience: *Sings the Cole Porter Song Book* sold over one hundred thousand copies within the first month of its release, and established Verve's credentials as a jazz label with aspirations to pop success.[34] Verve became a highly congenial home for vocal jazz, with Billie Holiday, Louis Armstrong, Blossom Dearie, and later, Astrud Gilberto and Nina Simone among the vocalists featured in its releases.

The Songbook series was a thematically organized collection of concept albums, made cogent to the marketplace through the consistent pairing of Fitzgerald with a sequence of popular song repertories. Pairings or duets, made up of juxtapositions between unexpectedly congenial collaborators (Louis Armstrong and Oscar Peterson, Ella Fitzgerald and Louis Armstrong, Ella Fitzgerald and Count Basie) constituted one of the most common handles for Verve as it sought to make its releases visible to record buyers. These albums anticipated the strategies taken up by jazz subsidiaries at contemporary major labels, where intergenerational matchups or "odd couple" pairings (for example, Wynton Marsalis and Willie Nelson's 2008 Blue Note release, *Two Men with the Blues,* or the similar Reprise album pairing Marsalis with Eric Clapton in 2011) allow labels to change consumers' perceptions of artists who are "known quantities."[35] Throughout his years overseeing the Clef, Norgranz, and Verve imprints, Granz also used the album series as an implicit conceptual referent, with sequential records bound together by shared artwork and title phrasing, as for example on *Oscar Peterson Plays Irving Berlin, Oscar Peterson Plays Jerome Kern,* and *Oscar Peterson Plays Duke Ellington,* each released on Clef, or the Oscar Peterson *Song Book* series from the late 1950s, released on Verve in the wake of Ella Fitzgerald's *Song Book* releases.[36] A consistent trope tying together many of these releases is the striking artwork of David Stone Martin, whose line drawings were featured on Granz's Clef and Verve covers, and in the trumpeter "logo" for Granz's Jazz at the Philharmonic series.[37] Quality of packaging would be another site of consistency; for instance, *The Jazz Scene,* a beautifully assembled collection of twelve 78-rpm records released on Clef, and devoted to a wide range of contemporary jazz, was issued for $25 in 1949 (about $245 in today's dollars).[38] Through this kind of branding consistency, Clef and Verve releases could serve as springboards for other Clef and Verve releases, and a distinctive label-wide identity could be established in the marketplace.

In 1961, Norman Granz sold Verve to MGM Records, the music subsidiary of the Metro-Goldwyn-Mayer film studio.[39] MGM Records was created in line with a pervasive trend in the postwar culture industry. In the wake of an antitrust case in the mid-1940s that required that film studios sell off their theater chains, companies such as MGM and Paramount found themselves in search of new sites of *vertical integration:* that is to say, the close coordination of units representing different stages of production.[40] MGM had founded MGM Records with the intention of "bringing home" profits generated by sales of recordings featuring MGM stars.[41] MGM Records had successfully diversified itself, and had become an important player in the country music market; the acquisition of the singular Verve jazz catalog and artist roster would allow MGM Records to build upon these strengths in a different area.[42] Nevertheless, as we shall see, Verve's new role as a component in a broader chain of vertical integration would temper its autonomy as a label during this period.

One crucial figure at MGM-Verve was Creed Taylor, a groundbreaking producer whose impact continues to be felt in the jazz recording industry.[43] Prior to his arrival at Verve, Taylor had been instrumental in the founding of the famed Impulse! label at ABC-Paramount, signing John Coltrane as a crucial addition to its roster. Following its acquisition by MGM Records in 1960, Taylor was brought in to head the Verve subsidiary, announcing that plans were under way to change the "logo, the label, and the look" of Verve Records.[44] Taylor sought to reposition the label in relation to the pop market, signing new artists and targeting new audiences for the label's existing artists. This transformation had consequences for the existing Verve stable of musicians built up under Granz. Taylor was disenchanted with what he saw as the absence of "nuance" in live or spontaneous "jam session" recordings, of the kind released by the Prestige label, or under the Jazz at the Philharmonic imprimatur at Granz's Clef and Verve labels.[45] In his new position, he suspended new releases for a period of six months, during which he reportedly undertook a downsizing of the Verve roster that would rival the effects of the Universal/PolyGram merger almost forty years later: of the myriad JATP veterans signed to the Granz independent imprint, Taylor kept only a handful of noteworthy artists, including Ella Fitzgerald, Stan Getz, Oscar Peterson, and Johnny Hodges, among others.[46]

Taylor worked carefully with musicians to develop a specific concept or generative idea for each project: "We work with the artist to find a new frame for his talent. Nothing gimmicky, just an original concept which showcases the artist's ability. I never ask the artist to change his style of playing, just to play sometimes within a new frame of reference."[47] Taylor was constantly alert to the pop potentiality of jazz recordings, and he would pursue a variety of tactics for locating that potential: demanding "two minutes of excitement" from his artists for each album project, and asking improvisers to "discipline" their impulse to take multiple choruses, he approached the jazz recording session with an ear open for music that might communicate to an audience beyond Verve's usual constituency.[48]

The introspective sound of bossa nova served as a key "frame of reference" for several important MGM/Verve recordings under Creed Taylor, yielding the tremendously popular Stan Getz collaborations *Jazz Samba,* recorded with Charlie Byrd in 1962, and *Getz/Gilberto,* recorded with the guitarist João Gilberto in 1964.[49] Elsewhere, many of Taylor's repertory choices for Verve jazz albums were shaped by his label's working relationship with MGM studios. Taylor had access to the musical numbers from current film offerings put out by the parent company. Taylor met regularly with studio executives to hear previews of music from the coming attractions, and he would sometimes be expected to use the subsidiary label's releases as promotional vehicles.[50] In this, MGM was taking advantage of a facet of vertical integration embraced by the music subsidiaries of other film companies, such as its rival, ABC-Paramount (parent company of Impulse!), and Warner Brothers.[51] At the same time, Verve's accountability to its MGM Records parent, and ultimately to the MGM film studios, would shape the Verve catalog in ways that may seem baffling to later observers: a select few film-music themes, such as Elmer Bernstein's title music for the 1962 film *Walk on the Wild Side,* would appear and reappear on a variety of 1960s Verve releases by Jimmy Smith, Bill Evans, and others.[52] In the case of Bill Evans, the track was part of a lushly orchestrated, baldly commercial album of film music settings, a project so out of keeping with the pianist's usual sensibilities that the Verve CD reissue team, releasing *The Complete Bill Evans on Verve* decades later, would quietly omit it from the anthology's offerings.[53]

For our purposes, what is significant about Creed Taylor's tenure at MGM/Verve is the degree to which it highlights the structural imperatives at work in the label's relationship with its parent corporations. As a descriptive term, *crossover* is usually used to designate efforts within the music industry to reach different *musical* markets, by way of stylistic fusions. However, the sense of crossover at work here is as much a reflection of Taylor's "synergistic" interactions with the film division of the MGM conglomerate as it is a description of musical genre-crossing. In this sense, the MGM/Verve years give us an insight into a period in which jazz was intimately bound up in the broader dynamics of vertical integration at the entertainment conglomerates.

VERVE UNDER POLYGRAM

As Michael James Roberts has argued, the late 1960s and early 1970s saw the major labels move toward a new focus on *federated* structures. Having historically operated largely via a model of vertical integration, with artist recruitment, development, recording, marketing, manufacturing, and distribution all managed under one figurative "roof," the major labels increasingly embraced a more loosely organized model in which the production and artist-development processes were either delegated to their subsidiary divisions or, in some cases, outsourced to smaller independent labels. At the same time, the majors intensified their control over distribution, establishing national networks. This new arrangement allowed the majors to harness the cultural capital of their diverse subsidiaries and affiliated independents, even as they maintained tight control over the music's network of circulation.[54] This emergent corporate structure helps to make sense of what Negus has referred to as the "loose-tight" managerial style of contemporary record companies: laissez-faire in their attitudes about values, dress code, and the day-to-day functioning of label subsidiaries, record companies were increasingly "tight" in their monitoring of the bottom line.[55]

This emergence of larger, more loosely federated record companies in the late 1960s took place against the backdrop of a new interest in the music industry taken by financial investors. As Russell Sanjek notes, industry observers in the late 1960s point to the increasing number of holding companies and outside investment firms with an increased stake in the record industry. In the waning years of the postwar boom, Wall Street investment firms looked to the steady growth of the youth market, with its considerable spending power, as an attractive area of investment. The period saw a variety of audacious acquisitions and mergers, including the entry of the Kinney National Service, a diversified firm controlling funeral, car rental, and airport concession services, into the record business with its acquisition of the Warner/7 Arts firm in 1969.[56]

In 1972, MGM/Verve was acquired by PolyGram, the Dutch music multinational under the ownership of Philips Electronics. In my view, there are a couple of important features of the corporate structure of Philips/PolyGram that inform the status of Verve as a PolyGram subsidiary. First, as a European multinational with an interest in the American market, PolyGram had an interest in adopting the new "federated" model increasingly employed by rival firms during this period: we might look here to the parallel development of Warner Communications, which treated its Warner, Elektra, and Atlantic entities as relatively autonomous divisions. In principle, this kind of loose, divisional structure allowed the parent corporation to benefit from the creative independence of its diverse subsidiaries, and to acquire market share in a variety of disparate regional contexts. PolyGram's acquisition of MGM/Verve and the United Distributing Corp. in 1972 formed part of its strategy of aggressive expansion into the U.S. market, with the Dutch corporation eventually acquiring Casablanca Records (the venerable disco label) and Decca. As it happens, the Dutch company may not have been well positioned to take advantage of its new position. The lavish cost overruns incurred by Casablanca at the height of the disco craze (with purchases of cocaine reportedly going on the company expense accounts) serve as a cautionary tale about the dangers inherent in the label autonomy of PolyGram's "federated" structure.[57]

The status of MGM and its Verve subsidiary in the years immediately following the PolyGram acquisition did not bode well for the jazz label's future under the Dutch firm's corporate umbrella. It should be noted that the late 1960s and early 1970s was a period of widespread retrenchment in the jazz economy, with the closure of record shops and jazz clubs also translating into a diminished market share for jazz recordings: sales of jazz records reached a reported low of 1.3 percent of the market in 1972. In their effort to keep pace with sweeping cultural changes, labels such as Columbia, which had historically been one of the key postwar benefactors of recorded jazz, pursued explicitly crossover strategies, looking for jazz-rock fusion and other hybrids to make inroads into the pop/rock market (which in 1972 accounted for 75 percent of all record sales).[58] Another factor was that industry observers were pointing to the negative impact of conglomeration on jazz labels, as the holding companies acquiring smaller, independent record companies often didn't seem to know what to do with their acquisitions.[59]

For its part, Verve did not initially benefit from its absorption into the federated structure of PolyGram. The label lay largely dormant during the first decade of its management by the Dutch multinational, with its parent MGM label folded into the Polydor subsidiary. In a *Billboard* interview during this period, interim Polydor manager Bob Fruin gave little evidence of his interest in assembling a new artist roster for Verve, which he seemed to view as an inexpensive source of low-maintenance back catalog.[60] Indeed, for much of the 1970s, labels such as Fantasy and Verve concentrated on inexpensive "twofer" (double LP) reissues of their classic catalog, frequently priced in the same range as a single-LP release.[61] However, with the development of a strong CD-reissue program in the 1980s, Richard Seidel would develop an important niche market for PolyGram. As a label with a deep jazz catalog and a cultural knowledge of jazz, Verve was able to maximize the impact of its role as a semi-autonomous jazz subsidiary under PolyGram during the crucial decade of the neoclassicist revival.

This question of CD reissues brings us to a second area where the structure of Philips/PolyGram would have implications for its jazz subsidiary. Through its partnership with Philips, PolyGram was able to draw upon its parent company's commitment to research and development in the area of sound reproduction technologies. This question of vertical integration, pairing home electronics "hardware" with the record companies' "software," dates to Philips NV's earliest interventions into the record business.[62] For our purposes here, though, what is perhaps most pertinent for our understanding of Verve's eventual success under Poly-Gram is the role that Philips played in the development of the compact-disc technology. The CD was developed in a joint partnership between Philips and the Japanese firm Sony in the early 1980s. Together, the two firms would establish what would be referred to as the "Red Book" standard, a set of precise technical specifications that they would license to third-party manufacturers elsewhere in the music industry.[63] Philips/PolyGram took a considerable risk in committing resources to the R&D plans behind the compact disc. Relative to other record companies, Poly-Gram was particularly exposed to the industry-wide downturn in record sales brought on by the recession of the late 1970s and early 1980s: the abrupt demise of the disco boom had severely undercut its Casablanca and RSO properties, and in this context, PolyGram's overconfident commitment to an expanded distribution network in the United States made them vulnerable to further losses.[64]

Nevertheless, PolyGram was especially well positioned to take advantage of the new CD technology. As the home of Deutsche Grammophon, with its prestigious catalog, PolyGram was the global leader in the classical market, a constituency that was both affluent enough to afford outlays in new consumer electronics and deeply committed to an ideology of sonic fidelity.[65] The compact disc, alongside other digital sound reproduction technologies, held out the promise of a sonic "cleanliness," a freedom from noise, that would have proven tremendously attractive to those invested in the ostensible autonomy of the musical work and in the disavowal of its mediation through mechanical sound reproduction. Moreover, by the time the compact disc emerged in the 1980s, an emergent audience of upwardly mobile jazz listeners, primed by the "clean," Apollonian sensibilities of the first wave of jazz neoclassicists, had also become quite amenable to the promise of sonic fidelity that accompanied the introduction of the compact disc.[66]

An important initial move in the recuperation of the Verve property under PolyGram was the relocation of the label from Polydor Records to PolyGram Classics in 1981. The move was designed to allow Verve to capitalize upon PolyGram Classics' expertise in marketing back catalog. As a classical imprint, PolyGram Classics looked to jazz and saw parallels with its own audience: according to Barry Feldman, then national jazz manager under PolyGram Classics, they approached jazz consumers not as a potential crossover market, but as a dedicated constituency with its own clearly defined boundaries. As such, it set sales and marketing expectations for the Verve catalog that were very much in line with their existing classical targets: "In the classical environment, over here, we're in an area where they're willing to work with jazz. They are not looking at it to cross over. They're looking at it to be out there, to be jazz records and to reach a jazz audience. We'd like to see pieces sell in the eighty thousands if we can do it, but we can live with a five thousand selling album. If we're going to put out Stockhausen records, and we can live with the expectations of those records, we can live with the expectations of jazz."[67] Feldman's comments about the initial rollout of PolyGram jazz shed light upon a variety of points that are salient to our understanding of this historical moment in the recording industry. First, his comments envision a sales horizon of modest expectations, and the subsidiary seems quite comfortable with those expectations: in contrast to the aggressive pop-market orientation of major-label jazz departments during the 1970s, there is a willingness here to allow jazz records to be marketed to a strictly defined taste public of jazz aficionados, and to adjust expectations accordingly. As Feldman notes, a classical subsidiary such as Deutsche Grammophon knows very well how to manage the slow, long-term sales trajectory of a chamber-music title, and is therefore in a good position to understand the usual time horizon of jazz sales. Indeed, as subsequent Verve A&R director Richard Seidel has pointed out, the reassignment of the Verve catalog to PolyGram Classics was most likely a necessary condition for its success: "The whole catalogue approach, which is commonly accepted for classical records—the feeling that they might not do bang-up business in the first month but will continue to sell for years and years—began to be applied to jazz records as well, at least within Polygram. And without that kind of an approach, I don't think a successful jazz-reissue program is possible."[68] PolyGram's decision to assign its jazz catalog to its classical subsidiary is prescient in its recognition of the unusual positioning of neoclassicism as a niche market: unlike the 1960s Verve label under MGM, which understood jazz as occupying a place on a pop continuum, Verve's new alignment with the priorities of PolyGram Classics seems to reflect an awareness that during the 1980s, jazz was gradually being redefined as another species of "classical music," set at a remove from pop.

A key element of the new Verve line was the introduction of an import series from Japan, with remastered recordings issued on high-quality vinyl, accompanied by new liner notes by prominent jazz critic Nat Hentoff, and released in the United States in packaging that wrapped the original cover art in a "bellyband" marked with English titling and Japanese calligraphy.[69] As I noted above with respect to Feldman's comments, the import project, with its high-quality materials, faithful art reproduction, and careful markers of import status, aligned PolyGram's jazz plans with its priorities for the classical division, which had been capably targeting the audiophile market: PolyGram Classics, along with its jazz wing, was being readied as early as 1980 to provide "software" for the Philips compact disc system then under development.[70]

However, as PolyGram Classics followed up on the results of its import campaign in the U.S. market in late 1982, it made note of important distinctions between the American and international markets. While initial sales were encouraging, sometimes these reissued imports of specific existing titles did not do as well as the aggressively repackaged compilations issued by some competitors: Barry Feldman noted that a sleekly repackaged Clifford Brown/Max Roach set issued by Elektra/Musician achieved greater domestic visibility than the straightforward Verve reissue of an unmodified classic album by the same quintet. Feldman argued that this had to do with the limited scope of the audiophile and record collector's market in the United States, compared to abroad, noting that "the U.S. is the home of jazz, so you don't have the same archivist mentality that you'll find overseas, where the emphasis on original packages is so significant."[71]

This intuition about the nature of the domestic American market for Verve records was instrumental in convincing label executives to pursue new strategies for packaging and promoting the label's prestigious catalog. Seidel argued that Verve was better served eschewing simple album reissues in favor of compilations with "a specific theme or concept other than the conventional 'best of' approach."[72] Seidel's compilation series strategy echoes aspects of the existing Verve ethos under Granz and Taylor, but it also anticipates the trajectory that Verve (and other labels) would take over the subsequent decades for both reissues and new releases, as conceptual hooks become an increasingly important tool in the marketing arsenal for neotraditional jazz releases.

In moving away from straightforward album reissues, the compilation strategy also allowed Verve to take advantage of the new format of the CD, which allows for a greater number of tracks than the LP. The Silver Collection, which consisted of Verve-branded CD compilations of recordings by historical Verve artists Oscar Peterson, Astrud Gilberto, Ella Fitzgerald, and Stan Getz, was marked with the caption "Over 60 Minutes of Music," elegantly linking the merits of the CD hardware format to the repackaging of Verve's software content. By 1986, in the midst of an industry-wide, reissue-driven boom in jazz record sales, PolyGram Classics and Jazz had leveraged its parent company's technological advantage and its extensive archive of Verve, EmArcy, and Mercury titles into the largest catalog of jazz material on CD in the U.S. market.[73]

To be sure, Verve's reissue strategy was not happening in a vacuum. Fantasy Records, a long-standing midcentury indie jazz label, had come under the A&R direction of Orrin Keepnews in 1973, and had been a leader in the reissues market ever since. They were among the first to pioneer the sale of "twofer" releases of their deep catalog (which comprised the classic Prestige label recordings, among other things), and by the mid-1980s they had developed the OJC (Original Jazz Classics) line of reissues, which rivaled that of Verve in scope.[74] Keepnews would later produce *Chronicle,* a ten-LP box set of the complete recordings of Miles Davis's Prestige materials, which was a first of its kind in the industry.[75] Reissues programs of the kind developed by Keepnews, along with carefully produced compilations and box-set releases, became a crucial lens through which the history of the music could be reconceived for a younger generation of consumers.

The success of the Verve reissue program under Seidel set the stage for the label's introduction of its first lineup of current artists since the label's acquisition by PolyGram in 1972. It is significant, in light of both the label's heritage and of its future direction, that an important part of this initial wave of "all new recordings from a vintage label" would consist of vocalists, performing live: leveraging Verve's association with Norman Granz's famous live recordings of the Jazz at the Philharmonic sessions, as well as its foundational affiliation with Ella Fitzgerald's Songbook series, the new *Live at Vine Street* discs featured direct-to-digital recordings of Nina Simone, Shirley Horn, and Joe Williams, performing as part of the Monday-night jazz showcase at the Vine Street Bar & Grill in Los Angeles.[76]

The renowned jazz vocalist Betty Carter would be among the most important additions to Verve's lineup during this period. The move to Verve was especially noteworthy in light of her earlier career: as a proud traditionalist facing the record industry's increasing ambivalence about mainstream jazz in the late 1960s, Carter decided to found an independent jazz label, Bet-Car, as an outlet for her own work. The label allowed her artistic control over her recorded work, but in the manner of many independent labels, it did not have access to the expansive distribution networks that ensured robust record sales for major labels. With the bebop revival of the late 1970s, though, Carter began to receive increased critical praise and public recognition, at a time when major labels were reentering the jazz market. In 1987, she was approached by Seidel at Verve about the possibility of joining the label: the resulting contract with the PolyGram subsidiary allowed her to retain complete artistic control over subsequent Verve releases, and would provide for the distribution of her complete Bet-Car catalog on compact disc.[77] Her first album with Verve, the 1987 title *Look What I Got!*, would go on to win a Grammy Award for best female jazz performance. The irony of this belated Grammy recognition was not lost on Carter: unlike her earlier Bet-Car releases, *Look What I Got!* had been the beneficiary of an aggressive media rollout, with Carter making appearances in contexts ranging from *Good Morning America* to David Sanborn's music variety show *Night Music* (where she traded fours with Branford Marsalis), and she was featured alongside comedian Bill Cosby in a television spot for Coca-Cola. In this context, Carter came to believe that it was only the media exposure afforded her through her PolyGram affiliation that secured her Grammy nomination.[78]

CONCLUSION

Given what we know about Verve's practices under Norman Granz and Creed Taylor, Seidel's intervention is particularly noteworthy for its ability to harness Verve's historical legacy as a catalyst for new artist development. The emphasis upon vocal jazz in the initial round of Seidel's newly recorded Verve releases is worth foregrounding here: they seem positioned to capitalize on the same kind of commercial accessibility achieved by such historical Verve titles as *Ella and Louis* or *Jazz Samba*. In particular, many of the tracks on the *Live at Vine Street* series, from Marlena Shaw's reading of Etta James's "At Last" (on the 1987 release *It is Love*) to Nina Simone's interpretation of the Everley Brothers hit "Let It Be Me" (from her contemporaneous album of the same name), present themselves in a self-consciously crossover vein. Seidel noted with respect to his contemporaneous CD-reissue program for Verve that his emphasis upon vocalists was a necessary concession to the "bottom-line people," and it is reasonable to assume that a similar logic is at work here.[79] In this connection, Verve reminds us that whatever contours the artist roster would assume in the 1990s, hybrid, crossover, and commercial sensibilities had long been at the core of the label's identity.

Against this backdrop, Verve's subsequent commitment to a largely instrumental wave of "young lion" and neoclassicist recordings in the early 1990s perhaps constitutes more of an anomaly in the Verve catalog than a straightforward return to historical form. This will be important to keep in mind further on, as we consider the diversification strategy that the Verve Music Group would pursue in the late 1990s and early 2000s.

CHAPTER 4

Bronfman's Bauble

The Corporate History of the
Verve Music Group (1990–2005)

In the preceding chapter, I outlined some of the ways in which the broader corporate context of Verve's ownership regime might inflect aspects of the label's aesthetic decision making, at the level of artist development and programming. In its guise as an independent label under Norman Granz, Verve was subject to the idiosyncratic vision of its private owners; when it became part of the music wing of Metro-Goldwyn-Meyer, Verve's programming and artist selection reflected a different range of pressures, such as Creed Taylor's micromanagerial style or the strategic priorities of MGM Records' corporate parent.

Under PolyGram, Verve would enjoy a position of relative autonomy in its relationship with PolyGram Classics. PolyGram's extensive experience in the classical market would serve as an important template for the revived jazz label, as it began to position itself in relation to the aesthetic and ideological priorities of neoclassicism in the early 1990s. However, as we shall soon see, the idiosyncratic practices of classical and jazz divisions would become particularly exposed to the vagaries of corporate strategy in the era of financialization: Edgar Bronfman Jr.'s 1998 orchestration of the PolyGram-Universal merger would impose a new logic upon formerly autonomous label subsidiaries, with important ramifications for Verve's long-standing roster of jazz instrumentalists.

POLYGRAM AND VERVE RECORDS IN THE 1990S

The beginning of the 1990s saw Philips, PolyGram's corporate parent, undergo a process of radical restructuring. With its position in the home electronics market increasingly threatened by competition from inexpensive manufacturers in Asia, Philips implemented a program entitled Operation Centurion, a sweeping reinvention of Philips's organizational structure and institutional culture. Initiated by incoming Philips chairman Jan Timmer, who was a former president at PolyGram, Centurion called for a 20 percent reduction in Philips's workforce worldwide, with the company spinning off its least profitable electronics divisions, outsourcing "noncore" operations formerly executed by Philips's well-salaried European workforce, and shifting its emphasis from production to customer service.[1] The new measures made precarious employment a fact of life in a multinational that had once been noted for its commitment to lifetime employment; they were also held up by financial sector observers as a textbook manifestation of the corporate abandonment of the stakeholder-driven conglomerate in the pursuit of shareholder value.

That PolyGram had not only survived the restructuring largely intact but had become one of the core drivers of Philips's return to profitability can be attributed in large part to changes that Timmer had implemented as PolyGram underwent a similarly draconian restructuring in the early 1980s, intensifying the development of its federated structure and strengthening its rights-based "software" business model. Gerben Bakker argues that PolyGram, as a federated structure, can be compared to the pharmaceutical industry, which moved to a similar structural model during the same period: Big Pharma firms reasserted their flagging control over the industry by investing in loosely controlled relationships with small biotech firms, allowing the smaller companies to harness their superior advantages in research and innovation, while maintaining control over product distribution and over the accumulation of "rents" from the holding of copyrights. Much like a small biotech firm, a small, nominally autonomous music subsidiary is better positioned to take advantage of its specialized knowledge of its market.[2]

At the same time, PolyGram benefited from its position as a "software" producer. In holding temporary monopoly rights over its accumulated intellectual properties, a major record company has access to a site of intellectual content that can be repackaged, reissued, and licensed in a variety of transient products and formats.[3] The higher profit margins accumulated through this rights-based "software" model were also enhanced during the period of the early 1990s, as PolyGram and other record companies benefited from the CD boom: as consumers replaced their LPs and cassettes with compact discs, PolyGram benefited from the higher margins per unit on these new sales. The so-called "library factor," the impulse to replace an existing record collection with titles in the new format, was a key driver of record sales through the middle years of the 1990s.[4]

We should also acknowledge the role that financialization played in placing PolyGram on a stronger foundation in this period. In 1989, following a two-year delay (owing to the market crash of 1987), PolyGram, which up until then had been a wholly-owned subsidiary of Philips NV, floated 20 percent of its company shares in an Initial Public Offering (IPO) on the New York and Amsterdam stock markets.[5] The IPO was initiated with the intention of helping PolyGram to finance its acquisition of two important labels, Island and A&M, as a means of increasing market share in the U.S. market.[6] This expansion into U.S. markets, along with the acquisition of an ever more diverse range of labels and artists, allowed PolyGram to harness its federated structure as a form of risk management, with the company arguing that "the size and diversity of its artist roster and of its catalogues of recordings give a measure of protection against sudden shifts in popular taste not available to smaller companies."[7] The PolyGram IPO initiated a decade of dramatic growth for the music multinational, with its real market value increasing from $2 billion in 1989 to approximately $11 billion at the time of the Seagram acquisition in 1998: over this same ten-year period, its share price tripled in value.[8] It is this dimension of strong shareholder value that would later make Polygram a particularly attractive target for corporate acquisition.

Verve Records, as a semi-autonomous subsidiary of PolyGram and as a key beneficiary of the CD-reissue boom, was in a unique position to capitalize upon its place in the jazz-record market of the early 1990s. Verve's reputation as a venerable jazz imprint would make the label attractive to new signatories, even as its CD-reissue program harnessed the new format to capture a new market for its existing properties. Moreover, the revitalization of the Verve label coincided with a period of new mainstream acceptance for jazz: in the wake of Wynton Marsalis's well-publicized career ascent, and with the music's youngest performers enjoying high-profile coverage in such venues as *Time* magazine, conditions seemed to be emerging in which the market had room for the development of a new roster of jazz artists.[9]

One of Verve's first ventures in this direction was its signing of the Harper Brothers, a quintet featuring trumpeter Philip Harper and drummer Winard Harper, alongside bassist Michael Bowie, pianist Stephen Scott, and alto saxophonist Justin Robinson. The quintet's work was brought to Seidel's attention through Betty Carter, whose working bands during the 1980s (which had featured Scott and Winard Harper) had taken on a mentorship role analogous to that of Art Blakey's Jazz Messengers.[10] Scott would see his own debut on the Verve label in 1991 with the release of *Something to Consider,* which featured trumpeter Roy Hargrove and drummer Lewis Nash.[11]

Towards the end of chapter 1, I discussed the way in which an earlier generation of neoclassicists (the Marsalis brothers, Terence Blanchard, Kenny Kirkland, Jeff "Tain" Watts, and others) emulated the harmonically ambiguous, rhythmically angular sound of 1960s postbop. By contrast, the Harper Brothers' musical sensibility was more closely wedded to the blues-inflected hard bop associated with the classic 1950s Blue Note label. By the early 1990s, there were a variety of artists making forays into this sound; for instance, Roy Hargrove's early releases on the Novus BMG imprint, including *Diamond in the Rough* (1990) and his collaboration with alto saxophonist Antonio Hart, *The Tokyo Sessions* (1992), see the trumpeter's band playing with the crisp drumming style, blues harmonies, stop-time, and blues gestures (scoops, bends, slides) that may previously have been most readily identified with the work of Lee Morgan, Horace Silver, or Julian "Cannonball" Adderley.[12] However, as influential a factor as any was the high-profile turn that Wynton Marsalis's music took in the late 1980s and early 1990s, as he turned away from his classical trumpet career to redouble his efforts in the jazz arena: as Alexander Stewart has noted, Marsalis's album *The Majesty of the Blues* (1989) documents the artist's embrace of more traditional harmonic progressions and more old-fashioned, bluesy sonorities, a change in style that derives from his commitment to the blues as a genre with the "emotional, harmonic, and technical depth to inform whatever you do in this music."[13]

A track such as "Kiss Me Right," from their 1989 Verve release *Remembrance: Live at the Village Vanguard,* gives us a good sense of the stylistic direction pursued by the Harper Brothers. The "head" arrangement that leads off the track is tautly constructed: in the opening eight-bar section, Philip Harper on trumpet and Justin Robinson on saxophone play a melodic figure harmonized a fourth apart, replete with triplets and other blues filigrees; in a call and response pattern, the rest of the band plays stop-time figures on the anticipation of the down-beat. This is followed by a second, more forthright eight-bar section, beginning with a simple two-quarter-note pickup on beats three and four; in rhythmic unison with the two horn players, drummer Winard Harper backs up the two-beat pickup with snare hits, and the rhythm section as a whole continues to reinforce the rhythmic unison through-out this section. These two eight-bar sections constitute the first half of a conventional thirty-two-bar form, with the remainder made up of a repetition of the initial two sections. In many respects, the overall affect here is close to a track such as Art Blakey's "Moanin'," with a similar call-response pattern in the opening section followed by the dramatic, two-beat quarter note hit leading into the song's bridge.[14] The style here is deliberately rootsy and stripped down, a departure from the more rhythmically and harmonically unstable forms featured in the postbop releases of many "young lion" artists during the 1980s.

If the "young lions" figured prominently in Verve's initial forays into contemporary neoclassicism, it was the addition of veteran saxophonist Joe Henderson to the Verve roster in 1991 that decisively established the label's commercial presence in this area. If Henderson was among the most distinctive tenor saxophonists to come of age in the century's middle decades, Henderson's profile would become more muted in the 1970s and 1980s: apart from his work with Blood, Sweat, and Tears in the early 1970s, Henderson's work did not receive much exposure beyond the jazz community, where he was seen as a kind of consummate "musician's musician," known primarily to aficionados.[15]

As with Betty Carter in the late 1980s, Henderson's arrival at Verve had a galvanizing impact on Henderson's career: with media appearances on the *Tonight Show* and *Good Morning America,* and with an aggressive touring schedule that took him to American cities well outside of conventional jazz markets, Henderson benefited from the tremendous visibility afforded him through his major-label affiliation. In a reprise of Carter's experience, following her transition to Verve, Henderson's first two records for the label were awarded Grammys in the Jazz Instrumental Solo category, and by 1995 they had collectively sold in the order of 450,000 copies, a tremendous accomplishment by jazz standards.[16] His first Verve project was the 1991 outing *Lush Life: The Music of Billy Strayhorn,* an album whose pairing of Henderson with the acclaimed Strayhorn repertory would link the record to the legacy of the Fitzgerald *Songbook* projects under Norman Granz. This concept-driven approach seems to have been built into Henderson's agreement with Verve, according to the press release announcing Henderson's signing to the label: as a feature of the "exclusive multi-project contract" to which Henderson was signed, "the [Strayhorn] date [would] commence a series of albums that spotlight the music of great jazz composers."[17] Over the course of the next decade, Henderson would record the Miles Davis tribute *So Near, So Far (Musing for Miles)* (1992), as well as *Double Rainbow: The Music of Antonio Carlos Jobim* (1994). These "songbook" projects may have been designed to repeat the success of earlier such Verve releases, but they also helped to distinguish Henderson's current output from his own earlier work: according to Seidel, they "put Joe in a new context. He didn't make records of other people's repertoire until he came to Verve."[18]

As a concept album in the classic Verve mold, Henderson's *Lush Life* employs a variety of overlapping strategies of packaging and programming. Its repertory is thoughtfully sequenced, with each track deploying a different combination of sidemen. "Isfahan" pairs Henderson in a duo setting with bassist Christian McBride; the performance of "Johnny Come Lately" employs the full quintet; "Take the 'A' Train" is an exhilarating sax-and-drums duo, with Greg Hutchinson propelling the action. The climactic final track is Henderson's intimate solo saxophone treatment of "Lush Life" itself, with Strayhorn's nuanced harmonic language given voice in Henderson's fluid arpeggiations and brittle intervallic leaps. As Henderson notes, the different small-group arrangements tend to enhance the album's continuity, its unifying meditation on Strayhorn and himself as the album's two key protagonists.[19] As I mention above, Seidel's central pairing of Henderson's interpretations with Strayhorn's songs resonates with Verve's "songbook" concept, dating to the earliest Norman Granz releases. Moreover, in superimposing two prominent jazz names (one historical, the other both historical and current), it allows consumers two potential avenues of entry into the record's concept.

In its self-conscious suturing of past and present, Verve's Henderson "brand" places considerable emphasis upon the depth of his experience, and its relationship with Verve's own longevity as a label. Henderson's backstory, his signing to Verve after a relatively long period of unrecorded obscurity, would become a crucial part of the narrative surrounding his recordings to the label. Profiles such as this one, penned by *New York Times* critic Peter Watrous, rarely failed to mention Verve's role in recuperating Henderson's career, framing his addition to the label roster as the redemptive culmination of a long period of struggle:

"The perception of greatness in jazz, as in the other arts, requires a consensus among the right people, money and often a bit of self-promotion. In 1991, Henderson was signed by Verve, and his status changed irrevocably. . . . Without the help of his new label, Henderson might still be laboring in obscurity."[20] For his part, Seidel argued that the timing of the Verve signing in 1991 positioned Henderson as the inheritor of a mantle passed down by Stan Getz and Dexter Gordon, recently deceased senior titans of the tenor saxophone.[21] The comparison with Gordon is particularly resonant, given that it echoes of one of the foundational moments in the neoclassicist revival. Verve's signing of Henderson, for its part, would be seen as highlighting a more specific subplot in the neoclassicist narrative, the question of renewed interest in the music's elder virtuosi. During this period, a variety of older musicians saw themselves returned to the limelight, enjoying new contracts with the major labels and new prominence on the live venue circuit. In many instances, the performer's biography would become a key element of the marketing push behind his or her return to prominence.[22]

Lush Life is one of numerous recordings from this period that pairs accomplished veterans with emerging artists. Henderson's rhythm section, made up of Christian McBride on bass, Greg Hutchinson on drums, and Stephen Scott on piano, comprises three of the most celebrated musicians in the then-emerging generation of jazz artists. The album also features Wynton Marsalis as a guest performer on a few of its tracks, and gives him prominent billing in Verve's promotional materials, tacitly linking both the young performers and the returning veteran to Marsalis's established persona. Stanley Crouch's liner notes serve as further confirmation of the project's commitment to the historical and stylistic parameters of neoclassicism. In the usual Crouchian manner, they map out a rhetoric of binary oppositions, with Strayhorn's elegant compositions and Henderson's uncompromising vision set in opposition to an encroaching miasma of superficial clichés and stylistic artifice. Henderson amplifies these oppositions in his own quoted remarks, citing what he perceived to be a near-total disappearance of Strayhorn's nuanced chord progressions and elegant melodies from the jazz world during the 1970s and 1980s. Situated against this backdrop, Henderson's youthful rhythm section on *Lush Life* is positioned as the embodiment of a return to enduring values:

> Something had disappeared from the music. It started about twenty years ago. You not only had gotten to the point where all of those beautiful songs had x's drawn through them, but then you had this other kind of stuff that

really didn't challenge a serious musician, and which I had no interest in whatsoever. . . . There was a dry spell of about ten years. Around 1980, things started changing for the better, but nobody knew if that was going to keep happening. . . . Now I look around and there are all of these young musicians coming up who have their heads on right and are focused on a zone that will benefit themselves as musicians and will benefit the listener who is out there seeking some quality.[23]

On *Lush Life*, Verve's A&R team proves to be adept in setting up various lines of association for the consumer, forging links between a veteran musician and the music's youthful vanguard, between Henderson's album and Marsalis's neoclassicist project, and over the long term, between Verve and Henderson's multi-album exploration of felicitous pairings. Nevertheless, these associations tend to point resolutely inward, exerting a kind of centripetal force: Verve's marketing strategy on this and contemporaneous projects redirects attention to the interior of the "young lions" movement, as neoclassicist collaborations become vectors for still further collaborations with other neoclassicists. Two Roy Hargrove albums for the Verve label from this period affirm this orientation: *Parker's Mood*, a 1995 outing with Stephen Scott and Christian McBride, takes up the same rhythm section employed on *Lush Life*, shorn of its drummer, in an album devoted to the music of Charlie Parker.[24] On his album *With the Tenors of our Time* from 1994, Hargrove is supported by a rhythm section made up of Hutchinson, bassist Rodney Whitaker, and pianist Cyrus Chestnut, each of whom are stylistically indebted to the hard-bop lineage of the neoclassicist sound. Here, the thematic kernel of the album is its showcasing of guest appearances by several important tenor saxophonists, ranging from the veterans Johnny Griffin, Joe Henderson, and Stanley Turrentine, to the celebrated current artists Joshua Redman and Branford Marsalis.[25] In all of these cases, there is a sense of mutual referentiality, in which a small community of stylistically like-minded artists make guest appearances on each other's sessions, reaffirming the acoustic instrumentation and swing-driven parameters of the neoclassicist sound.

As I have already noted, both Henderson's *Lush Life* and its follow-up album, *So Near, So Far*, both reached unit sales in the low six figures, achieving extraordinary volume by the standards of jazz releases. For their part, Henderson's younger label-mates also achieved respectable results during this time, with Hargrove's *Tenors of Our Time* also selling upward of a hundred thousand copies in the year following its release.[26] If anything, these numbers point to the unusual market environment that straightahead instrumental jazz enjoyed in this period, as the jazz charts saw numerous instances of successful releases working within the narrow confines of the neoclassicist hard-bop sound.

Nevertheless, the stylistic focus of Verve during this period manifests itself as something of a departure from the strategic positioning of the label at other moments in its history. In contrast to the inward, neotraditional gaze of many of the early 1990s U.S. Verve releases, the catalog during the Norman Granz and Creed Taylor years was frequently directed *outward:* to hybrid genre crossovers (organ-trio soul jazz, bossa nova, Afro-Cuban sounds), to pop-culture appropriations (jazz orchestrations of film music from the MGM archive), to the direct appeal of the singer and the populism of the crowd. During this period, concept albums, long a feature of the Verve catalog, were calibrated to dramatize unusual juxtapositions (matching, for example, "cool school" baritone saxophonist Gerry Mulligan with swing-era veteran Ben Webster on *Gerry Mulligan Meets Ben Webster*) or intriguing conceits (such as Bill Evans's overdubbed solo piano improvisations on *Conversations with Myself*).[27]

This is not to argue that Verve's strategy in the 1990s was any less commercially aggressive than that of the Granz and MGM years: as I have already argued, Richard Seidel was adamant about the need for an assertive media rollout of new releases, and for event- and narrative-driven promotional campaigns for its artists. What is different about the early 1990s is the degree to which the neoclassical conception of a homogenous, self-contained jazz legacy becomes a plausible vehicle for promotion during the heady years of the "young lions" boom. Contemporaneous accounts of strategic deliberations at Verve, Columbia, and Blue Note in the early 1990s see the labels engaging in heated bidding wars over such young players as Jackie Terrasson, Joshua Redman, Christian McBride, Roy Hargrove, and others. This generation of musicians, alert to the potential pitfalls of contractual negotiations, could make extensive demands upon their prospective labels, with Hargrove and trumpeter Wallace Roney arriving at deals with their respective labels worth approximately $80,000 per album.[28] This atmosphere of competitive bidding takes place in an environment transformed by the impact of an emerging array of high-profile music competitions, with winners of the Thelonious Monk Instrumental Competition and other contests enjoying considerable leverage. Richard Seidel, commenting upon the labels' tendency to use the competitions as a site for scouting new talent, argues that "there is an auction mentality at work. The competitions, with all their publicity and with all the A&R attention, have helped create a trading-floor atmosphere."[29] In their allocation of an explicit ranking to emerging artists, such competitions become an important means for record companies to translate aesthetic merit into market valuation.

Indeed, there is a case to be made that the environment of competitive bidding that characterized the major-label investment in the "young lions" phenomenon during the early 1990s adheres to a characteristic of the market psychology of speculative bubbles described by Robert Shiller, a kind of herd behavior wedded to the feedback loops of *information cascades:* market actors swept up in information cascades find themselves emulating other market actors through decisions based upon incomplete information.[30] To be sure, the analogy may not completely hold up in the context of major-label A&R departments, where figures such as Seidel, Matt Pierson, Steve Backer, George Butler, and others could each bring several decades' worth of expertise to bear in their evaluation of prospective artists, and would have access to much more than partial information about them. But the shared market consensus that seemed to settle upon a few key performers at that time, which was itself buttressed by the incomplete, partial information of prestigious competition rankings, suggests that the jazz divisions of the major labels may have been subject to a kind of "hype"-driven herd behavior. Pressed to make their roster choices intelligible to decision makers further up in the corporate hierarchy, A&R executives may have sought the comforting affirmation of a few familiar sounds and familiar names, of artists whose high ranking in the new jazz competitions seemed to lend them a precise (if not necessarily accurate) valuation of their potential. At the same time, the herd behavior of this "jazz bubble" may have been even more pronounced on the part of the performers themselves, as the intense media promotion of the "young lions" phenomenon in the early 1990s may have reinforced the conception that it was only performers of a specific profile who were deemed marketworthy.[31] In any case, it was these new major-label signatories, even more than the A&R executives, who would be most exposed to any significant changes in strategy at the top of the label hierarchy.

The artists who were subject to this neoclassical "brand" did not always agree with its precepts. For instance, the renowned bassist Christian McBride, who during this period was part of the rhythm section on countless releases in the neoclassicist mold, was by no means partisan about adhering to the antipop orthodoxies promulgated by some neoclassicists. It was rumored that McBride, whose father had played electric bass for such rhythm-and-blues groups as the Delfonics, had decided to sign with Verve (following an intense courtship by several major labels) because Verve's status as a subsidiary of PolyGram would give him access to the James Brown catalog.[32] McBride ultimately viewed the labels' preoccupation with the neoclassicists as inhibiting the creative freedom and growth of jazz artists during the 1990s. He suggests that it was the "young lions" phenomenon itself, and not smooth jazz or fusion, as it was so often argued, that had revealed itself to be the prevailing mode of commercial capitulation during this period: "The whole 'young lions' hype, which, unfortunately, I was part of, peaked in the early 1990s. I say 'unfortunately' because the hype was so strong, I don't think any musician from that 'movement' will ever be looked upon by certain people as serious musicians. We'll be looked at as puppets for record companies and managers, or *People* magazine–type personalities as opposed to, well, *Down Beat* magazine–type personalities."[33]

Here, McBride was also critical of the record companies' privileging of the concept album during this period. As I have already noted, the concept album, which McBride memorably describes as adhering to such formulas as "X plays the music of Y, X plays love songs, X plays music for driving to," was a marketing tactic that Verve and other labels had employed to complement the neoclassical brand during the early 1990s: the Joe Henderson album series was nothing if not a carefully calibrated execution of "X plays the music of Y."[34] By the middle years of this decade, though, the iconography of "young lions" neotradition-alism had yielded diminishing returns for the major labels. Stylistically, new contenders had made their presence felt, from the funk-driven organ trio music of Medeski, Martin, and Wood to the reinvention of the jazz "standard" under Brad Mehldau and Herbie Hancock, and new jazz hybrids, borrowing from such electronic genres as techno and house, had revealed neoclassicism to be merely one among several com-pelling narratives for the jazz legacy.[35]

In the absence of a prevailing story, the concept album became a fail-safe marketing posture for an industry in flux. Alongside McBride, numerous other major-label artists from the period recall the degree to which A&R executives pressed them to adopt this model. D.D. Jackson, a prominent Canadian pianist who was then signed to RCA, recalls meet-ings in which he was told that his creatively diverse albums had a ten-dency to "confuse the market," and that from a marketing standpoint, he was better served emulating the consistency of such multi-album projects as Brad Mehldau's *Art of the Trio* series.[36] For his part, Seidel, who had long advocated the concept album at Verve, found new applications for the practice that derived their appeal from the new sounds and formats of the late 1990s: if Roy Hargrove's 1994 album *The Tenors of Our Time* had been a straightforward hard-bop outing, his 1997 release *Habana* took Afro-Cuban music as its point of departure.[37] The guitar virtuoso John Scofield, newly added to the Verve roster, was featured fronting Medeski, Martin, and Wood on the funk-driven release *A Go Go* from the following year. In relation to these projects, Seidel once again noted that "the most important part of making a record these days is preproduction. Planning is key: finding a combination of the right repertoire and the right musicians."[38]

In the late 1990s, reissues at Verve were also subject to the logic of "X plays the music of Y, X plays love songs, X plays music for driving to." For instance, the Ultimate series was conceived by Seidel as a means of putting "a different spin on the 'Best Of' concept": this familiar phrasing, which almost precisely echoes his description of Verve's digitally repackaged catalog during his early years at PolyGram Classics in the 1980s, should alert us to the tenacity with which reissue teams at Verve, Columbia, and other major labels have set about locating new frames for their existing material.[39] Each Ultimate project invites a current jazz artist to compile a selection of their favorite tracks by a "classic" artist. Herbie Hancock picks his favorite Bill Evans selections; Roy Hargrove gives us his preferred Dizzy Gillespie recordings; Diane Reeves chooses her personal favorites from the Nina Simone discography. Verve artists were frequently chosen as either subjects or compilers for the series.[40] From the standpoint of branding, a disc such as *Ultimate Ray Brown,* a tribute to the Verve bassist by contemporary Verve bassist Christian McBride, offers at least three points of entry for the consumer, as a Brown listener might be led to McBride, a McBride listener to Brown, or both listeners to other artists in the Verve stable.

Reflecting on the Ultimate series, Seidel notes the considerable degree to which the featured artists became invested in the project, in many cases making different selections than those made by the usual curators of CD reissues.[41] In this way, the project holds out the promise of democratizing the CD reissue: to make contemporary artists into curators of the Verve archive is to invite them to become active interlocutors in the process of canon formation. In doing so, though, the Ultimate series also anticipates a much higher-profile Verve "reissue" project from the early 2000s, one that would index the extent to which Verve's back catalog of jazz "classics" had come to displace its active roster of jazz artists. Much like the Verve/Remixed series from the early 2000s, which tasked such DJs and electronic producers as Richard Dorfmeister, Felix da Housecatt, Carl Craig, and Diplo with reworking historic recordings from the Verve vault, the Ultimate series from the late 1990s eschews new studio recording in favor of revisiting extant recordings.[42] "X plays Y," in the case of Verve/Remixed, simply becomes X *spins* Y, the current artist relinquishing their role as active producer of a new sonic trace, and thus obviating the need for the label to assume the additional expense involved in committing live performance to disc. The Ultimate series in some sense prefigures the direction that Verve would pursue under its postmerger leadership, as the label's continued commitment to jazz increasingly favors a prestigious archive of the past over the cultivation of new talent in the present.

EDGAR BRONFMAN JR. AND THE UNIVERSAL/ POLYGRAM MERGER

In the first half of the 1990s, Verve profited from its stewardship of its midcentury legacy in the same moment that it pursued new work by contemporary artists. However, Verve would share the fate of far more prominent label subsidiaries in the second half of the 1990s, as it became subject to the volatile wave of entertainment megamergers that closed out the decade.[43] The architect of the Universal/PolyGram merger was Edgar Bronfman Jr., CEO of Seagram, a Canadian spirits company dating back to the Prohibition era. Bronfman Jr. has often been depicted as the naively ambitious enfant terrible of the powerful Bronfman family, whose members had long maintained a controlling stake in the company. Bronfman had already made an initial foray into the music industry in 1995, when his acquisition of MCA, parent company to Universal Studios, gave the magnate a controlling interest in Universal's music properties, which served as the basis for his formation of the Universal Music Group.[44] Seagram's acquisition of MCA, and subsequently Poly-Gram, presented itself to investors as a startling move into an industry that operated according to a different set of rules. While more bullish analysts, applauding Bronfman's deal with PolyGram in 1998, argued that entertainment simply constituted "a higher-margin industry" than spirits (yielding greater profit per unit), another contemporaneous observer noted that the company's strategic shift in emphasis from spirits to entertainment constituted the swapping of "a stable double-digit cash flow growth business for one that has more volatile cash flow characteristics."[45]

Indeed, PolyGram, like other actors in the culture industries, produced highly individuated commodities whose market potential was difficult to predict, making the company highly vulnerable to consumer whims.[46] PolyGram was also exposed to industry-specific shifts that came to reshape the music markets over the course of the 1990s. The company had experienced steady growth under the supervision of French CEO Alain Levy, benefiting from the boom in compact discs during this period, and from its accumulation of a pop roster through its investment in prominent U.S. labels (Island, A&M, and later Motown). By the late 1990s, though, PolyGram saw slowing performance as the music markets "matured," with consumers nearing the completion of their "libraries" of CDs.[47] As Levy points out, the compact disc boom had created a kind of artificial and unsustainable market bubble in record sales, with no new format emerging to fill the vacuum of diminished sales.[48] Anticipating these changed conditions, Levy's PolyGram had sought to absorb anticipated music declines by diversifying into other media markets, establishing its PolyGram Filmed Entertainment unit in 1992. However, PFE was ultimately unable to build the resources and distribution networks necessary to compete with Hollywood for market share.[49] It was these kinds of uncertainties that dramatically underscored the differences between Seagram's beverage empire on the one hand, and the culture industries it was in the process of embracing on the other.

A second reason that Bronfman's forays into music and film constituted a dramatic departure for Seagram that involved changes to the structure and corporate culture of the spirits company itself. For many decades, Seagram operated under the paternalistic gaze of the Bronfman family, under whose oversight the company had developed a consistent, stable business regimen. Edgar Bronfman Jr.'s assumption of the Seagram leadership in 1994 brought an end to this incremental approach: alongside his implementation of a sweeping internal reorganization of Seagram's wine-and-spirits operations, Bronfman Jr. made a series of investment decisions that significantly altered the company's risk profile, and transformed Seagram from an inwardly directed family-run firm to a corporation whose performance became much more intimately linked to the financial markets.[50] Bronfman's strategy aligned Seagram with a corporate trajectory that was becoming more pervasive toward the end of the 1990s: in place of long-term, "organic" growth, publicly traded companies increasingly harnessed heavily leveraged mergers and acquisitions in the pursuit of short-term spikes in stock valuation.[51]

At the time of the PolyGram acquisition, global media companies were increasingly in the business of creating integrated *brands,* with value produced less through any isolated strategies of vertical or horizontal integration than through a more thoroughgoing assembly of the components of "a wheel, with the brand at the hub and each of the spokes a means of exploiting it."[52] The coordinated cross promotion of a given work of intellectual property through film, television, music, theme park, and merchandizing outlets gives the holding company access to multiple revenue streams, even as each of these sites of exploitation reinforce the underlying brand. By comparison with its competitors, Seagram had thus far been relatively unsuccessful in integrating the necessary components, and its bid for PolyGram, with its combined music and film holdings, would put it in position to realize these synergies. Universal Music Group's pre-PolyGram music holdings were relatively small by comparison with other music majors, and in 1998, Bronfman Jr. sought to increase market share in this sector. Having initially pursued the acquisition of the British music major EMI, then home to the Beatles catalog, Bronfman Jr. entered into negotiations with Philips NV for the acquisition of Poly-Gram. The resulting $10.6 billion deal, announced in May 1998, would make the postmerger UMG into the largest record company in the world, with a total market share approaching 23 percent.[53]

Parties on all sides of the PolyGram/Universal merger consistently foregrounded the strategic primacy of shareholder value. Since the days of the draconian "Operation Centurion" reorganization in the early 1990s, Philips had undergone a steady process of divestment, shedding itself of properties that were seen as impeding its stock valuation on the financial markets. While PolyGram had been a lucrative holding for the electronics company in the 1990s, Philips had come to the conclusion that it was not adequately harnessing "synergies" between its PolyGram "software" and its electronic "hardware." By spinning off PolyGram and cutting costs, Philips could signal to Wall Street that it was successfully downsizing its unwieldy conglomerate structure and focusing upon its core business.[54] In line with these goals, Philips indicated in early 1998 that it was looking to sell off its 75 percent stake in the record company. Writing in the *Los Angeles Times,* Chuck Phillips notes that PolyGram president Alain Levy had not been informed of the decision to "sell the company out from under him."[55] Nevertheless, a spokesperson for PolyGram duly announced that the company's leadership would "embrace any strategic options which would maximize long-term value for our shareholders, as well as broaden opportunities for our management team, employees and talent."[56]

Seagram and Philips announced the initial framework for the Poly-Gram deal in May 1998. However, given its myriad legal intricacies, the sale of the firm would not be closed until the completion of the tender offer in December of that year.[57] In the intervening period, the merger was vulnerable to lapses in investor confidence, as Seagram's stock was affected by uncertainties in the Asian spirits market, and as fluctuations in the value of the dollar relative to the Dutch guilder threatened to magnify the cost of the PolyGram acquisition.[58] In June, after disappointing quarterly reports for Polygram led Seagram to renegotiate the original agreement with Philips the price for the acquisition of Philips's 75 percent stake had been reduced to $10.4 billion.[59] However, market observers, shareholders, and members of the Bronfman family continued to raise concerns about the prospect of Seagram taking on such a significant debt load. In the process, the deal would dramatically reduce Seagram's sizeable liquidity, a strategy at odds with the company's historically conservative management. To help fund the PolyGram acquisition, Seagram sought to sell off PolyGram Filmed Entertainment, as well as its Tropicana beverage property: Pepsi acquired Tropicana for $3.3 billion, but PolyGram failed to find a purchaser for PFE who would come close to their $1 billion asking price. In this context, analysts predicted that the PolyGram acquisition would magnify Seagram's debt-to-capital ratio from 15 to approximately 40 percent.[60] In early October, Moody's downgraded their bond rating for Seagram to just above junk-bond status, making it more difficult for the company to obtain financing.[61]

It was in the midst of this climate of grave concern about Seagram's prospects that Edgar Bronfman Jr. addressed shareholders at the company's annual meeting in November of 1998, arguing that "the combination of Universal and PolyGram will create a uniquely powerful competitor, and the acquisition will create significant shareholder value. . . . We believe that music will be the first and perhaps the largest industry among the entertainment businesses to benefit from the explosion of personal computing and the Internet."[62] It is worth noting here that the introduction of Napster was a mere months away (the platform was launched in May 1999), and the shepherds of the era's music multinationals would soon find themselves confronting the significant downside to a business model predicated upon the internet as a profit center.[63]

Despite shareholders' concerns about the PolyGram acquisition, the deal was successfully closed in December 1998 with the completion of Seagram's tender offer. However, the subsequent period of restructuring would have a truly seismic impact upon the company's artists, employees, and management, as Seagram pursued a promised $300 million in cost savings through downsizing and reorganization.[64] The question of debt is of considerable importance for our understanding of the nature of the PolyGram acquisition, and for the pressures that it placed upon the company's restructuring plan. Seagram took on tremendous debt in its bid for the music multinational, and it paid dearly to service this debt. In the midst of instability in the banking sector, driven by the Asian economic crisis of that year, Seagram faced difficulty in obtaining the $6.5 billion in bank loans required to complete the $10 billion acquisition. Consequently, it had to pay higher interest rates than it had anticipated at the time of the initial agreement.[65] To raise additional funding, Seagram also issued $3.5 billion in corporate bonds, with six different "tranches" priced according to their relative risk. Once again, in this case, the company sought to placate investor concerns by offering interest rates higher than what their credit rating would dictate: as it was, Seagram was barely considered an "investor-grade" company, meaning that its credit rating verged on "junk" status.[66] In the early weeks of 1999, a few weeks after the completion of the tender offer, the company's debt accounted for some $9 billion of its $27 billion market capitalization.[67]

Given the concerns raised by market observers in the runup to the Universal/PolyGram merger, and the degree to which the PolyGram acquisition altered the risk profile of Seagram, the jump in share price that the company experienced in the weeks following the deal may seem counterintuitive. One money manager at the time noted the way in which the merger seemed poised to dramatically alter the character of the company, and expressed surprise over the degree to which the market seemed willing to reward Seagram for this change: "This [Seagram] was a classic value play in the [share price of the] low 30s, a very liquid balance sheet, underleveraged. . . . What happened is they became much more leveraged, and the market decided they were worth 50% more. . . . You say to yourself, 'why has the stock gone from 30 to 48 [dollars per share]?'"[68] One answer to this question may reside in the contradictory attitudes about the relationship between debt and shareholder value that are often held among members of the investor class. From a certain standpoint, the transformation of Seagram from an underleveraged "value play" (a company with solid revenues and cash flow, and an undervalued stock) to a heavily leveraged company with diminished cash flow would seem to portend bad things. However, from the standpoint of shareholders, the additional expenses a company incurs in servicing debt during a merger are often seen as imposing a degree of *discipline* on corporate performance, forcing a company to pare down noncore and underperforming assets, and to attune its strategic priorities with the end goal of generating shareholder value.[69] Indeed, having taken on considerable debt as a result of the merger, Seagram looked to its PolyGram acquisition as the occasion of a more systemic imposition of "discipline," implementing dramatic restructuring plans in each of its operating divisions.[70]

Of course, the most dramatic repercussions of the new "discipline" imposed by the merger were felt most acutely among the combined workforce and artist roster of the postmerger UMG. Seagram's pursuit of $300 million in cost savings led UMG to significantly downsize both the Polygram and Universal artist rosters, as well as nearly 20 percent of the labels' combined workforce of fifteen thousand.[71] Many Universal and Polygram employees reportedly first learned about the probable shape of the cuts via a story leaked to the *Los Angeles Times* in November 1998, prior to the formal completion of the merger.[72] The comments of UMG chairman and CEO Doug Morris on the occasion of the formal announcement of staff cuts deploy a neoliberal rhetoric of nimble, protean maneuverability, asserting that the cuts would allow Universal to cultivate a "lean, flexible organization" with a management structure characterized by "strong local entrepreneurial spirit."[73] The postmerger reorganization constituted the most dramatic restructuring to date in the history of the music majors, and as such, it was a source of tremendous anxiety to personnel at the company's label subsidiaries. In a gesture of empathy, Morris announced that his leadership team would save discussion of the nature and scope of the layoffs until after the holiday season; he also announced that UMG would forgo its annual Grammy party, noting that "we [at UMG] want to be as thoughtful and sensitive as we can."[74]

THE "VERVE DIASPORA" AND THE POSTMERGER AFTERMATH AT VMG

The Universal/PolyGram merger brought significant organizational changes to Verve. The newly formed Verve Music Group brought together the complete jazz properties of both the Universal and

PolyGram label families: these included GRP, the erstwhile independent "contemporary jazz" label founded by Dave Grusin and Larry Rosen, together with the legendary catalog of the Impulse! label, the erstwhile home to avant-garde luminaries John Coltrane and Albert Ayler. Significantly, the emergent jazz division at Universal would be severed from classical operations, at least in the United States. It is important to recall that Verve's custodians at PolyGram had sought to harness the corporate culture and "catalog" marketing philosophy of its accomplished Classics division: a curatorial emphasis upon classic reissues in the 1980s had laid the initial groundwork for the neoclassical boom in the 1990s. The divorcing of jazz from classical at Universal suggests that a reprioritization of values and strategies was afoot at the revamped Verve Group.[75]

For an important clue regarding the shape of this reprioritization, we could look to UMG's installation of Tommy LiPuma and Ron Goldstein as chairman and president, respectively, of the new Verve Group.[76] LiPuma and Goldstein occupied these same senior management positions in the GRP label, prior to the PolyGram merger, and their assignment to the top Verve posts had the potential to significantly alter the existing corporate culture of the subsidiary. In particular, Goldstein would figure prominently in press accounts of Verve's new strategic vision, and his prior role at GRP provides us with a good sense of the direction that he would take following the merger. Goldstein was initially brought in at GRP in early 1998 with the specific intention of boosting the "star power" of its most prominent artist, pianist and singer Diana Krall. Goldstein had been instrumental in the renewal of the Warner Brothers jazz roster in the late 1970s, but more recently, he had been celebrated in the industry for his role at the "New Age" label Private Music, where he had transformed the multi-instrumentalist Yanni from a successful niche artist into a "multi-platinum-selling superstar." According to Zach Horowitz, president of UMG prior to the merger, Goldstein was explicitly hired in the hopes that this same "skill set" could be applied to the GRP artist roster, locating crossover potential in its jazz lineup: "Diana Krall, in our view, is a mass-appeal artist, not just a jazz artist. . . . There will be a number of artists at GRP, from time to time, who should be exposed to more than the traditional jazz audience. Certainly with Ron's background and skill set, he will help facilitate that."[77] This new emphasis upon a crossover, aggressively commercial position for the label clearly anticipates the shape of things to come: artists who had defined the Verve sensibility in the early 1990s, hard-bop artists in the neoclassicist mold (including Christian McBride, Nicholas Payton, and Roy Hargrove), would be among the most high-profile artists to depart from the label over the next few years, as Goldstein began to sign artists from an increasingly disparate range of stylistic orientations.

The financial impact of the Universal/PolyGram merger itself was an early and decisive factor in this exodus of mainstream jazz artists from the Verve label. Under LiPuma and Goldstein, Verve implemented a severe downsizing of the combined Verve/GRP roster and its support staff, in order to address its share of UMG's $300 million in targeted cost reductions. For Verve, this meant reducing its artist roster by nearly half: of the seventy-five to eighty artists signed to Verve under PolyGram, only forty-five were kept on by the new management team. In determining which artists would weather the purge at Verve, LiPuma and Goldstein cited CD sales as an important factor, but also considered the degree to which artists were actively working to generate interest in their CDs through touring and performance.[78] In early 1999, with the prospect of roster cuts on the immediate horizon, many Verve artists found themselves in an environment of uncertainty and anxiety. One artist affected by the changeover was Jason Lindner, a pianist and big-band director whose profile had been raised by a residency at Smalls, the prominent West Village jazz club. Alongside his friend and fellow Smalls regular Omer Avital, Lindner would count among the many artists who were dropped from the label as a result of the postmerger cuts. Originally slated to see his band's major-label debut album released by Impulse! in the late spring, Lindner had difficulty ascertaining whether the project would see the light of day: "You can't get your hopes up too high. . . . But they were really talking about pushing the band. The worst part about it was that they [Verve/GRP] really didn't tell me. I heard rumors for two weeks [in January], but we could not get in touch with any of the people at the label to find out if it was true. I had to call them."[79] According to Goldstein, the roster cuts were in large part dictated by the number of support staff that the label could continue to maintain in the wake of the cuts. In 1999, this number stood at fifty-eight employees, down twenty from the combined premerger staff. By 2004 (by which time Vivendi had acquired UMG), Goldstein's team had pared its staff down to forty-one employees, in tandem with further cuts to the artist roster.[80] In that year, it was possible for Dan Ouellette, writing in *Billboard,* to actually speak of a "Verve diaspora," a high-profile exodus comprising such prominent names as Michael Brecker, Chris Potter, or Danilo Perez, each of them searching for homes at the indie labels.[81] While we might be able to point to a number of "externalities" in explaining the severe downsizing at Verve (such as changes in the retail market for compact discs, or later on, the threat posed by file sharing), it is important to recognize the degree to which corporate restructuring had driven many of the most dramatic staff reductions and roster cuts: the "discipline" imposed by cost-cutting, which was itself imposed in response to the accumulation of new corporate debt under the conditions of the Seagram PolyGram acquisition, did as much to hasten Verve's divestment from its jazz commitments as any external market conditions.[82]

Goldstein's often outspoken remarks in the trade press during his tenure as president and CEO of VMG provide us with a useful measure of the label's shifting strategic relation to the instrumental jazz roster it had built up in the 1990s. In discussing his work with jazz instrumentalists, Goldstein frequently expressed frustration regarding what he saw as their myopic adherence to the aesthetic conventions of jazz, arguing that there was "a disconnect between artists who play instrumental jazz and the mass audience. The music is too intellectual, too heady. The playing is so far removed from what most audiences can comprehend. But if a singer renders an old Gershwin tune, people respond immediately."[83] From his perspective, such instrumentalists were also unnecessarily resistant to any encroachment upon their creative autonomy:

> Artists now take the viewpoint that it is their creativity and their music, so they are going to go into the studio and make the records that they want to make. . . . There is a real craftsmanship to recording. Producers help develop material, give an objective point of view, all the kinds of things that classic producers used to do. . . .
> I've argued until I was blue in the face with several artists about cutting back the length [of their albums]. The artists, in many cases, don't want to listen to the record company, which has somehow or other become the enemy.[84]

Where they did take place, signings of new instrumentalists at Verve under Goldstein and LiPuma tended toward the addition of established figures in the crossover/adult contemporary arena. Given his proclivity toward a melodic, accessible conception of jazz, it's perhaps not surprising that Goldstein was especially celebratory in his signing of smooth jazz saxophonist David Sanborn in late 2000, asserting that Sanborn was "the biggest talent out there, in terms of a sax player. . . . The guy is still the best. He's the originator."[85]

However, if smooth jazz in the Sanborn vein had once enjoyed a decisive commercial advantage over more traditional jazz releases, instrumental jazz in both categories was now being rapidly displaced by a new trend toward singers. Indeed, one of the most interesting features of the major-label jazz divestment has been the way that it has centered upon the divergent fortunes of instrumentalists on the one hand, and a new wave of jazz vocalists on the other. A range of accessible, melodic vocalists, from Verve's Diana Krall to Michael Bublé on Reprise, were beginning to receive considerable support from the record companies in the late 1990s and early 2000s. Jamie Callum, a twenty-three-year-old male crooner with a style reminiscent of Harry Connick Jr., was the object of aggressive major-label courting following the release of his album *Pointless Nostalgic* on the independent imprint Candid in 2002. After Verve succeeded in signing him to a reported $1.8 million contract, Callum's Verve/Universal debut *Twentysomething,* released initially to U.K. markets, rapidly achieved double-platinum certification in that country, with an aggressive pop promotional campaign slated for its U.S. release.[86] Verve's assertive push to sign Callum was itself an effort to capitalize on the staggering market potential revealed by Norah Jones, whose 2002 Blue Note recording, *Come Away with Me,* would achieve sales upward of 25 million units worldwide: as Ted Gioia has noted, the initial response to this recording was such that her record sales accounted for nearly half of *all* jazz CDs sold in many retail outlets.[87] As Stuart Nicholson has argued, Callum, Jones, Krall, and other such crossover-jazz vocalists benefited from their singular appeal to an upwardly-mobile-adult market demographic.[88] For his part, Goldstein hypothesized that the followers of the emergent crooners consisted in large part of "Boomers" channeling their erstwhile enthusiasm for Steely Dan or Van Morrisson into a new, upscale domain of pop.[89]

Instrumentalists figured most prominently in the wave of "young lions" signed to the labels in the early 1990s, and they figured just as prominently in accounts of slashed rosters at the close of the same decade. One *Billboard* article from 2002, entitled "Jazz Seeks Instrumental Stars," makes note of the near-total disappearance of titles by currently active instrumentalists from the Top Jazz Albums chart, and surveys key industry players about the circumstances that led to this situation. Radio and retail markets are held up as structural impediments to "straightahead" jazz, but several observers pointed to what they saw as problems with the music itself. Verve's Goldstein, reiterating a position we have seen him take in other contexts, focused on the question of repertory, asking, "When was the last time you could whistle a [jazz] song, over the last 30 years, since 'Take Five'?"[90] Similarly, Jeff Jones, then senior VP for jazz at Columbia Records, cites the need for "songs that are familiar and singable and have a memorable melody that people can latch onto."[91] If these statements seem to offer a straightforward fix for what ailed instrumental jazz recordings, the broader tone of the article is nevertheless saturated with an anxiety about the future of jazz in its entirety, one grounded in an idea of the music as *constitutively* instrumental in nature. Warner Brothers VP Matt Pierson, reflecting on the diminished commercial viability of jazz recordings, articulates this claim in particularly alarmist terms: "We talk about this all the time [at Warner Bros.], and I say, 'We're gonna lose this thing, we're gonna lose jazz, if we don't create new superstars in this music who are playing music that is fresh and hits you over the fucking head if you know nothing about music. This is major crisis mode.'"[92] Here, despite the sense that the failure to meet market expectations falls largely on the instrumental side of the ledger, this failing is nevertheless seen as a threat to the music in its entirety: the health of jazz and the survival of *instrumental* jazz are positioned as coextensive with one another.

At the same time, the critical reception of the new major-label vocalists in the 1990s and early 2000s often seemed to be couched in an unease about their ambivalent relation to jazz as a genre. Even as pop-centered marketing prerogatives dictate record executives' efforts to distance the crooners from jazz as a genre identity, jazz critics and enthusiasts have also worked to police genre boundaries from the other side. Here, gender often surfaces as a persistent (if persistently unexamined) source of unease. Just to cite one example, Nat Hentoff, in a 2001 column devoted to Diana Krall and Jane Monheit, positions the two artists as failed aspirants to a rigorous stylistic lineage: denouncing Krall's "sluggish" sense of time, and dismissing Monheit as little more than the beneficiary of clever marketing, Hentoff goes on to offer a set of "unsolicited [stylistic] suggestions for Monheit and Krall *and other artists with jazz eyes*."[93] When the president of Monheit's label at that time, Carl Griffin of N-Coded, strategically paired her on recording sessions with established musicians such as Ron Carter and Kenny Barron, it was in the service of responding to precisely this kind of critical barb, of forestalling anticipated criticisms from what he called the "jazz police": aggressively marketed as an attractive white female torch singer, with a potential appeal to an audience beyond the jazz world, Monheit would often find her jazz credentials held up to particular scrutiny.[94]

In examining the discourses that surround both the ascendency of the "nu-crooners" (Nicholson's term) and the depleted fortunes of instrumentalists at the major labels, we need to be cognizant of the historical devaluation of jazz singing in critical and scholarly accounts of the music. Lara Pellegrinelli has argued that a long-standing critical separation of instrumental jazz and vocal jazz falls along the crease of a gendered binary split, a dichotomy in which embodied vocality is marked as the intuitive, natural, and "feminine" other to the technical virtuosity of the instrumentalist.[95] This deeply established discourse helps to explain something of the ambivalence with which the new wave of jazz singers was received by the jazz world in the early 2000s, and it also helps to make some sense of the atmosphere of crisis that seemed to surround the commercial failings of instrumental jazz in some quarters.

Alongside other factors, these critical attitudes about the vocal crossover trend have served to position Verve, conventionally understood as a "jazz label" with a historical commitment to the music, as deviating from its primary mission. For instance, Stuart Nicholson, commenting on the period following the downsizings (in what is an otherwise nuanced analysis), argues that "by 2004, Universal's Verve had become a shadow of its past glories," its commitment to challenging instrumentalists such as Geri Allen jettisoned as part of its pursuit of "jazz-lite" vocalists: Nicholson describes the label's latter-day retention of a few high-profile mainstream jazz artists, including Wayne Shorter and Herbie Hancock (added to the Verve roster in 1995 and 1996, respectively), as a kind of fig leaf designed to lend the label a certain residual jazz respectability.[96] Such thinking, while understandable, tends to hinge upon a prelapsarian logic in which a putative "classic" midcentury Verve is presented as having been always already set at a remove from encroaching commercialism, its roster a triumphant catalog of a once-thriving "mainstream."

However, we need to remember that the Norman Granz Verve and the Creed Taylor Verve were by no means immune from the criticism of anticommercialist jazz aficionados: Granz, who is often seen as the first millionaire entrepreneur to derive his income entirely from the jazz business, was the object of critical barbs from those who saw his lucrative Jazz at the Philharmonic tours as unseemly concessions to commercial success.[97] Similarly, with respect to his MGM/Verve and later CTI recordings, Taylor would be the object of critical invective for relying too heavily upon MGM's film soundtracks for repertory, or for his lavishly orchestrated, melodically accessible Wes Montgomery releases, seen as early (and perhaps unwelcome) precursors to the smooth-jazz phenomenon.[98] Nor does VMG's postmerger embrace of vocalists radically distinguish the label from the commercial strategies employed by its various earlier incarnations. Whether under Granz, Taylor, or Richard Seidel's stewardship, vocalists—from Ella Fitzgerald to Astrud Gilberto, Billie Holiday to Shirley Horn—were absolutely pivotal figures in the Verve catalog from both an aesthetic and fiscal standpoint.

If there are meaningful distinctions to make between the market postures of Verve's "indie," MGM, PolyGram, and UMG manifestations, these have less to do with any putative "selling out" of Verve's respective ownership regimes, and much more to do with the label's *structural* position in the music industry, its changing exposure to the commercial pressures imposed respectively by independent ownership, vertical integration, and logics of financialization. In the context of early twenty-first-century neoliberal capitalism, meaningful decisions that affect the shape of artist rosters at the most granular level are determined from on high, linked to stock price via the mechanism of short-term metrics of performance. In the vast majority of cases, the aesthetic vision pursued by the leadership of a label subsidiary becomes *coextensive* with its specific financial targets, which are themselves determined by considerations elsewhere in the corporate hierarchy. The "loose-tight" management style associated with the federated structure of the music multinational limits its sphere of interest to the bottom line, an approach that is ostensibly designed to protect subsidiaries from day-to-day meddling in their affairs by the parent company. As it turns out, with subsidiary culture in the postmillennial era in large part determined by an ethos of ruthless cost-saving and short-term horizons of profitability, there could scarcely be any more disruptive intervention in a record company's culture than at the level of the balance sheet.

EPILOGUE: AN AQUAMARINE TWILIGHT AT
THE VERVE MUSIC GROUP

In spring 2006, *Office21* magazine, a trade periodical looking at contemporary office design, devoted a feature article to the Verve Group's newly renovated Manhattan headquarters. Ron Goldstein had tapped the prominent Los Angeles–based architect Josh Schweitzer to redesign the office: Goldstein wanted the renovations to reflect "a bit of L.A. in New York," and one imagines that Schweitzer's buoyant aquamarine color scheme did a lot to achieve this result.[99] Beyond this particular aesthetic issue, though, the designers (also comprising dTank, an L.A.-based custom furniture company) wanted to assemble a space that had the potential to encourage creative interactions among its workers. Schweitzer's design eschews compartmentalized offices in favor of open-concept spaces, with careful attention to lighting and acoustics: according to dTank president Henner Jahns, the project's juxtaposition of "industrial edge" and muted warmth had the potential to "increase productivity" and "encourage teamwork" among Verve's workers, presenting "a unique interior space" that communicated something of the vibrant energy of Verve's corporate culture.[100] Especially noteworthy in this respect is the area set aside for what Goldstein refers to as the "wild and boisterous" energy of the Promotions group: in order to harness their uniquely productive exuberance, the workspace would be located strategically next to the kitchen, its table equipped "with special stools that bounce up and down like pogo sticks."[101]

Goldstein's investment of company resources in a thoroughgoing redesign of VMG's corporate headquarters comes at an interesting moment in the company's history. As a statement of company values, it presents itself as a celebration of Verve's commitment to the playful, innovative proclivities of the twenty-first-century "creative class," that postindustrial vanguard identified by Richard Florida in his 2002 book on the subject.[102] Fortified with brightly-hued collaborative spaces and pogo-stick barstools, Verve's A&R and marketing staff were further empowered (or so it was hoped) to go forward and assemble an artist roster equal to the office's atmosphere of playful creativity.

However, Goldstein's testament to the creative zeal of his twenty-first-century Verve workplace environment does not entirely square with what we know of the reduced economic horizons of the label itself during this period. As I noted above, Goldstein had implemented at least two major purges of the artist roster between 1998 and 2006, with concomitant reductions in staffing. While the *content* of such downsizings did seem, in part, to reflect Goldstein's instincts about the commercially unsustainable nature of mainstream instrumental jazz, he makes clear that the downsizings themselves were largely driven by Verve's limited maneuverability within a corporate umbrella defined by its preoccupation with profit maximization: "Corporations own the major record companies. There is a bottom-line mentality, and it's not as entrepreneurial. And there's been a loss of certain executives and personalities who were in the business. . . . We're all subject to stock price. What that has to do with music is hard to justify, but that's where it is."[103] As the acting CEO for the subsidiary of a publically traded corporation, Goldstein's place was itself "subject to stock price," and both he and his subsidiary would soon face the business end of Universal's efforts to maximize shareholder value. In December 2006, just a few months after Verve's office makeover was proudly showcased for *Office21*'s readership, Goldstein "ankled" a third of the label's staff (in *Variety*'s colorful usage), with his own position eliminated and the rest of the label placed under the supervision of Universal Music Enterprises, UMG's catalog and reissue unit.[104] Verve would not be under its own autonomous management again until the appointment of David Foster to the CEO position in December 2011.

Such events proceed from UMG's application of managerial strategies that prioritize shareholder value as an overriding concern. In doing so, they highlight a fundamental contradiction residing at the core of our attempts to reconcile cultural productivity and financial logics. At the center of recent discourses about the importance of creativity and "disruptive innovation" in the contemporary economy is the idea that our most dynamic market actors give themselves over to a playful, disinhibited immersion in the life of risk. Indeed, as I noted in chapter 1, a number of jazz scholars have documented the proliferation of jazz-centered analogies in managerial training literatures, where they are harnessed in the attempt to cultivate nimble, spontaneous, and adaptive corporate cultures. However, even as business schools, investment banks, and Fortune 500 companies seek to learn the wisdom of creativity, improvisation, and nimble playfulness, the culture industry itself is in the process of eliminating these values from its own sphere of creative production: these values, when applied to the production of cultural commodities, bump up against the external limits imposed upon cultural production by logics of financialization.[105]

The downsizing of the Verve roster in 2002; the departure of many of the label's most prominent jazz instrumentalists in the early 2000s; the departure of the A&R executive that engineered the label's revival (Richard Seidel also departed from Verve at around this time); the further staff reductions and the label's ultimate reassignment to Universal's catalog division in 2006—all of these developments take place within a financial context shaped by the broader fate of the Universal Music Group since the 1998 merger. Edgar Bronfman Jr.'s decision in 2000 to sell Seagram and its Universal properties to Vivendi, which was at that time largely a water-and-waste management corporation, was in part driven by a desire to unload Seagram's $7 billion debt load, much of it generated as a result of the PolyGram merger of 1998.[106] However, the subsequent management of the Vivendi Universal empire, under CEO

Jean-Marie Messier, would expose the Universal properties to far greater financial risk. By 2002, Vivendi's pursuit of an aggressive "$77 billion acquisition spree" in the media and entertainment sectors in the late 1990s and early 2000s had brought the company to the edge of bankruptcy: having accumulated over $28 billion in debt as a result of the mergers, the company also faced losses of $12 billion in 2001, the worst such losses in French corporate history.[107] It was also revealed that Messier had approved a massive program of share buybacks in 2001, without the approval of his board of directors or his chief financial officer, in order to boost Vivendi's share price.[108] William Lazonick has demonstrated the degree to which such share repurchase initiatives redirect company funds away from productive capabilities (research and development, human resources) for the sake of an artificial boost in demand for company shares. In Vivendi's case, though, Messier's unauthorized share buybacks only further exacerbated the company's accumulation of debt.[109]

Messier's disastrous mismanagement of Vivendi had grave consequences for a wide variety of stakeholders, not the least of which were members of the Bronfman family, who had received Vivendi shares as compensation for the Seagram sale, and who had subsequently seen the value of their investments plummet some 200 percent over a two-year period.[110] However, Vivendi's accumulation of massive debt under Vivendi was perhaps most consequential for the employees of its many subsidiaries: significant cost-cutting was required to address the debt load incurred by Messier's risky strategy of aggressive diversification. The necessity of paring down debt imposed an austerity climate within the remaining Vivendi holdings, including UMG itself: in 2004, the London office for UMG experienced significant layoffs as part of what chairman and CEO Lucian Grainge referred to as a "cost rationalization" initiative affecting Universal's global workforce.[111] These conditions provide us with a context for understanding the numerous retrenchments in staffing and talent undertaken by the Verve Music Group in the first half of the 2000s.

The history of the Verve label since its 1980s "reboot" under Poly-Gram provides us with an instructive window onto a variety of developments relevant to our understanding of the late twentieth-century major-label jazz subsidiary. First, there was Richard Seidel's revitalization of the Verve catalog and active artist roster in the 1980s: both facets of Seidel's strategy served as testaments to the rekindling of public interest in acoustic jazz during this period. At the same time, the revitalization tells us a considerable amount about the strategic position of the major labels in this period: the Verve "reboot" reflects the majors' success in harnessing a distributed, federated structure in a post-Fordist era of niche markets and fragmented consumer tastes, but it also reflects the serendipitous market introduction of the compact disc, which provided the music industry with the basis for a spectacular and entirely temporary market expansion. Second, there was the period of intensive investment in the "young lions" of jazz and their neotraditionalist elders. The compact disc boom was particularly good to this neoclassicist jazz movement, which for a time benefited from a synergistic reinforcement of catalog sales and sales of new artist releases. However, in much the same way that excessive concentration of investment in the tech sector exposed 1990s market actors to an unsustainable asset bubble, the risky concentration of major-label investment in straightahead, acoustic, post-bebop instrumental jazz artists during this period would expose the jazz subsidiaries (and more pertinently, their artist rosters) to the consequences of a downturn precipitated by declining compact disc consumption and changing retail dynamics. Finally, there was the Universal/PolyGram merger, and its debt-driven installation of cost "rationalizations" in the day-to-day operation of the Verve Music Group: the adventurous risk proclivities of Bronfman Jr.'s investment strategies during this period imposed financial constraints at the level of UMG's subsidiaries, where managerial teams could no longer afford the kinds of long-term investment trajectories that allow aesthetically risky cultural production to see the light of day. By this standard, the 1990s Verve instrumental roster was riskier than most: in pursuit of what it initially saw as a profitable site of artist development, Verve had focused its resources very heavily in the niche domain of neoclassical jazz. This strategy exposed jazz instrumentalists to risk when the "young lions" sound could no longer find a niche in the emergent corporate ecology of postmillennial Verve.

The primary narrative about the jazz record business in the new millennium centers around this question of the demise of the major record labels as a viable commercial home for jazz, and highlights the subsequent rise of a scrappy league of "jazz indies." Here, we could point to the emergence of artist-founded labels, including Branford Marsalis's Marsalis Music or Ravi Coltrane's RKM, which sought to provide alternatives to the hit-driven logic of portfolio management employed at the major labels.[112] The decade also saw the introduction of new business models that sought to leverage the internet as a market portal and crowdsourcing tool: such new initiatives as Dave Douglas's Greenleaf Music or Brian Camelio's ArtistShare (home to bandleader Maria Schneider) envision a market for jazz recording that is less reliant upon conventional album sales as a revenue source.[113]

The strategy of downsizing and divestment employed by Verve, Warner Jazz, Columbia, and RCA in the late 1990s and early 2000s may seem to present itself as the only logical endgame for the major-label jazz subsidiary in the age of financialization. Nevertheless, other major-label imprints, such as Blue Note and Nonesuch Records, have demonstrated viable alternatives to the Verve model.[114] Nonesuch Records is an especially interesting case, in that alongside its promotion of other commercially offbeat genres, it has become an unexpected haven for major-label recorded jazz in the twenty-first century, under the stewardship of Robert Hurwitz. The boutique, "indie" sensibility and boldly eclectic roster of the long-standing Warner classical subsidiary helps to explain its success in taking over the recording careers for several artists displaced by the dismantling of Warner Jazz in the early 2000s.[115] Nonesuch, whose catalog boasts such divergent names as Steve Reich, Wilco, Emmylou Harris, and the Buena Vista Social Club, has produced a number of commercially successful recordings for Joshua Redman, Nicholas Payton, Brad Mehldau, and Pat Metheny. Nonesuch is particularly noteworthy for the way that it managed to protect its autonomy during the period of volatility surrounding the acquisition and restructuring of the Warner Music Group by a private-equity consortium.[116]

By behaving as "indies," by knowledgeably harnessing cultural capital and targeting highly specific taste publics, Blue Note and Nonesuch overcame many of the difficulties faced by competing jazz divisions in the new millennium. Indeed, these lessons do not seem to be entirely lost on other players in the industry. Sony Music, whose storied Columbia Records jazz division was shuttered around the turn of the century, has engineered a bold reentry into the jazz field with the resuscitation of the legendary OKeh imprint, following a singularly long period of disuse: the label that yielded Louis Armstrong's groundbreaking Hot Five and Hot Seven recordings in the 1920s will be put to work as the site of twenty-first-century releases by such artists as Sonny Rollins, Bill Frisell, Nils Petter Molvaer, and Branford Marsalis, among others.[117] Moreover, as this book goes to press, the Verve Music Group (now reconstituted as the Verve Label Group) seems to be on the verge of renewing its commitment to its jazz and classical properties, as Daniel Bennett, the aforementioned son of Tony Bennett, has taken over CEO duties from David Foster, and relocated the Verve Group headquarters to New York.[118]

Despite these encouraging signs, the sobering experience of the Verve Music Group highlights what is at stake in the contested relationship between the jazz world and the contemporary major labels. Seen at a comfortable distance, multinational media conglomerates, operating under a logic of financialization, are committed to ideals of fleet-footed dynamism that resonate with our most cherished models of postmodern subjectivity: it is a corporate personhood realized in financial capitalism's heroic self-image. It is at the level of the subsidiary units, where the lived texture of day-to-day operations unfolds, that the real problems with this model come into view. Debt-driven restructuring, the financial constraints of corporate austerity, the profit-centered logic of portfolio management: it is at the subsidiary level that these repercussions of "creative destruction" impose an unsustainable weight, undermining creative production and creating conditions of precarity for artists and employees. It is these troubling dimensions of the record industry that need to be kept in view as we develop a clearer understanding of the musical life of neoliberal culture.

CHAPTER 5

Jazz and the Right to the City

*Jazz Venues and the Legacy of Urban
Redevelopment in California*

Henri Lefebvre's notion of the "right to the city," which he outlined in
an essay of the same name in 1968, issues a call for a sweeping reevalu-
ation of urban life, a conception of the city that opens onto the fullness
of its human potentialities.[1] Lefebvre asks us to envision an urbanity that
repositions the ordinary inhabitants of the city as agents of urban transformation, and that privileges the use value of the city for its *citadins* (its
resident constituent-citizens) over its exchange value for speculators, its
imbrication in market processes. Along with its prioritization of citizen
participation in deliberations about the fate of the city, the right to the
city recognizes the right of its inhabitants to the radical *appropriation* of
urban space, an assertion that places Lefebvre's vision at odds with the
governing assumptions of capitalist regimes of accumulation.[2]

As David Harvey has pointed out, Lefebvre's essay resonates with the
cultural moment of its publication in Paris in the late 1960s. It is
indebted to the social vision articulated by the Situationists, with their
rigorous exploration of the "psychogeography" of the city, and anticipates the cultural upheaval that shook Paris during this period: the fes-
tive suspension of everyday social relations that attended the events of
May 1968 manifested itself, in part, as a response to the alienating
social conditions precipitated by unchecked urban redevelopment.[3]
However, the questions that Lefebvre raises about who has access to the
city, and what constituencies it serves, are especially relevant in our
present era of financialization. The economic polarization that has

disrupted the internal dynamics of such financial centers as New York and San Francisco in recent decades also maps onto a broader topography of uneven geographical development: during the same period that Rust Belt cities have reeled from the impact of a decades-long systemic disinvestment, the explosive growth of the financial sector has had a collateral effect upon the economies of the nation's financial metropoles, as the desire for urbanity itself becomes a catalyst for wealth extraction on an aggressive scale. Under these circumstances, the question of who will enjoy the right to the city assumes a heightened urgency.

Historically, the jazz venue has often served as a crucial site for the negotiation of contested claims to urban space. As numerous scholars have argued, jazz clubs and performance venues have worked to alter the social topography of the cities that they inhabit. In the early decades of the twentieth century, jazz performance sites offered spaces of potentiality that challenged prevailing urban patterns of racial segregation (in such contexts as the black-and-tans of South Side Chicago or Harlem's Savoy Ballroom), and that offered improvised responses to exploitative market conditions (as was the case with the use of rent parties by black tenants to stave off the prospect of eviction).[4] In the 1970s, the jazz loft scene in lower Manhattan, which gave rise to such artist-directed spaces as Rashied Ali's "Ali's Alley" and Sam and Bea Rivers's Studio Rivbea, yielded important new interventions in the political economy of cultural production: in the same moment that they offered an alternative business model to the conventional jazz club, they also (for better or for worse) marked an early moment in the city's repurposing of industrial spaces as postindustrial sites of creativity.[5] Presently, local jazz patrons in American cities continue to find a variety of unusual solutions for programming jazz, from the Sunday jazz concerts offered by Marjorie Eliot in the parlor of her Washington Heights brownstone home in New York, to Berkeley's Birdland Jazzista Social Club, whose owner, Michael Parayano, converted his six-car garage into a performance space for free Filipino barbeque and live jazz.[6]

The altered cultural status of jazz in the early twenty-first century has placed the music in a more complicated relationship with issues of social justice, and this in turn has had important implications for performance venues themselves. Where the music benefits from extensive corporate or philanthropic support, it tends to distance itself from its historical position at the leading edge of social change. As Daniel Fischlin, Ajay Heble, and George Lipsitz have argued, the corporate ecology inhabited by Jazz at Lincoln Center in Midtown Manhattan, its occupancy of a "highly bourgeois, corporatized space" alongside the luxury condominiums and upmarket boutiques of the Time Warner Center, embodies something of the ideological contradiction at the core of JALC's identity. Even as it projects an almost populist encomium to the democratic potentiality of "swing," this term is ultimately stripped of its experimental or insurgent possibilities: the tacitly conservative orientation of JALC's preoccupation with "swing" is the aesthetic correlate of the center's business model, which relies upon an affluent donor class and exclusionary ticket prices. Moreover, the neoclassicist bent of the JALC program casts a shadow over New York's jazz and improvised-music scene, shaping conditions of employment and economic opportunity for jazz musicians in the city.[7] The echoes of JALC can be found in jazz philanthropy across the United States, reflected in the formalization of jazz programming in the country's universities, concert halls, and other nonprofit spaces.

The outsized advantage enjoyed by large corporate and institutional actors in American urban economies is in many instances heavily underwritten by the public sector. In this, as in other dimensions of the neoliberal economy, the fact of public intervention flies in the face of prevailing ideological truisms: if "free-market" ideology presents its unevenly distributed prosperity as a triumph of private initiative within a scrupulously laissez-faire regulatory environment, the reality is more complicated, as state intervention is often required to clear the way for the private sector's most adventurous projects. In contexts ranging from the designation of "free-trade zones" by cash-strapped governments (which solicit private-sector investment through the suspension of local tax regimes and labor protections), to the effective subsidization of financial sector actors through the federal tax code (which imposes an arbitrary distinction between wages and capital gains as forms of taxable income), the "invisible hand" of the market is the beneficiary of considerable public largesse.[8] The aggressive intervention of contemporary government institutions on behalf of private sector actors operates as a hidden supplement to the regime of flexible accumulation, at once completely necessary for its operation, and yet subversive of its claims to legitimacy.[9]

In contemporary business discourses, the built environment in the neoliberal city is often understood as a temporary concretization of the fluid elasticities of the free market, a contingent materialization of dynamic capital flows. Residents experience the built environment in a very different way: they *inhabit* it as a functional assemblage of lasting, permanent structures. This relative material permanence of urban structures works to impede the drive for unchecked *liquidity* sought by real estate developers and property speculators. In this context, the state can intervene to facilitate the process of value extraction in the built environment: through the use of various legal devices, including "blight" designation and eminent domain, urban redevelopment agencies established by municipal governments (in concert with state and federal agencies) are empowered to free up "illiquid" urban space, making it available for redevelopment by the private sector.[10] In the jazz context, this state of affairs has a variety of implications: while performing-arts centers, universities, and other institutional venues for jazz programming are often brought into being through processes of urban redevelopment, the powerful legal mechanisms of the redevelopment agencies can pose a threat to smaller jazz establishments and their neighboring community stakeholders.[11]

In chapters 5 and 6, I examine one of the principal mechanisms through which federal, state, and municipal governments intervene in the market dynamics of the contemporary urban environment. Since the late 1940s, semi-autonomous community redevelopment agencies have allowed local governments to leverage state powers and public monies to make fundamental changes to the built environment. While community redevelopment is always framed in public-minded terms, the legal and financial tools at the agencies' disposal have, more often than not, been put to work on behalf of a small group of actors in the private sector, comprising developers, real estate speculators, and (more recently) investors in the financial markets. Moreover, during this period, redevelopment corporations have been agents of structural violence, with redevelopment initiatives resulting in the eviction and displacement of residents and the dismantling of long-standing neighborhood communities. At various points in their history, jazz venues have been affected by the actions of redevelopment agencies in a variety of ways, both as the targets of a racialized legacy of urban renewal, and as the beneficiaries of more contemporary efforts to harness cultural nostalgia as an engine of economic growth. Consequently, an account of twenty-first-century jazz urbanities must come to terms with the theory and practice of the community redevelopment agency.

COMMUNITY REDEVELOPMENT AGENCIES IN CALIFORNIA

In 1945, the California state legislature passed the Community Redevelopment Act in order to provide public authorities with tools for addressing "blight" conditions in major urban centers. California was the first state to pass legislation of this kind, but it was soon widely emulated in other parts of the country. In the postwar era, processes of suburbanization and white flight began to affect conditions in the inner cores of American cities, raising fears about the prospect of shuttered businesses, depressed property values, and a diminished tax base for governing municipalities. In this context, the introduction of community redevelopment agencies (CRAs) provided county and municipal governments with what they saw as an important policy counterweight to urban decline.[12] Nevertheless, outside of urban policymaking circles, the use of CRAs would become a source of controversy, owing to the powers that redevelopment legislation made available to the independent agencies, as well as the financing mechanism used to fund them: specific features of the redevelopment process potentially allowed the CRAs to redeploy public monies for the disproportionate benefit of the private sector, and often, as it would turn out, to the detriment to low-income residents and communities of color.[13]

The provisions of the Community Redevelopment Act allowed for the formation of redevelopment agencies entrusted with numerous powers: they had the authority to purchase real estate, or to acquire it via eminent domain; to develop the property and to sell it without competitive building, often at a discount, to private entities; to relocate persons who have interests in the properties obtained by the agencies; to finance the agency's activities by borrowing money from state and federal governments, or through the issuing of bonds; and to impose land-use controls for the purposes of development.[14] The act's redevelopment procedures constituted the only case in which eminent domain could be legally used for private, rather than public, purposes.[15] In the 1970s, California legislators made amendments to the redevelopment laws, committing resources to support low-income residents displaced by redevelopment initiatives.[16] CRAs remained a key instrument of urban planning in California until 2011, when the state legislature, at the urging of governor Jerry Brown, passed legislation abolishing the redevelopment agencies as a partial means of addressing the state's fiscal crisis.[17]

All of these developments take place against the backdrop of new federal housing laws introduced in the postwar era, with the 1949 American Housing Act providing "Title I" federal funding for "slum clearance" in the context of local urban renewal initiatives.[18] Title I urban renewal emulated the disturbing precedent set by California and other states with respect to the use of eminent domain on behalf of private interests. In Robert Caro's words, "for the first time in America, government was given the right to seize an individual's private property not for its own use but for reassignment to another individual for *his* [or her] use and profit."[19]

There are important differences between the ways that the midcentury Keynesian welfare state and the contemporary neoliberal "contract state" have made use of mechanisms of urban redevelopment. Under the earlier Keynesian regime, funding of municipal redevelopment derived in large part from federal block grants, made possible through the robust tax regime of the post–New Deal consensus. At the regional level, these federal funds were deployed under the stated pretext of a paternalistic focus upon moral uplift, with proponents of redevelopment citing lapses in health, hygiene, or morality as justifications for the designation of an improvement district. In many instances, these mechanisms were applied to "long-turnover" regions, areas with concentrated poverty and depressed real estate values, and their most draconian tools were used liberally.[20] Under the rubric of midcentury welfare capitalism, these acts of creative urban destruction always donned the vestments of public-minded, civic improvement.[21]

Even at the time, opponents of redevelopment frequently made note of the ways that projects undertaken in the name of civic amelioration tended to disproportionately benefit those private-sector actors who could exploit the ambiguous terms of "blight" for their own purposes. In this context, advocates of local urban stakeholders sought to use the courts to establish a crucial distinction between *blight* and *obsolescence:* if the category of obsolescence concentrated upon the market exchange value of a property within a designated project zone, *blight,* properly defined, centered upon the *use* value of the property for its various stakeholders. A clean, well-maintained older building located on a rapid-turnover land parcel, for example, may be construed as "obsolete" from the standpoint of its return on investment, even as it remains perfectly functional for the purposes of its inhabitants.[22]

Between 1949 and 1965, urban renewal was responsible for the displacement of approximately one million people, mostly low-income people of color, from existing high-density neighborhoods.[23] At the same time, the shape of redevelopment initiatives did evolve during this period. The 1954 Housing Act amended the law to allow for the rehabilitation of existing properties, and widened the scope of "blight" designation to include neighborhoods with the *potential* to experience decline at some point in the future. This modification allowed for the introduction of redevelopment projects in otherwise prosperous regions of the city, enabling municipal government to subsidize projects on behalf of the city's cultural elite (as for example with the building of Lincoln Center in New York), or to back the construction of profitable office developments for entrenched private real estate interests. By the mid-1960s, all of these efforts at redevelopment would run up against the organized opposition of various antigrowth constituencies, from supporters of Jane Jacobs's vision for a more scalable, walkable city, to those African-American communities that had borne the brunt of urban renewal's indifferent urbanism.[24]

The economic upheaval of the 1970s, which saw the intensification of global flows of capital, the shift to post-Fordist economic models, and the gradual retrenchment of the postwar Keynesian economic dispensation, established a new set of contexts for postwar models of urban redevelopment. One crucial change here was the degree to which advocates of redevelopment increasingly embraced the market value of designated properties as the primary motivation for pursuing redevelopment. This new stance constitutes an important reversal: in the wake of antiredevelopment campaigns initiated by civil rights activists and advocates for a post-Jacobs urbanism, the paternalistic tone of earlier urban-renewal campaigns had become unsustainable. In its place, cities have increasingly identified *obsolescence* (where existing structures prevent investors from realizing the full market value of a given property) as the primary factor in designating project areas, and have mobilized a rhetoric of entrepreneurialism to justify redevelopment.[25]

The shift to exchange value as the primary criterion for designation of project areas indexes a broader transformation in the funding climate surrounding redevelopment: over the last several decades, federal sources of funding have dried up (with the discontinuation of block grants for redevelopment agencies), and cities have increasingly turned to the market in municipal bonds to finance their initiatives. The terms of blight designation have been adjusted accordingly: earlier generations of civic activists had cited a distinction between blight and obsolescence precisely in order to guard against the undue exploitation of blight designation to benefit private developers. Activists insisted that the designation of a project zone on the basis of obsolescence alone (in other words, only on the basis of an unrealized market potential for developers) was an unjustifiable use of the redevelopment mechanism. However, under the market logic of neoliberalism, obsolescence has been recuperated as the *most* viable route to blight designation. Shorn of the moralizing implications of blight, the term obsolescence has come to provide civic leaders with what purported to be a politically neutral basis for the state-led appropriation of urban space. At the same time, a property's obsolescence, its objective failings in relation to market valuation, has also become a basis for translating regionally specific knowledge about the built environment into abstract terms understood by a deterritorialized, global body of distant investors. For the rentier class of far-flung investors, such techniques as securitization, through which debt obligations secured through real estate assets are bundled together as delocalized investment vehicles, hold out the promise of severing the illiquid, locally particular commodities of the built environment from their concrete urban specificity, resituating them in relation to the abstracting gaze of financialization.[26]

The specific means through which redevelopment agencies often enter into financing arrangements with the global bond market is through a mechanism referred to as tax-increment financing (or TIF). Tax-increment financing designates a specific taxing jurisdiction in an urban area targeted for redevelopment, and then allows for a portion of the municipal property taxes assessed in that area to be redirected to the financing of the redevelopment project. In recent decades, TIF mechanisms have served as security for globally traded municipal bonds, which in turn provide cities with the necessary up-front injection of capital necessary to initiate complex demolition and construction initiatives.[27] Beyond the funding of regular municipal services, which remains frozen at a Base Year rate coinciding with the first year of assessment, the remaining tax revenue, based upon the difference (or "increment") between property taxes assessed in the Base Year and those of subsequent years, is redirected toward redevelopment, or toward the repayment of municipal bonds financing redevelopment.[28]

California was one of the first states to pass legislation allowing for the use of TIF in redevelopment projects. However, the mechanism didn't truly come into its own until the late 1970s, with the passage of Proposition 13 by state referendum: under the new law, the result of a statewide conservative antitax revolt, severe constraints were imposed upon the property-tax rate and on permitted increases in the assessed value of a given property. In the tight new fiscal environment created by Proposition 13, municipalities were increasingly pressed to turn to the bond market to support capital-intensive projects, and tax increment financing came into extensive use.[29]

Tax increment financing has a variety of implications for fiscal policy at the municipal level. First, in an environment such as post–Proposition 13 California, where property-tax increases have effectively been placed politically off-limits, the re-allocation of accumulated "incremental" tax revenue to redevelopment projects amounts to a de facto tax cut on municipal services: monies that would otherwise have helped to fund police, fire department, and other critical services are redirected to the private-sector beneficiaries of redevelopment.[30] A second implication of TIF is that by creating a venue for the circulation of municipal tax revenue on the global bond markets, it incentivizes the designation of projects in areas of rapid turnover and dramatically escalating real estate values: because the revenue generated for the repayment of municipal bonds depends upon the "incremental" difference between the Base Year value and the property values at the completion of the project, the public sector is pressed to concentrate in areas of the city where state-acquired properties can be upgraded and reintroduced into "hot" real estate markets, so that the resulting spike in real estate values can help the municipality to justify up-front expenditures and to pay down outstanding debt on the bonds.[31] The result is a regime of redevelopment that Mark Davidson and Kevin Ward have referred to as *entrepreneurial speculative urbanism,* a strategy in which "cities speculate on future economic growth by borrowing against predicted future revenue streams to make this growth more likely": speculative urbanism of this kind embraces a heavily leveraged risk posture commensurate with the priorities of neoliberal development.[32]

One case study from the half-century history of California's redevelopment agencies may help us to understand the ways in which abstract policymaking and urban planning articulate with the urban life of jazz communities in the state during this period. Here, I will take up the redevelopment of San Francisco's storied Fillmore district in the 1950s and 1960s, a process that resulted in the displacement of thousands of African-American residents, the shuttering of countless local businesses, and the thoroughgoing destruction of one of the West Coast's most important midcentury jazz scenes.[33] In the early years of the new century, San Francisco's redevelopment agency sought to make amends for its catastrophic postwar venture through a jazz-centered revitalization initiative in the Fillmore district. However, as I will argue in the next chapter, the city's attempts to cultivate a twenty-first-century jazz "renaissance" in the Western Addition have not fared well, as the city faces the limitations of its top-down, debt-driven managerial approach in the project district.

THE FILLMORE DISTRICT

The story of the Fillmore district of San Francisco, an area also referred to as the Western Addition, constitutes an important chapter in the urban legacy of American jazz. It also entails one of the most infamous case studies in the use of state-sponsored redevelopment as a tool of "creative destruction": harnessing the tools of "blight" designation and eminent domain, the city's redevelopment agency pursued a scorched-earth program of urban renewal that resulted in the displacement of thousands of people and the systemic dismantling of the area's distinctive economic and cultural infrastructure.

The Fillmore district lays claim to a particularly distinctive role in the growth and development of the city of San Francisco. The formation of the district dates to the 1880s, with the city extending the reach of the urban grid to the west of City Hall in order to address chronic housing shortages and overcrowding. This new "Western Addition," served by a streetcar route along its north-south Fillmore Street commercial axis, became the site of a vibrant community of European, Jewish, and eventually Japanese immigrants, boasting a housing stock of ornate Victorian mansions and row houses. In the aftermath of the cataclysmic earthquake of 1906, Fillmore Street was one of the few largely undamaged commercial thoroughfares in the city, and it quickly became a hub for the relocated offices of the city's newspapers and government officials, and the new site of San Francisco's major department stores. To accommodate city residents displaced by the quake's path of destruction, many of the Fillmore's handsome Victorian houses were converted into boardinghouses. The resulting influx of Filipino/a, African-American, Russian, and Mexican residents transformed the Fillmore into one of the most diverse neighborhoods in the city.[34]

Up until the 1940s, the black population of the Western Addition was relatively small, held in check by housing discrimination and by the near-total exclusion of African Americans from the city's unionized workforce. However, with the outbreak of war, the neighborhood became a home to many Southern black workers, drawn to San Francisco by the availability of work in the city's massive shipyards. In many instances, the new black migrants took advantage of housing vacancies created in part by the internment of the district's Japanese-American residents. A wave of new black-owned businesses opened to meet the new residents' needs, contributing further to the economic vitality of the Fillmore's polyglot urban fabric. By the time of the 1950 census, the black population of the Fillmore stood at 42,520.[35]

The wartime growth of the black Fillmore saw the efflorescence of a bustling jazz scene in the neighborhood's venues. In the opening decades of the twentieth century, the Fillmore had already established itself as an important entertainment district for the city. The Majestic Hall on Geary Boulevard, decades prior to its legendary incarnation as Bill Graham's countercultural venue (renamed "the Fillmore"), presented dances and balls catering to a segregated audience; the National Hall on Post Street provided a regular platform for the young Al Jolson. With the growth of the area's African-American community in the 1940s, the Fillmore district began to serve as a West Coast fulcrum for the era's jazz movements: alongside such accomplished local performers as Earl Watkins, John Handy, and Frank Jackson, the Fillmore neighborhood would play host to national touring musicians, including Charlie Parker, Dizzy Gillespie, Billie Holiday, Dexter Gordon, Duke Ellington, Dinah Washington, and Miles Davis.[36]

The district's venues, vividly described in the first-person accounts collected in Elizabeth Pepin and Lewis Watts's book *Harlem of the West,* ranged from the Primalon Ballroom, a former German *biergarten* that doubled as a rollerskating rink during the week, to Jack's Tavern, an urbane, elegantly appointed club in which well-dressed clientele came to see and be seen. Countless other performing spaces, including the Long Bar, the New Orleans Swing Club, and the Club Alabam, contributed to the singularly vibrant atmosphere of the neighborhood.[37] One of the most important clubs was Jimbo's Bop City, located on Post Street two blocks east of the Fillmore commercial strip. First opened as Vout City, under the management of the celebrated multi-instrumentalist Slim Gaillard (purveyor of a scat-based language he referred to as "Vout"), the space was taken over by the local car salesman John Edwards in 1950, and reopened as a café and waffle house.[38] After musicians began using the back room of Jimbo's as a space for after-hours jams, the venue assumed a new role as Jimbo's Bop City, and soon became a major site for bebop on the West Coast. Bop City was regularly frequented by the likes of Count Basie, Dinah Washington, and Sammy Davis Jr., and the club's inexpensive chairs were painted with the names of jazz luminaries that had sat on them on one night or another: in the event that that artist returned, the occupant had to surrender their seat.[39] "Jimbo" Edwards reportedly ran a tight ship, closely monitoring his clientele's comings and goings, and stipulating numerous rules designed to keep the focus on the music: no dozing, note passing, or standing was allowed, and customers were expected to keep their hands above the table, to forestall the prospect of gambling or other illicit activities.[40] On any given night, between roughly two and six in the morning, its bandstand featured a range of legendary and soon-to-be legendary performers: the singer Johnny Mathis got his start at Bop City, and the young, then-unknown John Coltrane made an appearance at the club, with his developing sound provoking intense curiosity among local musicians.[41]

Edwards's celebrated venue served as a site of informal community for the Bay Area's nascent bebop scene. In the fashion of such East Coast after-hours spots as Milt's Playhouse or Monroe's, Jimbo's affirmed the jam session as a kind of meritocratic proving ground: an unseasoned newcomer like the young alto saxophonist John Handy could share the stage with established improvisers like Paul Gonsalves or Oscar Peterson. John Edwards encouraged many untested musicians to take to the bandstand, tactfully pulling them aside when things weren't working out. As Frank Jackson recalls, the informal atmosphere of the back room at Jimbo's made it an invaluable pedagogical environment for many young musicians: "There were quite a few after-hours spots in the Fillmore, but Bop City was the most famous. It was really a workshop for musicians, a place for learning. You got a chance to play with the good, the bad, and the ugly! Musicians would sit around and talk to each other about musical things, about chords and putting things together, and how they execute and how they finger things. You were surrounded by all of that."[42] However, this sense that the Fillmore's musical culture was an object of communal patrimony, spontaneously and publicly *shared*, extended beyond the informal jam sessions at Bop City. The back room at Jackson's Nook, a Creole restaurant on Buchanan Street, would often host an overflow jam session when Bop City got too crowded. Club Flamingo (later renamed the Texas Playhouse), a hotel and nightclub with an elegant Streamline façade, catered to a glamorous late-night crowd of musical luminaries as the venue's owner, Wesley Johnson Sr., played records for his clientele. Outside the nightclubs, the urban streetscape of the Fillmore also served as a site of ad hoc communal performances. "Sugar Pie" Desanto, a noted Filipina-American R&B singer from the area, recalls the pervasiveness of a capella doo-wop groups on the Fillmore's residential front porches and street corners; community activist Steve Nakajo also cites the sound of doo-wop ringing out from the district's storefronts, the singers "cutting it up, singing in the doorway because the marble floor gives a better sound."[43]

The local music scene occupied an environment of a kind that Richard Florida, writing in reference to later urbanisms, would hail as a densely overlapping "scene of scenes," each component contributing to a richly interwoven urban ecology.[44] Willie Brown, a resident of the Fillmore who would later serve as San Francisco's first African-American mayor, points out that the neighborhood served as an indispensable local center of African-American economic prosperity in the context of postwar urban segregation, of "stores that were as interesting and important as the ones in Union Square except they carried goods that primarily Blacks would purchase."[45] At the same time, the black Fillmore, whose tenements had been made available in part through the internment of Japanese-American residents during the Second World War, bordered upon another Western Addition community variously referred to as Japantown, Japanesetown, Nihonmachi, or Nihonjimachi: in the postwar era, with many of the district's Japanese-American residents returning to the area, the Fillmore's banks, barbeque joints, movie houses, barbershops, nightclubs, and countless other local amenities would cater to a multiethnic community of residents who had faced systemic exclusion.[46] As such, they helped to transform a shared experience of marginalization into a catalyst for shared economic and social vitality.

REDEVELOPMENT IN THE WESTERN ADDITION

However, in the years following the end of the Second World War, the polyglot community of the Fillmore would soon be faced with new and daunting structural obstacles. First, the conclusion of wartime hostilities led to severe downsizing in the shipbuilding industry, putting thousands of African-American laborers out of work, and undermining one of the key sources of the neighborhood's economic vitality.[47] Moreover, in the context of the city's segregated labor market, the Fillmore's black workers found themselves unable to secure new employment elsewhere in postwar San Francisco. This same period also saw the acceleration of a process of "white flight" in the Bay Area and other U.S. metropoles, as white middle-class migrants took advantage of the mortgage-subsidy provisions of the G.I. Bill to relocate to more racially homogeneous communities in the suburbs; such flight potentially endangered property values and tax revenue for inner cities.[48]

It is in this context that San Francisco's City Planning Commission, harnessing the new policy tools made available by the passage of California's Community Redevelopment Act in 1945, sought to develop a master plan for the wide-scale redevelopment of the city. Their project began in earnest with the publication of *The Redevelopment of Blighted Areas,* in the same year that saw the passage of the Community Redevelopment Act.[49] Drawing upon the findings of the 1939 Real Property Survey, a document commissioned by the federal Works Progress Administration, the authors of the 1945 master plan undertook a systematic evaluation of San Francisco's census data, neighborhood conditions, and property assessments, in order to target specific areas of the city for consideration as designated sites of redevelopment.[50] These detailed surveys armed city planners with a seemingly objective evidentiary basis for their claims regarding excessive "blight" in the Western Addition and other areas of the city. As Clement Lai has argued, the conclusions of the report, rendered in the dry administrative language of municipal policymakers, nevertheless engage in a "discursive slippage" linking physical and economic conditions prevailing in the built environment of the Western Addition to the racialized bodies of its inhabitants.[51] A pamphlet entitled *Blight and Taxes,* prepared by the San Francisco Planning and Housing Association in 1947, pointedly noted that the Geary-Fillmore neighborhood was "not white. It's gray, brown, and an indeterminate shade of dirty black. . . . A quarter of all those in [the area] are Negroes, Chinese, Japanese, and Filipinos." Elsewhere, the SFPHA report asserted that the Fillmore constituted "an unfortunate blot" on an otherwise proud city, further reinforcing its unsubtle pairing of blight with blackness.[52]

With the 1948 decision by the city's board of supervisors to assign blight designation to 280 blocks of the Western Addition, the newly formed San Francisco Redevelopment Agency entered into a decades-long, contentious, and often painful process of urban transformation in the Fillmore district. Upon assuming the position of SFRA director in 1959, Justin Herman set out to transform what he saw as an ineffective agency into a powerful tool of urban policy, securing federal funding and moving forward with an aggressive execution of the proposed redevelopment plans.[53]

The devastating impact of the redevelopment of the Western Addition, which unfolded in two phases (referred to as A-1 and A-2 respectively), has been chronicled at length elsewhere. The centerpiece of the first of these redevelopment areas was the widening of Geary Boulevard, to create a major east-west artery connecting downtown to the north-western area of the city. The A-1 project area would also include the establishment of a Japanese Cultural and Trade Center, an elaborate complex encompassing such elements as a Japanese-themed luxury hotel, commercial and office spaces catering to firms specializing in trade between Japan and the United States, and the regional Japanese consulate. Under Justin Herman's aggressive leadership, the demolition of properties falling within the A-1 project area began in 1958. Along the Geary Boulevard axis, the area slated for demolition was thirty blocks long, and would result in the dislocation of some four thousand families, many of whom were low-income African-American or Japanese-American households. Very few of these families were able to return to this area following redevelopment: given the spatial design of the A-1 redevelopment, only 2,009 new housing units were built in the project area (for an area that had once housed some eight thousand residents), and of these units, only 33 percent were priced appropriately for low- to middle-income residents, with the remaining housing made available at the going market rate. Some 20 percent of residents relocated outside of the A-1 project area were placed in substandard dwellings, and approximately 80 percent paid higher rents in their new residences following relocation. Moreover, since a quarter of the A-1 area's residents had been relocated to dwellings within the proposed A-2 area, they would need to undergo relocation a second time, as the redevelopment agency proceeded with the second phase of its project.[54]

Given the evident damage created by the initial A-1 phase of the Fillmore's redevelopment, the second project phase, beginning in the mid-1960s, faced much stronger resistance among community stakeholders. The Western Addition Community Organization (WACO), assembled by such area residents as Mary Rogers and Hannibal Williams, mobilized a coalition of community groups in opposition to the SFRA's redevelopment plans. WACO's methods were indebted to the tactics and values of nonviolent resistance enacted by the national civil rights movement, as, for example, when Williams and a group of activists padlocked a building slated for demolition, linking arms in front of the structure to bar the path of construction workers. On a broader, strategic level, WACO, working in concert with the San Francisco Neighborhood Legal Assistance Foundation (SFNLAF), succeeded in obtaining a federal injunction requiring the SFRA to negotiate with a panel of community leaders before moving forward with demolition of the A-2 project area: this injunction, issued in 1969, was one of the first to be applied to an urban redevelopment project anywhere in the country since the passage of urban-renewal legislation. Nevertheless, even these bold measures did not succeed in permanently delaying the implementation of the A-2 redevelopment project: ultimately, some 13,500 people were displaced by the second phase of the project, with the redevelopment agency failing to provide adequate affordable housing to replace the forty-five hundred housing units it had demolished. The effort contributed to a severe housing shortage for the city's low-income inhabitants, but it also decimated the ranks of small, black-owned businesses that had catered to the area's residents.[55]

THE TWILIGHT OF JAZZ ON FILLMORE STREET

The enormous destruction wrought by the process of redevelopment in San Francisco was spread across a wide range of small-business and residential locales, but in the present context, it is worth noting the particularly devastating implications that the A-1 and A-2 redevelopment projects had for the many small jazz venues and nightclubs in the Western Addition. In many instances, the direct displacements and indirect economic effects produced by the redevelopment agency's enactment of eminent domain worked in tandem with a variety of other factors to undermine the viability of nightclubs in the area: the vicissitudes of the national and local jazz economies played an important role here, and some observers point to the unexpected consequences of integration, in the wake of the passage of landmark civil rights legislation in the mid-1960s. Nevertheless, the destruction of the built environment enacted through the redevelopment of the Fillmore must count as a striking example of how structural violence can destroy a musical commons, a creative "scene of scenes."

Jimbo's Bop City, the aforementioned after-hours jam session venue run by John "Jimbo" Edwards, closed in 1965, and its fate reflects the complex factors that led to the shuttering of so many music nightspots in the Fillmore District during this era. To begin with, the 1960s was a period of change for Bay Area jazz musicians in general. The late 1950s saw the amalgamation of San Francisco's segregated union locals for the American Federation of Musicians, a situation that now permitted many black musicians to take gigs in a part of the city that had formerly been restricted to members of the all-white Local 6.[56] Philip Alley, son of prominent local drummer and bandleader Eddie Alley, argues that the new possibilities afforded by desegregation meant that many local favorites were now playing in upscale white venues elsewhere in the city that were inaccessible to the black Fillmore's working-class clientele.[57] Indeed, by this period, many jazz musicians were looking outside of the Bay Area altogether. Pianist Frank Jackson notes the centripetal pull that national touring, and the allure of New York City as a jazz center, had for local musicians:

> Starting in the late 1950s, a lot of musicians left the Fillmore clubs to tour or go to other cities. In order to get anywhere as musicians, you had to. Then you could come back as headliners in the bigger clubs around town. [Saxophonist] Jerome Richardson got disgusted. He was getting work, but he couldn't advance. You couldn't get any recognition in San Francisco. Jerome told me, "Frank, I'm moving to New York." . . . They left here together, and they did big things. Their careers took off.[58]

Indeed, part of the problem for Fillmore venues such as Bop City was that these shifting trends in the national jazz economy were changing the landscape for Bay Area jazz clubs outside the Fillmore. In the immediate postwar era, Bop City's late-night jam session scene (which often didn't get going until after two in the morning) depended upon an ecology of more prominent venues that were open during regular business hours. National touring artists would play clubs such as the Blackhawk or the Say When until closing time, and then head to Bop City after hours to socialize and to go head-to-head with local musicians.[59] However, by the early 1960s, both of these clubs had closed, and John Edwards's club became collaterally affected by this sudden contraction in the San Francisco jazz scene: "The time had ran out. I was there fifteen years from 1950 to 1965 and the time was over. It was all over. The Blackhawk was closed. The Say When was closed. All the clubs was closed and the musicians didn't come to San Francisco. So then I was setting with an empty club and nobody to draw from."[60] These pressures from within the jazz community were also exacerbated by pressures from without, including the emerging psychedelic rock scene flourishing in the nearby Haight-Ashbury neighborhood. In 1965 Charles Sullivan, the African-American proprietor of the Fillmore Auditorium, began subletting the space to Bill Graham, an aspiring concert promoter who would famously begin programming the music of Jefferson Airplane and the Grateful Dead at the venue.[61] These changes to the musical profile of Sullivan's theater, in the neighborhood from which it took its name, indicates something of the radically altered landscape in which jazz musicians were seeking to make their way.

In the end, though, what fatally undercut Jimbo's Bop City, along with the myriad other venues in the Western Addition, was the structural violence of redevelopment itself. Edwards's Bop City venue was located immediately across the street from the dozens of city blocks razed to the ground during the A-1 project phase of redevelopment, and so, even though the property in which Bop City was located did not come into the SFRA's possession until the mid-1970s, Bop City and myriad other local businesses were clearly affected by the displacement of residents and small businesses in the vicinity. Even without facing the immediate threat of the wrecking ball, businesses like Bop City were subject to the dismantling of the Fillmore district's "scene of scenes."[62]

At the same time, other venues were more directly affected by the actions of the SFRA. One of the most egregious instances of such systematic displacement and destruction can be seen in the agency's punitive handling of its interactions with Leola King, a proprietor of several musical and dining establishments and a central figure in the musical and economic life of the Fillmore. King opened her first nightclub, the Blue Mirror, in 1953, and the venue rapidly became one of the mandatory stops on the itineraries of both local and out-of-state blues and jazz musicians. Alongside such Bay Area artists as Frank Jackson, "Sugar Pie" Desanto, and Earl Grant, the club played host to Dinah Washington, T-Bone Walker, Sarah Vaughn, and Louis Armstrong.[63] Pianist Federico Cervantes describes the small club as having been "on the sophisticated side. . . . It and the Champagne Supper Club gave a little more prestige to the Fillmore."[64]

King had been overseeing a second establishment, a hugely popular barbeque restaurant called Oklahoma King's, whose clientele from nearby jazz clubs snaked out the door past midnight on busy nights.[65] During the first phase of redevelopment, Oklahoma King's became subject to eminent domain, along with many other local businesses in the vicinity, and one day King arrived at work to find the property gone.[66] In the wake of the bulldozing, she was retroactively forced to sell the property for less than the value of the land on which the restaurant stood, with no compensation forthcoming for the building or its equipment.[67] Following the shuttering of Oklahoma King's, King devoted her attention to the vibrant musical scene she had cultivated at the Blue Mirror. But she was to face the redevelopment authorities a second time in 1962, when the agency targeted her Blue Mirror location, along with other bars and late-night establishments, for violations of the municipal code as a pretext for shutting her down: "So the target was to close me down because I had such tremendous business. I was told by the business people . . . that my business would go for [a] big price and that's why they're trying to eliminate you. By putting police in the area, under-cover people, to give you violations to close you up. That's one way they were getting rid of us."[68] King recounts that the agency had a man bring a child into the Blue Mirror, ostensibly so they could use the bathroom, and the man then bought a drink and handed it to the child when none of the servers were looking. In this way, they were able to remove King's liquor license, and the Blue Mirror was swiftly padlocked and slated for demolition.

In the wake of the Blue Mirror's closure, King felt pressure to reopen in a new location to sustain her clientele. In 1964, she opened a new venue, the Bird Cage Tavern, on Fillmore Street. The space, which fea-tured a thirty-foot mahogany bar and a gilded birdcage, had both a juke-box and a piano, which she used to present music in the daytime; with the new space, King recalls, "I specialized in afternoon jazz."[69] Here too, though, Leola King once again faced the intransigent force of the city's redevelopment agency. Despite assurances that the property fell outside of the redevelopment project area, the SFRA acquired the property in which King was leasing space, and in 1974, all of the building's tenants were evicted to make way for the A-2 phase of redevelopment.[70]

The subsequent twenty-five years of King's life were spent negotiat-ing the terms of relocation, following the eviction at the Bird Cage Tav-ern, and seeking redress for the incalculable impact of the redevelop-ment agency's actions upon her livelihood. Indeed, throughout this period of protracted struggle, the SFRA continued to act in ways that raise questions about their commitment to addressing their prior actions toward King. As she was seeking to reopen her tavern, she chose to redeem a "certificate of preference" that the redevelopment agency had granted to her for a property lost to redevelopment; she used it to acquire a residential building on Eddy Street, with the backing of a fed-erally backed loan.[71] However, before the deed of ownership was for-mally transferred to her, thieves broke into the property and stripped its plumbing, light fixtures, windows, and doors. The agency immediately asserted that King had acquired the property "as is," and that they would not be responsible for existing damage.[72] It was in this broader context of these and other financial struggles that Leola King, by the late 1990s, found herself fighting bankruptcy proceedings without any real financial recognition from the redevelopment agency; indeed, in the late 1990s, the agency successfully filed an affidavit requiring that King's Chapter 11 bankruptcy be converted to Chapter 7, allowing creditors to go after her entire estate. Reflecting on her experience, King positions the agency's actions in the context of a broader legacy of structural expropriation in the Fillmore:

> This is why we have so much tragedy in America now. We've got people that's taking things that don't belong to them. Suffer the consequences. . . . [The] way they took everything—they gave away Fillmore—is criminal. . . . The Justice Department needs to have this on file. They need the whole story so that it don't happen round the world to other poor people, and the young people that's coming along now. It's criminal, the things that they were doing to people like me that worked hard.[73]

CONCLUSION

The destruction of the Fillmore by San Francisco's redevelopment agency had calamitous implications for the city's black population in the decades following the implementation of the 1945 Master Plan. San Francisco as a city has become singularly inhospitable to African Americans: the city saw its black population decline from 13.4 percent of the city's overall population in 1970 to just 6.5 percent in 2005, and this trend has only accelerated in the new millennium, as a tech-driven gentrification has exacerbated the city's crisis of affordable housing.[74] On a more granular level, many of the redevelopment agency's efforts to revitalize the Fillmore have also failed, for reasons that were perhaps predictable. The construction of the Fillmore Center, a $140-million mixed-use complex comprising residential and commercial units, failed to contribute to the area's revitalization in any meaningful way: beset by financial woes, owing in part to the refusal of local banks to finance a complex in the Western Addition neighborhood, the Fillmore Center was unable to fill its commercial storefront vacancies, and its residential units—even the 20 percent set aside for lower-income residents—were priced well out of the range of affordability for most of the community's former inhabitants.[75]

In the decades following the destruction of the Fillmore, the material traces of the neighborhood's storied jazz legacy would surface in unexpected places, ghostly remnants of the area's built environment. One of the more unusual news articles pertaining to the Fillmore in the 1960s and 1970s was a short piece in the *New York Times* announcing that the city of San Francisco was selling upward of forty Victorian buildings from the A-2 project area of the Western Addition. The initiative, in which the buildings were each priced at $500 (approximately $2,800 in current dollars), not including the cost of relocation, was a response to the public outcry following the demolition of over two hundred historic Victorian structures during the demolition phase of the A-1 redevelopment.[76] One of the Victorian structures that would eventually be relocated as part of the project was the home of Jimbo's Bop City itself: Essie Collins, a member of WACO, petitioned for the building to be physically moved from its former site on the 1686–1690 block of Post Street to a new location on the 1712–1716 block of Fillmore. In this new context, the building would become part of Victorian Square, a microproject of the city redevelopment agency that sought to assemble a cluster of recovered Victorian structures in a pattern evocative of the Fillmore's erstwhile streetscape. In 1980, the building that had once housed Jimbo Edwards's popular jazz club was acquired by Raye and Julian Richardson, who would use the structure as the new home of their storied bookstore Marcus Books, long a cornerstone of the intellectual life of the Fillmore's African-American community. In early 2014, the building was granted official landmark designation by the San Francisco Board of Supervisors.[77] In belatedly awarding official recognition to a jazz venue that no longer existed, by designating landmark status to a building whose address did not correspond with the jazz club's historical location, the city unwittingly highlighted the structural violence of the redevelopment process, its enactment of a strategy of dislocation that has denied black residents' claim to a right to the city.

CHAPTER 6

The "Yoshi's Effect"

Jazz, Speculative Urbanism, and Urban
Redevelopment in Contemporary
San Francisco

On a November night in 2007, the luminaries of the Bay Area political establishment turned out for a jazz concert in the Fillmore district, billed as an event of historic importance for the neighborhood, and for the Bay Area jazz community that had once called it home. The occasion of the event was the opening of Yoshi's, a San Francisco chapter of the storied Oakland jazz and sushi club: Yoshi's occupied the commercial anchor space in the new Fillmore Heritage Center, an ambitious mixed-use development built on property that had formerly belonged to the Western Addition A-2 redevelopment project area. The completion of the jazz club, and of the new residential space that surrounded it (along with a jazz heritage center, a film screening space, and a second commercial restaurant property), was the culmination of a decade-long effort to revitalize the Fillmore district, and in so doing, to add a redemptive coda to the agency's half-century legacy of destructive urban renewal. According to the project's champions, jazz was to become the explicit instrument of the district's revitalization: the city's political class sought to rebrand the erstwhile "Harlem of the West" as a jazz preservation district, harnessing the area's nostalgic associations as an engine of future economic growth.

Birds of a Feather, the band specially assembled for the opening-night set, comprised a lineup of jazz all-stars, with a horn line consisting of Nicholas Payton, Ravi Coltrane, and Kenny Garrett backed by Gary Burton on vibraphone, John Patitucci on bass, David Kikoski on piano, and the legendary bebop artist Roy Haynes as drummer and bandleader. What was perhaps just as noteworthy as the band was the reportedly exhaustive sequence of laudatory opening-night speeches that preceded it: by one account, the opening preliminaries lasted some seventy-five minutes, as mayor Gavin Newsom, developer Michael Johnson, and Yoshi's cofounders, Kaz Kajimura and Yoshie Akiba, alongside numerous other dignitaries, paid tribute to the new jazz center. The Reverend Arnold Townsend, a key figure in the community's midcentury fight against the A-2 redevelopment project, enjoined the initiative's benefactors to "lift every voice and sing! . . . We promise to praise you on the high-sounding cymbals."[1] The speeches culminated in a Buddhist purification ceremony intended to rid the space of evil spirits: in the context of the club's opening, the ceremony served as a nod to the damaging impact of the area's earlier redevelopment initiatives.[2]

Bay Area jazz critic Richard Scheinen, noting the considerable stakes riding on the success of the Heritage Center, recalled that "speaker after speaker seemed more than a little nervous" about the venue's prospects, many of them pleading for audiences to extend their patronage of Yoshi's beyond opening night.[3] The considerable political and financial capital marshaled on behalf of the Fillmore Heritage Center provides evidence of a genuine commitment to address the historical wrongs perpetrated by the Redevelopment Agency. Michael Johnson, the lead developer on the Heritage Center and its anchor jazz club, clearly viewed the project as a corrective to the tragic legacy of the SFRA's midcentury actions.[4]

January 2013 would see the opening of the new SF JAZZ Center in the nearby Hayes Valley neighborhood, a striking, freestanding jazz complex dedicated to concert programming for the community. Michael Johnson's project thus arrived on the cusp of a broader moment in which the city's leaders were beginning to commit considerable resources to the visibility and economic viability of jazz in San Francisco. However, despite these potentially encouraging signs, the prospects for the economic sustainability of the Heritage Center itself, and of the Fillmore Jazz Preservation District in general, would come to run up against the community's conflicting visions for the best way to address the region's economic and social recovery.

Moreover, there is a sense in which some of the problems that have dogged the jazz district derive from city boosters' deeply held procedural and ideological assumptions about successful urban planning in the neoliberal era. From a certain standpoint, the inefficacy of the redevelopment agency in arriving at a satisfactory and equitable solution for stakeholders in the Fillmore may be seen as a feature and not a bug. The very nature of the public-private partnership often ensures that projects undertaken with a nominal commitment to rectifying the wrongs of structural violence are actually committed to a different set of priorities. In this case, the terms of the tax increment financing process outlined in the previous chapter, which relies upon significant gains in property valuation to allow redevelopment agencies to pay off municipal bondholders, dictates a fairly narrow range of possible strategies through which governmental redevelopment agencies can intervene to right past wrongs. Nicholas Baham, in his historical study of the St. John Coltrane African Orthodox Church, has documented the extent to which these prevailing assumptions about the proper road to urbanism in San Francisco have made the city the antagonist of the Coltrane Church, and of other efforts to secure a right to the city for black San Franciscans.[5]

I will take up these issues as they pertain to two key moments in the long-standing effort to seek a jazz-themed "renaissance" in the Fillmore district. The first of these moments centered upon an unrealized proposal, sought by the SFRA and private developers in the 1990s, for a project that would have combined a West Coast iteration of the prominent Blue Note jazz club with an AMC movie theater; the second moment saw the realization of a mixed-use residential complex anchored, for a time, by the San Francisco branch of the well-known Yoshi's jazz venue.

"PARCEL 732" AND THE BLUE NOTE / AMC PROPOSAL

The idea of centering the economic revitalization of the Fillmore on the cultivation of a jazz-themed commercial district dates to the late 1980s. At that time, it came to the attention of Jim Jefferson, who was then serving as the president of the San Francisco Black Chamber of Commerce, that a plot of land known as "parcel 732," located at the corner of Fillmore and Eddy Streets, was the last remaining undeveloped land parcel under the jurisdiction of the SFRA's A-2 project area. The chamber seized upon parcel 732 as a potential site for the fostering of a thoroughgoing black business renaissance at the heart of the Western Addition. Soliciting proposals for the plot's development from a variety of bidders, the SFRA ultimately settled on the concept, put forward by Jefferson's consulting firm, of a Jazz Preservation District centering on the stretch of Fillmore Street extending south from Geary to Eddy. Jefferson's plan combined development of the property on the vacant lot with a program for populating existing storefronts with black-owned, Afro-centric businesses modeled on the district's theme: working in concert with a task force appointed by then-mayor Frank Jordan, the redevelopment agency would lease vacant retail locations from their respective landlords, at a rate of a dollar a square foot, and then identify local entrepreneurs whose prospective businesses fit the jazz concept to occupy the designated spaces.[6] Jefferson was frank about the fact that for him, the "jazz" focus of the Preservation District operated primarily as a branding mechanism that could translate the project's Afrocentric focus into terms accessible to a broader Bay Area public: "In my way of thinking jazz was a marketing tool. You have to be a magnet and since jazz has always been associated with African American culture[,] [t]hey . . . go hand in hand. It was a marketing strategy to create the jazz district so that it would resonate with everyone! That was the idea."[7] Working together, the SFRA and the mayor's task force narrowed down a list of prospective businesses to occupy the seven Fillmore street properties leased from area landlords.

However, the central focus of the redevelopment project was to be the question of what to do with "parcel 732." In the 1990s, the initial project proposed for development on 732 was the Fillmore Renaissance Project, an elaborate complex proposed by developer Chuck Collins of WDG Ventures, which would bring together a jazz club with movie theaters and parking availability. The final contours of the project would have combined an AMC movie multiplex with a Bay Area outpost of the famed Blue Note jazz club: preliminary architectural sketches for the prospective complex realize the Blue Note club as a glittering modernist box, set handsomely back from the tree-lined street.[8]

This component of the project, first envisioned by Kent Sims, then-economic development director for the SFRA, was intended as an anchor for the commercial district, a means of generating foot traffic on a perennially underused stretch of Fillmore Street.[9] Unlike the relatively prosperous commercial strip north of Geary, the southern part of Fillmore Street had languished economically, and civic leaders were now worried that the Lower Fillmore's remaining storefronts would soon be lost to "downmarket" fast food chains. The separation of Fillmore Street into "Upper" and "Lower" components is itself a marker of the continuing impact of the SFRA's midcentury redesign: the agency's construction of an expanded Geary corridor had effectively introduced a tacitly racialized line of demarcation through the middle of the Western Addition.[10]

A variety of obstacles—political, economic, and administrative—stood in the way of this initial effort at realizing the Fillmore Jazz District. One issue had to do with staffing turnover in the SFRA leadership, and with the shifting status of the task force initially appointed by the mayor to pursue planning for the Jazz District. Oversight of the task force's duties moved to the SFRA when Kent Sims, Jordan's point person on the jazz district, took a job under the redevelopment agency.[11] When Willie Brown took over as mayor in 1996, though, Sims and redevelopment director Clifford Graves were forced out at the SFRA. Project consultant Jim Jefferson, who had been instrumental in the formulation of the Jazz District concept, lamented the leadership vacuum that this created, and the unwillingness of the city to expend political capital for the project's execution: "I just don't see where the push is to make it happen. . . . Where is the impetus? Who is the advocate in The City?"[12]

Another complication affecting the realization of the Jazz District and its anchor Fillmore Renaissance Project component derived from the delicate local politics surrounding the project. In the numerous open meetings held by the Redevelopment Agency during this period, the SFRA and task-force members consistently found themselves at loggerheads with community activists over the project's direction. A key figure here was Mary Rogers, later eulogized by Mayor Gavin Newsom as the "true matriarch of community activism in San Francisco," who was instrumental in the foundation of WACO during the earlier struggles over the A-1 and A-2 project areas.[13]

Resistance from community activists regarding the Jazz District derived in large part from disappointment over the city's decision to prioritize commercial over residential development: in 1995, the redevelopment agency decided to rezone the remaining project area, which had previously been designated as housing only, in order to allow for the construction of a movie multiplex. Given the role of the Redevelopment Agency in displacing thousands of African-American residents from the Western Addition during the implementation of urban renewal, and given that San Francisco was, even then, experiencing a crisis of affordable housing, Rogers and other Fillmore activists believed that the priority of the SFRA should lie in the development of housing for the community's low-income residents. From their perspective, the proposed project invited a New York–based jazz club and a national theater chain to become the primary beneficiaries of local redevelopment money, directing much-needed resources away from local stakeholders.[14] Observers in the Bay Area jazz community also expressed their concern that the booking policies of a hypothetical Blue Note outpost would likely favor a heavily New York–centered coterie of nationally known musicians, many of whom adhered to a relatively conservative approach to the music, and who would opt to bring their own rhythm sections to the Bay Area rather than hire local artists.[15] For their part, local business owners and city officials believed that a major anchor tenant was necessary to generate foot traffic in the area. Here, the redevelopment agency could point to a study they commissioned which found that the Blue Note club could achieve a gross income of $29.2 million over the first five years of its operation, and that the combined Fillmore Renaissance Project could potentially generate $670,000 in tax revenue for the city, while creating upward of 228 permanent jobs for area residents.[16]

After a long and contentious process, and with the project seemingly shelved after the mayor declined to approve an initial startup loan of $7.5 million, Mayor Brown finally announced during his State of the City address in October 1997 that the Fillmore Renaissance Project would go forward.[17] With more details sorted out by late 1998, the city was prepared to adopt a financing plan in which the Redevelopment Agency would contribute $6 million in funds ($3 million of which constituted loans) to leverage $30 million in private financing for the construction of the Fillmore Renaissance Project. The SFRA would also contribute $5.5 million in streetscape improvements (designed to "beautify" Fillmore street and to encourage foot traffic from the Upper Fillmore), and the city's Parking Authority would provide $12.6 million in financing for the project's parking facilities.[18] The city seemed poised to proceed.

However, as subsequent events would demonstrate, the viability of the Renaissance Project was made vulnerable by its dependence upon a corporate anchor tenant with potentially malleable strategic priorities. During the period of negotiations between AMC, the city, and VDG Ventures in the late 1990s, AMC was overseen by Stanley Durwood, a legendary figure in the movie business who had been instrumental in the invention of the modern multiplex theater. In more recent years, Durwood's strategic vision for AMC was to harness the multiplex as a component of what real estate industry observers referred to as "urban entertainment destinations" (or UEDs): these large-scale developments, often targeting underutilized locations in central city neighborhoods, were often seen as potential instruments of urban revitalization.[19] From this perspective, the proposed Fillmore Renaissance Project could be seen as a more small-scale manifestation of the UED.

However, with Durwood's passing in the summer of 1999, AMC's corporate leadership revisited its strategic vision. Consequently, the Fillmore Renaissance Project, whose construction had been seen as a near certainty, was placed in doubt as AMC imposed new conditions on the deal: AMC made its participation in the Jazz District project contingent upon the city, or some unknown third party, assuming ownership of AMC's Kabuki Theater, located north of Geary in nearby Japantown, as it was unwilling to maintain both properties. The SFRA balked at AMC's proposal, which would have placed them in the position of developing the Fillmore district at Japantown's expense. With the city and the theater company unable to reach a new agreement, AMC walked away from the deal.[20] Despite Chuck Collins's efforts to try again with a new proposal for a mixed-use complex, the SFRA commissioners ultimately voted to terminate its agreement with WGD Ventures and to return the "parcel 732" site to competitive bids.[21]

The frustrating denouement of this initial run at the Fillmore Jazz Preservation District derives from a set of problems that are perhaps endemic to large-scale, top-down redevelopment projects of this kind. The linchpin of the city's hopes for redevelopment focused on the construction of an expensive high-profile flagship project on parcel 732. As noted above, this approach was itself contingent upon the successful completion of negotiations with two entertainment "brands" from outside the Bay Area, neither of which necessarily understood themselves as stakeholders with a commitment to the economic viability of the Western Addition. The outsized reliance of the redevelopment plan on AMC's participation made the viability of the entire economic plan for the Lower Fillmore vulnerable to any change of heart from that anchor tenant. The AMC management ultimately seemed to arrive at the unsurprising conclusion that avoiding market saturation in the Western Addition (AMC's Kabuki Theaters property was located a mere two blocks north of the proposed Blue Note/AMC site) was a more pressing concern than its commitment to bootstrapping economic revitalization in that neighborhood. Earlier on, amid ongoing concerns over the reputation of the Fillmore as an epicenter of urban "blight," Blue Note president Danny Bensusan had cited the club's potential "exposure to risk" as a factor that the city would need to mitigate going forward. In the end, when AMC pulled out of the project, and when the project developer was unable to secure a replacement for the principal anchor tenant, it is not surprising that Blue Note also decided to walk.[22]

Even as the Jazz District presented itself as the SFRA's effort to make amends with stakeholders in the Fillmore community itself, the entire orientation of the project pointed outward: the proposed venues for the anchor tenants targeted consumers from outside the neighborhood, and profits would flow back to these entities based outside of San Francisco. As then-director of the SFRA James Morales indicated, the inclusion of extensive parking facilities in the Renaissance Project was calibrated to appeal to moviegoers from outside the Western Addition, "adding to the sense of security, making people feel more comfortable entering a marginal neighborhood."[23] (One wonders, of course, how residents of the Fillmore would have reacted to seeing their neighborhood characterized in this way.) The proposed improvements to the neighborhood's streetscape prominently featured ornamental renovations to the bridge over the Geary underpass, connecting Upper Fillmore to Lower Fillmore. These measures emphasize flow, foot traffic from the Upper Fillmore, and the Fillmore's appeal to far-flung patrons; in this way, the Fillmore's role as an economic "destination" becomes privileged over its sustainability for area residents.

Beyond this initial proposal for a Renaissance development at the corner of Fillmore and Eddy, another component of the SFRA plan for the Jazz Preservation District during the 1990s might have had the potential to galvanize economic development in a manner that attended more closely to the needs of Western Addition constituents. As noted above, the SFRA implemented a program to lease vacant storefronts within the project area to prospective tenants, and loans were made available to allow these tenants to bring their small-business plans to fruition. However, a combination of factors, including the prohibitive terms of the SFRA's loans, as well as the agency's unwillingness to expend political capital to make the deals happen, ultimately frustrated the Redevelopment Agency's efforts during the 1990s to foster the development of a Jazz District in the Lower Fillmore. In many instances, the agency's insistence upon collateral as a term of the small-business loans posed barriers to entry.[24] Even in those circumstances where the terms of the Redevelopment Agency loans were not prohibitive, critics argued that the agency did not work to enable prospective tenants to circumvent other impediments to development. For instance, Roscoe's Chicken and Waffles, another business slated for inclusion in the Jazz District under the loan program, encountered problems when it entered into negotiations for the use of a space that the Redevelopment Agency had leased, in "as-is" condition, from property owner Richard Szeto. While the SFRA lease effectively subsidized a considerable part of the startup cost for the prospective tenant, Roscoe's and Szeto were unable to arrive at an agreement regarding the millions of dollars in seismic upgrades and structural improvements that would have been necessary to bring the building up to code. Consultant Todd Clayter, who had tried to mediate the dispute, argued that the deal might have gone through if the Redevelopment Agency had been willing to leverage its lease agreement to press Szeto to make the necessary upgrades.[25]

If the Blue Note/AMC development revealed itself to be something of a high-risk debacle, contingent upon the successful alignment of myriad working parts, one imagines that the SFRA's small-business loan/lease initiative, by comparison, might have served as an opportunity for the Redevelopment Agency to achieve success in its development of a viable economic climate for the Lower Fillmore. However, as of the early 2000s, following six years of meetings and negotiations, and with the cancellation of the Blue Note/AMC development, all the Redevelopment Agency had to show for its efforts was the opening of Agonafer Shiferaw's second Rasselas venue at 1534 Fillmore Street, as the lone "jazz-themed" business successfully brought online under the auspices of the Jazz District program.[26]

THE "YOSHI'S EFFECT" AND ITS VICISSITUDES

In the end, the city of San Francisco and its redevelopment agency ultimately *did* succeed in launching a high-profile anchor project for the Jazz Preservation District on "parcel 732." The aforementioned Yoshi's SF, a second location for the venerable Oakland-based jazz club and sushi emporium, would open in November 2007 to become the flagship tenant for a major mixed-use facility bringing together housing units, commercial storefronts, and a Jazz Heritage Center in the heart of the Lower Fillmore. Unsurprisingly, the opening of Yoshi's SF was remembered as a moment of profound emotional catharsis for the Fillmore's advocates, the culminating moment in a half-century struggle to revisit the cultural and economic vibrancy that this neighborhood enjoyed during its midcentury heyday as the "Harlem of the West" (see fig. 3).

At the same time, the jubilation that attended the opening of Yoshi's SF was tempered by a degree of ambivalence in the larger community, stemming from concerns over the club's economic impact, and its economic viability. Within a month of its grand opening, worried observers began referring to something that one writer called the "Yoshi's effect": the new Yoshi's outpost, they argued, may ultimately reveal itself to be little more than a local conduit for the rapid gentrification that was

FIGURE 3. Exterior of Yoshi's SF at the Fillmore Heritage Center, San Francisco, March 2012. Photo by Jason Debord (www.RockSubculture.com).

unfolding on the Upper Fillmore, north of Geary in Pacific Heights. Paolo Lucchesi, the founding editor of the *San Francisco Eater*, expressed concern regarding the impact that the bold new venue would have on Sheba Lounge, a piano bar located close to the Fillmore Heritage Center: "We've made no secret about our awe surrounding the project, but the money is still out whether Yoshi's will reinvigorate the immediate vicinity—remember the surrounding restaurants: Panda Express, Popeye's, Subway (Eat Fresh!)—or merely feed the continual rise north of the Fillmore in lower Pac Heights. True, a high tide floats all boats, but in the case of Sheba Lounge, a new competitor across the way + happy hour promotions + sidewalk signage + reports of small crowds often don't indicate a healthy situation."[27] A year prior to the opening of Yoshi's SF, the owners of the Sheba Lounge, Netsanet Alemayehu and her sister Israel Alemayehu, had benefited from the same SFRA small-business loan program that had enabled Agonafer Shiferaw to open his Rasselas venue in 1999.[28] However, as Lucchesi suggests here, the shadow cast by Yoshi's SF over smaller establishments like Sheba highlights the economic asymmetries that were already beginning to undermine the SFRA's own aspirations for successful economic development: to the extent that the SFRA's strategic actions prioritized highly capitalized projects like the Fillmore Heritage Center (or its failed Blue Note/AMC predecessor) over the need for more incremental contributions to neighborhood growth, how would this affect the economy of the Lower Fillmore?

In any event, there is reason to believe that Yoshi's SF eventually became a victim of its own "effect." A high-profile jazz venue of this kind, in hock to the Redevelopment Agency for the significant startup funds necessary to get things up and running, and facing the steep rents endemic to the San Francisco real estate market, would find it difficult to achieve a booking policy that would allow the club to maintain a level of profitability commensurate with the financial demands placed on its ownership. Even after its decision to forgo jazz acts in favor of a more eclectic calendar of artists, and despite pulling in an average of $10 million in revenue per year, the Fillmore satellite of the established Oakland club continued to encounter financial difficulties, and ultimately closed in the summer of 2014. Here again, the decision of the SFRA, area developers, and local commercial interests to pursue a strategy that relied upon the success of a small number of heavily leveraged "anchor" tenants would seem to have run up against the shortcomings of this preferred model of redevelopment.

In 2002 the SFRA, having reopened competitive bidding for the development of the Fillmore and Eddy site following the demise of the Blue Note/AMC project in the preceding year, settled on a new proposal put forward by Fillmore Development Associates, a consortium of local African-American developers headed by Michael Johnson. The proposal, which envisioned the construction of an elaborate mixed-use project combining a jazz museum and performance space, a jazz lounge-restaurant, the headquarters of the Transport Workers Union (which represented MUNI bus drivers), and a hundred units of affordable and mixed-income housing, had the backing of the Western Addition community from early on, a not-inconsiderable feat given the delicate political negotiations that attended the earlier effort to develop "parcel 732."[29] The community's supportive response to this plan was perhaps a reflection of its emphasis upon housing: the absence of a provision for affordable housing was one of the key sticking points for community activists with regard to the AMC/Blue Note proposal under consideration in the late 1990s. The enthusiasm of Fillmore residents may also have simply reflected the fact that action on this last significant parcel of SFRA land was long overdue. Commenting on the approval of the Yoshi's SF element of the redevelopment plan in 2004, Mary Rogers noted that, "I'm just glad to see this happen. . . . For twenty years, we tried to get something built on this site. This community has been cheated."[30]

However, the local financial sector was less supportive. It took four years for Michael Johnson's consortium of developers to accumulate the $83 million in financing necessary for the building's construction, and the process was further set back when one of Johnson's equity partners withdrew from the consortium. When Johnson and his associates eventually succeeded in assembling some thirteen funding sources for the project, Bay Area financial institutions were reportedly not counted among them. Beyond the SFRA itself, the largest funding source for the development of the Fillmore Heritage Center was the National Electrical Benefit Fund, a Maryland-based union pension fund providing retirement security for members of the International Brotherhood of Electrical Workers; the NEBF provided a $28.2 million construction loan in support of the project. Mugar Enterprises, a Boston-based real estate development firm, provided $6.7 million in financing to support the construction of the building's mezzanine. The SFRA contributed $15 million toward the realization of the Heritage Center, including a $6.5 million land loan, and $8.2 million in financing for tenant improvements, predevelopment activities, and the removal of contaminated soil from the building site. The mayor's Office of Community Development supplemented these loans with a further $5.5 million in financing.[31]

The difficulties Johnson faced in securing financial backing from local investors seem to echo the experience of developer Donald Tishman, who also had to turn to banks outside the Bay Area to realize construction of the Fillmore Center, an earlier mixed-use housing development built on A-2 Project Area land back in the 1980s.[32] In some ways, the absence of local banks in these deals seems to participate in a long legacy of racialized "risk assessment," dating back to the "redlining" practices that thwarted earlier generations of black Fillmore residents and small-business owners.

As I mentioned above, the promise of affordable housing was one of the key features of the Fillmore Heritage Center project that recommended it to Fillmore residents, as it quietly acknowledged (however partially and belatedly) the SFRA's responsibility for eliminating thousands of housing units under the aegis of its A-1 and A-2 project area redevelopment initiatives in the 1950s and 1960s. However, the ability of the new development to address the need for affordable housing in the region was severely constrained by the realities of the San Francisco real estate market, and by the specific pressures of tax increment financing. The sleek edifice, in which the building's clean lines converged on a series of gleaming window walls overlooking the corner of Fillmore and Eddy, would come to house some eighty residential units, of which only twelve would be designated as "affordable": while the market-rate properties would go for between $500,000 and $900,000 (one twelfth-floor two-bedroom unit would be listed for $1,100,000), "affordable," in this context refers to a small number of properties aimed at the middle-income market, and priced between $200,000 and $300,000. These units were set aside to comply with a policy put forward by the city of San Francisco that 15 percent of newly developed housing be offered to the public at "inclusionary," below-market rate pricing.[33] Some 858 applications were submitted by prospective residents seeking one of the FHC "affordable" properties.[34]

While these latter residential units may have been deemed affordable in relation to the inflated property values of a city undergoing rapid gentrification, they serve as a tacit admission that developments of this kind are not always wholly compatible with the provision of lower-income housing for an area's residents. The mechanism of tax increment financing places an onus upon property developers to realize projects with a demonstrated potential for economic growth: the rental and listing prices of residential properties in a project such as the FHC must be sufficient not only to recoup the debt incurred via the project's construction, but should also be sufficient to contribute, in a more general way, to increased property values in the designated project area.[35]

The conditions for expansion of affordable housing in San Francisco are, at the very least, challenging. The situation is made more daunting by other features specific to the San Francisco housing market: the prevalence of rent control (without a countervailing vacancy control to prevent sudden rent increases in vacated rent-control properties); the impact of the Ellis Act (which provides landlords with a mechanism for evicting tenants by going "out of business"); the role of Proposition 13 (which effectively locked in property taxes at a low rate during a period of growing property values, even as landlords declined to pass on these tax savings to tenants); the limitations on expansion imposed by the geography of the San Francisco peninsula—all of these dimensions of the San Francisco housing market make it difficult for affordable housing to be expanded, and also make the residential occupancy of existing low-income tenants vulnerable to the pressures of gentrification and economic expansion.[36]

BOOKING POLICIES AND THE YOSHI'S "BRAND"

With respect to the jazz club component of the Fillmore Heritage Center, the overriding economic concern about Yoshi's SF, prior to its opening, was that it would undercut its own Oakland predecessor, rerouting audiences for the Bay Area's most prestigious jazz bookings to San Francisco. Indeed, in the months following the club's opening, Yoshi's SF seemed to be encroaching upon the market share of its sibling in Oakland's Jack London Square: a frequent booking strategy for the clubs, in which artists would be brought in for successive week-long runs at both the San Francisco and Oakland clubs, often resulted in diminished attendance at both venues, and many of the Oakland regulars began heading in to San Francisco.[37] However, very soon both the Oakland and San Francisco venues would be faced with the significant impact of the 2008 financial crisis. Burdened with debt from its inception, and facing the formidable commercial rental rates of contemporary San Francisco, Yoshi's SF in particular struggled to maintain a revenue flow adequate to cover its daunting expenses.

To a large extent, the financial difficulties faced by Yoshi's derived from its position in an interlocking chain of debt, binding Yoshi's troubles to those faced by the club's landlord, the equity partners owning the Fillmore Heritage Center. In 2004, the SFRA had issued a $4.4 million loan in support of the venue's construction, but Yoshi's ownership soon faced significant cost overruns, with over $15 million spent on tenant improvements alone, almost double the sum initially budgeted. In September and December of 2008, the SFRA would extend two additional loans to Yoshi's owners, totaling $1.3 million and $1.5 million respectively, in order to enable the San Francisco venue to weather the effects of the economic downturn.[38] By themselves, these accumulated debts may not have been unduly onerous to a club whose annual revenue would approach an average of $10 million. However, Yoshi's SF was also subleasing its commercial space at an exorbitant rate, from developers who were themselves facing considerable debt: the team of developers assembled by Michael Johnson to construct the Fillmore Heritage Center, having come in well over budget in the completion of the larger mixed-use project, owed $5.5 million to the city of San Francisco, as they paid a lease on the land parcel made available by the SFRA. The debt load carried by Johnson's consortium of developers in relation to the Fillmore Heritage Center was an important part of the context for Yoshi's troubles, as the venue sought to keep up with occupancy costs of over $60,000 a month (comprising the sublease, maintenance fees, and taxes), which according to co-owner Kajimura was between two to three times what similar institutions paid elsewhere in the industry.[39] Another factor that further complicated the relationship between the Fillmore Heritage Center and its anchor tenant was the fact that Michael Johnson and other members of the FHC developer consortium (Fillmore Development Commercial, LLC) held minority stakes in the jazz club's ownership, alongside majority owner Kajimura, cofounder of the original Yoshi's venue.[40]

The difficult economic circumstances facing Yoshi's prompted its management to explore a range of booking strategies at both of its Bay Area locations. In the months immediately following the launch of Yoshi's SF, the long-standing Yoshi's artistic director Peter Williams set the calendar for both sites, with a lineup of such established jazz artists as Pat Metheny, Pharoah Sanders, and Cassandra Wilson at the Fillmore Yoshi's complementing similar engagements at the Oakland club.[41] In some instances, Yoshi's would book back-to-back engagements for particular artists at both of its venues. As he noted around the time of the club opening, Williams experimented with the idea of featuring its headline artists in contrasting ensemble settings at its two venues, in order to draw out distinct audiences for each engagement:

> We feel like the opening of the San Francisco club provides an opportunity for some cross-marketing between the two locations. . . . For example, Taj Mahal is playing with his Phantom Blues Band this week in San Francisco but will move over to Oakland next week to play in a trio setting. It's good for the artist because they can stay in the Bay Area and not have to travel anywhere, but they get to stretch out and play at two different clubs in two totally different contexts for two different audiences.[42]

However, as I mentioned above, the larger Yoshi's organization soon found itself in the strange position of seeing its two clubs compete with one another for market share. Williams's innovative strategy of back-to-back residencies for prominent performers did not bear fruit: rather than attend engagements at both venues to see artists in contrasting settings, audiences would forgo the Oakland residency. Even the Fillmore venue, however, was earning only 70 percent of its revenue projections, and Kajimura soon found himself looking for increasingly experimental ways to generate additional revenue, with the venue hosting monthly DJ nights and offering membership promotions.[43]

With respect to live programming, Kajimura sought to address its thinly spread jazz audience by assigning Williams to concentrate upon jazz bookings at the Oakland venue. In the Fillmore location, a new artistic director, the formerly Minneapolis-based arts manager Bill Kubeczko, was given a mandate to introduce a more expansive, multigenre booking policy for Yoshi's SF.[44] However, Kubeczko's efforts to build a calendar around such artists as singer-songwriter Michelle Shocked, New Orleans R&B singer Irma Thomas, and 1960s pop artist Lesley Gore constituted a significant departure from Yoshi's "brand" as a programmer of adventurous jazz.

Once again, Kajimura changed course, and in mid-2009 he hired Jason Olaine, Yoshi's erstwhile booking manager at its Oakland venue, who had been instrumental in bringing the Yoshi's name to West Coast prominence during the 1990s. During that period, Olaine had scheduled a range of adventurous engagements, such as the oft-noted multiweek residencies that paired pianist McCoy Tyner together with such jazz heavyweights as Michael Brecker, Joshua Redman, Billy Higgins, or Bobby Hutcherson.[45] These 1990s engagements had effectively rescued the Oakland club from a financial slump, and Olaine sought to employ the same assertive jazz focus in his programming for the Yoshi's SF venue: these ranged from a series of appearances by Charlie Haden, to the experimental showcase known as Go Left Fest, which featured such prominent avant-garde artists as Matthew Shipp, Sunny Murray, and Marshall Allen of the Sun Ra Arkestra, alongside the renowned Oakland poet Ishmael Reed.[46] Olaine's initiative seemed to portend a decisive return to consistent jazz programming at the San Francisco venue.

However, with the continued impact of the recession, Yoshi's SF was unable to sustain the jazz-centered bookings that had historically been associated with the "brand" of the Oakland-based club. If we look to the venue's calendar toward the end of its run, we can see that Yoshi's SF had reverted to a more eclectic artist lineup, in which jazz bookings played an increasingly minor role. While the club continued to program such jazz artists as Roy Hargrove and Cassandra Wilson, the venue's schedule between 2010 and 2014 featured a stylistically diverse range of attractions, in which nostalgia seemed to offer a key draw: their calendar included such acts as Oakland rapper Too $hort, electroclash group Ladytron, and a series of dubstep DJ nights, but also 1960s psychedelic rockers the Zombies, 1980s funk artist Cameo (headlining a Halloween party), and 1980s folk-rock band the Cowboy Junkies.[47] This movement away from exclusively jazz-related programming can be readily understood in light of the significant financial pressures that were facing the Fillmore branch of the Yoshi's club franchise. Nevertheless, the overall effect of this strategy was to undermine the already tenuous connection between the Yoshi's "brand," on the one hand, and the jazz-themed business improvement district for which it was serving as an anchor venue, on the other.

"WALL STREET . . . WITH SLIGHTLY SMALLER NUMBERS"

Under normal circumstances, one might be tempted to attribute the untimely demise of Yoshi's SF solely to issues of booking policy, business strategy, or market timing (among other things, during this period the new SF JAZZ concert venue was being built a short distance away in Hayes Valley). Yoshi's SF was made particularly vulnerable, though, by its structural position in the complex public/private ecology of the Fillmore Heritage Center redevelopment project. As noted earlier, the San Francisco branch of the Yoshi's chain was bound up in a structure of concatenated debt, a delicate construct of fiscal interdependence that was itself made possible (and desirable) by the high political stakes of redevelopment. In its bid to establish a major anchor tenant on "parcel 732," the SFRA "green-lit" a project that was reliant upon large quantities of debt for its realization. However, with this degree of public investment (including an outlay of millions from the city itself), the prospect of default would present itself not merely as an economic failure but also as a political one. Positioned as the potential instruments of the SFRA's redemption, and as markers of the city's investment in its communities, the FHC and its well-appointed venue were in some respects considered too important to fail, assets that the city should endeavor to protect from the full vicissitudes of the open market. It is perhaps for this reason that commentator Chris Barnett, addressing the club's financial restructuring in 2014, wryly alluded to the so-called TARP federal bailout of financial institutions in the wake of the subprime lending crisis in 2008, describing the Yoshi's situation as "an arcane, complex 'workout,' a long drawn-out mediation straight out of Wall Street but with slightly smaller numbers."[48]

The paper trail of correspondence between Michael Johnson's Fillmore Development Commercial Group, the SFRA (and its successor agency in the municipal government, the Office of Community Investment and Infrastructure), and the mayor's Office of Housing and Community Redevelopment, along with local reportage and other documents archived by the San Francisco city government, traces a complex history of negotiations pertaining to the disposition of the Fillmore Heritage Center, on the one hand, and its chief commercial tenant, the Yoshi's venue, on the other. Much of the ensuing conflict surrounded the venue's complicated ownership structure, in which the venue's effective landlord was also a co-owner of the venue: Yoshie Akiba and Kaz Kajimura, the proprietors of Yoshi's Oakland venue, held a majority, two-thirds stake in the Fillmore club, with FHC developer Michael Johnson and other minority partners holding the remaining one-third under an entity known as Fillmore Jazz Clubs.[49]

As noted earlier, Yoshi's SF already carried a significant debt load when it came online in 2007. With the impact of the subsequent economic slowdown, Yoshi's SF increasingly had trouble meeting its rent obligations (payable to Johnson's Fillmore Development Commercial) and covering its day-to-day operating expenses. Kajimura wanted out, and in 2012 he approached his minority partners about the possibility of restructuring the ownership arrangement. Michael Johnson and the other minority owners were not interested in restructuring, arguing that they were invested in the long-term success of the venue. In June 2012, Kajimura unilaterally sought bankruptcy protection, pressing the court to consider a reduction in the club's rent and a restructuring of its debt. Michael Johnson, who was simultaneously the club's landlord and its chief minority partner, heatedly opposed the push toward bankruptcy: the move would potentially result in a loss of revenue for Johnson's developer consortium, Fillmore Development Commercial, which had fallen into arrears on its repayment of the city's $5.5 million construction loan.[50]

Eventually, the conflicting demands of Yoshi's majority and minority partners were resolved via a mediated settlement, overseen by a bankruptcy judge. All of the partners lost their invested equity in the venue: for Kajimura and Akiba, this amounted to $2 million in lost equity, while Johnson and the minority partners collectively lost approximately

$1.2 million. However, the mediated settlement allowed the venue to avoid Chapter 7 bankruptcy, in which all assets would be liquidated: instead, the venue's debt was restructured, and the establishment was left in the hands of Fillmore Live Entertainment, a new entity in which Johnson's Fillmore Development Commercial group held a majority stake. With the dissolution of Yoshi's, Johnson and the other FLE partners each invested $500,000 in capital to bring the venue back online under a new brand.[51]

The disposition of the debt burden of $7.2 million in redevelopment agency funds that Yoshi's had accumulated between 2004 and 2009 was a key source of uncertainty for all parties during the negotiation of the settlement. Ultimately, under the terms of the agreement, Johnson's Fillmore Live Entertainment would assume responsibility for his one-third liability of $2.4 million. However, the remaining sum, comprising Kajimura's $4.8 million share of the debt to the SFRA's successor agency, would reportedly be written off as unsecured debt. This significant loss of public redevelopment money would expose a key shortcoming of the SFRA's strategy of pursuing a high-stakes investment in a single anchor tenant for the Fillmore Jazz District: as Ian Port noted in the *SF Weekly* at the time, the write-off of the redevelopment loan "likely means that $5 million of public money meant to seed the growth of a now-foundering jazz district will simply disappear."[52]

When the terms of the mediated settlement were made known, a spokesperson for the city was careful to emphasize that "we did not forgive this [redevelopment] loan to Kaz [Kajimura]. It was lost with the bankruptcy."[53] Here, the city's redevelopment wing argued that there was no question of a purposeful decision to relinquish public monies, that legal restrictions simply prevented the city from collecting on the unsecured debt. Nevertheless, it is clear from the larger context of the Yoshi's redevelopment project that the state and municipal agencies entrusted with the public financing of the Fillmore Heritage Center and its anchor tenant had invested considerable economic and political capital in the project's realization, and were reluctant to undermine its chances for success, either through too rigid an adherence to the terms of their loans, or through the provision of loans that were insufficiently magnanimous to begin with. Speaking in 2009, in the wake of the SFRA's decision to supplement their initial $4.4 million tenant improvement loan with two additional loans amounting to $2.8 million, James Morales, general counsel to the redevelopment agency, argued that, "We [the SFRA] struggled for many years to get a movie theater or club to the Fillmore. . . . This project [the Yoshi's/FHC complex] came forward, and it became the key ingredient in bringing back a jazz district. No one's talking about the club failing, but clearly the city and the agency have made keeping Yoshi's there a high priority."[54] This reluctance of the city and its redevelopment agency (or successor agency) to impede the success of the "parcel 732" project meant that collecting on the city's $5.5 million loan to Fillmore Development Commercial, in support of the construction of the Fillmore Heritage Center, was for a time also politically off-limits: an anonymous source familiar with the terms of the Yoshi's restructuring noted that, "even though they [FDC] weren't making payments, the city would be reluctant to foreclose. The club would go dark, which would have been disastrous for the neighborhood—and the city would still have to find a new tenant."[55]

Nevertheless, correspondence between the city and the FHC ownership group (who were now primary owners of Yoshi's SF) reflects a frequently tense negotiation process, as the city expressed frustration over the FDC's delays in meeting the terms of its initial agreement for the repayment of its $5.5 million construction loan, and for Johnson's request that $6.2 million of the $7.2 million tenant improvement loan for Yoshi's SF be forgiven.[56] For its part, the mayor's Office of Housing, which had derived funds for its $5.5 million construction loan from a so-called federal Section 108 loan, pointed to the absence of flexibility in its repayment schedule with the Department of Housing and Urban Development.[57]

Matters escalated in late 2013, with the city giving notice that FDC was delinquent on its $5.5 million loan, owing approximately $1.4 million in outstanding payments, accumulated interest, and fees: the city would foreclose upon the lease if the developer consortium did not repay the remaining sum by a date set in November of that year.[58] Olsen Lee, director of the mayor's Office of Housing and Community Development, implied that the FDC partners, in pressing for a further restructuring of their loan even as they failed to honor their existing financial obligations, was in some sense asking city taxpayers to underwrite private-sector losses: "Given the City's commitment to the Fillmore Heritage Center and desire to see the Fillmore Street commercial corridor thrive, my office has held off foreclosing on its secured loan for more than two years while waiting for Borrower [the FHC developer consortium] to put forth a viable plan to restructure the project's finances. . . . My office's goal was to support the Western Addition neighborhood, not provide an ongoing subsidy to the benefit of short-term investors."[59]

In the end, Michael Johnson and the other FDC partners were granted a stay on the outstanding amount from the $5.5 million loan, with the city allowing a reduction in rent payments as the FHC underwent a transition to a new anchor tenant: Johnson's Fillmore Live Entertainment Group had assumed a complete ownership stake in the former Yoshi's site, and they rebranded and relaunched the space as the Addition. However, despite the rebrand, the venue remained a difficult enterprise to sustain. Local observers argued that the space was simply "too big" to fill to capacity—in its guise as Yoshi's SF, the cavernous 420-seat club was supplemented by 370 additional restaurant seats in its Japanese-themed lounge—and that it could be more profitably reconfigured as a set of smaller eateries or performance spaces.[60] Ultimately, in January 2015, barely three months after its relaunch, the Addition was itself shuttered.[61]

AGONAFER SHIFERAW AND THE RASSELAS JAZZ CLUB

What the Yoshi's-centered Fillmore Heritage Center has in common with its conceptual predecessor, the Blue Note/AMC partnership proposed for the Fillmore Renaissance Project in the late 1990s, is the notion that a high-profile "destination" site targeting tourists and patrons from outside the Fillmore district can, or should, serve as the principal driver of local economic development. The "urban destination" of a major anchor project provides city officials with an attractive narrative hook, with its tacit promise that a single transformative alteration in the built environment can have a sweepingly dramatic ameliorative impact on the surrounding neighborhood.

However, the prioritization of major anchor projects as the engine of redevelopment in the Fillmore has been problematic for a variety of reasons. For one thing, the scenario at least loosely resembles the "jazz bubble" I discussed in chapter 4: here, the idea of jazz as a beacon for economic growth serves as the catalyst for city officials, private developers, and other entities to pursue a heavily leveraged investment in a single "urban destination," even as a project of this magnitude exposes them and the surrounding community to the ramifications of failure. Moreover, as I noted earlier, this approach has come at the expense of smaller local stakeholders within the redevelopment project area, whose role in the cultivation of the jazz redevelopment district has been eclipsed by the primacy of "Parcel 732," and whose importance resides in their contribution to the kind of densely sustainable urban fabric that no one larger project can sustain.

What kind of entity sought to make use of the SFRA's small-business loan program, and how did this manifest itself on the ground? The case of Rassalas Jazz Club, a jazz club and Ethiopian eatery owned by proprietor Agonafer Shiferaw, is useful not only because it provides us with a compelling window onto the approach taken by the SFRA in its oversight of its small-business loan program, but because for a time, at least, it constituted the only other prominent jazz club in the district outside of Yoshi's.[62] Born in Addis Ababa, Agonafer Shiferaw moved to the Bay Area in 1970 to study at San Francisco State University, where he concentrated in management. After having served in the city government of San Francisco for ten years, Shiferaw set out on his own to become an entrepreneur. His ultimate intention was to open a restaurant specializing in Ethiopian food (an as-yet untapped market in the Bay Area in the mid-1980s), but he started in business with a hardware store, which he set up in 1984 while laying the groundwork for his restaurant business. Finally in 1986, Shiferaw found an opportunity to lease a bar across the street from his hardware store, at the corner of California and Divisadero Streets a few blocks north of the Western Addition.[63]

It was at this location that Shiferaw first opened Rasselas, an Ethiopian restaurant that would soon come to double as a live jazz venue. Shiferaw approached the jazz business with the same practicality that he had brought to the business of hardware sales. He began traveling all over the country to scout for different musicians, and to understand how other club promoters made things work. Even as he acknowledged the paramount importance of artistic quality, Shiferaw noted, "I figured out that there is a difference between the business of jazz, and the art of jazz and what I needed to do was what I did best: Manage the business of jazz, rather than the art of jazz."[64]

Shiferaw had maintained contacts in the municipal government, owing to his work for the city in his postcollege years, and in the mid 1990s, he was approached by the agency about the possibility of opening a new, Fillmore outpost for his jazz club, to be located within the Fillmore Jazz District. The resulting agreement stipulated an initial $737,000 loan for tenant improvements to the existing property; Shiferaw in turn initially invested upward of $1 million in equity and private-sector loans in the new project.[65] Rassellas was built on the site of a former fish market dating to the 1930s; the design for Shiferaw's club maintained the exposed brick walls of the original space, detailed with art-deco gestures, and featured an open, multitiered space for performance and a café open to clientele during the daytime.[66]

From a programming standpoint, the new Rasselas venue became an important site for presenting local jazz in San Francisco, alongside a variety of other genres. Shiferaw cites one successful early residency involving the working quartet of prominent local bandleader and Afro-Cuban percussionist Babatunde Lea, comprising Hilton Ruiz, Ernie Watts, and Geoff Brennan; Lea's record label, Motema Music, assisted by co-sponsoring a number of concerts with Rasselas.[67] Building upon its existing reputation at its previous location, Rasselas was able to program a variety of music, ranging from jazz artists such as Pharoah Sanders and John Handy, to pop and R&B figures such as Tracy Chapman, Sheila E., and Ledisi; the latter artist established herself in the Bay Area in large part through frequent residencies at the club in the early 2000s.[68] Moreover, Rasselas became an important home for local jazz in San Francisco, featuring music extending from the hard bop and funk of Bohemian Knuckleboogie (formerly led by the late trumpeter Mike Pitre) to the straightahead jazz of tenor saxophonist Charles Unger, who would hold down a weekly Sunday-night slot at the club.[69] The venue would also serve as an after-hours stop during the Fillmore Jazz Festival, an annual free music festival held on Fillmore Street in early July.[70]

Despite these musical successes, Shiferaw would face some of the same struggles as other small businesses, along with other challenges particular to jazz venues operating in the context of the Fillmore Jazz District. A 2011 article cites the economic difficulties faced by local jazz musicians, who individually faced a going rate at the time of $40 a night (or roughly $13 an hour) at venues such as Rassellas or the neighboring Sheba Piano Lounge, run by fellow Ethiopian-American Netsanet Alemayehu. Indeed, local artists such as bassists Ollie Dudek and Caroline Chung had gone so far as to press the city for a wage floor for jazz musicians in the Fillmore Jazz District. For their part, though, Shiferaw, Alemayehu, and other club owners argued that from their perspective, the modest pay for musicians was justifiable given the additional operating costs involved in running a jazz venue. Alemayehu argued that compensation for musicians and other aspects of the nightly entertainment constituted upward of a third of her nightly operating expenses; Shiferaw pointed out that alongside such regular business expenses, he was also facing licensing fees imposed by ASCAP for any live music making use of nonoriginal musical covers. Shiferaw in particular cited frustration with the image of jazz club owners as "greedy," mentioning the economic realities faced by live music venues, and the reluctance of many jazz fans to run up the kind of food and beverage tab that would be

adequate to sustain the range of musical acts they had come to see:
"Like the night before last, we had a jam session. . . . We made two
hundred dollars. You know how much I paid the band? One hundred
sixty dollars. . . . People come in and don't drink, but they jam. I say,
'Put yourself in my position, and tell me how I can pay you more.'"[71]
Part of the disconnect regarding artist wages in the Fillmore lay in the
vicissitudes of the redevelopment initiative itself, which for some observers was seen to create an expectation that professional jazz artists,
working in the historically resonant jazz district during a period of city-
backed revitalization, would receive compensation commensurate with
the spirit of the initiative. Artists pointed out that clientele at Yoshi's,
Sheba, and Rasselas, perhaps deceived by the polished, upmarket trappings of the venues, might find it difficult to imagine that they were
receiving the same pay as many low-wage service workers in the area.[72]

The particulars of the redevelopment agency's engagement with
small business in the Jazz District posed particular problems for Shiferaw's operation. As noted earlier, an early barrier to Shiferaw's move
into the Fillmore, and one that affected other businesses subject to the
small-business loan program, were the stringent collateral requirements
imposed on the projects. In one account, Shiferaw indicates that he had
set about leveraging his previous property on California Street, valued
at $4 million, to invest in the new club, when the SFRA belatedly asked
him to provide collateral for a $737,000 loan supporting renovations.
At the very least, Shiferaw succeeded in seeing through the realization
of his project; in at least one other case, the collateral requirement
proved to pose an insurmountable problem for the prospective client.
Hasan Al-Ghani's Oakland-based restaurant, Rosalies Taste of New
Orleans, had been tapped to serve as a potential addition to the Jazz
District. Al-Ghani was three years into planning, having spent over
$8,000 on architectural plans, when he learned that the $214,600 loan
he had negotiated with the Redevelopment Agency was contingent
upon the provision of collateral: while Al-Ghani offered to put up
kitchen equipment and other assets as a surety on the loan, the Redevelopment Agency declined to accept these as collateral, and consequently
the Rosalies project fell through. While a spokesperson from the SFRA
defended its insistence upon collateral property as a condition of the
loans, arguing that it served as a means of confirming that a prospective
business had "skin in the game," local business consultant Derf Butler
pointed out that the SFRA's request for collateral was unrealistic for
many small, black-owned businesses, whose proprietors often did not

own property that could be used to secure a loan. Butler argued that the Redevelopment Agency should have underwritten the loans, noting that the existing program "was not [properly] designed to get black businesses in those spaces."[73]

Alongside the collateral issue, Shiferaw would later point to a variety of areas where he felt that the SFRA had not been entirely supportive of his efforts to keep Rasselas financially sustainable. He argues that when he sought to acquire the property housing Rasselas in 2004, "certain Agency staff discouraged me in my pursuit to achieve ownership of the commercial real estate, and in some instances actually frustrated my aspiration for ownership."[74] Elsewhere, Shiferaw has argued that the redevelopment agency had never prioritized black ownership, that the SFRA "consider[s] economic development in terms of people getting employed for $8, $9, $10 per hour. . . . We consider economic development to be helping African Americans to own their own business."[75]

In 2004, Shiferaw did successfully acquire the property, with the assistance of private financing, but by 2008, with the advent of the global financial crisis, he was facing mounting financial pressures, alongside other businesses in the Fillmore. In early 2009, Shiferaw requested an alteration of the terms of his loan with the SFRA, to allow for an additional amount to be added to the principal of the loan, and with a two-year deferral of loan repayments. The minutes of the SFRA meeting in early 2009, in which Shiferaw put forth his request, provide us with an interesting look into deliberations surrounding the terms imposed upon loan recipients by the SFRA, as the agency sought a degree of tight managerial control over projects under the agency's oversight.

As Shiferaw had set about making improvements to his business, in line with the stipulations of preceding loan adjustments, the agency had required that a restaurant consultant be present to make recommendations to Shiferaw about how best to increase revenue, reduce expenses, broaden the audience for the venue, and develop marketing strategies.[76] Presented with Shiferaw's request for an adjustment of the loan terms at the January 2009 meeting, SFRA commissioner Rick Swig noted that he was "not satisfied" with Shiferaw's figures, and sought to make the disbursement of new funds contingent upon the recommendations of the appointed restaurant consultant, and subject to the judgment of the executive director of the redevelopment agency.[77] In response, other commissioners expressed concerns about the barriers that such a stipulation would impose. Linda Cheu pointed out that in the context of grim economic circumstances brought about by the recession, there was a danger of losing the very businesses that the SFRA was charged with supporting. Francee Covington, for her part, argued that, "the businesses belong to the people who started the business, they do not belong to the restaurant consultant, no business consultant comes in and tells you exactly what you're supposed to do."[78] To be sure, this moment constituted one isolated point of friction in a longer meeting, and in any case, the SFRA commissioners did ultimately vote unanimously to approve Shiferaw's request, without additional conditions attached. Nevertheless, the incident provides us with a useful glimpse into the powers at the disposal of the redevelopment agency, and its ability to impose lending conditions of a kind that small-business loan recipients might find onerous or potentially damaging.

Indeed, throughout his period of collaboration with the SFRA, Shiferaw has been vocal about his disappointment with the city and the redevelopment agency as stewards of the Fillmore Jazz District initiative. When Rasselas finally closed in 2013, after years of weathering a difficult postrecession economic climate, Shiferaw penned a letter to the mayor's office, arguing that the closure of his establishment was indicative of a larger failure on the part of the redevelopment agency, which he saw as providing insufficient follow-through on its promise of policies and programming designed to benefit the jazz district:

> Many times, I felt as if certain Agency staff wanted me to fail. Once I opened Rasselas there was, in my opinion, a demonstrable lack of energy and interest by the Agency staff to follow through on important policies and programs. . . . In a report to the Agency Commission in 1995 then Executive Director Clifford Graves, stated that the success and sustainability of the Jazz Preservation District required . . . that recruitment of theme and supporting tenants is essential and that "financing sources" and "financing methods" associated with the unique environment of lower Fillmore Street must be devised; this call to pro-active and creative support from the City and County of San Francisco was never materialized in my opinion.[79]

Agonafer Shiferaw's experience with the SFRA, following his opening of a second Rasselas club on Fillmore, illustrates some of the pitfalls facing small businesses in their collaboration with the redevelopment agency. Among other issues, Shiferaw and other small-business owners in the Fillmore point to what they see as the unwillingness of the redevelopment agency to offer generous credit terms to the establishments in its rolling small-business loan program, even as considerable sums were loaned to help realize the Yoshi's/FHC venture. As important as anything here was the generalized sense that the redevelopment agency needed to devote more resources and time toward cultivating the more granular dimensions of a neighborhood economy, a task that depends as much upon small successes as on large ones.

YOSHI'S SF, THE FILLMORE JAZZ DISTRICT, AND SPECULATIVE URBANISM

Alongside the SFRA's marginalization of small businesses, a second issue with the prioritization of major anchor projects in the Fillmore is that neither the AMC/Blue Note project nor the subsequent Yoshi's/FHC project seemed to prioritize the existing residents of the Fillmore district. As noted earlier, the civic posture of the all-commercial AMC/Blue Note project fell afoul of criticism by local activists, who pointed to the project's failure to address the neighborhood's crisis of affordable housing. The mixed-use FHC development, whose provision of "inclusory" housing paled in comparison to its surfeit of market-rate properties for affluent homebuyers, was itself only partially responsive to this earlier criticism, particularly in the sense that it stood to exacerbate the gentrification of the Fillmore.

Moreover, one larger, overriding problem with both projects is that the financial model of speculative urbanism that favors large, stand-alone anchor projects is dependent upon the accumulation of substantial amounts of debt for its realization. This amassing of debt around a small number of major projects exposes both debtors and creditors to a significant level of risk, particularly in the context of the kind of market downturn that we witnessed in 2008: the losses of municipal bondholders may have been mitigated by the general robustness of the San Francisco real estate market, but the exposure of the SFRA, the Yoshi's ownership consortium, and the FDC developer partnership to accumulated debt made them vulnerable to any delays or setbacks in the construction or operation of the Fillmore Heritage Center project and its principal commercial tenant.

In addition to being creditors to development projects in the FHC mold, California's redevelopment agencies were also debtors, reliant upon so-called "tax allocation bonds" to provide the up-front financing necessary to support development initiatives. As one such entity, the San Francisco Redevelopment Agency weathered the 2008 financial downturn better than many California CRAs. As Davidson and Ward have argued, a great many municipalities have belatedly discovered the downside to their reliance upon the debt-supported financing mechanism of the redevelopment agencies: with the dissolution of the CRAs under

Jerry Brown in 2011 and 2012, these municipalities struggled to meet operating expenses in the absence of bond proceeds, even as they faced onerous debt burdens left over from the winding down of the redevelopment agencies; in some cases, the municipalities were forced to enter into bankruptcy proceedings.[80] In the case of the SFRA, the former CRA has not placed its parent municipality in such a grave position, though it continues to be subject to scrutiny from the ratings agencies. The Moody's rating agency has issued a somewhat lackluster "Ba1" rating on the debt held by San Francisco's successor agency, arguing that its immersion in a real estate market with robust valuations was not sufficient to bring the former CRA up to "investment grade" status (a rating of Baa3 or higher), because it was not able to consistently maintain a certain threshold of cash flow over and beyond its specific debt repayment obligations.[81]

Even as it constitutes one component of the former SFRA's initiatives, the precarious financial status of the Yoshi's/FHC project perhaps helps to illuminate the context in which the redevelopment agency of a booming city could receive an anemic rating on its debt. The inability of the SFRA or its successor agency to recoup its $7.2 million investment in the Yoshi's SF venture is one component of a larger picture of financial underperformance in the SFRA's Fillmore project area. An audit of the A-2 project area conducted by the city controller's office in 2010 (prior to Yoshi's de facto bankruptcy) faulted the SFRA for having failed to properly track its loan disbursements to project recipients, and to collect upon outstanding loans.[82]

In some cases, the SFRA and city agencies may have created the conditions in which collecting upon loan repayments would become impossible. For example, in the case of Powell's Place, a popular Hayes Valley barbeque establishment that the redevelopment agency had tapped for relocation to Fillmore Street, bureaucratic delays contributed heavily to its failure as a potential showcase for the SFRA "jazz district." To realize the relocation project, proprietor Emmitt Powell had mortgaged his home, in addition to a second Oakland property, and had taken on $360,000 in loans from the SFRA's revolving lending program. However, a six-month delay in the city's issuing of the necessary permits kept the establishment closed, even as Powell continued to face lease payments for the new site. Finding himself over $60,000 in arrears on loan payments by the time the restaurant opened in February 2005, Powell was forced to close the new location only two years later, having lost his home in the process. After a successful thirty-year run in the Hayes

Valley location, there was a sense in which the renowned soul-food eatery and its long-standing owner were fatally undermined by the good intentions of the city and its redevelopment agency.[83]

In a context where the success of redevelopment projects (and the recouping of loan disbursements by the SFRA or its successor agency) was contingent upon the ability of loan recipients to repay their debts, a good part of the problem with the A-2 project area initiatives seems to derive from basic issues of administrative coordination between the city, the redevelopment agency, and the loan recipients. In such cases, the failure of major debt-dependent redevelopment projects will often place all parties concerned in a worse place financially than if the project were never initiated to begin with.

CONCLUSION: JAZZ, NEOLIBERAL URBANISM, AND THE RIGHT TO THE CITY

In the previous chapter, I argued that the contested place of jazz in contemporary urbanisms could be understood against the backdrop of our ongoing deliberations over the right to the city: if we proceed from the understanding that the public has a claim to a built environment given over to use values that are not wholly reducible to commodification or market logics, then our sense of jazz within the urban environment is necessarily altered. Seen from this vantage point, it is often difficult to see how our conventional business models could provide a space for jazz performance sites that faithfully attend to the right to the city, that meaningfully engage with a city's citizens as stakeholders in the urban compact.

The model of public-private partnership discussed in this chapter adds a further layer of complexity to these deliberations. Proceeding from an elitist and technocratic set of assumptions, an earlier generation of advocates for urban renewal harnessed the powerful legal and funding mechanisms of midcentury urban redevelopment agencies to impose sweeping changes upon the built environment, displacing and dismantling those residents and commercial enterprises whose mixed-use "scene of scenes," with their dense overlay of mutually supportive restaurants, family businesses, and live performance venues, helped to establish sites of community for urban stakeholders. More recently, a newer generation of urban boosters have promised to make amends for the excessive zeal of their modernist predecessors, leveraging bold new instruments of financial capital in the pursuit of urban revitalization.

Here, music becomes at once a symbolic touchstone for urban redemption and a conduit for the reimagining of urban space necessary for any process of gentrification.

In this context of urban gentrification and corporatization, would another model of urbanism been possible, one in keeping with a recognition of the right to the city? In this connection, it is worth noting the proposal put forward by Nicholas Louis Baham III, in concert with Frederick Harris and a consortium of architects and developers, to secure financing from the SFRA to establish a St. John Coltrane University of Arts and Social Justice; as its name suggests, the university was a proposed initiative of the locally renowned St. John Coltrane Church, directed by Archbishop Franzo King. The proposal was one of several put forward for the refurbishing of a former municipal railway substation, one of the last remaining land parcels held by the SFRA as part of the A-2 project area. The group seeking to acquire the property for the use of the Coltrane Church did so on behalf of Leola King, who as I noted above was among those most egregiously affected by the redevelopment agency's use of eminent domain during the midcentury dismantling of the Western Addition.[84]

The project sought to further the values of social justice pursued by the Coltrane Church since its founding in the mid-1960s. The proposed institution would have become a site for the instruction of a community-engaged jazz pedagogy consistent with the aims of such institutions as Horace Tapscott's UGMAA in Los Angeles: in the proposal, which featured a curriculum that harnessed the field of African-American studies as a point of departure for inquiries into music, literature, or film, instruction in aesthetic traditions would be self-consciously linked to the exploration of the cultural, material, and political circumstances in which they were developed. As Baham recounts, the institution "would place central importance on the ability of the arts to form communities and counter-narratives to discursive formations and practices in other social domains. . . . This progressive pedagogy of the arts was a specific attempt . . . to teach improvisation as a cultural act that could inform all social domains including politics and spirituality."[85] In the event that it had taken place, the greenlighting of this Coltrane Church proposal would have constituted an important shift in priorities for the SFRA Jazz District project, given the plan's decidedly noncommercial focus, its furtherance of the goals of a long-standing Bay Area institution, and most importantly, its basic orientation toward the inhabitants of the Fillmore community.

When the SFRA turned down the proposal, and suggested instead that the Coltrane Church become a tenant of the SFRA, with the redevelopment agency retaining control over the site, the archbishop refused: at the core of this refusal, according to Baham, was an unwillingness to cede the autonomy of the church, and its "long-standing reputation as a fundamentally counterhegemonic community organization."[86] In the end, monies ostensibly earmarked for the Muni substation proposals were quietly redirected toward Yoshi's and the Fillmore Heritage Center. In the meantime, the Coltrane Church itself, which leased a storefront space in the West Bay Conference Center on Fillmore for many years, left the district after a long dispute with its landlord.[87]

The SFRA's decision to use redevelopment funds to salvage the struggling Yoshi's project, rather than to help realize a project more in keeping with the distinctive social justice vision of the Coltrane Church, is perhaps unsurprising in light of the larger ideological priorities of redevelopment agencies in the neoliberal era. Here, as with the New Orleans Peoples Jazz Health Market project outlined in the introduction to this book, the jazz legacy becomes bound up in the neoliberal economy in a tangential and unexpected way: it is made monetizeable not by way of music's historically conventional relation to the commodity form (that is, via sales of recordings), but as an idea of playful, soulful spirit that may be commandeered in favor of what Ana Y. Ramos-Zayas, in her discussion of the affective life of Latino/a residents in contemporary Newark, refers to as "the feel that sells," an "emotional commonsense" that serves to align our affective predispositions with the needs of the market.[88] A neighborhood that attends to its historical jazz legacy is not only engaged in a process of nostalgic recuperation, but is also aligning itself with a mode of black musical production that has been "made safe" for urban consumption in the early twenty-first century.[89]

The difficulty here is that from a certain standpoint, neither jazz nor the city can be understood solely, or even primarily, as a conduit of financial capital or vectors of consumerism. At a certain level, both jazz performance and urban centers are spaces (physical or sonic) that people *inhabit:* the city is not simply a repository of leveraged assets, but home to the people that live in it; the jazz performance, for its part, is always a society in miniature, and its energy (like that of the city's) is driven as much by the internal relationships of its participants as by any external force of commerce or market pressure. I have meditated at length, here, in this chapter and in previous ones, about the inextricable relationship between jazz and the present regime of accumulation, about the ways in which neoliberal ideas and market logics inhabit our contemporary understanding of jazz culture, and shape it from within. In the end, though, the challenge for us is to locate those aspects of the jazz legacy that contain within them the seeds of other possibilities, of those worlds that might unfold beyond the parameters of exchange value. At stake here, alongside the right to the city, is a struggle over a right to a *culture,* a collective effort to ensure that the promise latent within the music's improvised and dynamic relationships can continue to be realized in the face of a daunting and turbulent historical moment.

Notes

INTRODUCTION

1. "The New Orleans Jazz Orchestra (NOJO) Kicks Off the Grand Opening of the People's Health New Orleans Jazz Market." Goldman Sachs, posted 3 April 2015, www.goldmansachs.com/what-we-do/investing-and-lending/impact-investing/case-studies/nojo-multimedia/press-release.pdf (accessed 24 October 2017); "About NOJO," New Orleans Jazz Orchestra, http://thenojo.thecanary collective.com/pages/detail/141/About-NOJO (accessed 23 October 2017).

2. "New Orleans Jazz Orchestra (NOJO)."

3. Lydia DePillis, "Goldman Sachs Thinks It Can Make Money by Being a Do-Gooder," *Washington Post,* 5 November 2013; "Social Impact Bonds," GoldmanSachs.com, posted October 2014, www.goldmansachs.com/our-thinking /pages/social-impact-bonds.html (accessed 7 November 2017). For specific cases, see Eduardo Porter, "Wall St. Money Meets Social Policy at Rikers Island," *New York Times,* 28 July 2015.

4. On social bonds and the "pay-for-success" model, see Drew Von Glahn and Caroline Whistler, "Pay for Success Programs: An Introduction," *Policy and Practice,* June 2011, 19–22.

5. Irvin Mayfield, in "Impact Investing: New Orleans Jazz Orchestra, New Orleans, LA," Goldman Sachs, www.goldmansachs.com/what-we-do/investing-and-lending/impact-investing/case-studies/nojo-nola.html (accessed 4 January 2016).

6. Owen Courrèges, "Irvin Mayfield's Jazz Market and the Forced Gentrifi-cation of Central City," UptownMessenger.com, posted 8 June 2015, http:// uptownmessenger.com/2015/06/owen-courreges-irwin-mayfields-jazz-market-and-the-forced-gentrification-of-central-city (accessed 28 October 2017). May-field has been criticized for what observers see as a misuse of his fundraising authority; on this point, see Richard Rainey, "Irvin Mayfield Steered Library

Donations to His Jazz Education Project, TV Station Reports," *Times-Picayune*, 6 May 2015.

7. On CDOs and mortgage-backed securities, see Gérard Duménil and Dominique Lévy, *The Crisis of Neoliberalism* (Cambridge, MA: Harvard University Press 2011), 191; David Kotz, *The Rise and Fall of Neoliberal Capitalism* (Cambridge, MA: Harvard University Press, 2015), 133.

8. Clara Miller, "Social Impact Bonds' Slippery Slope," HuffingtonPost.com, posted 9 February 2016, www.huffingtonpost.com/clara-miller/social-impact-bonds-slipp_b_7170474.html (accessed 24 October 2017).

9. See, for instance, Mark Rosenman, "Why Let Financial Institutions Profit From Financing Services for the Needy?" *Chronicle of Philanthropy*, 12 December 2013, https://philanthropy.com/article/Why-Let-Financial-Institutions/153901 (accessed 26 October 2017).

10. Lloyd Blankfein, in "Goldman Sachs Weighs In on Social Impact Bonds," Governing.com, posted 14 November 2013, www.governing.com/topics/finance/gov-goldman-sachs-weighs-social-impact-bonds.html (23 October 2017). Investment banks may be far less financially "vested" in social amelioration schemes than their touted publicity may imply. See Jessica Toonkel, "Analysis: Wall Street Sees Social-Impact Bonds as Way to Do Good and Do Well," Reuters.com, posted 12 November 2013, www.reuters.com/article/us-goldman-social-impact-bond-analysis-idUSBRE9AB0ZD20131112 (accessed 28 October 2017).

11. Toonkel, "Wall Street Sees Social-Impact Bonds." On Goldman Sachs's image problem in particular, see Matt Taibbi, "The Great American Bubble Machine," *Rolling Stone*, 5 April 2010.

12. Jazz critic Gary Giddins first popularized this moniker in 1982. See Gary Giddins, "Jazz Turns Neoclassical," *Atlantic Monthly*, September 1982, 156–59. The frequent application of the phrase "young lions" to refer to the youthful musicians of the neoclassicist movement likely derives from an important concert at the 1982 Kool Jazz Festival in New York, billed as the "Young Lions of Jazz," and featuring such artists as Wynton Marsalis, Kevin Eubanks, Anthony Davis, and Bobby McFerrin. See Robert Palmer, "Perils Confront the Young Lions of Jazz," *New York Times*, 22 May 1982.

In citing the same music, critic Joachim-Ernst Berendt, in his idiosyncratic taxonomy of 1970s and 1980s jazz, refers to jazz "classicism"; Berendt assigns the label of "neoclassicist" to a more experimental and expansive vein of late 1970s jazz traditionalism, comprising such artist as Henry Threadgill, David Murray, and Arthur Blythe. See Joachim-Erenst Berendt and Günther Huessman, *The Jazz Book: From Ragtime to the 21st Century*, 7th ed. (Chicago: Lawrence Hill Books, 2009), 45–50.

13. For discussions of the neoclassicist sensibility in jazz, see Berendt and Huessman, *Jazz Book*, 45–50; David Ake, *Jazz Cultures* (Berkeley: University of California Press, 2002), 146–77; Herman Gray, *Cultural Moves: African Americans and the Politics of Representation* (Berkeley: University of California Press, 2005), 32–51; Scott DeVeaux, "Constructing the Jazz Tradition: Jazz Historiography," *Black American Literature Forum* 25/3 (Fall 1991): 527–29.

14. For a good overview of many of the key artists associated with the neoclassicist revival in the 1980s and early 1990s, see Stuart Nicholson,

Jazz: The 1980s Resurgence (New York: Da Capo Press, 1995), 221–54 and *passim*.

15. See Scott DeVeaux, *The Birth of Bebop: A Social and Musical History* (Berkeley: University of California Press, 1997); Aaron Johnson, "Jazz and Radio in the United States: Mediation, Genre, and Patronage" (Ph.D. diss., Columbia University, 2014).

16. See Ake, *Jazz Cultures;* Gabriel Solis, *Thelonious Monk Quartet with John Coltrane at Carnegie Hall* (New York: Oxford University Press, 2014); Mark Laver, *Jazz Sells: Music, Marketing, and Meaning* (New York: Routledge, 2014); Tracy McMullen, "Identity for Sale: Glenn Miller, Wynton Marsalis, and Cultural Replay in Music," in *Big Ears: Listening for Gender in Jazz Studies,* edited by Nichole Rustin and Sherrie Tucker (Durham, NC: Duke University Press, 2008), 129–56.

17. Adam Krims, *Music and Urban Geography* (New York: Routledge, 2007); Timothy Taylor, *Music and Capitalism: A History of the Present* (Chicago: University of Chicago Press, 2016). See also Andrea Moore, "Neoliberalism and the Musical Entrepreneur," *Journal of the Society for American Music* 10/1 (February 2016): 33–53; for an account of the relationship between twentieth-century music and consumer subjectivities, see Robert Fink, *Repeating Ourselves: American Minimal Music as Cultural Practice* (Berkeley: University of California Press, 2005), 62–166.

18. For discussions of the theory, practice, and geopolitical impact of neoliberalism, see Gérard Duménil and Dominique Lévy, *Capital Resurgent: Roots of the Neoliberal Revolution,* translated by Derek Jeffords (Cambridge, MA: Harvard University Press, 2004); David Harvey, *A Brief History of Neoliberalism* (New York: Oxford University Press, 2005); Thomas Lemke, "'The Birth of Biopolitics'—Michel Foucault's Lecture at the Collège de France on Neoliberal Governmentality," *Economy and Society* 30/2 (May 2001): 190–207; Wendy Brown, "Neoliberalism and the End of Liberal Democracy," *Theory and Event* 7/1 (2003): n.p., https://muse.jhu.edu/article/48659 (accessed 23 October 2017).

19. Harvey, *Brief History of Neoliberalism,* 2.

20. Jodi Dean, *Democracy and Other Neoliberal Fantasies: Communicative Capitalism and Left Politics* (Durham, NC: Duke University Press, 2009), 53–54; see also Harvey, *Brief History of Neoliberalism,* 23–26.

21. On the promulgation of neoliberal ideologies in think tanks, academia, and contemporary media, see Harvey, *Brief History of Neoliberalism,* 39–44.

22. Michel Foucault, *The Birth of Biopolitics: Lectures at the Collège de France 1978–79,* edited by Michel Senellart et al., translated by Graham Burchell (Basingstoke, England: Palgrave Macmillan, 2008), 222–30.

23. Alongside the construction of the Jazz Market in New Orleans, the Jazz at Lincoln Center facilities in New York and the SF Jazz Center in San Francisco, plans have been under way to construct a new home for the Jazz Bakery performance venue in Culver City, designed by Frank Gehry. See Chris Barton, "What's Frank Gehry Designing for the Jazz Bakery? Drawings Shown at LACMA," *Los Angeles Times,* 7 September 2015.

24. As David LaRosa has pointed out, Nielsen's end-of-year report on music consumption in 2014 situates jazz as "the least popular genre" in the United

States, in terms of album sales, downloads, and streaming statistics. See David LaRosa, "Jazz Has Become the Least-Popular Genre in the U.S.," TheJazzLine. com, posted 9 March 2015, http://thejazzline.com/news/2015/03/jazz-least-popular-music-genre (accessed 23 October 2017).

25. See Michael Heller, *Loft Jazz: Improvising New York in the 1970s* (Berkeley: University of California Press, 2017), 55–56.

26. Steve Isoardi, *The Dark Tree: Jazz and the Community Arts in Los Angeles* (Berkeley: University of California Press, 2006), 143; Heller, *Loft Jazz,* 55; Giovanni Rusonello, "David Murray: A Jazz Innovator Leads from the Center to the Edge," *Washington Post,* 27 February 2015.

27. Larry Kart, "The Death of Jazz," *Chicago Tribune,* 24 February 1985. On the range of neoclassicist artists in this vein, see Berendt and Huesmann, *Jazz Book,* 46.

28. Heller, *Loft Jazz,* 89.

29. Stanley Crouch, in Robert Boyton, "The Professor of Connection: A Profile of Stanley Crouch," *New Yorker,* 6 November 1995, 113–16.

30. Eric Porter, *What Is This Thing Called Jazz? African American Musicians as Artists, Critics, and Activists* (Berkeley: University of California Press, 2002), 293–95.

31. Ibid.

32. Larry Kart, who we last encountered in his mildly critical assessment of neoclassicism in the mid-1980s, had become sufficiently disenchanted with the ascendency of what he called "neo-con" jazz that by the close of the decade, he had left his position as jazz critic at the *Chicago Tribune.* See Peter Margasak, "The Last Good Jazz Critic at the Trib: Larry Kart, Back in Print," *Chicago Reader,* 20 January 2005.

33. See for example Monica Prassad's discussion of the efficacy of Ronald Reagan's "welfare queen" trope in winching white racial resentment to conservative fiscal policy. Monica Prassad, *The Politics of Free Markets: The Rise of Neoliberal Economic Policies in Britain, France, Germany, and the United States* (Chicago: University of Chicago Press, 2006), 86–87.

34. On the complex problems posed by reissues for the "young lions," see Stuart Nicholson, *Is Jazz Dead? (Or Has It Just Moved to a New Address)* (New York: Routledge, 2005), 15.

35. Ronald Radano, *New Musical Figurations: Anthony Braxton's Cultural Critique* (Chicago: University of Chicago Press, 1993), 270–71.

36. McMullen, "Identity for Sale," 143.

37. Farah Jasmine Griffin, *If You Can't be Free, be a Mystery: In Search of Billie Holiday* (New York: Free Press, 2001), 143; see also George Lewis, *A Power Stronger Than Itself: The AACM And American Experimental Music* (Chicago: University of Chicago Press, 2008), 443–44.

38. Matthew Shipp, in Howard Mandel, "Matthew Shipp: My Feature for *The Wire,* 1998," Jazz beyond Jazz, posted 19 April 2013, www.artsjournal.com /jazzbeyondjazz/2013/04/matthew-shipp-my-feature-for-the-wire-1998.html (accessed 24 October 2017); on the "Jazz Left," see Gray, *Cultural Moves,* 52–73.

39. See Mark Laver, "Improvise!™: Jazz Consultancy and the Aesthetics of Neoliberalism," *Critical Studies in Improvisation* 9/1 (2013); Ken Prouty, "Find-

ing Jazz in the Jazz-as-Business Metaphor," *Jazz Perspectives* 7/1 (2013): 31–55. Laver is a coguest editor for the issue of *Critical Studies in Improvisation* from which "Improvise!™ is drawn, entitled "Ethics and the Improvising Business."

40. On the status of the jazz musician as an independent contractor, and its relation to the labor struggles of the American Federation of Musicians, see Paul Chevigny, *Gigs: Jazz and the Cabaret Laws in New York City* (New York: Routledge, 1991), 14–23. In my review of the organizational theory "jazz metaphor" literature, I located one article that considered hiring practices for jazz gigs—from the perspective of the bandleader. See Mary Jo Hatch, in William Pasmore, "Organizing for Jazz," *Organization Science* 9/5 (September–October 1998): 568. On jazz historiography and the "gig economy," see Dale Chapman, "A Prehistory of the 'Gig Economy': Jazz Musicians as Independent Contractors in Midcentury American Culture," paper presented at the annual meeting of the Society for American Music, Montreal, Canada, March 2017.

41. Penny Von Eschen, *Satchmo Blows Up the World: Jazz Ambassadors Play the Cold War* (Cambridge, MA: Harvard University Press, 2009).

42. On these points, see Gray, *Cultural Moves*, 32–51; Porter, *What Is This Thing Called Jazz?* 287–334; Daniel Fischlin et al., *The Fierce Urgency of Now: Improvisation, Rights, and the Ethics of Cocreation* (Durham, NC: Duke University Press, 2013), 121–27.

43. On this point, see Von Eschen, *Satchmo Blows Up the World*, 251–54.

44. Mark Laver, "Freedom of Choice: Jazz, Neoliberalism, and the Lincoln Center," *Popular Music and Society* 37/5 (2014): 538–56. On the conflation of democratic governance with laissez-faire economic principles, see Thomas Frank, *One Market under God: Extreme Capitalism, Market Populism, and the End of Economic Democracy* (New York: Anchor Books, 2001), 15.

45. On jazz and the targeting of affluent consumers, see Krin Gabbard, "Introduction: The Jazz Canon and Its Consequences," in *Jazz among the Discourses*, edited by Krin Gabbard (Durham, NC: Duke University Press, 1995), 1–2; McMullen, "Identity For Sale," 142. On the broader relationship between jazz and advertising, see Laver, *Jazz Sells*.

46. Gerald Epstein, "Financialization, Rentier Interests, and Central Bank Policy," paper prepared for PERI Conference on "Financialization of the World Economy," University of Massachusetts, Amherst, 7–8 December 2001.

47. Scholars in anthropology, political science, and cognate fields have begun to devote their attention to the critical examination of the financial sector, with frequently exciting results. See for instance Edward LiPuma and Benjamin Lee, *Financial Derivatives and the Globalization of Risk* (Durham, NC: Duke University Press, 2004); Arjun Appadurai, *The Future as Cultural Fact: Essays on the Global Condition* (London: Verso, 2013); Karen Ho, *Liquidated: An Ethnography of Wall Street* (Durham, NC: Duke University Press, 2009); Louis Hyman, *Debtor Nation: The History of America in Red Ink* (Princeton, NJ: Princeton University Press, 2011).

48. Hyman, *Debtor Nation*, 168–69.

49. For a profile of the impact of payday lending on low-income communities, see Daniel Brook, "Usury Country: Welcome to the Birthplace of Payday Lending," *Harper's*, April 2009, 41–48.

50. Randy Martin, *Financialization of Daily Life* (Philadelphia: Temple University Press, 2002).

51. David Harvey, *Spaces of Global Capitalism: Towards a Theory of Uneven Geographical Development* (London: Verso, 2006), 69–116.

52. Saskia Sassen, *The Global City: New York, London, Tokyo* (Princeton, NJ: Princeton University Press, 1991), 3.

53. Miriam Greenberg, *Branding New York: How a City in Crisis was Sold to the World* (New York: Routledge, 2008), 124–25.

54. Bruce Berg, *New York City Politics: Governing Gotham* (New Brunswick, NJ: Rutgers University Press, 2007), 22.

55. On the economic decline of Rust Belt cities in the late twentieth and early twenty-first centuries, and the culpability of Wall Street in their decline, see Thomas Sugrue, *The Origins of the Urban Crisis: Race and Inequality in Postwar Detroit* (Princeton, NJ: Princeton University Press, 2014 [1996]), xx, 3, 13, and *passim*.

56. Ta-Nehisi Coates, "Take Down the Confederate Flag—Now," TheAtlantic.com, 18 June 2015, www.theatlantic.com/politics/archive/2015/06/take-down-the-confederate-flag-now/396290/ (accessed 15 August 2016).

57. Patrick Wolfe, "Settler Colonialism and the Elimination of the Native," *Journal of Genocide Research* 8/4 (December 2006): 388.

58. Michelle Alexander, *The New Jim Crow: Mass Incarceration in the Age of Colorblindness* (New York: New Press, 2012). On "racism without racists," see Eduardo Bonilla-Silva, *Racism without Racists: Color-Blind Racism and the Persistence of Racial Inequality in America*, 5th ed. (Lanham, MD: Rowman & Littlefield, 2018).

59. Jack Hitt, "To Collect and Serve: The Dangers of Turning Police Officers into Revenue Generators," *Mother Jones*, September–October 2015, 5–8.

60. See for instance recent work on high mortality rates among middle-aged white noncollege educated men. See David Squires and David Blumenthal, "Mortality Trends among Working-Age Whites: The Untold Story," Commonwealth Fund, January 2016, www.commonwealthfund.org/publications/issue-briefs/2016/jan/mortality-trends-among-middle-aged-whites (accessed 27 October 2017); Anne Case and Angus Deaton, "Rising Mortality and Morbidity in Midlife among White Non-Hispanic Americans in the 21st Century," *Proceedings of the National Academy of Sciences* 112/49 (December 2015): 15078–83. See also Olga Khazan, "Why Are So Many Middle-Aged White Americans Dying?" *The Atlantic.com*, 29 January 2016, www.theatlantic.com/health/archive/2016/01/middle-aged-white-americans-left-behind-and-dying-early/433863 (accessed 29 October 2017). .

61. The former President Bill Clinton, a noted jazz aficionado, participated in a symposium moderated by Charlie Rose and sponsored by Jazz at Lincoln Center, with Wynton Marsalis, Farah Jasmine Griffin, and Michael Kammen among the other interlocutors in the discussion. See Ben Ratliff, "Marsalis, Clinton, and Others Dissect Jazz at Symposium," *New York Times*, 11 December 2003. Numerous TED and "TEDx" talks have situated jazz in relation to such issues as creativity, cognition, and group collaboration; see for instance Charles Limb, "Your Brain On Improv," presentation for TEDx Mid Atlantic,

November 2010, www.ted.com/talks/charles_limb_your_brain_on_improv? language = en (23 October 2017); Jim Kalbach, "Jazz Improvisation as a Model for Radical Collaboration," TEDx Jersey City, 30 March 2015, www.youtube .com/watch?v = j8Gmp194zbI (23 October 2017). At least two different figures have drawn attention to jazz analogies for the high-profile attendees of the Davos World Economic Forum; see Steve Lohr, "The Yin and the Yang of Corporate Innovation," *New York Times*, 26 January 2012; Georgette Jasen, "Music Propels Chris Washburne from Ohio Farm to Career as Jazz Teacher, Bandleader," Columbia News, posted 8 July 2015, http://news.columbia.edu/content/music-propels-chris-washburne-ohio-farm-career-jazz-teacher-bandleader (accessed 28 October 2017).

62. On rule-bound pedagogies in jazz in the wake of neoclassicism, David Ake has written about the codification, for instance, of "scale-chord" methods in jazz pedagogy; see Ake, *Jazz Cultures*, 122–26. The valorization of a concept of jazz as driven by the rule-bound adherence to a "musical grammar" dates to the earliest examinations of the "jazz metaphor" in organizational theory, and coincide roughly with the efflorescence of neoclassical jazz. See David Bastien and Todd Hostager, "Jazz as a Process of Organizational Innovation," *Communication Research* 15/5 (October 1988): 586–87.

63. Randy Martin, *An Empire of Indifference: American War and the Financial Logic of Risk Management* (Durham, NC: Duke University Press, 2007), 37–38.

64. Ibid., 38–39.

65. Stanley Crouch, "Blues to Be Contitutional: A Long Look at the Wild Wherefores of Our Democratic Lives as Symbolized in the Making of Rhythm and Tune," in *The Jazz Cadence of American Culture*, edited by Robert O'Meally (New York: Columbia University Press, 1998), 159.

66. Porter, *What Is This Thing Called Jazz?* 320.

67. Crouch, "Blues to Be Constitutional," 159.

68. Porter, *What Is This Thing Called Jazz?* 316.

69. Clyde Woods, *Development Arrested: The Blues and Plantation Power in the Mississippi Delta* (London: Verson, 1998), 16–19.

70. See for example Loren Kajikawa, *Sounding Race in Rap Songs* (Berkeley: University of California Press, 2015), 85–114.

71. On financial deregulation and the rise of alternative savings instruments for consumers, see Martin, *Financialization of Daily Life*, 23–24; on the shift from defined-benefit to defined-contribution plans, see Paul Langley, *The Everyday Life of Global Finance: Saving and Borrowing in Anglo-America* (New York: Oxford University Press, 2008), 81–86; on the rise of interest in gambling as symptomatic of a broader rise in neoliberal sensibilities, see Jean Comaroff and John Comaroff, "Millennial Capitalism: First Thoughts on a Second Coming," in *Millennial Capitalism and the Culture of Neoliberalism*, edited by Jean Comaroff and John Comaroff (Durham, NC: Duke University Press, 2001), 5–7.

72. Howard Reich, "Herbie's Blues," *Chicago Tribune*, 21 March 2004.

73. One important example of formal jazz/music education in the rise of the "young lions" can be found in Terence Blanchard's discussion of the New Orleans Center for the Creative Arts (or NOCCA). Anthony Magro, *Contemporary*

Cat: Terence Blanchard with Special Guests (Lanham, MD: Scarecrow Press, 2002), 22–26 and *passim*.

74. For a brief account of the rise of the Jazz Education Network following the dissolution of the International Association of Jazz Educators in 2008, see Melissa Daniels, "Jazz Education Network Formed to Fill Void Left By IAJE Collapse," JazzTimes.com, 6 June 2008, http://jazztimes.com/articles/24026-jazz-education-network-formed-to-fill-void-left-by-iaje-collapse (accessed 23 October 2017).

75. David Ake, *Jazz Matters: Sound, Place, and Time since Bebop* (Berkeley: University of California Press, 2010), 103.

76. See Eitan Wilf, *School for Cool: The Academic Jazz Program and the Paradox of Institutionalized Creativity* (Chicago: University of Chicago Press, 2014), 113; Stephanie Horsley, "Facing the Music: Pursuing Social Justice Through Music Education in a Neoliberal World," in *The Oxford Handbook of Social Justice in Music Education,* edited by Cathy Benedict et a. (New York: Oxford University Press, 2015), 69.

77. See, for instance, Joyce Canaan and Wesley Shumar, "Higher Education in the Era of Globalization and Neoliberalism," in *Structure and Agency in the Neoliberal University,* edited by Joyce Canaan and Wesley Shumar (New York: Routledge, 2008), 1–32.

78. See Wilf, *School for Cool;* Ajay Heble and Mark Laver, eds., *Improvisation and Music Education: Beyond the Classroom* (New York: Routledge, 2016). Another useful discussion in this area can be found in Ken Prouty, *Knowing Jazz: Community, Pedagogy, and Canon in the Information Age* (Jackson: University of Mississippi Press, 2011), 46–77.

79. On the ways in which a politics of gender, for instance, informs the long-standing exclusion of women from the Lincoln Center Jazz Orchestra, a crucial institution of jazz neoclassicism, see McMullen, "Identity For Sale," 144–46; on the gendered social dynamics of Wall Street investment banking, see Ho, *Liquidated,* 270–71.

CHAPTER 1. "CONTROLLED FREEDOM": JAZZ, RISK, AND POLITICAL ECONOMY

1. Stefon Harris, "There Are No Mistakes on the Bandstand," TED.com, posted December 2011, www.ted.com/talks/stefon_harris_there_are_no_mistakes _on_the_bandstand.html (accessed 23 October 2017).

2. See, for example, David Baker, *Jazz Pedagogy: A Comprehensive Method of Jazz Education for Teacher and Student* (Los Angeles: Alfred Music Publishing, 1989), 160; Peter Boonshaft, *Teaching Music with Promise: Conducting, Rehearsing, and Inspiring* (Galesville, MD: Meredith Music Publications, 2009), 166–67; Paul Berliner, *Thinking in Jazz: The Infinite Art of Improvisation* (Chicago: University of Chicago Press, 1994), 210–16.

3. See "Shlomo Benartzi: Saving for Tomorrow, Tomorrow," Allianzgi.com, posted November 2011, http://befi.allianzgi.com/en/befi-tv/Pages/shlomo-benartzi .aspx (accessed 28 October 2017).

4. Hersh Shefrin, *Beyond Greed and Fear: Understanding Behavioral Finance and the Psychology of Investing* (New York: Oxford University Press, 2002), 3–9. Among the key early analyses in this field are Richard Thaler and Hersh Shefrin, "An Economic Theory of Self-Control," *Journal of Political Economy* 89/2 (April 1981): 392–406; and Daniel Kahneman, Paul Slovic, and Amos Tversky, *Judgment under Uncertainy: Heuristics and Biases* (Cambridge: Cambridge University Press, 1982).

5. Mark Laver, "Improvise!™: Jazz Consultancy and the Aesthetics of Neo-liberalism," *Critical Studies in Improvisation* 9/1 (2013), Criticalimprov.com, www.criticalimprov.com/article/view/2897/3229 (accessed 28 October 2017).

6. See, for example, A. Neilson, "A New Metaphor for Strategic Fit: All That Jazz," *Leadership and Organization Development Journal* 13/5 (1992): 3–6; Ken Kamoche and Miguel Pina e Cunha, "Minimal Structures: From Jazz Improvisation to Product Innovation," *Organization Studies* 22/5 (2001): 733–64.

7. See Michael Gold, "World Class Musicians," Jazz Impact, www.jazz-impact.com/who-we-are (accessed 23 October 2017); Linda Stern, "How to Jazz Up Innovation," *Newsweek,* 14 November 2005, E4. Michael Gold is profiled in Laver, "Improvise!™" On jazz at the World Economic Forum in Davos, see Georgette Jasen, "Music Propels Chris Washburne from Ohio Farm to Career as Jazz Teacher, Bandleader," Columbia News, posted 8 July 2015, http://news.columbia.edu/content/music-propels-chris-washburne-ohio-farm-career-jazz-teacher-bandleader (accessed 28 October 2017); Steve Lohr, "The Yin and the Yang of Corporate Innovation," *New York Times*, 26 January 2012.

8. On "entrepreneurial selfhood," see Michel Foucault, *The Birth of Biopolitics: Lectures at the Collège de France, 1978–79,* edited by Michel Senellart et al., translated by Graham Burchell (Basingstoke, England: Palgrave Macmillan, 2008), 226.

9. Philip Mirowski, *Never Let a Serious Crisis Go to Waste: How Neoliberalism Survived the Financial Meltdown* (London: Verso, 2013), 119.

10. Randy Martin, *Financialization of Daily Life* (Philadelphia: Temple University Press, 2002), 112–14.

11. On the debate between swing's advocates and their traditionalist, "moldy fig" opponents, see Bernard Gendron, "Moldy Figs and Modernists: Jazz at War (1942–1946)," in *Jazz among the Discourses,* edited by Krin Gabbard (Durham, NC: Duke University Press, 1995), 31–56; on the divergent threads of jazz culture in the 1990s and early twenty-first century, see for example Herman Gray, *Cultural Moves: African Americans and the Politics of Representation* (Berkeley: University of California Press, 2005), 32–76.

12. Jonathan Levy, *Freaks of Fortune: The Emerging World of Capitalism and Risk in America* (Cambridge, MA: Harvard University Press, 2010), 4.

13. David Dequench, "Uncertainty and Economic Sociology: A Preliminary Discussion," *American Journal of Economics and Sociology* 62/3 (July 2003): 514; Martin Hollis and Edward Nell, *Rational Economic Man: A Philosophical Critique of Neo-Classical Economics* (Cambridge: Cambridge University Press, 1975), 210–11.

14. On this point, see Dimitris Milonakis and Ben Fine, *From Political Economy to Economics: Method, the Social, and the Historical in the Evolution of Economic Theory* (Abingdon, England: Routledge, 2009), *passim*.

15. Frank Knight, *Risk, Uncertainty, and Profit* (Boston: Houghton Mifflin, 1921). On the intellectual challenges posed by Knight's work to his fellow "Chicago School" economists, see Angus Burgin, *The Great Persuasion: Reinventing Free Markets since the Depression* (Cambridge, MA: Harvard University Press, 2012), 34–35.

16. Richard Langlois and Metin Cosgel, "Frank Knight on Risk, Uncertainty, and the Firm: A New Interpretation," *Economic Inquiry* 31 (July 1993): 459–60.

17. S. Nuri Erbaş and Chera L. Sayers outline some of the ways that weak governance structures (in the form of increased political corruption) may convert something like the simple Knightian "risk" of the fire insurance situation into the more ambiguous terrain of Knightian uncertainty. See S. Nuri Erbaş and Chera L. Sayers, 2006, "Institutional Quality, Knightian Uncertainty, and Insurability: A Cross-Country Analysis," Working Paper 06/179 (International Monetary Fund, 2006), www.imf.org/external/pubs/ft/wp/2006/wp06179.pdf (accessed 1 May 2014).

18. Nigel Bowles, *Nixon's Business: Authority and Power in Presidential Politics* (College Station: Texas A&M University Press, 2005), 161–65.

19. John Eatwell and Lance Taylor, *Global Finance at Risk: The Case for International Regulation* (New York: New Press, 2000), 1–3.

20. Arjun Appadurai, *The Future as Cultural Fact: Essays on the Global Condition* (London: Verso, 2013), 240–41.

21. On this emergent breed of "rock n' roll CEOs," and hip anticonformism in postmodern corporate style, see Naomi Klein, *No Logo: Taking Aim at the Brand Bullies* (New York: Picador, 1999), 81; Thomas Frank, *One Market under God: Extreme Capitalism, Market Populism, and the End of Economic Democracy* (New York: Anchor Books, 2001), 33.

22. Frank Barrett, *Yes to the Mess: Surprising Leadership Lessons from Jazz* (Boston: Harvard Business School Publishing, 2012), 37.

23. Laver, "Improvise!™"

24. Michael Gold, "About," Jazz Impact, www.jazz-impact.com/about (accessed 23 October 2017).

25. John Kao, *Jamming: The Art and Discipline of Business Creativity* (New York: HarperCollins, 1996), 35, 163. Joseph Schumpeter's conception of "creative destruction" proposes an evolutionary model of the market economy in which the adoption of new technologies or strategic innovations "revolutionize[s] the economic structure from within." See Joseph A. Schumpeter, *Capitalism, Socialism, and Democracy,* 6th ed., with an introduction by Richard Swedberg (London: Routledge, 2006), 83.

26. Edward LiPuma and Benjamin Lee, *Financial Derivatives and the Globalization of Risk* (Durham, NC: Duke University Press, 2004), 119–22.

27. On the relation of the "jazz metaphor" to other managerial discourses, See Laver, "Improvise!™"

28. On Marsalis and Evelyn Brooks Higginbotham's concept of the "politics of respectability," see Farah Jasmine Griffin and Salim Washington, *Clawing at*

the Limits of Cool: Miles Davis, John Coltrane, and the Greatest Jazz Collaboration Ever (New York: St. Martin's Press, 2008), 245–46.

29. On the rise of "shareholder value" as a central value in corporate governance, see Karen Ho, *Liquidated: An Ethnography of Wall Street* (Durham, NC: Duke University Press, 2009); on the ideology of risk as a social abstraction, see LiPuma and Lee, *Financial Derivatives*, 119–22.

30. LiPuma and Lee, *Financial Derivatives*, 119.

31. Levy, *Freaks of Fortune*, 3–5.

32. Ibid., 22.

33. Walter Johnson, *Soul by Soul: Life inside the Antebellum Slave Market* (Cambridge, MA: Harvard University Press, 1999), 164, 176–77.

34. Saidiya Hartman, *Scenes of Subjection: Terror, Slavery, and Self-Making in Nineteenth-Century America* (New York: Oxford University Press, 1997), 17–48.

35. See Ronald Radano, *Lying Up a Nation: Race and Black Music* (Durham, NC: Duke University Press, 2003), 149; Johnson, *Soul by Soul*, 19.

36. Ira Berlin, *The Making of African America: The Four Great Migrations* (New York: Viking Penguin, 2010), 139–43; Jeannie M. Whayne, *A New Plantation South: Land, Labor, and Federal Favor in Twentieth-Century Arkansas* (Charlottesville: University Press of Virginia, 1996).

37. Levy, *Freaks of Fortune*, 135–36.

38. Melvin Oliver and Thomas Shapiro, *Black Wealth / White Wealth: A New Perspective on Racial Inequality,* 10th anniversary ed. (New York: Routledge, 2006), 14–15, 11–34.

39. On this point, see Kimberley Johnson, *Reforming Jim Crow: Southern Politics and State in the Age before Brown* (New York: Oxford University Press, 2010), 43–45.

40. Peter Rodriguez et al., "Government Corruption and the Entry Strategies of Multinationals," *Academy of Management Review* 30/2 (April 2005): 386.

41. Ira Katznelson, *When Affirmative Action Was White: An Untold History of Racial Inequality in Twentieth-Century America* (New York: W. W. Norton, 2005), 42–52.

42. Ibid., 111–41; Suzanne Mettler, *Soldiers to Citizens: The G.I. Bill and the Making of the Greatest Generation* (New York: Oxford University Press, 2005), 101–2.

43. Oliver and Shapiro, *Black Wealth*, 19–23. See also the exploitative practice of "on contract" property sales to African Americans, outlined in Amanda Seligman, *Block by Block: Neighborhoods and Public Policy on Chicago's West Side* (Chicago: University of Chicago Press, 2005), 158–59; and Ta-Nehisi Coates, "The Case for Reparations," *Atlantic Monthly,* June 2014, 54–71.

44. Louis Hyman, *Debtor Nation: The History of America in Red Ink* (Princeton, NJ: Princeton University Press, 2011), 174–82.

45. Scott DeVeaux, *The Birth of Bebop: A Social and Musical History* (Berkeley: University of California Press, 1997), *passim.*

46. Clyde Woods, *Development Arrested: The Blues and Plantation Power in the Mississippi Delta* (London: Verso, 1998), 16.

47. John Szwed, *So What: The Life of Miles Davis* (New York: Simon & Schuster, 2004), 236–37; Keith Waters, *The Studio Recordings of the Miles Davis Quintet, 1965–68* (New York: Oxford University Press, 2011), 5.

48. For a useful stylistic overview of this sequence of recordings, see Waters, *Studio Recordings of the Miles Davis Quintet.*

49. Ingrid Monson, *Freedom Sounds: Civil Rights Call Out to Jazz and Africa* (New York: Oxford University Press, 2010), 216; see also Ron Carter, in Jonah Jonathan, "Ron Carter: Every Note Counts," Jazz Musicians Voice, interview posted 4 December 2012, www.youtube.com/watch?v = w3Rw1s6L-OA (accessed 23 October 2017).

50. Miles Davis and Quincy Troupe, *Miles: The Autobiography* (New York: Simon & Schuster, 1989), 266.

51. Christopher Banks, "A Sense of the Possible: Miles Davis and the Semiotics of Improvised Performance," *TDR* 39/3 (Autumn 1995): 42.

52. Davis and Troupe, *Miles,* 220.

53. Robert Walser, "'Out of Notes': Signification, Interpretation, and the Problem of Miles Davis," in *Jazz among the Discourses,* edited by Krin Gabbard (Durham, NC: Duke University Press, 1995), 173–79.

54. On this point, see for example Joachim-Ernst Berendt and Günther Huesmann, *The Jazz Book: From Ragtime to the 21st Century,* 7th ed. (Chicago: Chicago Review Press, 2009), 170; Ingrid Monson, *Saying Something: Jazz Improvisation and Interaction* (Chicago: University of Chicago Press, 1994), 175; Berliner, *Thinking in Jazz,* 340–41.

55. Herbie Hancock, in Mark Obenhaus and Yvonne Smith, producers, *Miles Ahead: the Music of Miles Davis* (New York: WNET/Thirteen and Obenhaus Films in association with Channel 4 Television, London, 1986).

56. Herbie Hancock, in Michelle Mercer, *Footprints: The Life and Work of Wayne Shorter* (New York: Penguin Books, 2007), chap. 7.

57. Bob Gluck, *You'll Know When You Get There: Herbie Hancock and the Mwandishi Band* (Chicago: University of Chicago Press, 2012), 43.

58. Steven Strunk, "Notes on Harmony in Wayne Shorter's Compositions, 1964–67," *Journal of Music Theory* 49/2 (Fall 2005): 303, 326.

59. Waters, *Studio Recordings of the Miles Davis Quintet,* 26–27; Strunk, "Notes on Harmony," 327.

60. One important example that we might cite here is the "burnout" aesthetic pursued by Branford and Wynton Marsalis on their early recordings for Columbia. See Ben Ratliff, *Coltrane: The Story of a Sound* (New York: Farrar, Strauss and Giroux, 2007), 197. For an analytical discussion of "time, no changes" in Davis's work, see Waters, *Studio Recordings of the Miles Davis Quintet,* 79 and *passim.*

61. On Williams as playing "on top of the beat," see Davis and Troupe, *Miles,* 274.

62. Waters, *Studio Recordings of the Miles Davis Quintet,* 67–69.

63. Tony Williams, in Ben Sidran, *Talking Jazz: An Oral History* (New York: Da Capo Press, 1995), 277.

64. Herbie Hancock, in Herbie Hancock and Ron Carter, "Miles and the 1960s Quintet," in *Miles Davis: The Complete Illustrated History,* Sonny Rollins, Francis Wolff, et al. (Minneapolis: Voyageur Press, 2012), 130.

65. On the *tihai* in Hindustani music, see Thom Lipiczky, "Tihai Formulas and the Fusion of 'Composition' and 'Improvisation' in North Indian Music," *Musical Quarterly* 71/2 (1985): 159.

66. Herbie Hancock, in Hancock and Carter, "Miles and the 1960s Quintet," 130.

67. The video footage from the concert, which took place on 31 October 1967, can be found on Miles Davis Quintet, *Live in Europe, 1967 (The Bootleg Series, Vol. 1)*, 2011 by Columbia Records, CBS 88697 94053 2, Bonus DVD, track 1.

68. See David Such, *Avant-Garde Jazz Musicians: Performing "Out There"* (Iowa City: University of Iowa Press, 1993), 47; Kimberley Benston, *Performing Blackness: Enactments of African-American Modernism* (New York: Routledge, 2000), 137–38.

69. See, for example, Dan Morgenstern, "Caught in the Act: Miles Davis," *Down Beat*, 13 January 1966, 32.

70. Woods, *Development Arrested*, 16.

71. On V.S.O.P., see Waters, *Studio Recordings of the Miles Davis Quintet, 1965–68*, 275–76; Jack Chambers, *Milestones: The Music and Times of Miles Davis* (New York: Da Capo Press, 1998), 293–94.

72. Waters, *Studio Recordings of the Miles Davis Quintet*, 280.

73. On Blanchard's admiration for the sound of the Davis Quintet, see Herbert Wong, "Terence Blanchard: Joyful Jazz Journeys," *Jazz Educators Journal* 34/2 (September 2001): 39.

74. Waters, *Studio Recordings of the Miles Davis Quintet*, 279; Berendt and Huesmann, *Jazz Book*, 170.

75. Wynton Marsalis, in Ethan Iverson, "Interview with Wynton Marsalis (Part 2)," Do the Math, posted 15 June 2010, https://ethaniverson.com /interviews/interview-with-wynton-marsalis-part-2 (accessed 23 October 2017).

76. Wynton Marsalis, in Lolis Eric Elie, "An Interview with Wynton Marsalis," *Callaloo* 13/2 (Spring 1990): 274.

77. For example, on Jeff Watts's stylistic debt to Tony Williams, see David Glover, "Style and Analysis: Jeff 'Tain' Watts," *Modern Drummer*, October 2009, 64.

78. Herbie Hancock, in Mark Obenhaus and Yvonne Smith, producers, *Miles Ahead: A Tribute to Miles Davis*, New York: WNET/Thirteen and Obenhaus Films in association with Channel 4 Television (London, 1986). See also Christopher Smith's analysis of rhythm section dynamics in "Gingerbread Boy," taken from the same documentary, in Smith, "Sense of the Possible," 44–47.

79. Wynton Marsalis, in Iverson, "Interview with Wynton Marsalis (Part 2)."

80. Larry Kart, "Part II of the Death of Jazz: An Update on the Status of the Neoclassical Trend," *Chicago Tribune*, 4 May 1986, section 13, pp. 10–11.

81. Wynton Marsalis, in Stanley Crouch, liner notes to Wynton Marsalis, *Marsalis Standard Time Vol. 1*, compact disc, Columbia, CK 40461, 1987.

82. LiPuma and Lee, *Financial Derivatives and the Globalization of Risk*, 119–22.

83. Jean Comaroff and John Comaroff, "Millennial Capitalism: First Thoughts on a Second Coming," in *Millennial Capitalism and the Culture of*

Neoliberalism, edited by Jean Comaroff and John Comaroff (Durham, NC: Duke University Press, 2001), 5. On Alan Greenspan's coining of the phrase "irrational exuberance," see Robert Shiller, *Irrational Exuberance,* 2nd ed. (New York: Broadway Books, 2005), xi–xii.

84. Martin, *Financialization of Daily Life,* 108–9.

85. William Rothstein, *Public Health and the Risk Factor: A History of an Uneven Medical Revolution* (Rochester, NY: University of Rochester Press, 2003), 3–5.

86. U.S. Department of Education, National Commission on Excellence in Education, *A Nation at Risk: The Imperative for Educational Reform* (Washington, DC: Government Printing Office, 1983), 5.

87. See, for example, Cathy Cohen, *The Boundaries of Blackness: AIDS and the Breakdown of Black Politics* (Chicago: University of Chicago Press, 1999), 82–83.

88. James Patterson, *Freedom Is Not Enough: The Moynihan Report and America's Struggle over Black Family Life; From LBJ to Obama* (New York: Basic Books, 2010), 68–71.

89. On this point, see Daniel Geary, *Beyond Civil Rights: The Moynihan Report and Its Legacy* (Philadelphia: University of Pennsylvania Press, 2015), 1–11, 81, and *passim.*

90. See U.S. Department of Labor, Office of Policy Planning and Research, *The Negro Family: A Case for National Action,* by Daniel Patrick Moynihan (Washington, DC: United States Government Printing Office, 1965), 3; Michael Katz, *The Undeserving Poor: America's Enduring Confrontation with Poverty,* 2nd ed. (New York: Oxford University Press, 2013), 18.

91. U.S. Department of Labor, *Negro Family,* 29–30.

92. Randy Martin, *An Empire of Indifference: American War and the Financial Logic of Risk Management* (Durham, NC: Duke University Press, 2007), 136–37. On the use of race-neutral legal language in pursuing the discriminatory policies of the War on Drugs, see Doris Marie Provine, *Unequal under Law: Race in the War on Drugs* (Chicago: University of Chicago Press, 2007), 91–119; on the targeting of economically disadvantaged minorities via the subprime lending industry, see Stephen Ross and John Yinger, *The Color of Credit: Mortgage Discrimination, Research Methodology, and Fair-Lending Enforcement* (Cambridge, MA: MIT Press, 2002), 24–27.

CHAPTER 2. "HOMECOMING": DEXTER GORDON AND
THE 1970S FISCAL CRISIS IN NEW YORK CITY

1. Don Heckman, "Midnight Jam Session at Music Hall," *New York Times,* July 5, 1972, 31.

2. The title of my chapter, "Homecoming," derives from the title of Gordon's first album for Columbia after the signing, a live album recorded at a subsequent Village Vanguard performance.

3. On the contested place of the 1970s in recent jazz histories, see Scott DeVeaux, "Constructing the Jazz Tradition: Jazz Historiography." *Black American Literature Forum* 25/3 (Fall 1991): 527, 554; Eric Porter, "Introduc-

tion: Rethinking Jazz through the 1970s," *Jazz Perspectives* 4/1 (April 2010): 1—2.

4. See Miriam Greenberg, *Branding New York: How a City in Crisis Was Sold to the World* (New York: Routledge, 2008), 185–87.

5. Ibid., 185–91.

6. This is, for instance, the approach taken by Ken Burns in his high-profile ten-part documentary *Jazz* in 2000, where the final episode hinges upon Dexter Gordon's return as a moment of redemption for a jazz tradition ostensibly placed in jeopardy by avant-garde experimentation and the encroachment of rock. See the final episode of Ken Burns, director, *Jazz: A Film,* produced by Joe Thomas, 10 episodes, aired January 2001, DVD, 1140 min. (PBS, 2005).

7. See Bruce Schulman and Julian Zelizer, eds., *Rightward Bound: Making America Conservative in the 1970s* (Cambridge, MA: Harvard University Press, 2008), *passim.*

8. See Robert A. Beauregard, *Voices of Decline: The Postwar Fate of US Cities* (Oxford: Blackwell, 1993), 176.

9. See ibid., 174.

10. Greenberg, *Branding New York,* 189.

11. For accounts of Times Square both prior to and following its early-1990s redevelopment, see Greenberg, *Branding New York,* 61–63; Lynne B. Sagalyn, *Times Square Roulette: Remaking the City Icon* (Cambridge, MA: MIT Press, 2003), 338–72; Andreas Huyssen, *Present Pasts: Urban Palimpsests and the Politics of Memory* (Stanford, CA: Stanford University Press, 2003), 85—93.

12. Greenberg, *Branding New York,* 153–57.

13. ABC, whose WABC-TV affiliate in New York introduced the format in the early 1970s, came up with the moniker "Eyewitness News" as a brand for this practice. Jeremy Harris Lipschultz and Michael L. Hilt, *Crime and Local Television News: Dramatic, Breaking, and Live from the Scene* (Manwah, NJ: Lawrence Erlbaum Associates, 2003), 13.

14. Caroline O'Meara's work on the "No Wave" experimental scene of the late 1970s and early 1980s offers a compelling portrait of the urban geography of blight in New York during this period. Caroline O'Meara, "New York Noise: Music in the Post-Industrial City, 1978–1985" (Ph.D. diss., University of California, Los Angeles, 2006).

15. The very concept of urban "blight," which I will examine in chapter 5, has a highly contested and problematic history in relation to urban development since the Second World War.

16. See for example Robert A. Caro, *The Power Broker: Robert Moses and the Fall of New York* (New York: Alfred A. Knopf, 1974); Marshall Berman, *All That Is Solid Melts into Air: The Experience of Modernity* (New York: Simon & Schuster, 1983).

17. Tricia Rose, *Black Noise: Rap Music and Black Culture in Contemporary America* (Middletown, CT: Wesleyan University Press, 1994), 30–33. On the noise of the freeway overpasses and its indelible imprint on the soundscape of the South Bronx, see O'Meara, "New York Noise," 188–94.

18. Greenberg, *Branding New York,* 123–24.

19. In particular, see Kim Moody, *From Welfare State to Real Estate: Regime Change in New York City, 1974 to the Present* (New York: New Press, 2007); Eric Lichten, *Class, Power, and Austerity: The New York City Fiscal Crisis* (Amherst, MA: Greenwood Press, 1986); Robert Fitsch, *The Assassination of New York* (New York: Verso, 1993).

20. Greenberg, *Branding New York,* 124–25.

21. Ibid., 100–101.

22. Ibid., 128–29.

23. Ibid., 208. Travis Jackson situates some key transformations of the jazz scene in late twentieth-century New York in relation to this same set of developments: the city redirected resources away from the provision of necessary services, and into a prioritization of increased traffic for its entertainment and financial districts. This had important consequences for the city's jazz venues, which were increasingly clustered around the highly gentrified environs of the Village Vanguard. See Travis Jackson, *Blowin' the Blues Away: Performance and Meaning on the New York Jazz Scene* (Berkeley: Universiry of California Press, 2012), 63–64.

24. David Harvey, *A Brief History of Neoliberalism* (New York: Oxford University Press, 2005), 48.

25. Ibid., 39–40.

26. Leslie Savan, *The Sponsored Life: Ads, TV, and American Culture* (Philadelphia: Temple University Press, 1994), 17–22.

27. Greenberg, *Branding New York,* 149. George L. Kelling and James Q. Wilson, the creators of "broken windows" theory, introduced their ideas in 1982 in an article for *The Atlantic.* They would go on to expand their theory in a 1996 publication, entitled *Fixing Broken Windows.* See George L. Kelling and James Q. Wilson, "Broken Windows," *The Atlantic,* March 1982, 29–38; George Kelling and James Wilson, *Fixing Broken Windows: Restoring Order and Reducing Crime in Our Neighborhoods* (New York: Simon & Schuster, 1997). For a sustained critique of broken windows theory, see Bernard E. Harcourt, *Illusion of Order: The False Promise of Broken Windows Policing* (Cambridge, MA: Harvard University Press, 2001).

28. See Jerry DeMuth, "Phil Woods: Working More And Enjoying It, No Less," *Down Beat,* 11 January 1979, 14–16; Lee Jeske, "Scott Hamilton grew up in the '70s but Swing's His Thing," *Down Beat,* December 1979, 28–30.

29. On this point, see Porter, "Introduction," 1–5; for examples, see Grover Sales, *Jazz: America's Classical Music* (New York: Da Capo Press, 1984), 201–2; Stuart Nicholson, *Jazz: The 1980s Resurgence* (New York: Da Capo Press, 1995), 146.

30. John S. Wilson, "Jazz Attracting Some Younger Fans," *New York Times,* 23 October 1970, 28.

31. John S. Wilson, "A New Jazz Club, Wein's Storyville, on the City Scene," *New York Times,* 27 February 1976, 18; John S. Wilson, "Where One Man Hopes the Jazz Will Be Heavenly," *New York Times,* 15 October 1976, 65; John S. Wilson, "Jazz: Ron Carter Quartet," *New York Times,* 13 April 1979, C13; John S. Wilson, "Jazz Haunts in Town for the Jazz Fan," *New York Times,* 26 January 1979, C1; John Wilson, "Jazz Notes: New Clubs and a Big Band Bash," *New York*

Times, 2 February 1975, X17; Gary Giddins, "The Beat Goes On: New Jazz Clubs," *New York*, 10 March 1980, 44–49.

32. Nicholson, *Jazz*, 72–74; Stan Britt, *Dexter Gordon: A Musical Biography* (New York: Da Capo Press, 1989), 81–83.

33. Leonard Feather, "A Tale of Two Citizens—Abroad," *Los Angeles Times*, 18 January 1976, M52.

34. See Akbar DePriest with Arlynn Nellhaus, "The Impossible Dream: A Cat's View of 'Cope,'" *New York Times*, 9 November 1975, XX7; "Jazz Mecca Reopens in Copenhagen: One of the World's Great Jazz Clubs to Reopen in Copenhagen," Politiken, 22 February 2010, http://politiken.dk/newsinenglish /art4847960/Jazz-Mecca-reopens-in-Copenhagen (accessed 23 October 2017).

35. In the wake of the Algerian War, many black expatriates were confronted with the limitations of Parisian tolerance, witnessing the city's brutal persecution of its Arab minorities. See Tyler Stovall, "The Fire This Time: Black Expatriates and the Algerian War," *Yale French Studies* 98 (2000): 182–200.

36. Dexter Gordon, in Jenny Armstrong, "Dexter Gordon: Transcontinental Tenorist," *Down Beat*, 20 June 1972, 17.

37. Indeed, jazz tenorist Johnny Griffin recalls that at one rally in Copenhagen's Town Hall Square, student protesters carried signs saying, "We Want Dexter—We Don't Want NATO." See Johnny Griffin, in Britt, *Dexter Gordon*, 97.

38. Dexter Gordon, in Peter Keepnews, "A Jazzman Returns," *New York Post*, 27 October 1976.

39. Nicholson, *Jazz*, 71–72; on MsManagement, the jazz booking firm cofounded by Gregg, see Robin D. G. Kelley, "The Jazz Wife: Muse and Manager," NYTimes.com, 21 July 2002, www.nytimes.com/2002/07/21/arts/music-the-jazz-wife-muse-and-manager.html (accessed 28 October 2017).

40. Chuck Berg, "Dexter Gordon: Making His Great Leap Forward," *Down Beat*, 10 February 1977, 12.

41. "Dexter Returns," *Down Beat*, 16 December 1976, 11.

42. See Robert Palmer, "Jazz: Return of Saxophonist Packs Club," *New York Times*, 22 October 1976, 71; Robert Palmer, "A Native Son Returns to Make Jazz History," *New York Times*, 29 October 1976, 58.

43. Dexter Gordon, in Pete Hamill, "On Jazz: 'Dex Is Comin' Back,'" *New York Daily News*, 6 November 1977, 5.

44. "Dexter Returns," 11.

45. Dexter Gordon, in Ira Gitler, "Dexter Gordon Loves In," *Radio Free Jazz*, January 1977, 6.

46. Ira Gitler, "People: New York," *Jazz* 1/3 (Spring 1977): 14.

47. "Dexter Returns," 11.

48. Bruce Lundvall, Gary Giddins, and Joe Lovano, "Blue Note at 70: Behind an Iconic Label," CUNY Media, posted 17 November 2009, www .youtube.com/watch?v=1m7Ft-cBRWs (accessed 23 October 2017); Gitler, "People," 15.

49. Gitler, "People," 15.

50. On his friendship with, and his admiration for Dexter Gordon, see Lundvall, Gidden, and Lovano, "Blue Note at 70"; Bruce Lundvall, in Ted Panken, "25 Years at Blue Note: Bruce Lundvall Reflects on a Quarter-Century at the

Helm of Jazz's Most Storied Label," Jazziz, posted 17 June 2009, 2 June 2012, www.jazziz.com/interviews/2009/06/17/bruce-lundvall, Internet Archive, https://web.archive.org/web/20120602144206/http://www.jazziz.com/interviews/2009/06/17/bruce-lundvall (accessed 26 October 2017).

51. Eliot Tiegel, "Coexistence of Pure Jazz and Fusion to Continue," *Billboard*, 7 January 1978, 3, 102.

52. Ibid., 3; Panken, "25 Years at Blue Note."

53. Clarence Waldron, "Dr. George Butler, Retired Jazz Record Executive, Dies," *Jet*, 5 May 2008, 37. Interestingly, Richard Cook attributes the decision to sign Marsalis to Bruce Lundvall, rather than George Butler. See Richard Cook, *Blue Note Records: The Biography* (Boston: Justin, Charles & Company, 2003), 212.

54. Unlike Columbia, many of these revitalized jazz projects at other major labels would not get under way in earnest until the ebbing of recession in the early 1980s. On this point, see Peter Keepnews, "Rhythm of Revival Is Cautiously Upbeat: It's Never Been Away, but . . . Jazz Is Back!" *Billboard*, 28 June 1986, J-3–J-8; for an earlier (and bleaker) perspective on jazz subsidiaries and reissue programs during the 1970s, see Gary Giddins, "Verve and Savoy Join Reissue Parade," *Village Voice*, 12 July 1976, 99. See also "Columbia Jazz Assault," *Down Beat*, 20 October 1977, 11.

55. "Blackout—Chapter 2," *Down Beat*, 6 October 1977, 10. On the contrast between the 1977 blackout and its more muted predecessor in 1965, see Greenberg, *Branding New York*, 185, 188.

56. "Punk Comes to Village Gate," *Down Beat*, 6 October 1977, 10.

57. On the odd gloominess of the 1976 bicentennial year, see Bruce Schulman, *The Seventies: The Great Shift in American Culture, Society, and Politics* (New York: Da Capo Press, 2002), 124.

58. Bruno E. Strapko, "Punk Backlash," *Down Beat*, 5 October 1978, 8.

59. Max Gordon, "Confusing Mish Mash," *Down Beat*, 19 October 1978, 9.

60. K. Goerner and William Woolley, in "Contemporary Readers," *Down Beat*, 25 January 1979, 8.

61. See Herb Nolan, review of *Small Change*, by Tom Waits, *Down Beat*, 24 February 1977, 26; Tim Schneckloth, review of *Studio Tan*, by Frank Zappa, *Down Beat*, 11 January 1979, 24; Mikal Gilmore, review of *Low*, by David Bowie, *Down Beat*, 9 May 1977, 33; Arnold Shaw, review of *Animal*, by Pink Floyd, *Down Beat*, 5 May 1977, 24, 28; Larry Birnbaum, review of *Go West*, by the Village People, *Down Beat*, 21 June 1979, 38. For this last review, in which the Village People record received three stars from *Down Beat*, the magazine was swiftly castigated by a letter writer in the subsequent "Chords and Discords" section; see Glenn Riley, "Disco in Perspective," *Down Beat*, 6 September 1979, 8.

62. Jimmy Heath and Percy Heath, in Bret Primack, "The Heath Brothers: Bebop above and beyond the Fads," *Down Beat*, 22 March 1979, 17, 36.

63. Grover Washington Jr., in S. Bloom, "Grover Washington Jr.: Class Act of Commercial Jazz," *Down Beat*, 19 April 1979, 42.

64. Charles Carson, "'Bridging the Gap': Creed Taylor, Grover Washington Jr., and the Crossover Roots of Smooth Jazz," *Black Music Research Journal* 28/1 (Spring 2008): 13.

65. On this point, see for example John Gennari's discussion of Stanley Crouch, in *Blowin' Hot and Cool: Jazz and Its Critics* (Chicago: University of Chicago Press, 2010), 354–55.

66. Indeed, as John Gennari points out, one of the most adamant critics of this turn toward post-Moynihan discourses of black pathology in social science was Albert Murray, whose book *The Omni-Americans* was formative in the intellectual history of jazz neoclassicism. See Gennari, *Blowin' Hot and Cool*, 348.

67. Primack, "Heath Brothers," 16.

68. Percy Heath and Jimmy Heath, in ibid., 16–17.

69. Heath and Heath, in ibid., 17.

70. See Tim Lawrence, *Love Saves the Day: A History of American Dance Music Culture, 1970–1979* (Durham, NC: Duke University Press, 2003), 373–82. For an example of this strain of critical invective against disco, particularly as it applies to R&B, see Nelson George, *The Death of Rhythm and Blues* (New York: Pantheon Books, 1988), 147–70.

71. For an engaging overview of the history of disco, see Lawrence, *Love Saves the Day;* see also Alice Echols, *Hot Stuff: Disco and the Remaking of American Culture* (New York: W. W. Norton, 2010).

72. On Maynard Ferguson's *Carnival,* see Jeff Litt, "Stop the Carnival," *Down Beat,* 16 November 1978, 8; John B. Salmon and Frank Gambino, in "Carnival Controversy Continues," *Down Beat,* 11 January 1979, 9. On Weather Report's *Mr. Gone,* see David Less, review of *Mr. Gone,* by Weather Report, *Down Beat* 11 January 1979; Bob Jones et al., in "Mr. Gone," *Down Beat,* 22 February 1979, 12.

73. Neil Lusby, "And What Is Jazz, Then?" *Down Beat,* 21 December 1978, 8.

74. See ibid.

75. Alongside several "straightahead" projects, many of Hubbard's recordings from this period seemed crafted to appeal to a crossover market. See for example Freddie Hubbard, *Bundle of Joy,* produced by Bert DeCoteaux (Columbia JC 34902, 1977); *The Love Connection,* produced by Clause Ogerman (Columbia JC 36015, 1979).

76. Chuck Estes, "Contemporary Readers," *Down Beat,* 25 January 1979, 8.

77. Several jazz artists also weigh in on disco in contemporaneous *Down Beat* interviews. See Dave Holland, in Bret Primack, "Dave Holland: Diverse and Dedicated," *Down Beat,* 18 May 1978, 20; Herbie Hancock, in Bret Primack, "Herbie Hancock: Chameleon in His Disco Phase," *Down Beat,* 17 May 1979, 42.

78. John Yarling, "Disgusting Funk," *Down Beat,* 10 March 1977, 8.

79. For analyses of the critical devaluation of repetition in western musical discourse, see Susan McClary, *Rap, Minimalism, and Structures of Time in Twentieth-Century Music* (Lincoln: University of Nebraska Press, 1998); Rose, *Black Noise,* 62–98.

80. Peter Fallico, "Curson Encore," *Down Beat,* 10 March 1977, 8.

81. On the Disco Demolition Derby, see Tim Lawrence, *Love Saves the Day,* 373–78.

82. George, *Death of Rhythm and Blues,* 154.

83. Lee Edelman, *No Future: Queer Theory and the Death Drive* (Durham, NC: Duke University Press, 2004), 13.

84. See "Will Disco Stranglehold Choke Off Black Music?" *Jet,* 10 May 1979, 22, 24; Lawrence, *Love Saves the Day,* 381.

85. See Walter Hughes, "In the Empire of the Beat," in *Microphone Fiends,* edited by Andrew Ross and Tricia Rose (New York: Routledge, 1994), 147–57.

86. Hamill, "On Jazz: 'Dex is comin' back.'"

87. Bob Blumenthal, "Meat-and-Potatoes Tenor: Long Tall Dexter Is Still the Boss," *Boston Phoenix,* 26 November 1976, 6.

88. Gitler, "Dexter Gordon Loves In," 6.

89. Ibid.

90. A key point of reference here is Dale Turner, the character played by Dexter Gordon in the 1986 film *'Round Midnight,* directed by Bertrand Tavernier. On this point, see Krin Gabbard, *Black Magic: White Hollywood and African American Culture* (Piscataway, NJ: Rutgers University Press, 2004), 215–16.

91. Edelman, *No Future,* 2–3.

92. The lineage of representations that posit homosocial bonds between black men and white men is extensive. On this point, see for instance Charles Nero's account of "operatic tutelage," in Charles I. Nero, "Diva Traffic and Male Bonding in Film: Teaching Opera, Learning Gender, Race, and Nation," *Camera Obscura* 19/2 (2004): 47–73.

93. Richard Sudhalter, *Lost Chords: White Musicians and their Contributions to Jazz, 1915–1945* (New York: Oxford University Press, 1999); see also Nicholas Evans's critique of Sudhalter in his *Writing Jazz: Race, Nationalism, and Modern Culture in the 1920s* (New York: Garland Publishing, 2000), 1–10.

94. Richard Sudhalter, "Sax Man's Old Gold Horn Suits Him to a 'C,'" *New York Post,* 6 April 1978, 47.

95. On the beauty and design innovation of the Cord Phaeton, see "The Single, Most Beautiful American Car," *American Heritage,* November 1996, 6.

96. Among other things, album titles from this period reinforced Gordon's links to New York: *Biting the Apple,* on the SteepleChase label, and Columbia's *Gotham City* and *Manhattan Symphonie* all attempt to capitalize on Gordon's renewed affiliation with New York.

97. See Peter Keepnews, "The Lionization of Dexter Gordon," *Jazz* 1/4 (Summer 1977): cover image, 29–31.

98. Ira Gitler, liner notes for Dexter Gordon, *Sophisticated Giant,* produced by Michael Cuscuna (CBS Records 34989, 1977).

99. On the question of disco's multitracked articifice and the threat it was perceived to pose to musical authenticity, see Jeremy Gilbert and Ewan Pearson, *Discographies: Dance Music, Culture, and the Politics of Sound* (London: Routledge, 1999), 113.

100. See Rufus Reid, in Paul Berliner, *Thinking in Jazz: The Infinite Art of Improvisation* (Chicago: University of Chicago Press, 1994), 424–25.

101. I use "Coltrane changes" here in a dual sense: Coltrane's distinctive arrangement of the head centers around a repeated Ebm-EbmM7-Ebm7-

EbmM6-Ebm7-EbmM7 vamp progression introduced in the introduction and held through the first four bars of the song proper. These could be seen as "Coltrane's changes" for the tune. At the same time, the bridge of Coltrane's arrangement uses a chord sequence popularly known as the "Coltrane changes," a progression that briefly tonicizes each successive major third below the root of the initial chord in the sequence. See Lewis Porter, *John Coltrane: His Life and Music* (Ann Arbor: University of Michigan Press, 1998), 145–54.

102. See Samuel L. Floyd, *The Power of Black Music* (New York: Oxford University Press, 1995), 35–57; Olly Wilson, "The Heterogenous Sound Ideal in African-American Music," in *Signifyin(g), Sanctifyin', and Slam Dunking,* edited by Gena Dagel Caponi (Amherst: University of Massachusetts Press, 1999), 157–71.

103. More recently, scholars have pointed to the potentially essentializing dimension of Wilson's formulation; on this point, see Ronald Radano, *Lying Up A Nation: Race and Black Music* (Durham, NC: Duke University Press, 2003).

104. See Tracy McMullen, "Identity for Sale: Glenn Miller, Wynton Marsalis, and Cultural Replay in Music," in *Big Ears: Listening for Gender in Jazz Studies,* edited by Nichole Rustin and Sherrie Tucker (Durham, NC: Duke University Press, 2008), 142.

105. Karen Ho, *Liquidated: An Ethnography of Wall Street* (Durham, NC: Duke University Press, 2009), 337–38 n. 10.

106. The recuperation of New York punk, disco, No Wave, hip hop, and other aspects of the late 1970s, early 1980s New York scene has been taken up in a variety of recent texts. See for example Simon Reynolds, *Rip It Up and Start Again: Postpunk, 1978–1984* (New York: Penguin Books, 2006); Mark Masters, *No Wave* (London: Black Dog Publishing, 2007); Jeff Chang, *Can't Stop Won't Stop: A History of the Hip-Hop Generation* (New York: St. Martin's Press, 2005); Lawrence, *Love Saves the Day.*

CHAPTER 3. SELLING THE SONGBOOK: THE POLITICAL ECONOMY OF VERVE RECORDS (1956–1990)

1. Scott DeVeaux, *The Birth of Bebop: A Social and Musical History* (Berkeley: University of California Press, 1997), 301.

2. For other recent discussions of the dynamics of jazz at the major labels, see Travis Jackson, *Blowin' the Blues Away: Performance and Meaning on the New York Jazz Scene* (Berkeley: Universiry of California Press, 2012), 92–99; Gabriel Solis, *Thelonious Monk Quartet with John Coltrane at Carnegie Hall* (New York: Oxford University Press, 2014), 156–59; Jeremy Smith, "'Sell It Black': Race and Marketing in Miles Davis's Early Fusion Jazz," *Jazz Perspectives* 4/1 (April 2010): 7–33.

3. On this point, see Tim Anderson, *Popular Music in a Digital Music Economy: Problems and Practices for an Emerging Service Industry* (New York: Routledge, 2014).

4. Keith Negus, *Music Genres and Corporate Cultures* (London: Routledge, 1999), 47–49. For a discussion of portfolio management in the jazz divisions of major labels, see Jackson, *Blowin' The Blues Away,* 98.

5. For a useful journalistic overview of Edgar Bronfman Jr.'s interventions into the music industry, see Fred Goodman, *Fortune's Fool: Edgar Bronfman Jr., Warner Music, and an Industry in Crisis* (New York: Simon & Schuster, 2010).

6. An important new model for musicians outside the major labels is the rise of crowdfunding sites such as ArtistShare, which employ a model analogous to the Kickstarter platform. See Paul de Barros, "Taking Control: Maria Schneider Uses a New Model to Distribute Her Music," *Down Beat,* November 2004, 56–59.

7. Anderson, *Popular Music,* 155.

8. For an account of Nonesuch Records' success in this area, see Russel Shorto, "The Industry Standard," *New York Times Magazine,* 3 October 2004, 50–58.

9. Stuart Nicholson, *Is Jazz Dead? (Or Has It Moved to a New Address)* (New York: Routledge, 2005), 82.

10. This situation may be about to change: May 2016 saw the formation of the Verve Label Group, under the stewardship of Danny Bennett (son of and manager to vocalist Tony Bennett), who is replacing David Foster as CEO. The move may portend a renewed commitment to the jazz and classical properties overseen by the label group. See "Universal Music Group Forms Verve Label Group," Universal Music, posted 19 May 2016, www.universalmusic.com /universal-music-group-forms-verve-label-group (accessed 27 October 2017). Also, with Universal Music Group's acquisition of EMI in 2012, both the Verve Group and Blue Note Records presently operate under the same corporate umbrella. See Georg Szalai, "Universal Music Completes $1.9 Million EMI Recorded Music Acquisition," HollywoodReporter.com, 28 September 2012, www.billboard.com/biz/articles/news/1083616/universal-completes-19-billion-emi-recorded-music-acquisition (27 October 2017).

11. Karen Ho, *Liquidated: An Ethnography of Wall Street* (Durham, NC: Duke University Press, 2009), 123.

12. Ibid., 194–99.

13. Ibid., 173–75.

14. On the role of financial markets in reallocating capital, see Thomas Palley, *Financialization: The Economics of Finance Capital Domination* (Basingstoke, England: Palgrave Macmillan, 2013), 2–3; on the shift from Fordist models of production to "flexible accumulation," see Steven Vallas, "Rethinking Pos-Fordism: The Meaning of Workplace Flexibility," *Sociological Theory* 17/1 (March 1999): 90–91.

15. Ho, *Liquidated,* 205–12.

16. For a discussion of the 1980s takeover movement and its impact upon subsequent corporate mergers, see ibid., 129–50.

17. I used the Google Books search function to find instances of the phrase "shareholder value" in its complete online run of *Billboard* issues; the search yielded forty-five citations of the phrase between 1994 and 2007. See for example Ray Waddell, "Concert Outlook Bright as Biz Weighs Mega-Merger: SFX/ Clear Channel Concerns Raised," *Billboard,* 11 March 2000, 1, 82; Frank Saxe, "Clear Channel's Sights on Web," *Billboard,* 16 September 2000, 5, 92;

Ed Christman, "Is Warner Music Group IPO on the Horizon?" *Billboard,* 15 January 2005, 37.

18. See Geraldine Fabrikant, "Deal Is Expected for Sony to Buy Columbia Pictures," *New York Times,* 26 September 1989; on the UMG/Polygram merger and market share, see Adam Sandler, "U Music Group Picks New Leaders," *Daily Variety,* 15 June 1998, 1.

19. Fabian Muniesa, "A Flank Movement in the Understanding of Valuation," *Sociological Review* 59, supplement (December 2011): 24–38; Daniel Beunza and Raghu Garud, "Calculators, Lemmings or Frame-Makers? The Intermediary Role of Market Analysts," *Sociological Review* 55, supplement (October 2007): 13–39.

20. "Official: David Foster Named Chairman of Verve Music Group," Hollywood Reporter, posted 15 December 2011, www.hollywoodreporter.com /news/official-david-foster-named-chairman-274299 (accessed 24 October 2017).

21. David Foster, *Hitmaker: Forty Years Making Music, Topping the Charts, and Winning Grammys* (New York: Pocket Books, 2008).

22. "Universal Music Group Expands Verve Music with Appointment of Grammy Award-Winning Producer, Songwriter, and Artist, David Foster," Universal Music Group, 15 December 2011, 22 August 2014, www.universalmusic .com/corporate/detail/867, Internet Archive, https://web.archive.org/web /20140822165502/www.universalmusic.com/corporate/detail/867 (accessed 27 October 2017).

23. Hassahn Liggins, "Smokey Robinson Signs with Verve Music Group to Release First-Of-Its-Kind Duets Album," RadioFacts.com, posted 28 March 2013, www.radiofacts.com/smokey-robinson-signs-with-verve-music-group-to-release-first-of-its-kind-duets-album (accessed 23 October 2017); Chris Payne, "Sarah McLachlan Signs to Verve: New Album 'Shine On' Coming May 6," Billboard.com, 30 January 2014, www.billboard.com/articles/news/5892795 /sarah-mclachlan-signs-to-verve-new-album-shine-on-coming-may-6 (accessed 26 October 2017); "Ruben Studdard to Release New CD Unconditional Love on Verve Records, Feb. 4th," PR Newswire, 18 November 2013, www .prnewswire.com/news-releases/ruben-studdard-to-release-new-cd-unconditional-love-on-verve-records-feb-4th-232328521.html (accessed 27 October 2017); Jem Aswad, "Danny Bennett and Graham Parker Talk the New Verve Label Group: Exclusive," Billboard.com, 26 May 2016, www.billboard.com /articles/news/7385216/danny-bennett-graham-parker-new-verve-label-group-exclusive (accessed 28 October 2017).

24. Verve Records publicity brochure, "Verve Records" folder, record company files, Institute of Jazz Studies, Rutgers University, Newark.

25. John Jurgensen, "Carla Bruni's 'Little French Songs': Exclusive First Listen," *Wall Street Journal* online, 9 April 2013, http://blogs.wsj.com /speakeasy/2013/04/09/carla-brunis-little-french-songs-exclusive-first-listen (accessed 28 October 2017); "Dirty Loops: Loopified," Dirty Loops, www .dirty-loops.com/about (accessed 23 October 2017).

26. On Trombone Shorty's addition to the Verve Forecast roster, see Gail Mitchell, "The Real Deal," *Billboard,* 3 April 2010, 35; on the revival of the

Verve Forecast imprint, Michael Paoletta, "Brazilian Girls Forecast: Catching On, with Verve," *Billboard*, 29 January 2005), 5.

27. Paoletta, "Brazilian Girls Forecast," 5.

28. For D.D. Jackson's reflections on his departure from RCA/Victor, see D.D. Jackson, "Riding The Wave: My Major-Label Journey," *Down Beat*, September 2001, 30–33. For accounts of the downsizing of major labels in the postmillenial era, see Jackson, *Blowin' the Blues Away*, 213–14; Nicholson, *Is Jazz Dead?* 1–22.

29. Nicholson, *Is Jazz Dead?* 8–15, 82–86.

30. See Jackson, *Blowin' the Blues Away*, 98–99; see also Negus, *Music Genres and Corporate Cultures*, 49–50.

31. See Bob Margolis, "Ravi Coltrane, Dave Douglas, Others in Limbo after BMG Shakeup," MTV.com, posted 13 June 2000, www.mtv.com/news/971968 /ravi-coltrane-dave-douglas-others-in-limbo-after-bmg-shakeup (accessed 24 October 2017); Steven Graybow, "Jazz Notes: Downsizing," *Billboard*, 31 May 2003, 18; Jackson, "Riding The Wave," 30–33; Brian Garrity, "Newsline . . . " *Billboard*, 29 July 2000, 112.

32. Tad Hershorn, *Norman Granz: The Man Who Used Jazz for Justice* (Berkeley: University of California Press, 2011), 4.

33. Ibid., 81–84.

34. Ibid., 216–21.

35. See Ben Ratliff, review of *Two Men with the Blues* by Wynton Marsalis and Willie Nelson, *New York Times*, 7 July 2008; Jon Pareles, "Pairing Their Sounds and Sharing the Blues," review of *Wynton Marsalis and Eric Clapton Play the Blues* by Wynton Marsalis and Eric Clapton, *New York Times*, 10 April 2011.

36. Richard Havers, *Verve: The Sound of America* (London: Thames & Hudson, 2013), 157, 274–75.

37. Hershorn, *Norman Granz*, 84–85.

38. Philip Elwood, "Granz's 'Jazz Scene' Album Reissued on CD," *Chicago Tribune*, 8 December 1994.

39. Hershorn, *Norman Granz*, 292–94; Ren Grevatt and Lee Zhito, "M-G-M Buys Verve; Maxin Tops Combo," *Billboard*, 21 November 1960, 2.

40. Michael Conant, "The Paramount Decrees Reconsidered," in *Hollywood: Critical Concepts in Media and Cultural Studies*, edited by Thomas Schatz (New York: Routledge, 2004), 3: 280.

41. "Soundtracks Are Big Business," MGM Records advertising supplement, *Billboard*, 21 January 1967, MGM-44.

42. "Hank Williams: MGM's Country Tradition," MGM Records advertising supplement, *Billboard*, 21 January 1967, MGM-33.

43. On Creed Taylor, see Charles Carson, "'Bridging the Gap': Creed Taylor, Grover Washington Jr., and the Crossover Roots of Smooth Jazz," *Black Music Research Journal* 28/1 (Spring 2008): 1–15.

44. "Taylor to Do Job on Verve's Image Under MGM Pres.," *Billboard*, 1 May 1967, 5.

45. See Creed Taylor, in Ted Panken, "The Right Groove: Creed Taylor," *Down Beat*, October 2005, 59–61.

46. Raymond Horricks, *Profiles in Jazz: From Sidney Bechet to John Coltrane* (New Brunswick, NJ: Transaction Publishers, 1991), 179.

47. Creed Taylor, in "Formula: Build for Jazz, Score Pop," *Billboard*, 9 February 1963, 17.

48. Ibid.

49. On the Verve bossa nova recordings produced by Creed Taylor, see Ruy Castro, *Bossa Nova: The Story of the Brazilian Music That Seduced the World* (Chicago: Chicago Review Press, 2000), 256–58.

50. Creed Taylor, in Marc Myers, "Interview: Creed Taylor (Part 12)," JazzWax, posted 5 November 2008, 5 September 2015, www.jazzwax.com /2008/11/interview-cre-2.html, Internet Archive, https://web.archive.org/web /20150905151843/http://www.jazzwax.com/2008/11/interview-cre-2.html (accessed 26 October 2017).

51. Peter Tschmuck, *Creativity and Innovation in the Music Industry* (Berlin: Springer Verlag, 2012), 134.

52. "Verve Gets Jimmy Smith," *Billboard*, 9 February 1963, 3; on Bill Evans's reading of "Walk on the Wild Side," see Peter Pettinger, *Bill Evans: How My Heart Sings* (New Haven, CT: Yale University Press, 1998), 146.

53. Gary Giddins, *Weather Bird: Jazz at the Dawn of its Second Century* (New York: Oxford University Press, 2004), 185.

54. Michael James Roberts, *Tell Tchaikovsky the News: Rock 'n Roll, the Labor Question, and the Musician's Union, 1942–1968* (Durham, NC: Duke University Press, 2014), 201–4.

55. Negus, *Music Genres and Corporate Cultures*, 50.

56. Russell Sanjek, *American Popular Music and Its Business: The First Four Hundred Years: Volume III, from 1900 to 1984* (New York: Oxford University Press, 1988), 508; Steve Chapple and Reebee Garofalo, *Rock n' Roll is Here to Pay: The History and Politics of the Music Industry* (Chicago: Nelson-Hall, 1977), 201–4.

57. See Frederic Dannen, *Hit Men: Power Brokers and Fast Money inside the Music Business* (New York: Vintage Books, 1991), 161–81; Gerben Bakker, "The Making of a Music Multinational: Polygram's International Business, 1945–1998," *Business History Review* 80/1 (Spring 2006): 106–7.

58. Fabian Holt, *Genre in Popular Music* (Chicago: University of Chicago Press, 2007), 86–87.

59. Mike Gross, "Labels Start New Drive to Aid Down (but Not Out) Jazz," *Billboard*, 30 March 1968, 1.

60. Eliot Tiegel, "Interim MGM Plans Summarized by Fruin," *Billboard*, 1.

61. On "twofers," see Scott Yanow, "Retro: Boxing with the Past," *Jazziz*, September 1998, 68–70; Alan Penchansky, "Mercury Kills Emarcy Twofers," *Billboard*, 25 February 1978, 64.

62. Bakker, "Making of a Music Multinational," 96–102.

63. Kieran Downes, "'Perfect Sound Forever': Innovation, Aesthetics, and the Re-making of Compact Disc Playback," *Technology and Culture* 51/2 (April 2010): 305–31.

64. Bakker, "Making of a Music Multinational," 106, 115–16.

65. Ibid., 106, 116–17.

66. On this point, see John Corbett's discussion of "fetishistic audiophilia," in *Extended Play: Sounding Off from John Cage to Dr. Funkenstein* (Durham,

NC: Duke University Press, 1994), 41; see also John Gennari's distinction between "Apollonian" and "Dionysian" approaches to jazz aesthetics, in John Gennari, "Jazz Criticism: Its Development and Ideologies," *Black American Literature Forum* 25/3 (Autumn 1991), 465.

67. Barry Feldman, in Don Palmer, "The New Jazz Majors," *Musician,* February 1986, 20.

68. Richard Seidel, in Larry Kart, "Reissue Riches: Polygram's Catalogue, Commitment Are a Boon," *Chicago Tribune,* 21 December 1986, 8.

69. "Verve's Marketing Moves to London Administration," *Billboard,* 10 January 1981, 4.

70. Alan Penchansky, "Polygram: Classics on Digital," *Billboard,* 27 December 1980, 38; Sam Sutherland, "Reactivation of Verve Line Sparks PolyGram Catalog," *Billboard,* 14 November 1981, 53.

71. Sam Sutherland, "PolyGram Classics Jazzing it Up: New Verve Reissue Series Debuted; Midlines Planned," *Billboard,* 4 December 1982, 6, 44.

72. Ibid., 44.

73. Sam Sutherland, "The Compact Impact: Carving Renaissance Out of Technology," *Billboard,* 28 June 1986, J16.

74. Sam Sutherland and Peter Keepnews, "Blue Notes," *Billboard,* 27 July 1985, 58; Chris Morris, "Jazz Lives Thanks to Handful of Vets," *Billboard,* 7 July 2001, 1, 68.

75. Morris, "Jazz Lives," 68.

76. "Now's the Time for All New Recordings from a Vintage Label," Poly-Gram Classics press release, n.d., "PolyGram" folder, record label files, Institute of Jazz Studies, Rutgers University, Newark; "Verve Live Series Set," *Billboard,* 20 September 1986, 6.

77. William Bauer, *Open the Door: The Life and Music of Betty Carter* (Ann Arbor: University of Michigan Press, 2002), 182.

78. Ibid., 189–90.

79. Richard Seidel, in Kart, "Reissue Riches," 8.

CHAPTER 4. BRONFMAN'S BAUBLE: THE CORPORATE HISTORY OF THE VERVE MUSIC GROUP (1990–2005)

1. See Keith Negus, *Music Genres and Corporate Cultures* (London: Routledge, 1999), 42–43; "Philips: A Brighter Future?" *Economist,* 13 August 1994, 60, 63.

2. Gerben Bakker, "The Making of a Music Multinational: Polygram's International Business, 1945–1998," *Business History Review* 80/1 (Spring 2006): 122–23.

3. Ibid.; Negus, *Music Genres and Corporate Cultures,* 42.

4. On the ebb and flow of profit margins during the CD boom, see Don Jeffrey, "Labels' Profit Margin Flat, Study Says: Completion of CD Libraries, Diverging Tastes Blamed," *Billboard,* 26 November 1994, 5.

5. Bakker, "Making of a Music Multinational," 117.

6. PolyGram NV, 1989 Prospectus for initial public offering, David Kronemyer, 14 December 1989, 10, www.kronemyer.com/Polygram/PolyGram%20Prospectus%2012-14-1989.pdf (accessed 30 August 2014; link no longer active).

7. Ibid., 7.

8. Gerben Bakker, "Making of a Music Multinational," 117; Adam White and Melinda Newman, "Inside EMI's New Leadership Strategy," *Billboard,* 27 October 2001, 96.

9. Thomas Sancton, "Horns of Plenty," *Time,* 22 October 1990, 64–71.

10. On the contentious circumstances surrounding the signing of the Harper Brothers—Carter had apparently not been notified of the separate signing of her working band—see William Bauer, *Open the Door: The Life and Music of Betty Carter* (Ann Arbor: University of Michigan Press, 2002), 184–85.

11. Mark Miller, "Recordings of Note," review of *Something to Consider* by Stephen Scott, *Globe and Mail,* 9 March 1992, C1.

12. See for instance Hargrove and Hart's interpretation of Nat Adderley's "Work Song," on Roy Hargrove and Antonio Hart, *The Tokyo Sessions,* compact disc, produced by Ikuyoshi Hirakawa and Larry Clothier (Novus 01241 63164 2, 1992).

13. Wynton Marsalis, in Alexander Stewart, *Making the Scene: Contemporary New York City Big Band Jazz* (Berkeley: University of California Press, 2007), 296.

14. "Kiss Me Right," from the Harper Brothers, *Remembrance: Live at the Village Vanguard,* compact disc, produced by Brian Bacchus (Verve Records 841 723-2, 1990).

15. On Henderson's period of relative inactivity in the 1980s, see Richard Seidel, in Chris Morris, "Joe Henderson Leaves Jazz Legacy," *Billboard,* 14 July 2001, 8, 59.

16. Elaine Guregian, "Grammys Open Doors for Tenor Saxophonist," *Wichita Eagle,* 23 April 1994, 6C.

17. "Legendary Tenor Saxophonist Joe Henderson Joins Verve Records' Jazz Roster," Verve Records press release, September 1991, "Joe Henderson" folder, artist files, Institute of Jazz Studies, Rutgers University, Newark.

18. Richard Seidel, in Morris, "Joe Henderson Leaves Jazz Legacy," 59.

19. Joe Henderson, in Stanley Crouch, liner notes for Joe Henderson, *Lush Life,* compact disc, produced by Don Sickler and Richard Seidel (Verve Records 314 511 779-2, 1991).

20. Peter Watrous, "Joe Henderson Pushes the Limits," *New York Times,* 28 February 1993, H28.

21. Richard Seidel, in Morris, "Joe Henderson Leaves Jazz Legacy," 59.

22. See, for example, this discussion of veteran saxophonist Frank Morgan, in Marke Andrews, "Frank Morgan Rejoices in His Reversal of Fortune," *Vancouver Sun,* 21 June 1991, D6.

23. Joe Henderson, in Stanley Crouch, liner notes for Joe Henderson, *Lush Life.*

24. Matt Schudel, "Hargrove Calls Up Spirit of Parker," *Sun-Sentinel* (Broward County, FL), 21 May 1996.

25. Richard Woodward, "On the Run With: Roy Hargrove; Have Trumpet, Will Frolic," *New York Times,* 7 September 1994, C1, C6.

26. Zoë Anglesey, "Artists in Conversation: Roy Hargrove," *Bomb,* Fall 1995.

27. See Richard Havers, *Verve: The Sound of America* (London: Thames & Hudson, 2013), 41, 313, 335.

28. Billboard notes that this $80,000 figure accounts for "production costs and the artists' upfront take"; as such, it is likely recoupable against album sales. See Jeff Levenson, "Emerging Jazz Artists Learn Art of the Deal," *Billboard,* 2 April 1994, 72.

29. Richard Seidel, in ibid.

30. Robert Shiller, *Irrational Exuberance,* 2nd ed. (New York: Broadway Books, 2005), 159–60.

31. On this point, see Stuart Nicholson, *Is Jazz Dead? (Or Has It Moved to a New Address)* (New York: Routledge, 2005), 7–8.

32. Jeff Levenson, "McBride Gets to It with Verve Release," *Billboard,* 7 January 1995, 108.

33. Christian McBride, in "Artists Perspectives of the '90s," *Down Beat,* January 2000, 33.

34. Ibid.

35. Jim Macnie, "Trend Spotting: Requiem for a Straight Line," *Billboard,* 28 June 1997, 31.

36. D. D. Jackson, "Riding the Wave: My Major-Label Journey," *Down Beat,* September 2001, 33.

37. Macnie, "Trend Spotting," 31.

38. Richard Seidel, in ibid.

39. Richard Seidel, in Bret Primack, "Playing Favorites," *Jazz Times,* May 1998, 86.

40. Ibid.

41. Ibid.

42. Nicholson, *Is Jazz Dead?* 138.

43. For an overview of the Universal/PolyGram deal set in relation to the broader context of the contemporary music industry, see Negus, *Music Genres and Corporate Cultures,* 42–45.

44. Ibid., 44.

45. Jill Krutick, in Martin Peers, "Street Toasts Deal: Seagram Stock Climbs; Analyst Reactions Mixed," *Daily Variety,* 26 May 1998, 6.

46. For an account of the unpredictable dynamics of the culture industries, as it pertains to film, see Arthur DeVany, *Hollywood Economics: How Extreme Uncertainty Shapes the Film Industry* (New York: Routledge, 2004).

47. Adam Dawtrey and Benedict Carver, "Showbiz must face the music: media giants ponder bids for Polygram, EMI," *Variety,* 11 May 1998, 1.

48. Alain Levy, in Chuck Philips, "Levy Sounds Off on Legacy at PolyGram," *Los Angeles Times,* 1 July 1998.

49. Geoffrey MacNab, "The Europeans Are Coming: Why Our Film-Makers Don't Need Hollywood Any More," *The Independent,* 31 August 2011, 16; Geoffrey MacNab, "Rushes: News: Comeback Kid," *Sight and Sound,* August 2011, 6.

50. Mitchell Sparks, *Charging Back Up the Hill: Workplace Recovery after Mergers, Acquisitions, and Downsizings* (San Francisco: Jossey-Bass, 2003), 131–32.

51. Here, Bronfman's approach to the acquisition of E. I. du Pont de Namours, the prominent chemical concern, is highly relevant. See Nicholas Faith, *The*

Bronfmans: The Rise and Fall of the House of Seagram (New York: St. Martin's Press, 2006), 246.

52. "Size Does Matter," *Economist,* 21 May 1998.

53. Don Jeffrey, "P'Gram Accepts Seagram Bid—World's Largest Record Company to Result from Merger," *Billboard,* 30 May 1998, 5.

54. Johan Seilbron and Sander Quak, "Changing Labor Policies of Transnational Corporations: The Decrease and Polarization of Corporate Social Responsibility," in *The Transformation of Solidarity: Changing Risks and the Future of the Welfare State,* edited by Romke van der Meen et al. (Amsterdam: Amsterdam University Press, 2012), 149–50.

55. Philips "Levy Sounds Off."

56. PolyGram company statement, cited in Dawtrey and Carver, "Polygram Up for Grabs."

57. Alice Rawsthorn, "Philips Denies Renegotiation of PolyGram," *Financial Times,* 8 October 1998, 26.

58. Peter Bart, *The Gross: The Hits, the Flops—The Summer That Ate Hollywood* (New York: St. Martin's Press, 1999), 279.

59. Adam White, "A New Universal Emerges as a Global Force: Morris' Team Puts Plan into Action," *Billboard,* 19 December 1998, 75.

60. Anthony Wilson-Smith, "Seagram's Shift in Direction," Macleans, 16 November 1998, www.thecanadianencyclopedia.ca/en/article/seagrams-shift-in-direction (accessed 27 October 2017).

61. Brian Milner, "Seagram Sells Polygram Movie Library to MGM: Price Less Than Expected; Two Agencies Cut Ratings," *Globe and Mail,* 23 October 1998, B1.

62. Edgar Bronfman Jr., in Larry LeBlanc, "Bronfman Assures Shareholders About P'Gram Deal," *Billboard,* 14 November 1998, 3.

63. Tom Lamont, "Napster: The Day the Music Was Set Free," *The Observer,* 23 February 2013.

64. "Seagram Closes Offer to Acquire PolyGram in $10.4 Billion Deal," *Wall Street Journal,* 7 December 1998, B8.

65. Alice Rawsthorn, "Waiting for the Music to Stop before Striking a Deal: After the Market Turmoil Seagram May Try to Renegotiate the Price It Pays for Polygram," *Financial Times,* 21 October 1998, 28.

66. "New Securities Issues," *Wall Street Journal,* 14 December 1998, C23; David Lieberman, "CEO Must Face Analysts Today about Seagram's Future," *USA Today,* 14 December 1998, 03B.

67. Alex Berenson, "No Sea Change at Seagram," TheStreet.com, posted 25 January 1999, www.thestreet.com/story/684822/1/no-sea-change-at-seagram.html (accessed 1 October 2017).

68. Anonymous money manager, in ibid.

69. Karen Ho, *Liquidated: An Ethnography of Wall Street* (Durham, NC: Duke University Press, 2009), 146.

70. Brian Milner, "Seagram Revamps Spirits Business: New Strategy for Flagship Multi-Billion Dollar Division Is to Focus on Handful of Leading Brands, Markets," *Globe and Mail,* 11 November 1998, B1.

71. Brenda Bouw, "Is Universal Too Big? Losing Key Relationships—and Unhappy Artists—Could Pose a Problem for Seagram Co. as It Orchestrates a Mammoth Merger of Polygram and Universal Music," *National Post*, 11 December 1998, C09.

72. White, "New Universal Emerges," 75.

73. Doug Morris, in Adam Sandler, "Universal Will Boot 3,000," *Daily Variety*, 11 December 1998, 1.

74. Doug Morris, in White, "New Universal Emerges," 75.

75. Ibid., 76.

76. Ibid.

77. Zach Horowitz, in Craig Rosen, "GRP Recording Co. Shuffles Executives, Aims for Wide Appeal," *Billboard*, 9 May 1998, 84.

78. John Janowiak and Jason Koransky, "Verve + GRP = Verve Music Group," *Down Beat*, May 1999, 14.

79. Ibid. Similar stories emerged from other major label jazz subsidiaries during this period; see for example pianist D. D. Jackson's account of his departure from RCA, in Jackson, "Riding the Wave," 32–33.

80. "Universal: One Year Later; Merger Behind It, UMG Looks Ahead," *Billboard*, 25 December 1999, 80; Erica Farber, "Publisher's Profile: Ron Goldstein," RadioandRecords.com, posted 14 May 2004, http://radioymusica.com/Profiles/Pages/Goldstein_R.asp (accessed 23 October 2017).

81. Dan Ouellette, "Hancock Plays Playboy Fest: Indies Go for Verve Acts," *Billboard*, 12 June 2004, 13. Brecker and Perez were among those GRP/Impulse! artists who were transferred to the Verve roster in the wake of the Universal/PolyGram merger in 1998.

82. See White, "New Universal Emerges."

83. Ron Goldstein, in Dan Ouellette, "All Those Vocals: More Singers in Labels' Jazz Mix," *Billboard*, 20 September 2003, 80.

84. Ron Goldstein, in "Industry Q&A: Ron Goldstein," *Jazzweek*, 6 March 2006, 11–12.

85. Ron Goldstein, in Melinda Newman, "Sanborn Joins Verve Music Group: Friendship with LiPuma, Musical Vision Lure Sax Player from Elektra," *Billboard*, 9 December 2000, 99.

86. Nicholson, *Is Jazz Dead?* 84–85; Dan Ouellette, "Verve Hopes Callum Has That 'Something,'" *Billboard*, 15 May 2004, 11.

87. Ted Gioia, *The History of Jazz*, 2nd ed. (New York: Oxford University Press, 2011), 374.

88. See Nicholson, *Is Jazz Dead?* 89.

89. Ron Goldstein, in Lara Pellegrinnelli, "Singing for Our Supper," *Jazz Times*, December 2003, 56–62.

90. Ron Goldstein, in Chris Morris, "Jazz Seeks Instrumental Stars: Lack of Industry Support for Young Player Reaches Crisis Level," *Billboard*, 20 April 2002, 81.

91. Jeff Jones, in ibid., 81.

92. Matt Pierson, in ibid.

93. Nat Hentoff, *At the Jazz Band Ball: Sixty Years on the Jazz Scene* (Berkeley: University of California Press, 2010), 79–80; emphasis mine.

94. Alexander Gelfand, "The Great White Hype?" *Jazziz,* December 2001, 40–43, 44.

95. Lara Pellegrinelli, "Separated at 'Birth': Singing and the History of Jazz," in *Big Ears: Listening for Gender in Jazz Studies,* edited by Nichole Rustin and Sherrie Tucker (Durham, NC: Duke University Press, 2008), 32–34.

96. Nicholson, *Is Jazz Dead?* 13. On Wayne Shorter's Verve debut, *High Life,* see Jim Macnie, "Verve's Shorter Living 'High Life,'" *Billboard,* 9 September 1995, 1, 130; Herbie Hancock's Verve debut, *The New Standard,* was released in 1996. See "HH on LP and CD: A Selected Discography," Herbie Hancock tribute supplement, *Billboard,* 1 May 1999, H-6.

97. Iain Anderson, *This Is Our Music: Free Jazz, the Sixties, and American Culture* (Philadelphia: University of Pennsylvania Press, 2007), 31.

98. See Charles Carson, "'Bridging the Gap': Creed Taylor, Grover Washington Jr., and the Crossover Roots of Smooth Jazz," *Black Music Research Journal* 28/1 (Spring 2008): 1–15; Michael Stephans, *Experiencing Jazz: A Listener's Companion* (Lanham, MD: Scarecrow Press, 2013), 425.

99. Ron Goldstein, in Carmen Walsh, "West Coast Hip: A New York City Music Label Shows Off Its L.A. Connections with a Redesign," *Office21,* Spring 2006, 32.

100. Henner Jahns, in ibid., 34.

101. Ibid.

102. Richard Florida, *The Rise of the Creative Class: And How It's Transforming Work, Leisure, Community and Everyday Life* (New York: Basic Books, 2002).

103. Ron Goldstein, in Farber, "Publisher's Profile."

104. Phil Gallo, "Less Verve at U Music," *Daily Variety,* 13 December 2006, 4.

105. Thomas Frank, "TED Talks Are Lying to You," Salon.com, posted 13 October 2013, www.salon.com/2013/10/13/ted_talks_are_lying_to_you (accessed 23 October 2017). For an excellent discussion of the relationship between "creativity" and the culture of financialization, see Max Haiven, "The Creative and the Derivative: Historicizing Creativity Under Post-Bretton Woods Financialization," *Radical History Review* 118 (Winter 2014): 113–38.

106. Leo Kolber and Ian MacDonald, *Leo: A Life* (Montreal: McGill-Queens University Press, 2003), 52; Brian Garrity, "Seagram, Vivendi in Buyout Talks," *Billboard,* 24 June 2000, 122.

107. See Marie Mawad and Amy Thompson, "Vivendi Takes M&A Pause to Decide How to Spend $14 Bln," Bloomberg.com, posted 22 November 2013, www.bloomberg.com/news/2013-11-21/vivendi-takes-m-a-pause-to-decide-how-to-spend-14-billion-cash.html (accessed 24 October 2017); Matthew Benz, "Sentiment Shifts against Messier," *Billboard,* 15 June 2002, 3; Brian Garrity, "Vivendi Universal: What Now?" *Billboard,* 22 June 2002, 1, 79.

108. John Carreyrou and Martin Peers, "How Messier Kept Cash Crisis at Vivendi Hidden for Months," *Wall Street Journal,* 31 October 2002.

109. Ibid. See also William Lazonick, "The Quest for Shareholder Value: Stock Repurchases in the US Economy," *Louvain Economic Review* 74/4 (2008): 479-540.

110. Laura Holson and Geraldine Fabrikant, "Shake-up at Vivendi: The Family; a Wealthy Family Humbled by Its Own Moves," *New York Times*, 3 July 2002, C4.

111. Frank Ahrens, "GE, Vivendi Give Rise to a Giant: New NBC Universal a $43 Billion Concern," *Washington Post*, 13 May 2004, E01; "Universal U.K. to Make Staff Cuts," Billboard.com, 22 January 2004, www.billboard.com/biz /articles/news/1447266/universal-uk-to-make-staff-cuts (accessed 27 October 2017).

112. See Steve Graybow, "Jazz Notes: Downsizing," *Billboard*, 31 May 2003, 18; Steve Graybow, "Jazz Notes: Climbing the Mountain," *Billboard*, 9 March 2002, 39.

113. David Adler, "ArtistShare Remakes Distribution Model," *Down Beat*, September 2004, 14; Michael West, "Dave Douglas' Greenleaf Music Label: Defining Success in Today's Online Music Biz," Jazztimes.com, posted 11 November 2012, http://jazztimes.com/articles/58950-dave-douglas-greenleaf-music-label (accessed 27 October 2017).

114. See EMI vice-president Howard Handler's discussion of the "consumer equity" of the Blue Note brand, in Larry Blumenfeld, "Blue Note: Still Spry at 70," *Billboard*, 28 March 2009, 26.

115. Warner Jazz was one of many subsidiaries axed or downsized by Warner Music Group following its acquisition by a private equity group led by Edgar Bronfman Jr. in 2004. See Ed Christman, "WMG Speeds Into New Era: 1,000 Jobs Going; Fresh A&R Sources Sought," *Billboard*, 13 March 2004, 1, 85; Gregory Robb, "Going the Distance: March-April 2004," Allaboutjazz.com, posted 8 March 2004, www.allaboutjazz.com/going-the-distance-march-april-2004-by-gregory-j-robb.php#.VCclASldVhM (accessed 26 October 2017).

116. See Russell Shorto, "The Industry Standard," *New York Times Magazine*, 3 Ocober 2004.

117. See "OKeh—Artists," Okey Records, www.okeh-records.com/artists (accessed 24 October 2017); "Sony Classical Relaunching OKeh Records Jazz Imprint," Billboard.com, posted 11 January 2013, www.billboard.com/biz /articles/news/retail/1484243/sony-classical-relaunching-okeh-records-jazz-imprint (accessed 27 October 2017).

118. "UMG Creates Verve Label Group, Danny Bennett to Lead," Billboard. com, 19 May 2016, www.billboard.com/articles/news/7377729/umg-verve-label-group-danny-bennett (accessed 27 October 2017).

CHAPTER 5. JAZZ AND THE RIGHT TO THE CITY: JAZZ VENUES AND THE LEGACY OF URBAN REDEVELOPMENT IN CALIFORNIA

This chapter takes its inspiration from a white paper issued by a consortium of community scholars in Los Angeles, devoted to furthering a just urbanism in Leimert Park, Lincoln Heights, and other Los Angeles communities. See "Fighting for a Right to the City: Collaborative Research to Support Community Organizing in L.A.," UCLA Luskin Capstone Database, June 2007, https://ucla.app.box. com/s/tsd5py7sbynj187hov9i325eu2d25gba (accessed 23 October 2017). .

1. See Henri Lefebvre, *Writings on Cities,* translated and introduced by Eleonore Kofman and Elizabeth Lebas (Oxford: Blackwell, 1996).

2. See Mark Purcell, "Excavating Lefebvre: The Right to the City and Its Urban Politics of the Inhabitant," *GeoJournal* 58/2–3 (2002): 103.

3. David Harvey, *Rebel Cities: From the Right to the City to the Urban Revolution* (London: Verso, 2012), xi.

4. See William Howland Kenney, *Chicago Jazz: A Cultural History, 1904–1930* (New York: Oxford University Press, 1994), 16–19; David Stowe, *Swing Changes: Big-Band Jazz in New Deal America* (Cambridge, MA: Harvard University Press, 1994), 41–42; Paul Machlin, *Stride: The Music of Fats Waller* (Boston: Twayne Publishers, 1985), 9; Caroline Rosenthal, *New York and Toronto Novels after Postmodernism* (Rochester, NY: Camden House, 2011), 161.

5. George Lewis, "Experimental Music in Black and White: The AACM in New York, 1970–1985," in *Uptown Conversations: The New Jazz Studies,* edited by Robert G. O'Meally (New York: Columbia University Press, 2004), 68–69. For an account of repurposed lofts and their role in changing patterns of urbanization, see Sharon Zukin, *Loft Living: Culture and Capital in Urban Change* (New Brunswick, NJ: Rutgers University Press, 1989); see also Michael Heller, *Loft Jazz: Improvising New York in the 1970s* (Berkeley: University of California Press, 2017), 34–64.

6. See Ron Scott, "Parlor Jazz Tradition," *New York Amsterdam News,* 3 March 2004, 23. Due to its sidewalk traffic and its policy of offering free food, Parayano's Birdland Jazzista venue was frequently cited by the City of Berkeley for municipal code violations. In spite of widespread support from the East Bay community, the venue was eventually shut down by police. See Emilie Raguso, "End of an Era for Berkeley Rustic Birdhouses, Birdland Jazz," Berkeleyside, posted 10 December 2012, www.berkeleyside.com/2012/12/10/end-of-an-era-for-berkeley-rustic-birdhouses-birdland-jazz/comment-page-1.

7. Daniel Fischlin et al., *The Fierce Urgency of Now: Improvisation, Rights, and the Ethics of Cocreation* (Durham, NC: Duke University Press, 2013), 120–27.

8. On "free trade zones," see Naomi Klein, *No Logo: Taking Aim at the Brand Bullies* (New York: Picador, 1999), 202–9; on the capital gains tax rate as an effective subsidy of the financial sector, see Gautam Makunda, "The Price of Wall Street's Power," *Harvard Business Review* (June 2014), https://hbr.org/2014/06/the-price-of-wall-streets-power (accessed 2 October 2017).

9. On this contradiction, see David Harvey, *A Brief History of Neoliberalism* (New York: Oxford University Press, 2005), 20–21. For a discussion of the blurred boundaries between public and private sectors in public-private partnerships, see Sanford Schram, *The Return of Ordinary Capitalism: Neoliberalism, Precarity, Occupy* (New York: Oxford University Press, 2015), 164.

10. See Rachel Weber, "Extracting Value from the City: Neoliberalism and Urban Development," *Antipode* 34/3 (July 2002): 519–40.

11. See, for instance, the case of the Los Angeles Community Redevelopment Agency and its efforts to intervene in Leimert Park, home to the World Stage and other black-owned cultural institutions. See "Fighting for a Right to the City," 3–2–3–22.

12. Christy Leffall et al., "Redevelopment: After the Fall," *Race, Poverty, and the Environment* 19/1 (2012): 57; Mara Parks, "Shifting Ground: The Rise and Fall of the Los Angeles Community Redevelopment Agency," *Southern California Quarterly* 86/3 (Fall 2004): 241.

13. Michael Dardia, *Subsidizing Redevelopment in California* (San Francisco: Public Policy Institution of California, 1998), 3–4.

14. Mara Parks, "Shifting Ground," 245; Jeff Chapman, "Tax Increment Financing and Fiscal Stress: The California Genesis," in *Tax Increment Financing and Economic Development: Uses, Structures, and Impact*, edited by Craig Johnson and Joyce Man (Albany: State University of New York Press, 2001), 114.

15. Dardia, *Subsidizing Redevelopment*, 3.

16. Parks, "Shifting Ground," 245.

17. The law abolishing the state's redevelopment agencies survived a legal challenge in the California Supreme Court. See Maura Dolan et al., "California High Court Puts Redevelopment Agencies out of Business," *Los Angeles Times*, 29 December 2011.

18. On Title I of the Housing Act and urban renewal, see Samuel Zipp, *Manhattan Projects: The Rise and Fall of Urban Renewal in Cold War New York* (New York: Oxford University Press, 2010), 7–8.

19. Robert A. Caro, *The Power Broker: Robert Moses and the Fall of New York* (New York: Alfred A. Knopf, 1974), 12; emphasis in original text.

20. On this point, see ibid., *passim*.

21. Weber, "Extracting Value from the City," 527.

22. Ibid.

23. Ibid., 528; Peter Hall, *Cities of Tomorrow: An Intellectual History of Urban Planning and Design since 1880*, 4th ed. (Oxford: Blackwell, 1996), 276–77.

24. Weber, "Extracting Value from the City," 528; Hall, *Cities of Tomorrow*, 277.

25. Weber, "Extracting Value from the City," 532–33.

26. Ibid., 530–31.

27. Ibid., 534.

28. "Sector Study: California Redevelopment and Tax Allocation Bonds," paper issued by the National Public Finance Guarantee, January 2010, 2.

29. Ibid., 2; on the politics and policy impact of Proposition 13, see Peter Schrag, *Paradise Lost: California's Experience, America's Future*, rev. ed. (Berkeley: University of California Press, 2004), 129–88.

30. California's school system is to some extent shielded from this implication of TIF. See Dardia, *Subsidizing Redevelopment*, 4–5.

31. Weber, "Extracting Value from the City," 534–35.

32. See Mark Davidson and Kevin Ward, "'Picking Up the Pieces': Austerity Urbanism, California and Fiscal Crisis," *Cambridge Journal of Regions, Economy and Society* 7/1 (2014): 84.

33. For a compelling account of the midcentury Fillmore / Western Addition jazz scene that addresses the social and psychological impact of redevelopment,

see Nicholas Baham, *The Coltrane Church: Apostles of Sound, Agents of Social Justice* (Jefferson, NC: McFarland, 2016).

34. Elizabeth Pepin and Lewis Watts, *Harlem of the West: The San Francisco Fillmore Jazz Era* (San Francisco: Chronicle Books, 2006), 30.

35. Ibid., 32.

36. Ibid., 38, 87, and *passim*.

37. Ibid., *passim*; Martha Ackmann, *Curveball: The Remarkable Story of Toni Stone* (Chicago: Chicago New Press, 2010), 57–58.

38. On Slim Gaillard's humorous performances, and his development of the "Vout" language, see Charles Hiroshi Garrett, "The Humor of Jazz," in *Jazz/Not Jazz*, edited by David Ake et al. (Berkeley: University of California Press, 2012), 57.

39. Carol Chamberland, "The House That Bop Built," *California History* 75/3 (Fall 1996): 275.

40. Bop City, like many of the black-owned clubs in the neighborhood, was subject to countless police raids during this period. See Historic Preservation Committee, "Landmark Designation Report: Marcus Books/Jimbo's Bop City, 1712–1716 Fillmore Street," 13 February 2014, p. 3, www.sf-planning.org/ftp/files/Preservation/landmarks_designation/Final_Adopted_LM_Designation Report_266_Marcus.pdf (accessed 26 October 2017).

41. On Jimbo's Bop City, see also Baham, *Coltrane Church*, 63–76.

42. Frank Jackson, in Pepin and Watts, *Harlem of the West*, 141.

43. Steve Nakajo, in ibid., 40.

44. Richard Florida, *Rise of the Creative Class: And How It's Transforming Work, Leisure, Community, and Everyday Life* (New York: Basic Books, 2002), 183.

45. Willie Brown, in Pepin and Watts, *Harlem of the West*, 38.

46. See Meredith Akemi Oda, "Remaking the 'Gateway To The Pacific': Urban, Economic, and Racial Redevelopment in San Francisco, 1945–1970" (Ph.D. diss., University of Chicago, 2010).

47. See Robert Self, *American Babylon: Race and the Struggle for Postwar Oakland* (Princeton, NJ: Princeton University Press, 2003), 82.

48. Ira Katznelson, *When Affirmative Action Was White: An Untold History of Racial Inequality in Twentieth-Century America* (New York: W. W. Norton, 2005), 116.

49. Oda, "Remaking the 'Gateway to the Pacific,'" 68.

50. City Planning Commission, *The Redevelopment of Blighted Areas: Report on Conditions Indicative of Blight and Redevelopment Policies* (San Francisco: City Planning Commission, 1945).

51. Clement Lai, "The Racial Triangulation of Space: The Case of Urban Renewal in San Francisco's Fillmore District," *Annals of the Association of American Geographers* 102/1 (2012): 157.

52. San Francisco Planning and Housing Association, *Blight and Taxes* (San Francisco: San Francisco Planning and Housing Association, 1947), 3–8.

53. See James Bassett, "Christopher Goal for S.F. in Sight: Redevelopment, Long a Political Football, Gives Mayor Stature in Race for Governor," *Los Angeles Times*, 10 July 1961, 27.

54. Paul Miller, *The Postwar Struggle for Civil Rights: African Americans in San Francisco, 1945–1975* (New York: Routledge, 2010), 106–26; Chester Hartman with Sarah Carnochan, *City for Sale: The Transformation of San Francisco* (Berkeley: University of California Press, 2002), 65–66.

55. Miller, *Postwar Struggle for Civil Rights,* 121–26.

56. Leta Miller, "Racial Segregation and the San Francisco Musicians' Union," *Journal of the Society for American Music* 1/2 (May 2007): 161–206.

57. Philip Allen, in Pepin and Watts, *Harlem of the West,* 171–72.

58. Frank Jackson, in ibid., 169.

59. Historic Preservation Committee, "Landmark Designation Report."

60. John "Jimbo" Edwards, in Chamberland, "House that Bop Built," 282.

61. Gary Carr, "Who Shot the Mayor of Fillmore?" *New Fillmore,* 4 September 2014, http://newfillmore.com/2014/09/04/who-shot-the-mayor-of-fillmore (accessed 29 October 2017); Rob Lowman, "Skirball Center Opens 'Bill Graham and the Rock & Roll Revolution,'" *Los Angeles Daily News,* 29 May 2015.

62. Historic Preservation Committee, "Landmark Designation Report."

63. Lance Burton, "Legendary 'Queen of Fillmore' Leola King Leaves Proud Legacy of Struggle against Redevelopment," *San Francisco BayView,* 12 February 2015; Pepin and Watts, *Harlem of the West,* 114.

64. Federico Cervantes, in Pepin and Watts, *Harlem of the West,* 112.

65. Jason Dearen, "50 Years of Urban Renewal Nearly Over in San Francisco," *Charleston Gazette,* 10 November 2008, A10.

66. Leola King, in the Urban School of San Francisco, "Leola King," in *Telling Their Stories: Oral History Archives Project,* Tellingstories.org, 12 May 2007, http://tellingstories.org/fillmore/leola_king/index.html (accessed 14 April 2017).

67. Dearen, "50 Years of Urban Renewal."

68. Leola King, in the Urban School of San Francisco, "Leola King."

69. Leola King, in G.W. Schultz, "A Half-Century of Lies," *San Francisco Bay Guardian,* 20 March 2009.

70. Ibid.

71. Ibid.; San Francisco Mayor's Office of Housing and Community Development, "Certificate of Preference Program Frequently Asked Questions," http://sfmohcd.org/sites/default/files/FileCenter/Documents/7515-COPP_FAQs_120513.pdf (accessed 15 April 2017).

72. Schultz, "Half-Century of Lies."

73. Leola King, in the Urban School of San Francisco, "Leola King."

74. Michael E. Ross, "Why Are Black Folks Leaving San Francisco?" TheRoot.com, posted 6 May 2009, 23 May 2016, www.theroot.com/articles/culture/2009/05/why_are_black_folks_leaving_san_fran.1.html, Internet Archive, https://web.archive.org/web/20160523002627/www.theroot.com/articles/culture/2009/05/why_are_black_folks_leaving_san_fran.1.html (accessed 26 October 2017). Between 2000 and 2010, San Francisco saw a 20.4 percent loss in its African-American population; on this development, see Eric Tang, "Recent College Graduates Are Pushing Lower-Income African Americans out of Cities," *Washington Post* online, posted 29 October 2014, www.washingtonpost.com

/posteverything/wp/2014/10/29/college-graduates-are-pushing-african-americans-out-of-cities (accessed 29 October 2017).

75. On the Fillmore Center, see Hartman, *City for Sale*, 413 n. 2; Julia Gilden, "San Francisco: 20-Year Rehabilitation About to Bear Fruit," *New York Times*, 5 February 1989, A9; John McCloud, "Tenanting a Big, Controversial Project," *New York Times*, 9 December 1990, R5.

76. "Old Houses Sold by San Francisco: Victorian Buildings Offered in Redevelopment Area," *New York Times*, 23 July 1972, 49.

77. Historic Preservation Committee, "Landmark Designation Report."

CHAPTER 6. THE "YOSHI'S EFFECT": JAZZ, SPECULATIVE
URBANISM, AND URBAN REDEVELOPMENT IN
CONTEMPORARY SAN FRANCISCO

1. Reverend Arnold Townsend, in Richard Scheinen, "Yoshi's Shines, Sizzles on Opening Night in S.F.: Drummer Haynes Perfect for Jazz Club's Gala Event," *San Jose Mercury News*, 30 November 2007.

2. Ibid.

3. Ibid.

4. See, for example, Johnson's discussion of the project in Kathy Perry's profile of the developer, Kathy Perry, "Fillmore Heritage Center's Michael Johnson: Preserving the Fillmore Legacy," *Harlem West*, June 2008, 4.

5. On these points, see Nicholas Baham, *The Coltrane Church: Apostles of Sound, Agents of Social Justice* (Jefferson, NC: McFarland, 2016), 89–94.

6. Venise Wagner, "Trying to Jazz Up Fillmore: Dream of Jazz District Rebirth in Neighborhood Is Fading," *San Francisco Examiner*, 9 July 2000, C1.

7. Jim Jefferson, in "Fillmore Jazz District, Open for Business: An Interview with Jim Jefferson," *Harlem West*, January 2008, 9.

8. Philip Elwood, "S.F. Jazz 'Renaissance' Detailed Fillmore Complex Will Cost $35 Million," *San Francisco Examiner*, 7 October 1998, C1. A reproduction of the proposed Blue Note/AMC Theater complex is posted at the website for "The Fillmore," the fourth part in a documentary series on San Francisco's neighborhoods prepared by the PBS affiliate KQED. See "Fillmore Timeline," PBS, www.pbs.org/kqed/fillmore/learning/time.html (accessed 6 April 2015).

9. Wagner, "Trying to Jazz Up Fillmore," C1.

10. On the renaming of the Upper Fillmore as "Lower Pacific Heights," see Emily Landes, "If You Rename It, Will They Come?" *San Francisco Apartment Magazine*, November 2006. A well-known account of this phenomenon, as it applies to property values in Southern California, can be found in Mike Davis's *City of Quartz: Excavating the Future in Los Angeles* (London: Verso, 2006), 152–56.

11. Gregory Lewis, "Mayor Moves on Fillmore Project: Brown to Appoint New Jazz District Advisory Panel under His Office," *San Francisco Examiner*, 17 October 1996, D1.

12. Wagner, "Trying to Jazz Up Fillmore," C1.

13. Demian Bulwa, "Obituary: Mary Rogers—S.F. Community Activist," *SFGate*, 6 March 2006; Rachel Brahinski, "'Hush Puppies,' Communalist

Politics, and Demolition Governance: The Rise and Fall of the Black Fillmore," in *Ten Years That Shook the City: San Francisco 1968–1978,* edited by Chris Carlsson (San Francisco: City Lights Books, 2011), 147.

14. Gregory Lewis, "Mayor Moves on Fillmore Project," *SFGate,* 17 October 1996.

15. Amanda Nowinski, "Straight Ahead: The New Generation of Jazz in San Francisco," *The Metropolitan,* 29 March 1999.

16. Gerald Adams, "City's Proposed Jazz District Back on Track," *SFGate,* 28 October 1997.

17. "All That Jazz: The Mayor, in a Turnabout, Will Invest Funds in the Proposed Jazz Renaissance District in the City where 'Jazz' Was First Printed," *San Francisco Examiner,* 10 November 1997, A18.

18. Jesse Hamlin, "Blue Note, AMC Renew Fillmore Project Plans," *SFGate,* 7 October 1998.

19. See Diana Henriques, "Obituary: Stanley Durwood, 78, Inventor of Multiplex," *New York Times,* 16 July 1999; Joe Gose, "In Kansas City, the Battle Continues Over a Big Downtown Entertainment Complex," *Barrons,* 10 May 1999. For a more extensive account of UEDs and their political and economic impact, see John Hannigan, *Fantasy City: Pleasure and Profit in the Postmodern Metropolis* (New York: Routledge, 1998), *passim.*

20. Venise Wagner, "Jazz District Project Struggling," *SFGate,* 7 April 2000; Venise Wagner, "AMC pulls out of Jazz District," *SFGate,* 5 April 2000.

21. Dan Levy, "Agency Axes Jazz District Developer: City Seeking New Partner for Project," *SFGate,* 14 June 2001.

22. Gerald Adams, "Jazz Greats Staking Out Space in San Francisco," *Chicago Tribune,* 18 December 1995, Tempo section 4; Levy, "Agency Axes District Developer."

23. James Morales, in Victoria Colliver, "Silver Screens with Silver Linings," *SFGate,* 26 July 1998.

24. Wagner, "Trying to Jazz Up Fillmore."

25. Ibid., C1.

26. Paolo Lucchesi, "Rasselas Jazz Club Closes, as Its Owner Calls Upon Mayor Lee to Salvage Jazz Preservation District Vision," *SF Gate,* 19 August 2013.

27. Paolo Lucchesi, "Uh-Oh Alert: Sheba's Lounge Feeling the Yoshi's Effect?" Eater.com, 12 December 2007, http://sf.eater.com/2007/12/12/6807869/uh-oh-alert-sheba-lounge-feeling-the-yoshis-effect.

28. San Francisco Redevelopment Agency, agenda item 4(h), San Francisco Office of Community Investment and Infrastructure, 19 June 2005, http://sfocii.org/ftp/archive/sfarchive.org/index4c4f.html?dept = 1051&sub = &dtype = 3456&year = 6157&file = 62342 (accessed 27 October 2017); Carolyn Alburger, "Sheba Piano Lounge Owner Sources from Ethiopia," *SFGate,* 13 September 2009.

29. Michael Johnson, "Next Time, Consider the Community," letter to the editor, *SFGate,* 1 September 2002; Dan Levy, "Fillmore Update," *SFGate,* 22 September 2002.

30. Mary Rogers, in Charlie Goodyear, "Jazz Coming Back to Fillmore: After Years Of Delay, City Oks Financing for Club-Restaurant," *SFGate,* 20 October 2004.

31. Linda Castrone, "Jazzy Upgrades up and down Fillmore: Resurgent Activity Livens a City Favorite," *Registry: Bay Area Real Estate Journal,* June 2008, 12; Dan Levy, "Neighborhood Dream Fulfilled—Fillmore Again a Place of Note," *SFGate,* 16 October 2005; Jim Harrington, "Yoshi's at the Fillmore," *Alameda Times-Star,* 21 September 2005, n.p.

32. Julia Gilden, "San Francisco: 20-Year Rehabilitation About to Bear Fruit," *New York Times,* 5 February 1989, A9.

33. On additional regulations facing community redevelopment agencies involved in the production of new housing and mixed-use developments, see Michael Dardia, *Subsidizing Redevelopment in California* (San Francisco: Public Policy Institution of California, 1998), 79–86.

34. Castrone, "Jazzy Upgrades up and down Fillmore," 13.

35. Ralph Conant and Daniel Myers, *Towards a More Perfect Union: The Governance of Metropolitan America* (Novato, CA: Chandler and Sharp Publishers, 2002), 39–40.

36. On these points, see Kim-Mai Cutler, "How Burrowing Owls Lead to Vomiting Anarchists (or SF's Housing Crisis Explained)," TechCrunch.com, 14 April 2014, http://techcrunch.com/2014/04/14/sf-housing (accessed 23 October 2017).

37. Jesse Hamlin, "Yoshi's SF Changes Its Repertoire," *SFGate,* 10 January 2009.

38. Andrew Gilbert, "Redevelopment Agency Loans Millions to Keep Yoshi's in S.F.," *San Jose Mercury News,* 23 January 2009, n.p.

39. Ian Port, "Coda: The End of Yoshi's SF," *SF Weekly,* 18 June 2014.

40. Ibid.

41. Yoshi Cato, "Sax master Pharaoh Sanders Returns to Bay Area," *Inside Bay Area,* 3 January 2008; Jim Harrington, "Cassandra Wilson Heats Up Yoshi's SF," *Contra Costa Times,* 30 January 2008, n.p.; Jim Harrington, "Don't Fret: Pat Metheny Is Finally at Yoshi's in S.F.," *Inside Bay Area,* 19 February 2008.

42. Peter Williams, in Andy Tennille, "Yoshi's San Francisco: Sushi and Standards," *Jazz Times,* January–February 2008.

43. Jennifer Maertz, "Tough Economic Times Hit Yoshi's, Vips, and Your CD Collection," *SF Weekly,* 10 December 2008.

44. Gilbert, "Redevelopment Agency Loans Millions."

45. Dan Ouellette, "Pianist McCoy Tyner Settles In at Yoshi's: Legendary Jazzman Is Making It an Annual Tradition," *SF Gate,* 27 January 1999.

46. Dave Pehling, "Yoshi's Steps Up Its Game with Free-Jazz Fest," *SF Weekly,* 17 June 2009.

47. Tamara Palmer, "Oakland Rapper Too $hort Makes His Fillmore District Debut at Yoshi's," *SF Weekly,* 7 March 2011; Jim Harrington, "8 Scary Good Shows for Oct. 31," *Contra Costa Times,* 21 October 2013, n.p.; Jim Harrington, "Cowboy Junkies Singer Talks Tunes, Life on the Road," *San Jose*

Mercury News, 26 April 2013, n.p.; Jim Harrington, "Zombies Are Coming—and That's Good News," *San Jose Mercury News,* 27 August 2013, n.p.

48. Chris Barnett, "How the Yoshi's Deal Went Down," *New Fillmore,* 4 July 2014.

49. Ibid.

50. Ibid.

51. Ibid.

52. Ian Port, "Coda."

53. Unnamed city official, in Barnett, "How the Yoshi's Deal Went Down."

54. James Morales, in Gilbert, "Redevelopment Agency Loans Millions."

55. Anonymous source, in Barnett, "How the Yoshi's Deal Went Down."

56. Office of Community Investment and Infrastructure, San Francisco, Informational Memorandum, Attachment 3, "Recent Communications Between OCII/City and FDC's Investor Group," San Francisco Office of Community Investment and Infrastructure, 23 September 2013, 3–4, http://sfocii.org/sites/default/files/ftp/meetingarchive/oversight_board/sfocii.org/modules/InfoMemoAttachment3-Fillmore-documentid = 5366.pdf (accessed 26 October 2017).

57. Ibid., 5–6; Office of Community Investment and Infrastructure, "Final Workshop on the Long-Range Property Management Plan Pursuant to Section 34191.5 of Assembly Bill 1484," San Francisco Office of Community Investment and Infrastructure, 5 November 2013, attachment 6, 2, http://sfocii.org/sites/default/files/ftp/meetingarchive/commission/www.sfocii.org/modules/5cWorkshopMemoAtt6-documentid = 5683.pdf (accessed 26 October 2017).

58. "Final Workshop on Long-Range Property Management Plan," attachment 6, 2.

59. Office of Community Investment and Infrastructure, "Final Workshop on the Long-Range Property Management Plan Pursuant to Section 34191.5 of Assembly Bill 1484," San Francisco Office of Community Investment and Infrastructure, 5 November 2013, attachment 7, 2, http://sfocii.org/sites/default/files/ftp/meetingarchive/commission/www.sfocii.org/modules/5cWorkshopMemoAtt7-documentid = 5684.pdf (accessed 26 October 2017).

60. Chris Barnett, "A New Era Begins at Yoshi's," *New Fillmore,* 4 July 2014.

61. Peter Williams, in Richard Scheinin, "The Addition Nightclub in San Francisco to Close Jan. 14," *San Jose Mercury News,* 12 January 2015.

62. The Sheba Piano Lounge opened in 2006. For a profile of its principal owner, Netsanet Alemayehu, see Chris Barnett, "Keeing Jazz Alive on the Fillmore," *New Fillmore,* 1 July 2016.

63. Peter Gebre, *Making It in America: Conversations with Successful Ethiopian American Entrepreneurs* (Washington, DC: AASBEA Publishers, 2004), 79–83.

64. Agonafer Shiferaw, in ibid., 84–85.

65. San Francisco Redevelopment Agency, Memorandum, Agenda item 4(a), meeting of 13 January 2009, http://sfocii.org/sites/default/files/ftp/archive/sfarchive.org/indexoe3b.html; Gebre, *Making It in America,* 86–87.

66. Greg Heller, "Jazz Club Opens on Fillmore," *SFGate,* 17 October 1999.

67. Gebre, *Making It in America,* 83–84.

68. Paolo Lucchesi, "Rasselas Jazz Club to Close This Month," *SFGate,* 5 August 2013; Ian Port, "With Rassela's Gone, Is the Fillmore Jazz District Working?" *SF Weekly,* 28 August 2013; Silke Tudor, "*SF Weekly* Whammies 2000," *SF Weekly,* 4 October 2000.

69. Anthony Torres, "Farewell to a Big Man with a Tiny Trumpet," *New Fillmore,* 4 January 2012; Anthony Torres, "A Great Player Who Loves What He's Doing," *New Fillmore,* 1 May 2011.

70. Matt Crawford, "Fillmore Jazz Festival Highlights," SF Station, posted 1 July 2011, www.sfstation.com/2011/07/01/fillmore-jazz-festival-highlights / (accessed 3 October 2017); "Fillmore Jazz Festival," Steven Restivo Event Services, www.sresproductions.com/events/fillmore-jazz-festival/ (accessed 19 April 2017).

71. Agonafer Shiferaw, in Rachel Swan, "Jazz Musicians Sing the Blues," *East Bay Express,* 15 June 2011.

72. Swan, "Jazz Musicians Sing the Blues."

73. Derf Butler, in Wagner, "Trying to Jazz Up Fillmore."

74. Agonafer Shiferaw, in Lucchesi, "Rasselas Jazz Club Closes."

75. Agonafer Shiferaw, in Cathy Bussewitz and William Love, "S.F. Aims to Jazz Up Fillmore," *East Bay Times,* 27 March 2006.

76. San Francisco Redevelopment Agency, Memorandum, Agenda item 4(a), meeting of 13 January 2009.

77. San Francisco Redevelopment Agency, "Minutes of a Regular Meeting of the Redevelopment Agency of the City and County of San Francisco," Archive.org, https://archive.org/stream/73minutesregular2009sanf/73minutesr egular2009sanf_djvu.txt (accessed 19 April 2017).

78. Ibid.

79. Agonafer Shiferaw, in Lucchesi, "Rasselas Jazz Club Closes."

80. Mark Davidson and Kevin Ward, "'Picking Up the Pieces': Austerity Urbanism, California and Fiscal Crisis," *Cambridge Journal of Regions, Economy, and Society* 7/1 (2014): 89–91.

81. "Moody's Confirms Ba1 on Successor Agency to the San Francisco RDA (CA) TABs," Moodys.com, posted 5 September 2013, www.moodys.com /research/Moodys-Confirms-Ba1-on-Successor-Agency-to-the-San-Francisco— PR_281717 (accessed 24 October 2017).

82. Office of the Controller, City Services Auditor, "San Francisco Redevelopment Agency: Audit of Seven Programs in the Western Addition A-2 Redevelopment Plan," 20 December 2011, http://sfcontroller.org/sites/default/files/File Center/Documents/2799-SFRA%20Western%20Addition%20Report%20 12–20–11.pdf (accessed 27 October 2017).

83. Matt Smith and Zusha Ellinson, "Fillmore District Audit Shows Little Oversight," *New York Times,* 5 January 2012.

84. The story behind this proposal is outlined in Nicholas Baham, *Coltrane Church,* 180–91.

85. Ibid., 186.

86. Ibid., 191.

87. Sam Whiting, "Coltrane Church to Vacate Western Addition at End of April," *SFGate*, 21 March 2016.

88. Ana Y. Ramos-Zayas, *Street Therapists: Race, Affect, and Neoliberal Personhood in Latino Newark* (Chicago: University of Chicago Press, 2012), 7.

89. Nicholas Baham has also suggested as much in *Coltrane Church*, 91.

Works Cited

"About NOJO." New Orleans Jazz Orchestra, http://thenojo.thecanarycollective
.com/pages/detail/141/About-NOJO (accessed 23 October 2017).

Ackmann, Martha. *Curveball: The Remarkable Story of Toni Stone.* Chicago:
Chicago New Press, 2010).

Adler, David. "ArtistShare Remakes Distribution Model." *Down Beat,* September 2004, 14.

Ake, David. *Jazz Cultures.* Berkeley: University of California Press, 2002.

———. *Jazz Matters: Sound, Place, and Time since Bebop.* Berkeley: University
of California Press, 2010.

Alexander, Michelle. *The New Jim Crow: Mass Incarceration in the Age of
Colorblindness.* New York: New Press, 2012.

Anderson, Iain. *This Is Our Music: Free Jazz, the Sixties, and American Culture.* Philadelphia: University of Pennsylvania Press, 2007.

Anderson, Tim. *Popular Music in a Digital Music Economy: Problems and
Practices for an Emerging Service Industry.* New York: Routledge, 2014.

Anglesey, Zoë. "Artists in Conversation: Roy Hargrove." *Bomb,* Fall 1995.

Appadurai, Arjun. *The Future as Cultural Fact: Essays on the Global Condition.* London: Verso, 2013.

Armstrong, Jenny. "Dexter Gordon: Transcontinental Tenorist." *Down Beat,*
20 June 1972, 17

"Artists Perspectives of the '90s." *Down Beat,* January 2000, 33–35, 37.

Aswad, Jem. "Danny Bennett and Graham Parker Talk the New Verve Label
Group: Exclusive." Billboard.com, 26 May 2016, www.billboard.com
/articles/news/7385216/danny-bennett-graham-parker-new-verve-label-
group-exclusive (accessed 28 October 2017).

Baham, Nicholas. *The Coltrane Church: Apostles of Sound, Agents of Social
Justice.* Jefferson, NC: McFarland, 2016.

Baker, David. *Jazz Pedagogy: A Comprehensive Method of Jazz Education for Teacher and Student.* Los Angeles: Alfred Music Publishing, 1989.

Bakker, Gerben. "The Making of a Music Multinational: Polygram's International Business, 1945–1998." *Business History Review* 80/1 (Spring 2006): 81–123.

Baldwin, James. *The Fire Next Time.* New York: Vintage Books, 1993 [1962].

Banks, Christopher. "A Sense of the Possible: Miles Davis and the Semiotics of Improvised Performance." *Drama Review* 39/3 (Autumn 1995): 41–55.

Barrett, Frank. *Yes to the Mess: Surprising Leadership Lessons from Jazz.* Boston: Harvard Business School Publishing, 2012.

Bart, Peter. *The Gross: The Hits, the Flops; The Summer That Ate Hollywood.* New York: St. Martin's Press, 1999.

Bastien, David, and Todd Hostager. "Jazz as a Process of Organizational Innovation." *Communication Research* 15/5 (October 1988): 582–602.

Bauer, William. *Open the Door: The Life and Music of Betty Carter.* Ann Arbor: University of Michigan Press, 2002.

Beauregard, Robert A. *Voices of Decline: The Postwar Fate of US Cities.* Oxford: Blackwell, 1993.

Benston, Kimberley. *Performing Blackness: Enactments of African-American Modernism.* New York: Routledge, 2000.

Benz, Matthew. "Sentiment Shifts against Messier." *Billboard,* 15 June 2002, 3.

Berendt, Joachim-Erenst, and Günther Huessman. *The Jazz Book: From Ragtime to the 21st Century,* 7th ed. Chicago: Lawrence Hill Books, 2009.

Berenson, Alex. "No Sea Change at Seagram." TheStreet, posted 25 January 1999, www.thestreet.com/story/684822/1/no-sea-change-at-seagram.html (accessed 1 October 2017).

Berg, Bruce. *New York City Politics: Governing Gotham.* New Brunswick, NJ: Rutgers University Press, 2007.

Berg, Chuck. "Dexter Gordon: Making His Great Leap Forward." *Down Beat,* 10 February 1977, 12.

Berlin, Ira. *The Making of African America: The Four Great Migrations.* New York: Viking Penguin, 2010.

Berliner, Paul. *Thinking in Jazz: The Infinite Art of Improvisation.* Chicago: University of Chicago Press, 1994.

Berman, Marshall. *All That Is Solid Melts into Air: The Experience of Modernity.* New York: Simon & Schuster, 1983.

Beunza, Daniel, and Raghu Garud. "Calculators, Lemmings or Frame-Makers? The Intermediary Role of Market Analysts." *Sociological Review* 55, supplement (October 2007): 13–39.

Birnbaum, Larry. Review of *Go West,* by the Village People. *Down Beat,* 21 June 1979, 38.

"Blackout—Chapter 2." *Down Beat,* 6 October 1977, 10.

Bloom, S. "Grover Washington Jr.: Class Act of Commercial Jazz." *Down Beat,* 19 April 1979, 12.

Blumenfeld, Larry. "Blue Note: Still Spry at 70." *Billboard,* 28 March 2009, 26.

Bonilla-Silva, Eduardo. *Racism without Racists: Color-Blind Racism and the Persistence of Racial Inequality in America.* 5th ed. Lanham, MD: Rowman & Littlefield, 2018.

Boonshaft, Peter. *Teaching Music with Promise: Conducting, Rehearsing, and Inspiring*. Galesville, MD: Meredith Music Publications, 2009.

Bowles, Nigel. *Nixon's Business: Authority and Power in Presidential Politics*. College Station: Texas A&M University Press, 2005.

Boyton, Robert. "The Professor of Connection: A Profile of Stanley Crouch." *New Yorker*, 6 November 1995, 113–16.

Brahinski, Rachel. "'Hush Puppies,' Communalist Politics, and Demolition Governance: The Rise and Fall of the Black Fillmore." In *Ten Years That Shook the City: San Francisco 1968–1978*, edited by Chris Carlsson, 141–53. San Francisco: City Lights Books, 2011.

Britt, Stan. *Dexter Gordon: A Musical Biography*. New York: Da Capo Press, 1989.

Brook, Daniel. "Usury Country: Welcome to the Birthplace of Payday Lending." *Harper's*, April 2009, 41–48.

Brown, Wendy. "Neoliberalism and the End of Liberal Democracy." *Theory and Event* 7/1 (2003): n.p., available at Project Muse, https://muse.jhu.edu/article/48659 (accessed 23 October 2017).

Burgin, Angus. *The Great Persuasion: Reinventing Free Markets since the Depression*. Cambridge, MA: Harvard University Press, 2012.

Burns, Ken, director. *Jazz: A Film*. Produced by Joe Thomas. 10 episodes, aired January 2001. DVD, 1140 min. PBS, 2005.

Canaan, Joyce, and Wesley Shumar. "Higher Education in the Era of Globalization and Neoliberalism." In *Structure and Agency in the Neoliberal University*, edited by Joyce Canaan and Wesley Shumar, 1–32. New York: Routledge, 2008.

"Carnival Controversy Continues." *Down Beat*, 11 January 1979, 9.

Caro, Robert A. *The Power Broker: Robert Moses and the Fall of New York*. New York: Alfred A. Knopf, 1974.

Carr, Gary. "Who Shot the Mayor of Fillmore?" *New Fillmore*, 4 September 2014, http://newfillmore.com/2014/09/04/who-shot-the-mayor-of-fillmore (accessed 29 October 2017).

Carson, Charles. "'Bridging the Gap': Creed Taylor, Grover Washington Jr., and the Crossover Roots of Smooth Jazz." *Black Music Research Journal* 28/1 (Spring 2008): 1–15.

Case, Anne, and Angus Deaton. "Rising Mortality and Morbidity in Midlife among White Non-Hispanic Americans in the 21st Century." *Proceedings of the National Academy of Sciences* 112/49 (December 2015): 15078–83.

Castro, Ruy. *Bossa Nova: The Story of the Brazilian Music that Seduced the World*. Chicago: Chicago Review Press, 2000.

Castrone, Linda. "Jazzy Upgrades up and down Fillmore: Resurgent Activity Livens a City Favorite." *Registry: Bay Area Real Estate Journal*, June 2008, 12.

Chamberland, Carol. "The House That Bop Built." *California History* 75/3 (Fall 1996): 272–83.

Chambers, Jack. *Milestones: The Music and Times of Miles Davis*. New York: Da Capo Press, 1998.

Chang, Jeff. *Can't Stop Won't Stop: A History of the Hip-Hop Generation*. New York: St. Martin's Press, 2005.

Chapman, Dale. "A Prehistory of the 'Gig Economy': Jazz Musicians as Independent Contractors in Midcentury American Culture." Paper presented at the Annual meeting of the Society for American Music, Montreal, Canada, March 2017.

Chapman, Jeff. "Tax Increment Financing and Fiscal Stress: The California Genesis." In *Tax Increment Financing and Economic Development: Uses, Structures, and Impact,* edited by Craig Johnson and Joyce Man, 113–36. Albany: State University of New York Press, 2001.

Chapple, Steve, and Reebee Garofalo. *Rock n' Roll Is Here to Pay: The History and Politics of the Music Industry.* Chicago: Nelson-Hall, 1977.

Chevigny, Paul. *Gigs: Jazz and the Cabaret Laws in New York City.* New York: Routledge, 1991.

Christman, Ed. "Is Warner Music Group IPO on the Horizon?" *Billboard,* 15 January 2005, 37.

———. "WMG Speeds into New Era: 1,000 Jobs Going; Fresh A&R Sources Sought." *Billboard,* 13 March 2004, 1, 85.

City Planning Commission, San Francisco. *The Redevelopment of Blighted Areas: Report on Conditions Indicative of Blight and Redevelopment Policies.* San Francisco: City Planning Commission, 1945.

Coates, Ta-Nehisi. "The Case for Reparations." *Atlantic Monthly,* June 2014, 54–71.

———. "Take Down the Confederate Flag—Now." Atlantic.com, 18 June 2015, www.theatlantic.com/politics/archive/2015/06/take-down-the-confederate-flag-now/396290 (accessed 15 August 2016).

Cohen, Cathy. *The Boundaries of Blackness: AIDS and the Breakdown of Black Politics.* Chicago: University of Chicago Press, 1999.

"Columbia Jazz Assault." *Down Beat,* 20 October 1977, 11.

Comaroff, Jean, and John Comaroff. "Millennial Capitalism: First Thoughts on a Second Coming." In *Millennial Capitalism and the Culture of Neoliberalism,* edited by Jean Comaroff and John Comaroff, 1–56. Durham, NC: Duke University Press, 2001.

Conant, Michael. "The Paramount Decrees Reconsidered." In *Hollywood: Critical Concepts in Media and Cultural Studies,* edited by Thomas Schatz, 3: 279–311. New York: Routledge, 2004.

Conant, Ralph, and Daniel Myers. *Towards a More Perfect Union: The Governance of Metropolitan America.* Novato, CA: Chandler and Sharp Publishers, 2002.

Cook, Richard. *Blue Note Records: The Biography.* Boston: Justin, Charles & Company, 2003.

Courrèges, Owen. "Irvin Mayfield's Jazz Market and the Forced Gentrification of Central City." UptownMessenger.com, posted 8 June 2015, http://uptownmessenger.com/2015/06/owen-courreges-irwin-mayfields-jazz-market-and-the-forced-gentrification-of-central-city/ (accessed 28 October 2017).

Corbett, John. *Extended Play: Sounding Off from John Cage to Dr. Funkenstein.* Durham, NC: Duke University Press, 1994.

Crouch, Stanley. "Blues to Be Constitutional: A Long Look at the Wild Wherefores of Our Democratic Lives as Symbolized in the Making of Rhythm and

Tune." In *The Jazz Cadence of American Culture,* edited by Robert O'Meally, 154–65. New York: Columbia University Press, 1998.

Cutler, Kim-Mai. "How Burrowing Owls Lead to Vomiting Anarchists (or SF's Housing Crisis Explained)." TechCrunch, 14 April 2014. http://techcrunch .com/2014/04/14/sf-housing (accessed 23 October 2017).

Daniels, Melissa. "Jazz Education Network Formed to Fill Void Left by IAJE Collapse." JazzTimes.com, 6 June 2008, http://jazztimes.com/articles/24026-jazz-education-network-formed-to-fill-void-left-by-iaje-collapse (accessed 23 October 2017).

Dannen, Frederic. *Hit Men: Power Brokers and Fast Money inside the Music Business.* New York: Vintage Books, 1991.

Dardia, Michael. *Subsidizing Redevelopment in California.* San Francisco: Public Policy Institution of California, 1998.

Davidson, Mark, and Kevin Ward. "'Picking Up the Pieces': Austerity Urbanism, California and Fiscal Crisis." *Cambridge Journal of Regions, Economy, and Society* 7/1 (2014): 81–97.

Davis, Mike. *City of Quartz: Excavating the Future in Los Angeles.* London: Verso, 2006.

Davis, Miles, and Quincy Troupe. *Miles: The Autobiography.* New York: Simon & Schuster, 1989.

Dawtrey, Adam, and Benedict Carver. "Showbiz must face the music: media giants ponder bids for Polygram, EMI."

Dean, Jodi. *Democracy and Other Neoliberal Fantasies: Communicative Capitalism and Left Politics.* Durham, NC: Duke University Press, 2009.

de Barros, Paul. "Taking Control: Maria Schneider Uses a New Model to Distribute Her Music." *Down Beat,* November 2004, 56–59.

DeMuth, Jerry. "Phil Woods: Working More and Enjoying It, No Less." *Down Beat,* 11 January 1979, 14–16.

Dequench, David. "Uncertainty and Economic Sociology: A Preliminary Discussion." *American Journal of Economics and Sociology* 62/3 (July 2003): 509–32.

DeVany, Arthur. *Hollywood Economics: How Extreme Uncertainty Shapes the Film Industry.* New York: Routledge, 2004.

DeVeaux, Scott. *The Birth of Bebop: A Social and Musical History.* Berkeley: University of California Press, 1997.

———. "Constructing the Jazz Tradition: Jazz Historiography." *Black American Literature Forum* 25/3 (Fall 1991): 527–29.

"Dexter Returns." *Down Beat,* 16 December 1976, 11.

"Dirty Loops: Loopified." Dirty Loops, www.dirty-loops.com/about (accessed 23 October 2017).

Downes, Kieran. "'Perfect Sound Forever': Innovation, Aesthetics, and the Remaking of Compact Disc Playback." *Technology and Culture* 51/2 (April 2010): 305–31.

Duménil, Gérard, and Dominique Lévy. *Capital Resurgent: Roots of the Neoliberal Revolution.* Translated by Derek Jeffords. Cambridge, MA: Harvard University Press, 2004.

———. *The Crisis of Neoliberalism.* Cambridge, MA: Harvard University Press 2011.

Eatwell, John, and Lance Taylor. *Global Finance at Risk: The Case for International Regulation*. New York: New Press, 2000.

Echols, Alice. *Hot Stuff: Disco and the Remaking of American Culture*. New York: W. W. Norton, 2010.

Edelman, Lee. *No Future: Queer Theory and the Death Drive*. Durham, NC: Duke University Press, 2004.

Elie, Lolis Eric. "An Interview with Wynton Marsalis." *Callaloo* 13/2 (Spring 1990): 270–90.

Epstein, Gerald. "Financialization, Rentier Interests, and Central Bank Policy." Paper prepared for PERI Conference on the "Financialization of the World Economy." University of Massachusetts, Amherst, 7–8 December 2001.

Erbaş, See S. Nuri, and Chera L. Sayers. 2006. "Institutional Quality, Knightian Uncertainty, and Insurability: A Cross-Country Analysis." Working Paper 06/179 (International Monetary Fund, 2006), www.imf.org/external/pubs/ft/wp/2006/wp06179.pdf (accessed 1 May 2014).

Estes, Chuck. "Contemporary Readers." *Down Beat,* 25 January 1979, 8.

Evans, Nicholas. *Writing Jazz: Race, Nationalism, and Modern Culture in the 1920s*. New York: Garland Publishing, 2000.

Faith, Nicholas. *The Bronfmans: The Rise and Fall of the House of Seagram*. New York: St. Martin's Press, 2006.

Fallico, Peter. "Curson Encore." *Down Beat,* 10 March 1977, 8.

Farber, Erica. "Publisher's Profile: Ron Goldstein." RadioandRecords.com, 14 May 2004, http://radioymusica.com/Profiles/Pages/Goldstein_R.asp (accessed 23 October 2017).

"Fighting for a Right to the City: Collaborative Research to Support Community Organizing in L.A." UCLA Luskin Capstone Project Database. June 2007, https://ucla.app.box.com/s/tsd5py7sbynj187hov9i325eu2d25gba (accessed 23 October 2017).

Fink, Robert. *Repeating Ourselves: American Minimal Music as Cultural Practice*. Berkeley: University of California Press, 2005.

Fischlin, Daniel, et al. *The Fierce Urgency of Now: Improvisation, Rights, and the Ethics of Cocreation*. Durham, NC: Duke University Press, 2013.

Fitsch, Robert. *The Assassination of New York*. New York: Verso, 1993.

Florida, Richard. *The Rise of the Creative Class: And How It's Transforming Work, Leisure, Community, and Everyday Life*. New York: Basic Books, 2002.

Floyd, Samuel L. *The Power of Black Music*. New York: Oxford University Press, 1995.

"Formula: Build for Jazz, Score Pop." *Billboard,* 9 February 1963, 17.

Foster, David. *Hitmaker: Forty Years Making Music, Topping the Charts, and Winning Grammys*. New York: Pocket Books, 2008.

Foucault, Michel. *The Birth of Biopolitics: Lectures at the Collège de France, 1978–79*. Edited by Michel Senellart et al. Translated by Graham Burchell. Basingstoke, England: Palgrave Macmillan, 2008.

Frank, Thomas. *One Market under God: Extreme Capitalism, Market Populism, and the End of Economic Democracy*. New York: Anchor Books, 2001.

———. "TED Talks Are Lying to You." Salon.com, posted 13 October 2013, www.salon.com/2013/10/13/ted_talks_are_lying_to_you (accessed 23 October 2017).

Gabbard, Krin. *Black Magic: White Hollywood and African American Culture.* New Brunswick, NJ: Rutgers University Press, 2004.

———. "Introduction: The Jazz Canon and Its Consequences." In *Jazz among the Discourses,* edited by Krin Gabbard, 1–30. Durham, NC: Duke University Press, 1995.

Gallo, Phil. "Less Verve at U Music." *Daily Variety,* 13 December 2006, 4.

Garrett, Charles Hiroshi. "The Humor of Jazz." In *Jazz/Not Jazz,* edited by David Ake et al., 49–69. Berkeley: University of California Press, 2012.

Garrity, Brian. "Newsline . . . " *Billboard,* 29 July 2000, 112.

———. "Seagram, Vivendi in Buyout Talks." *Billboard,* 24 June 2000, 1, 122.

———. "Vivendi Universal: What Now?" *Billboard,* 22 June 2002, 1, 79.

Geary, Daniel. *Beyond Civil Rights: The Moynihan Report and Its Legacy.* Philadelphia: University of Pennsylvania Press, 2015.

Gebre, Peter. *Making It in America: Conversations with Successful Ethiopian American Entrepreneurs.* Washington, DC: AASBEA Publishers, 2004.

Gelfand, Alexander. "The Great White Hype?" *Jazziz,* December 2001, 40–44.

Gendron, Bernad. "Moldy Figs and Modernists: Jazz at War (1942–1946)." In *Jazz among the Discourses,* edited by Krin Gabbard, 31–56. Durham, NC: Duke University Press, 1995.

Gennari, John. *Blowin' Hot and Cool: Jazz and Its Critics.* Chicago: University of Chicago Press, 2010.

———. "Jazz Criticism: Its Development and Ideologies." *Black American Literature Forum* 25/3 (Autumn 1991): 449–523.

George, Nelson. *The Death of Rhythm and Blues.* New York: Pantheon Books, 1988.

Giddins, Gary. "The Beat Goes On: New Jazz Clubs." *New York,* 10 March 1980, 40–49.

———. "Jazz Turns Neoclassical." *Atlantic Monthly,* September 1982, 156–59.

———. "Verve and Savoy Join Reissue Parade." *Village Voice,* 12 July 1976, 99–100.

———. *Weather Bird: Jazz at the Dawn of Its Second Century.* New York: Oxford University Press, 2004.

Gilbert, Jeremy, and Ewan Pearson. *Discographies: Dance Music, Culture, and the Politics of Sound.* London: Routledge, 1999.

Gilmore, Mikal. Review of *Low,* by David Bowie. *Down Beat,* 9 May 1977, 33.

Gioia, Ted. *The History of Jazz.* 2nd ed. New York: Oxford University Press, 2011.

Gitler, Ira. "Dexter Gordon Loves In." *Radio Free Jazz,* January 1977, 6.

———. "People: New York." *Jazz* 1/3 (Spring 1977): 15.

Glover, David. "Style and Analysis: Jeff 'Tain' Watts." *Modern Drummer,* October 2009, 64.

Gluck, Bob. *You'll Know When You Get There: Herbie Hancock and the Mwandishi Band.* Chicago: University of Chicago Press, 2012.

Goerner, K., and William Woolley. "Contemporary Readers." *Down Beat,* 25 January 1979, 8.

Gold, Michael. "About." Jazz Impact, www.jazz-impact.com/about (accessed 23 October 2017).

———. "World Class Musicians." Jazz Impact, www.jazz-impact.com/who-we-are (accessed 23 October 2017).

Goodman, Fred. *Fortune's Fool: Edgar Bronfman Jr., Warner Music, and an Industry in Crisis*. New York: Simon & Schuster, 2010.

"Goldman Sachs Weighs In on Social Impact Bonds." Governing.com, posted 14 November 2013, www.governing.com/topics/finance/gov-goldman-sachs-weighs-social-impact-bonds.html (accessed 23 October 2017).

Gordon, Dexter. *Sophisticated Giant*. Produced by Michael Cuscuna. CBS Records 34989, 1977.

Gordon, Max. "Confusing Mish Mash." *Down Beat*, 19 October 1978, 9.

Gray, Herman. *Cultural Moves: African Americans and the Politics of Representation*. Berkeley: University of California Press, 2005.

Graybow, Steven. "Jazz Notes: Climbing the Mountain." *Billboard*, 9 March 2002, 39.

———. "Jazz Notes: Downsizing." *Billboard*, 31 May 2003, 18.

Greenberg, Miriam. *Branding New York: How a City in Crisis Was Sold to the World*. New York: Routledge, 2008.

Griffin, Farah Jasmine. *If You Can't Be Free, Be a Mystery: In Search of Billie Holiday*. New York: Free Press, 2001.

Griffin, Farah Jasmine, and Salim Washington. *Clawing at the Limits of Cool: Miles Davis, John Coltrane, and the Greatest Jazz Collaboration Ever*. New York: St. Martin's Press, 2008.

Gross, Mike. "Labels Start New Drive to Aid Down (but Not Out) Jazz." *Billboard*, 30 March 1968, 1, 8.

Haiven, Max. "The Creative and the Derivative: Historicizing Creativity under Post-Bretton Woods Financialization." *Radical History Review* 118 (Winter 2014): 113–38.

Hall, Peter. *Cities of Tomorrow: An Intellectual History of Urban Planning and Design since 1880*. 4th ed. Oxford: Blackwell, 1996.

Hancock, Herbie, and Ron Carter. "Miles and the 1960s Quintet." In *Miles Davis: The Complete Illustrated History*, by Sonny Rollins, Francis Wolff, et al., 130–41. Minneapolis: Voyageur Press, 2012.

"Hank Williams: MGM's Country Tradition." MGM Records advertising supplement, *Billboard*, 21 January 1967, MGM-33.

Hannigan, John. *Fantasy City: Pleasure and Profit in the Postmodern Metropolis*. New York: Routledge, 1998.

Harcourt, Bernard E. *Illusion of Order: The False Promise of Broken Windows Policing*. Cambridge, MA: Harvard University Press, 2001.

Hargrove, Roy, and Antonio Hart. *The Tokyo Sessions*. Compact disc. Produced by Ikuyoshi Hirakawa and Larry Clothier. Novus 01241 63164 2, 1992.

Harper Brothers. *Remembrance: Live at the Village Vanguard*. Compact disc. Produced by Brian Bacchus. Verve Records 841 723–22, 1990.

Harris, Stephon. "There Are No Mistakes on the Bandstand." TED.com, posted December 2011, www.ted.com/talks/stefon_harris_there_are_no_mistakes_on_the_bandstand.html (accessed 23 October 2017).

Hartman, Chester, with Sarah Carnochan. *City for Sale: The Transformation of San Francisco.* Berkeley: University of California Press, 2002.

Hartman, Saidiya. *Scenes of Subjection: Terror, Slavery, and Self-Making in Nineteenth-Century America.* New York: Oxford University Press, 1997.

Harvey, David. *A Brief History of Neoliberalism.* New York: Oxford University Press, 2005.

———. *Rebel Cities: From the Right to the City to the Urban Revolution.* London: Verso, 2012.

———. *Seventeen Contradictions and the End of Capitalism.* New York: Oxford University Press, 2014.

———. *Spaces of Global Capitalism: Towards a Theory of Uneven Geographical Development.* London: Verso, 2006.

Havers, Richard. *Verve: The Sound of America.* London: Thames & Hudson, 2013.

Heble, Ajay, and Mark Laver, eds. *Improvisation and Music Education: Beyond the Classroom.* New York: Routledge, 2016.

Heller, Michael. *Loft Jazz: Improvising New York in the 1970s.* Berkeley: University of California Press, 2017.

Henderson, Joe. *Lush Life.* Compact disc. Produced by Don Sickler and Richard Seidel. Verve Records 314 511 779-2, 1991.

Hentoff, Nat. *At the Jazz Band Ball: Sixty Years on the Jazz Scene.* Berkeley: University of California Press, 2010.

Hershorn, Tad. *Norman Granz: The Man Who Used Jazz for Justice.* Berkeley: University of California Press, 2011.

"HH on LP and CD: A Selected Discography." Herbie Hancock tribute supplement. *Billboard,* 1 May 1999, H-6.

Hitt, Jack. "To Collect and Serve: The Dangers of Turning Police Officers into Revenue Generators." *Mother Jones,* September–October 2015, 5-8.

Ho, Karen. *Liquidated: An Ethnography of Wall Street.* Durham, NC: Duke University Press, 2009.

Hollis, Martin, and Edward Nell. *Rational Economic Man: A Philosophical Critique of Neo-Classical Economics.* Cambridge: Cambridge University Press, 1975.

Holt, Fabian. *Genre in Popular Music.* Chicago: University of Chicago Press, 2007.

Horricks, Raymond. *Profiles in Jazz: From Sidney Bechet to John Coltrane.* New Brunswick, NJ: Transaction Publishers, 1991.

Horsley, Stephanie. "Facing the Music: Pursuing Social Justice through Music Education in a Neoliberal World." In *The Oxford Handbook of Social Justice in Music Education,* edited by Cathy Benedict et al., 62–77. New York: Oxford University Press, 2015.

Hubbard, Freddie. *Bundle of Joy.* Produced by Bert DeCoteaux. Columbia JC 34902, 1977.

———. *The Love Connection.* Produced by Clause Ogerman. Columbia JC 36015, 1979.

Hughes, Walter. "In the Empire of the Beat." In *Microphone Fiends,* edited by Andrew Ross and Tricia Rose, 147–57. New York: Routledge, 1994.

Huyssen, Andreas. *Present Pasts: Urban Palimpsests and the Politics of Memory*. Stanford, CA: Stanford University Press, 2003.

Hyman, Louis. *Debtor Nation: The History of America in Red Ink*. Princeton, NJ: Princeton University Press, 2011.

"Impact Investing: New Orleans Jazz Orchestra, New Orleans, LA." Goldman Sachs, www.goldmansachs.com/what-we-do/investing-and-lending/impact-investing/case-studies/nojo-nola.html (accessed 4 January 2016).

"Industry Q&A: Ron Goldstein." *Jazzweek*, 6 March 2006, 10–13.

International Monetary Fund, 2006. IMF website, www.imf.org/external/pubs/ft/wp/2006/wp06179.pdf (accessed 1 May 2014).

Isoardi, Steve. *The Dark Tree: Jazz and the Community Arts in Los Angeles*. Berkeley: University of California Press, 2006.

Iverson, Ethan. "Interview with Wynton Marsalis (Part 2)." Do the Math. Posted 15 June 2010, https://ethaniverson.com/interviews/interview-with-wynton-marsalis-part-2/ (accessed 23 October 2017).

Jackson, D.D. "Riding The Wave: My Major-Label Journey." *Down Beat*, September 2001, 30–33.

Jackson, Travis. *Blowin' the Blues Away: Performance and Meaning on the New York Jazz Scene*. Berkeley: University of California Press, 2012.

Janowiak, John, and Jason Koransky. "Verve + GRP = Verve Music Group." *Down Beat*, May 1999, 14.

Jasen, Georgette. "Music Propels Chris Washburne from Ohio Farm to Career as Jazz Teacher, Bandleader." Columbia News, posted 8 July 2015, http://news.columbia.edu/content/music-propels-chris-washburne-ohio-farm-career-jazz-teacher-bandleader (accessed 28 October 2017).

"Jazz Mecca Reopens in Copenhagen: One of the World's Great Jazz Clubs to Reopen in Copenhagen." Politiken, 22 February 2010, http://politiken.dk/newsinenglish/art4847960/Jazz-Mecca-reopens-in-Copenhagen (accessed 23 October 2017).

Jeffrey, Don. "Labels' Profit Margin Flat, Study Says: Completion of CD Libraries, Diverging Tastes Blamed." *Billboard*, 26 November 1994, 5.

———. "P'Gram Accepts Seagram Bid: World's Largest Record Company to Result from Merger." *Billboard*, 30 May 1998, 5, 99.

Jeske, Lee. "Scott Hamilton Grew Up in the '70s but Swing's His Thing." *Down Beat*, December 1979, 28–30.

Johnson, Aaron. "Jazz and Radio in the United States: Mediation, Genre, and Patronage." Ph.D. diss., Columbia University, 2014.

Johnson, Kimberley. *Reforming Jim Crow: Southern Politics and State in the Age before Brown*. New York: Oxford University Press, 2010.

Johnson, Walter. *Soul by Soul: Life inside the Antebellum Slave Market*. Cambridge, MA: Harvard University Press, 1999.

Jonathan, Jonah. "Ron Carter: Every Note Counts." Jazz Musicians Voice, interview posted 4 December 2012, www.youtube.com/watch?v=w3Rw1s6L-OA (accessed 23 October 2017).

Kahneman, Daniel, Paul Slovic, and Amos Tversky. *Judgment under Uncertainy: Heuristics and Biases*. Cambridge: Cambridge University Press, 1982.

Kajikawa, Loren. *Sounding Race in Rap Songs*. Berkeley: University of California Press, 2015.

Kalbach, Jim. "Jazz Improvisation as a Model for Radical Collaboration." TEDx Jersey City, 30 March 2015, www.youtube.com/watch?v = j8Gmp194zbI (accessed 23 October 2017).

Kamoche, Ken, and Miguel Pina e Cunha. "Minimal Structures: From Jazz Improvisation to Product Innovation." *Organization Studies* 22/5 (2001): 733–64.

Kao, John. *Jamming: The Art and Discipline of Business Creativity*. New York: HarperCollins, 1996.

Katz, Michael. *The Undeserving Poor: America's Enduring Confrontation with Poverty*. 2nd ed. New York: Oxford University Press, 2013.

Katznelson, Ira. *When Affirmative Action Was White: An Untold History of Racial Inequality in Twentieth-Century America*. New York: W. W. Norton, 2005.

Keepnews, Peter. "The Lionization of Dexter Gordon." *Jazz* 1/4 (Summer 1977): cover image, 29–31.

———. "Rhythm of Revival Is Cautiously Upbeat: It's Never Been Away, but . . . Jazz Is Back!" World of Jazz & Fusion supplement. *Billboard*, 28 June 1986, J-3, J-20.

Kelling, George, and James Wilson. "Broken Windows." *The Atlantic*, March 1982, 29–38.

———. *Fixing Broken Windows: Restoring Order and Reducing Crime in Our Neighborhoods*. New York: Simon & Schuster, 1997.

Kenney, William Howland. *Chicago Jazz: A Cultural History, 1904–1930*. New York: Oxford University Press, 1994.

Khazan, Olga. "Why Are So Many Middle-Aged White Americans Dying?" *The Atlantic*, 29 January 2016, www.theatlantic.com/health/archive/2016/01/middle-aged-white-americans-left-behind-and-dying-early/433863 (accessed 29 October 2017).

Klein, Naomi. *No Logo: Taking Aim at the Brand Bullies*. New York: Picador, 1999.

Kolber, Leo, and Ian MacDonald. *Leo: A Life*. Montreal: McGill-Queens University Press, 2003.

Kotz, David. *The Rise and Fall of Neoliberal Capitalism*. Cambridge, MA: Harvard University Press, 2015.

KQED. "Fillmore Timeline." PBS, www.pbs.org/kqed/fillmore/learning/time.html (accessed 6 April 2015).

Knight, Frank. *Risk, Uncertainty, and Profit*. Boston: Houghton Mifflin, 1921.

Krims, Adam. *Music and Urban Geography*. New York: Routledge, 2007.

Lai, Clement. "The Racial Triangulation of Space: The Case of Urban Renewal in San Francisco's Fillmore District." *Annals of the Association of American Geographers* 102/1 (2012): 151–70.

Landes, Emily. "If You Rename It, Will They Come?" *San Francisco Apartment Magazine*, November 2006.

Langley, Paul. *The Everyday Life of Global Finance: Saving and Borrowing in Anglo-America*. New York: Oxford University Press, 2008.

Langlois, Richard, and Metin Cosgel. "Frank Knight on Risk, Uncertainty, and the Firm: A New Interpretation." *Economic Inquiry* 31 (July 1993): 456–65.

LaRosa, David. "Jazz Has Become the Least-Popular Genre in the U.S." TheJazzLine.com, posted 9 March 2015, http://thejazzline.com/news/2015/03/jazz-least-popular-music-genre (accessed 23 October 2017).

Laver, Mark. "Freedom of Choice: Jazz, Neoliberalism, and the Lincoln Center." *Popular Music and Society* 37/5 (2014): 538–56.

———. "Improvise!™: Jazz Consultancy and the Aesthetics of Neoliberalism." *Critical Studies in Improvisation* 9/1 (2013), Criticalimprov.com, www.criticalimprov.com/article/view/2897/3229 (accessed 28 October 2017).

———. *Jazz Sells: Music, Marketing, and Meaning.* New York: Routledge, 2014.

Lawrence, Tim. *Love Saves the Day: A History of American Dance Music Culture, 1970–1979.* Durham, NC: Duke University Press, 2003.

Lazonick, William. "The Quest for Shareholder Value: Stock Repurchases in the US Economy." *Louvain Economic Review* 74/4 (2008): 479–540.

LeBlanc, Larry. "Bronfman Assures Shareholders about P'Gram Deal." *Billboard,* 14 November 1998, 3, 90.

Lefebvre, Henri. *Writings on Cities.* Translated and introduced by Eleonore Kofman and Elizabeth Lebas. Oxford: Blackwell, 1996.

Leffall, Christy, et al. "Redevelopment: After the Fall." *Race, Poverty, and the Environment* 19/1 (2012): 57–59.

"Legendary Tenor Saxophonist Joe Henderson Joins Verve Records' Jazz Roster." Verve Records press release, September 1991, "Joe Henderson" folder, artist files, Institute of Jazz Studies, Rutgers University, Newark.

Lemke, Thomas. "'The Birth of Biopolitics'—Michel Foucault's Lecture at the Collège de France on Neoliberal Governmentality." *Economy and Society* 30/2 (May 2001): 190–207.

Less, David. Review of *Mr. Gone,* by Weather Report. *Down Beat* 11 January 1979.

Levenson, Jeff. "Emerging Jazz Artists Learn Art of the Deal." *Billboard,* 2 April 1994, 1, 72.

———. "McBride Gets to It with Verve Release." *Billboard,* 7 January 1995, 1, 108.

Levy, Jonathan. *Freaks of Fortune: The Emerging World of Capitalism and Risk in America.* Cambridge, MA: Harvard University Press, 2010.

Lewis, George. "Experimental Music in Black and White: The AACM in New York, 1970–1985." In *Uptown Conversations: The New Jazz Studies,* edited by Robert G. O'Meally 50–101. New York: Columbia University Press, 2004.

——— *A Power Stronger Than Itself: The AACM And American Experimental Music.* Chicago: University of Chicago Press, 2008.

Lichten, Eric. *Class, Power, and Austerity: The New York City Fiscal Crisis.* Amherst, MA: Greenwood Press, 1986.

Liggins, Hassahn. "Smokey Robinson Signs with Verve Music Group to Release First-of-Its-Kind Duets Album." RadioFacts.com, posted 28 March 2013, www.radiofacts.com/smokey-robinson-signs-with-verve-music-group-to-release-first-of-its-kind-duets-album (accessed 23 October 2017).

Limb, Charles. "Your Brain on Improv." Presentation for TEDx Mid Atlantic, November 2010, www.ted.com/talks/charles_limb_your_brain_on_improv?language = en (accessed 23 October 2017).

Lipiczky, Thom. "Tihai Formulas and the Fusion of 'Composition' and 'Improvisation' in North Indian Music." *Musical Quarterly* 71/2 (1985): 157–71.

Lipschultz, Jeremy Harris, and Michael L. Hilt. *Crime and Local Television News: Dramatic, Breaking, and Live from the Scene.* Manwah, NJ: Lawrence Erlbaum Associates, 2003.

LiPuma, Edward, and Benjamin Lee. *Financial Derivatives and the Globalization of Risk.* Durham, NC: Duke University Press, 2004.

Litt, Jeff. "Stop the Carnival." *Down Beat,* 16 November 1978, 8.

Lundvall, Bruce, Gary Giddins, and Joe Lovano. "Blue Note at 70: Behind an Iconic Label." CUNY Media, posted 17 November 2009, www.youtube.com/watch?v=1m7Ft-cBRWs (accessed 23 October 2017).

Lusby, Neil. "And What Is Jazz, Then?" *Down Beat,* 21 December 1978, 8.

Machlin, Paul. *Stride: The Music of Fats Waller.* Boston: Twayne Publishers, 1985.

MacNab, Geoffrey. "Rushes: News: Comeback Kid." *Sight and Sound,* August 2011, 6.

Macnie, Jim. "Trend Spotting: Requiem for a Straight Line." *Billboard,* 28 June 1997, 31, 34.

———. "Verve's Shorter Living 'High Life.'" *Billboard,* 9 September 1995, 1, 130.

Magro, Anthony. *Contemporary Cat: Terence Blanchard with Special Guests.* Lanham, MD: Scarecrow Press, 2002.

Makunda, Gautam. "The Price of Wall Street's Power." *Harvard Business Review* (June 2014), https://hbr.org/2014/06/the-price-of-wall-streets-power (accessed 2 October 2017).

Mandel, Howard. "Matthew Shipp: My Feature for *The Wire,* 1998." Jazz beyond Jazz, posted 19 April 2013, www.artsjournal.com/jazzbeyondjazz/2013/04/matthew-shipp-my-feature-for-the-wire-1998.html (accessed 24 October 2017).

Margolis, Bob. "Ravi Coltrane, Dave Douglas, Others in Limbo after BMG Shakeup." MTV.com, posted 13 June 2000, www.mtv.com/news/971968/ravi-coltrane-dave-douglas-others-in-limbo-after-bmg-shakeup (accessed 24 October 2017).

Marsalis, Wynton. *Marsalis Standard Time Vol. 1.* Compact disc. Columbia, CK 40461. 1987.

Martin, Randy. *An Empire of Indifference: American War and the Financial Logic of Risk Management.* Durham, NC: Duke University Press, 2007.

———. *Financialization of Daily Life.* Philadelphia: Temple University Press, 2002.

Masters, Mark. *No Wave.* London: Black Dog Publishing, 2007.

Mawad, Marie, and Amy Thompson. "Vivendi Takes M&A Pause to Decide How to Spend $14 Bln." Bloomberg.com, posted 22 November 2013, www.bloomberg.com/news/2013-11-21/vivendi-takes-m-a-pause-to-decide-how-to-spend-14-billion-cash.html (accessed 24 October 2017).

McClary, Susan. *Rap, Minimalism, and Structures of Time in Twentieth-Century Music.* Lincoln: University of Nebraska Press, 1998.

McMullen, Tracy. "Identity for Sale: Glenn Miller, Wynton Marsalis, and Cultural Replay in Music." In *Big Ears: Listening for Gender in Jazz Studies,* edited by Nichole Rustin and Sherrie Tucker, 129–56. Durham, NC: Duke University Press, 2008.

Mercer, Michelle. *Footprints: The Life and Work of Wayne Shorter.* New York: Penguin Books, 2007.

Mettler, Suzanne. *Soldiers to Citizens: The G.I. Bill and the Making of the Greatest Generation.* New York: Oxford University Press, 2005.

Miles Davis Quintet. *Live in Europe, 1967 (The Bootleg Series, Vol. 1).* Compact disc. Columbia Records, CBS 88697 94053, 2011.

Miller, Clara. "Social Impact Bonds' Slippery Slope." HuffingtonPost.com, posted 9 February 2016, www.huffingtonpost.com/clara-miller/social-impact-bonds-slipp_b_7170474.html (accessed 24 October 2017).

Miller, Leta. "Racial Segregation and the San Francisco Musicians' Union." *Journal of the Society for American Music* 1/2 (May 2007): 161–206.

Miller, Paul. *The Postwar Struggle for Civil Rights: African Americans in San Francisco, 1945–1975.* New York: Routledge, 2010.

Milonakis, Dimitris, and Ben Fine. *From Political Economy to Economics: Method, the Social, and the Historical in the Evolution of Economic Theory.* Abingdon, England: Routledge, 2009.

Mirowski, Philip. *Never Let a Serious Crisis Go to Waste: How Neoliberalism Survived the Financial Meltdown.* London: Verso, 2013.

Mitchell, Gail. "The Real Deal." *Billboard,* 3 April 2010, 35.

Monson, Ingrid. *Freedom Sounds: Civil Rights Call Out to Jazz and Africa.* New York: Oxford University Press, 2010.

———. *Saying Something: Jazz Improvisation and Interaction.* Chicago: University of Chicago Press, 1994.

Moody, Kim. *From Welfare State to Real Estate: Regime Change in New York City, 1974 to the Present.* New York: New Press, 2007.

"Moody's Confirms Ba1 on Successor Agency to the San Francisco RDA (CA) TABs." Moodys.com, posted 5 September 2013, www.moodys.com/research/Moodys-Confirms-Ba1-on-Successor-Agency-to-the-San-Francisco--PR_281717 (accessed 24 October 2017).

Moore, Andrea. "Neoliberalism and the Musical Entrepreneur." *Journal of the Society for American Music* 10/1 (February 2016): 33–53.

Morgenstern, Dan. "Caught in the Act: Miles Davis." *Down Beat,* 13 January 1966, 32.

Morris, Chris. "Jazz Lives Thanks to Handful of Vets." *Billboard,* 7 July 2001, 1, 68–69.

———. "Jazz Seeks Instrumental Stars: Lack of Industry Support for Young Player Reaches Crisis Level." *Billboard,* 20 April 2002, 1, 81.

———. "Joe Henderson Leaves Jazz Legacy." *Billboard,* 14 July 2001, 8, 59.

"Mr. Gone." *Down Beat,* 22 February 1979, 12.

Muniesa, Fabian. "A Flank Movement in the Understanding of Valuation." *Sociological Review* 59, supplement (December 2011): 24–38.

Myers, Marc. "Interview: Creed Taylor (Part 12)." JazzWax, posted 5 November 2008, www.jazzwax.com/2008/11/interview-cre-2.html, Internet Archive, https://web.archive.org/web/20150905151843/http://www.jazzwax.com/2008/11/interview-cre-2.html (accessed 26 October 2017).

Negus, Keith. *Music Genres and Corporate Cultures*. London: Routledge, 1999.

Neilson, A. "A New Metaphor for Strategic Fit: All That Jazz." *Leadership and Organization Development Journal* 13/5 (1992): 3–6.

Nero, Charles I. "Diva Traffic and Male Bonding in Film: Teaching Opera, Learning Gender, Race, and Nation." *Camera Obscura* 19/2 (2004): 47–73.

"The New Orleans Jazz Orchestra (NOJO) Kicks Off the Grand Opening of the People's Health New Orleans Jazz Market." Goldman Sachs, posted 3 April 2015, www.goldmansachs.com/what-we-do/investing-and-lending/impact-investing/case-studies/nojo-multimedia/press-release.pdf (accessed 24 October 2017).

Newman, Melinda. "Sanborn Joins Verve Music Group: Friendship with LiPuma, Musical Vision Lure Sax Player from Elektra." *Billboard,* 9 December 2000, 99.

Nicholson, Stuart. *Is Jazz Dead? (Or Has It Moved to a New Address)*. New York: Routledge, 2005.

———. *Jazz: The 1980s Resurgence*. New York: Da Capo Press, 1995.

Nolan, Herb. Review of *Small Change,* by Tom Waits, *Down Beat,* 24 February 1977, 26.

"Now's the Time for All New Recordings from a Vintage Label." PolyGram Classics press release, n.d., "PolyGram" folder, record label files, Institute of Jazz Studies, Rutgers University, Newark.

Obenhaus, Mark, and Yvonne Smith, producers. *Miles Ahead: A Tribute to Miles Davis*. New York: WNET/Thirteen and Obenhaus Films in association with Channel 4 Television, London, 1986.

Oda, Meredith Akemi. "Remaking the 'Gateway to the Pacific': Urban, Economic, and Racial Redevelopment in San Francisco, 1945–1970." Ph.D. diss., University of Chicago, 2010.

"Official: David Foster Named Chairman of Verve Music Group." Hollywood Reporter, posted 15 December 2011, www.hollywoodreporter.com/news/official-david-foster-named-chairman-274299 (accessed 24 October 2017).

"OKeh—Artists." Okeh Records, www.okeh-records.com/artists (accessed 24 October 2017).

Oliver, Melvin, and Thomas Shapiro. *Black Wealth / White Wealth: A New Perspective on Racial Inequality*. 10th anniversary ed. New York: Routledge, 2006.

O'Meara, Caroline. "New York Noise: Music in the Post-Industrial City, 1978–1985." Ph.D. diss., University of California, Los Angeles, 2006.

Ouellette, Dan. "All Those Vocals: More Singers in Labels' Jazz Mix." *Billboard,* 20 September 2003, 5, 80.

———. "Hancock Plays Playboy Fest: Indies Go for Verve Acts." *Billboard,* 12 June 2004, 13.

———. "Verve Hopes Callum Has That 'Something.'" *Billboard,* 15 May 2004, 11–12.

Palley, Thomas. *Financialization: The Economics of Finance Capital Domination*. Basingstoke, England: Palgrave Macmillan, 2013.

Palmer, Don. "The New Jazz Majors." *Musician*, February 1986.

Panken, Ted. "The Right Groove: Creed Taylor." *Down Beat*, October 2005, 58–61.

———. "25 Years at Blue Note: Bruce Lundvall Reflects on a Quarter-Century at the Helm of Jazz's Most Storied Label." Jazziz, posted 17 June 2009, www.jazziz.com/interviews/2009/06/17/bruce-lundvall, Internet Archive, https://web.archive.org/web/20120602144206/http://www.jazziz.com/interviews/2009/06/17/bruce-lundvall (accessed 26 October 2017).

Paoletta, Michael. "Brazilian Girls Forecast: Catching On, with Verve." *Billboard*, 29 January 2005, 5, 11–12.

Parks, Mara. "Shifting Ground: The Rise and Fall of the Los Angeles Community Redevelopment Agency." *Southern California Quarterly* 86/3 (Fall 2004): 241–90.

Pasmore, William. "Organizing for Jazz." *Organization Science* 9/5 (September–October 1998): 562–68.

Patterson, James. *Freedom Is Not Enough: The Moynihan Report and America's Struggle over Black Family Life; From LBJ to Obama*. New York: Basic Books, 2010.

Payne, Chris. "Sarah McLachlan Signs to Verve: New Album 'Shine On' Coming May 6." Billboard.com, 30 January 2014, www.billboard.com/articles/news/5892795/sarah-mclachlan-signs-to-verve-new-album-shine-on-coming-may-6 (accessed 26 October 2017).

Peers, Martin. "Street Toasts Deal: Seagram Stock Climbs; Analyst Reactions Mixed." *Daily Variety*, 26 May 1998, 6.

Pellegrinelli, Lara. "Separated at 'Birth': Singing and the History of Jazz." In *Big Ears: Listening for Gender in Jazz Studies*, edited by Nichole Rustin and Sherrie Tucker, 31–47. Durham, NC: Duke University Press, 2008.

———. "Singing for Our Supper." *Jazz Times*, December 2003, 56–62.

Penchansky, Alan. "Mercury Kills Emarcy Twofers." *Billboard*, 25 February 1978, 64.

———. "Polygram: Classics on Digital." *Billboard*, 27 December 1980, 38.

Pepin, Elizabeth, and Lewis Watts. *Harlem of the West: The San Francisco Fillmore Jazz Era*. San Francisco: Chronicle Books, 2006.

Pettinger, Peter. *Bill Evans: How My Heart Sings*. New Haven, CT: Yale University Press, 1998.

"Philips: A Brighter Future?" *Economist*, 13 August 1994, 60, 63.

PolyGram NV. Prospectus for initial public offering, 14 December 1989, David Kronemyer, www.kronemyer.com/Polygram/PolyGram%20Prospectus%20 12-14-1989.pdf (accessed 30 August 2014; link no longer active).

Porter, Eric. "Introduction: Rethinking Jazz through the 1970s." *Jazz Perspectives* 4/1 (April 2010): 1–5.

———. *What Is This Thing Called Jazz? African American Musicians as Artists, Critics, and Activists*. Berkeley: University of California Press, 2002.

Porter, Lewis. *John Coltrane: His Life and Music*. Ann Arbor: University of Michigan Press, 1998.

Prassad, Monica. *The Politics of Free Markets: The Rise of Neoliberal Economic Policies in Britain, France, Germany, and the United States.* Chicago: University of Chicago Press, 2006.

Primack, Bret. "Dave Holland: Diverse and Dedicated." *Down Beat,* 18 May 1978, 18–20, 46.

———. "The Heath Brothers: Bebop above and beyond the Fads." *Down Beat,* 22 March 1979, 16–17, 36–39.

———. "Herbie Hancock: Chameleon in His Disco Phase." *Down Beat,* 17 May 1979, 12.

———. "Playing Favorites." *Jazz Times,* May 1998, 86, 176.

Prouty, Ken. "Finding Jazz in the Jazz-as-Business Metaphor." *Jazz Perspectives* 7/1 (2013): 31–55.

———. *Knowing Jazz: Community, Pedagogy, and Canon in the Information Age.* Jackson: University of Mississippi Press, 2011.

Provine, Doris Marie. *Unequal under Law: Race in the War on Drugs.* Chicago: University of Chicago Press, 2007.

"Punk Comes to Village Gate." *Down Beat,* 6 October 1977, 10

Purcell, Mark. "Excavating Lefebvre: The Right to the City and Its Urban Politics of the Inhabitant." *GeoJournal* 58/2–3 (2002): 99–108.

Radano, Ronald. *Lying Up a Nation: Race and Black Music.* Durham, NC: Duke University Press, 2003.

———. *New Musical Figurations: Anthony Braxton's Cultural Critique.* Chicago: University of Chicago Press, 1993.

Ramos-Zayas, Ana Y. *Street Therapists: Race, Affect, and Neoliberal Personhood in Latino Newark.* Chicago: University of Chicago Press, 2012.

Ratliff, Ben. *Coltrane: The Story of a Sound.* New York: Farrar, Strauss and Giroux, 2007.

Reynolds, Simon. *Rip It Up and Start Again: Postpunk, 1978–1984.* New York: Penguin Books, 2006.

Riley, Glenn. "Disco in Perspective." *Down Beat,* 6 September 1979, 8

Robb, Gregory. "Going the Distance: March-April 2004." Allaboutjazz.com, posted 8 March 2004, www.allaboutjazz.com/going-the-distance-march-april-2004-by-gregory-j-robb.php#.VCclASldVhM (accessed 26 October 2017).

Roberts, Michael James. *Tell Tchaikovsky the News: Rock 'n Roll, the Labor Question, and the Musician's Union, 1942–1968.* Durham, NC: Duke University Press, 2014.

Rodriguez, Peter, et al. "Government Corruption and the Entry Strategies of Multinationals." *Academy of Management Review* 30/2 (April 2005): 383–96.

Rose, Tricia. *Black Noise: Rap Music and Black Culture in Contemporary America.* Middletown, CT: Wesleyan University Press, 1994.

Rosen, Craig. "GRP Recording Co. Shuffles Executives, Aims for Wide Appeal." *Billboard,* 9 May 1998, 6, 84.

Rosenman, Mark. "Why Let Financial Institutions Profit from Financing Services for the Needy?" *Chronicle of Philanthropy,* 12 December 2013, https://philanthropy.com/article/Why-Let-Financial-Institutions/153901 (accessed 26 October 2017).

Rosenthal, Caroline. *New York and Toronto Novels after Postmodernism.* Rochester, NY: Camden House, 2011.

Ross, Michael E. "Why Are Black Folks Leaving San Francisco?" TheRoot.com, posted 6 May 2009, www.theroot.com/articles/culture/2009/05/why_are_black_folks_leaving_san_fran.1.html, Internet Archive, https://web.archive.org/web/20160523002627/www.theroot.com/articles/culture/2009/05/why_are_black_folks_leaving_san_fran.1.html (accessed 26 October 2017).

Ross, Stephen, and John Yinger. *The Color of Credit: Mortgage Discrimination, Research Methodology, and Fair-Lending Enforcement.* Cambridge, MA: MIT Press, 2002.

Rothstein, William. *Public Health and the Risk Factor: A History of an Uneven Medical Revolution.* Rochester, NY: University of Rochester Press, 2003.

"Ruben Studdard to Release New CD Unconditional Love on Verve Records, Feb. 4th." PR Newswire, 18 November 2013, www.prnewswire.com/news-releases/ruben-studdard-to-release-new-cd-unconditional-love-on-verve-records-feb-4th-232328521.html (accessed 27 October 2017).

Sagalyn, Lynne B. *Times Square Roulette: Remaking the City Icon.* Cambridge, MA: MIT Press, 2003.

Saillant, John. "The Black Body Erotic and the Republican Body Politic, 1790–1820." *Journal of the History of Sexuality* 5/3 (January 1995): 403–28.

Sales, Grover. *Jazz: America's Classical Music.* New York: Da Capo Press, 1984.

Salmon, John, and Frank Gambino. "Carnival Controversy Continues." *Down Beat,* 11 January 1979, 9.

Sancton, Thomas. "Horns of Plenty." *Time,* 22 October 1990, 64–71.

Sandler, Adam. "U Music Group Picks New Leaders." *Daily Variety,* 15 June 1998, 1.

———. "Universal Will Boot 3,000." *Daily Variety,* 11 December 1998, 1.

San Francisco Historic Preservation Committee. "Landmark Designation Report: Marcus Books/Jimbo's Bop City, 1712–1716 Fillmore Street." City and County of San Francisco Planning Department, 13 February 2014, www.sf-planning.org/ftp/files/Preservation/landmarks_designation/Final_Adopted_LM_DesignationReport_266_Marcus.pdf (accessed 26 October 2017).

San Francisco Mayor's Office of Housing and Community Development. "Certificate of Preference Program Frequently Asked Questions." San Francisco Mayor's Office of Housing and Community Development, http://sfmohcd.org/sites/default/files/FileCenter/Documents/7515-COPP_FAQs_120513.pdf (accessed 26 October 2017).

San Francisco Office of Community Investment and Infrastructure. "Final Workshop on the Long-Range Property Management Plan Pursuant to Section 34191.5 of Assembly Bill 1484." San Francisco Office of Community Investment and Infrastructure, 5 November 2013, attachment 6, http://sfocii.org/sites/default/files/ftp/meetingarchive/commission/www.sfocii.org/modules/5cWorkshopMemoAtt6-documentid = 5683.pdf (accessed 26 October 2017).

———. "Final Workshop on the Long-Range Property Management Plan Pursuant to Section 34191.5 of Assembly Bill 1484." San Francisco Office of Community Investment and Infrastructure, 5 November 2013, attachment

7, http://sfocii.org/sites/default/files/ftp/meetingarchive/commission/www.sfocii .org/modules/5cWorkshopMemoAtt7-documentid = 5684.pdf (accessed 26 October 2017).

———. Informational Memorandum, Attachment 3. "Recent Communications Between OCII/City and FDC's Investor Group." San Francisco Office of Community Investment and Infrastructure, 23 September 2013, 3–4, http:// sfocii.org/sites/default/files/ftp/meetingarchive/oversight_board/sfocii.org /modules/InfoMemoAttachment3-Fillmore-documentid = 5366.pdf (accessed 26 October 2017).

San Francisco Office of the Controller, City Services Auditor. "San Francisco Redevelopment Agency: Audit of Seven Programs in the Western Addition A-2 Redevelopment Plan." San Francisco Office of the Controller, 20 December 2011, http://sfcontroller.org/sites/default/files/FileCenter/Documents/2799-SFRA%20Western%20Addition%20Report%202012–20–11.pdf (accessed 27 October 2017).

San Francisco Planning and Housing Association. *Blight and Taxes*. San Francisco: San Francisco Planning and Housing Association, 1947.

San Francisco Redevelopment Agency. Agenda item 4(h), San Francisco Office of Community Investment and Infrastructure, 19 June 2005, http://sfocii .org/ftp/archive/sfarchive.org/index4c4f.html?dept = 1051&sub = &dtype = 3456&year = 6157&file = 62342 (accessed 27 October 2017).

———Memorandum, Agenda item 4(a), meeting of 13 January 2009, http:// sfocii.org/sites/default/files/ftp/archive/sfarchive.org/indexoe3b.html (accessed 27 October 2017).

———. "Minutes of a Regular Meeting of the Redevelopment Agency of the City and County of San Francisco." Archive.org, https://archive.org/stream /73minutesregular2009sanf/73minutesregular2009sanf_djvu.txt (accessed 19 April 2017).

Sanjek, Russell. *American Popular Music and Its Business: The First Four Hundred Years: Volume III, from 1900 to 1984*. New York: Oxford University Press, 1988.

Sassen, Saskia. *The Global City: New York, London, Tokyo*. Princeton, NJ: Princeton University Press, 1991.

Savan, Leslie. *The Sponsored Life: Ads, TV, and American Culture*. Philadelphia: Temple University Press, 1994.

Saxe, Frank. "Clear Channel's Sights on Web." *Billboard*, 16 September 2000, 7, 92.

Schneckloth, Tim. Review of *Studio Tan*, by Frank Zappa, *Down Beat*, 11 January 1979, 24.

Schrag, Peter. *Paradise Lost: California's Experience, America's Future*. Rev. ed. Berkeley: University of California Press, 2004.

Schram, Sanford. *The Return of Ordinary Capitalism: Neoliberalism, Precarity, Occupy*. New York: Oxford University Press, 2015.

Schulman, Bruce. *The Seventies: The Great Shift in American Culture, Society, and Politics*. New York: Da Capo Press, 2002.

Schulman, Bruce, and Julian Zelizer, eds. *Rightward Bound: Making America Conservative in the 1970s*. Cambridge, MA: Harvard University Press, 2008.

Schumpeter, Joseph A. *Capitalism, Socialism, and Democracy*. 6th ed. With an introduction by Richard Swedberg. London: Routledge, 2006.

"Sector Study: California Redevelopment and Tax Allocation Bonds." Paper issued by the National Public Finance Guarantee, January 2010.

Seilbron, Johan, and Sander Quak. "Changing Labor Policies of Transnational Corporations: The Decrease and Polarization of Corporate Social Responsibility." In *The Transformation of Solidarity: Changing Risks and the Future of the Welfare State,* edited by Romke van der Meen et al., 139–64. Amsterdam: Amsterdam University Press, 2012.

Self, Robert. *American Babylon: Race and the Struggle for Postwar Oakland.* Princeton, NJ: Princeton University Press, 2003.

Seligman, Amanda. *Block by Block: Neighborhoods and Public Policy on Chicago's West Side.* Chicago: University of Chicago Press, 2005.

Shaw, Arnold. Review of *Animal,* by Pink Floyd. *Down Beat,* 5 May 1977, 24, 28.

Shefrin, Hersh. *Beyond Greed and Fear: Understanding Behavioral Finance and the Psychology of Investing.* New York: Oxford University Press, 2002.

Shiller, Robert. *Irrational Exuberance.* 2nd ed. New York: Broadway Books, 2005.

"Shlomo Benartzi: Saving for Tomorrow, Tomorrow." Allianzgi.com, posted November 2011, http://befi.allianzgi.com/en/befi-tv/Pages/shlomo-benartzi.aspx (accessed 28 October 2017).

Shorto, Russel. "The Industry Standard." *New York Times Magazine,* 3 October 2004, 50–58.

Sidran, Ben. *Talking Jazz: An Oral History.* New York: Da Capo Press, 1995.

"The Single, Most Beautiful American Car." *American Heritage,* November 1996, 6.

"Size Does Matter." *Economist,* 23 May 1998, 57.

Smith, Jeremy. "'Sell It Black': Race and Marketing in Miles Davis's Early Fusion Jazz." *Jazz Perspectives* 4/1 (April 2010): 7–33.

"Social Impact Bonds." GoldmanSachs.com, posted October 2014, www.goldmansachs.com/our-thinking/pages/social-impact-bonds.html (accessed 28 October 2017).

Solis, Gabriel. *Thelonious Monk Quartet with John Coltrane at Carnegie Hall.* New York: Oxford University Press, 2014.

"Sony Classical Relaunching OKeh Records Jazz Imprint." Billboard.com, posted 11 January 2013, www.billboard.com/biz/articles/news/retail/1484243/sony-classical-relaunching-okeh-records-jazz-imprint (accessed 27 October 2017).

"Soundtracks Are Big Business." MGM Records advertising supplement, *Billboard,* 21 January 1967, MGM44.

Sparks, Mitchell. *Charging Back Up the Hill: Workplace Recovery after Mergers, Acquisitions, and Downsizings.* San Francisco: Jossey-Bass, 2003.

Squires, David, and David Blumenthal. "Mortality Trends among Working-Age Whites: The Untold Story." Commonwealth Fund, January 2016, www.commonwealthfund.org/publications/issue-briefs/2016/jan/mortality-trends-among-middle-aged-whites (accessed 27 October 2017).

Stephans, Michael. *Experiencing Jazz: A Listener's Companion.* Lanham, MD: Scarecrow Press, 2013.

Stern, Linda. "How to Jazz Up Innovation." *Newsweek,* 14 November 2005, E4.

Steven Restivo Event Services. "Fillmore Jazz Festival." Steven Restivo Event Services, www.sresproductions.com/events/fillmore-jazz-festival/ (accessed 19 April 2017).

Stewart, Alexander. *Making the Scene: Contemporary New York City Big Band Jazz.* Berkeley: University of California Press, 2007.

Stovall, Tyler. "The Fire This Time: Black Expatriates and the Algerian War." *Yale French Studies* 98 (2000): 182–200.

Stowe, David. *Swing Changes: Big-Band Jazz in New Deal America.* Cambridge, MA: Harvard University Press, 1994.

Strapko, Bruno E. "Punk Backlash," *Down Beat,* 5 October 1978, 8.

Strunk, Steven. "Notes on Harmony in Wayne Shorter's Compositions, 1964–67." *Journal of Music Theory* 49/2 (Fall 2005): 301–32.

Such, David. *Avant-Garde Jazz Musicians: Performing "Out There."* Iowa City: University of Iowa Press, 1993.

Sudhalter, Richard. *Lost Chords: White Musicians and Their Contributions to Jazz, 1915–1945.* New York: Oxford University Press, 1999.

Sugrue, Thomas. *The Origins of the Urban Crisis: Race and Inequality in Postwar Detroit.* Princeton, NJ: Princeton University Press, 2014 [1996].

Sutherland, Sam. "The Compact Impact: Carving Renaissance Out of Technology." *Billboard,* 28 June 1986, N-3, N-21, N-22.

———. "PolyGram Classics Jazzing It Up: New Verve Reissue Series Debuted; Midlines Planned." *Billboard,* 4 December 1982, 6, 44.

———. "Reactivation of Verve Line Sparks PolyGram Catalog." *Billboard,* 14 November 1981, 4, 53.

Sutherland, Sam, and Peter Keepnews. "Blue Notes." *Billboard,* 27 July 1985, 58, 73.

Szalai, Georg. "Universal Music Completes $1.9 Million EMI Recorded Music Acquisition." HollywoodReporter.com, 28 September 2012, www.billboard.com/biz/articles/news/1083616/universal-completes-19-billion-emi-recorded-music-acquisition (accessed 27 October 2017).

Szwed, John. *So What: The Life of Miles Davis.* New York: Simon & Schuster, 2004.

Taibbi, Matt. "The Great American Bubble Machine." *Rolling Stone,* 5 April 2010.

Taylor, Timothy. *Music and Capitalism: A History of the Present.* Chicago: University of Chicago Press, 2016.

"Taylor to Do Job on Verve's Image under MGM Pres." *Billboard,* 1 May 1967.

Tennille, Andy. "Yoshi's San Francisco: Sushi and Standards." *Jazz Times,* January–February 2008, 37–38.

Thaler, Richard, and Hersh Shefrin. "An Economic Theory of Self-Control." *Journal of Political Economy* 89/2 (April 1981): 392–406.

Tiegel, Eliot. "Coexistence of Pure Jazz and Fusion to Continue." *Billboard,* 7 January 1978, 3, 102.

———. "Interim MGM Plans Summarized by Fruin." *Billboard,* September 22, 1973, 1, 62.

Tschmuck, Peter. *Creativity and Innovation in the Music Industry.* Berlin: Springer Verlag, 2012.

"UMG Creates Verve Label Group, Danny Bennett to Lead." Billboard.com, 19 May 2016, www.billboard.com/articles/news/7377729/umg-verve-label-group-danny-bennett (accessed 27 October 2017).

"Universal Music Group Expands Verve Music with Appointment of Grammy Award-Winning Producer, Songwriter, and Artist, David Foster." Universal Music Group, 15 December 2011, www.universalmusic.com/corporate /detail/867, Internet Archive, https://web.archive.org/web/20140822165502 /www.universalmusic.com/corporate/detail/867 (accessed 27 October 2017).

"Universal Music Group Forms Verve Label Group." Universal Music, post 19 May 2016, www.universalmusic.com, www.universalmusic.com/universal-music-group-forms-verve-label-group (accessed 27 October 2017).

"Universal: One Year Later; Merger behind It, UMG Looks Ahead." Billboard, 25 December 1999, 5, 78, 80.

"Universal U.K. to Make Staff Cuts." Billboard.com, 22 January 2004, www .billboard.com/biz/articles/news/1447266/universal-uk-to-make-staff-cuts (accessed 27 October 2017).

Urban School of San Francisco. Telling Their Stories: Oral History Archives Project. Tellingstories.org, 12 May 2007, http://tellingstories.org/fillmore/leola _king/index.html (accessed 14 April 2017).

U.S. Department of Education, National Commission on Excellence in Education. A Nation at Risk: The Imperative for Educational Reform. Washington, DC: Government Printing Office, 1983.

U.S. Department of Labor, Office of Policy Planning and Research. The Negro Family: A Case for National Action. By Daniel Patrick Moynihan. Washington, DC: United States Government Printing Office, 1965.

Vallas, Steven. "Rethinking Pos-Fordism: The Meaning of Workplace Flexibility." Sociological Theory 17/1 (March 1999): 68–101.

"Verve Gets Jimmy Smith." Billboard, 9 February 1963, 3.

"Verve Live Series Set." Billboard, 20 September 1986, 6.

Verve Records Publicity Brochure. Verve Records folder, record company files, Institute of Jazz Studies, Rutgers University, Newark.

"Verve's Marketing Moves to London Administration." Billboard, 10 January 1981, 4.

Von Eschen, Penny. Satchmo Blows Up the World: Jazz Ambassadors Play the Cold War. Cambridge, MA: Harvard University Press, 2009.

Von Glahn, Drew, and Caroline Whistler. "Pay for Success Programs: An Introduction." Policy and Practice, June 2011, 19–22.

Waddell, Ray. "Concert Outlook Bright as Biz Weighs Mega-Merger: SFX/ Clear Channel Concerns Raised." Billboard, 11 March 2000, 1, 82.

Waldron, Clarence. "Dr. George Butler, Retired Jazz Record Executive, Dies." Jet, 5 May 2008, 37.

Walser, Robert. "'Out of Notes': Signification, Interpretation, and the Problem of Miles Davis." In Jazz among the Discourses, edited by Krin Gabbard, 165–88. Durham, NC: Duke University Press, 1995.

Walsh, Carmen. "West Coast Hip: A New York City Music Label Shows Off Its L.A. Connections with a Redesign." Office21, Spring 2006.

Waters, Keith. *The Studio Recordings of the Miles Davis Quintet, 1965–68.* New York: Oxford University Press, 2011.

Weber, Rachel. "Extracting Value from the City: Neoliberalism and Urban Development." *Antipode* 34/3 (July 2002): 519–40.

West, Michael. "Dave Douglas' Greenleaf Music Label: Defining Success in Today's Online Music Biz." Jazztimes.com, posted 11 November 2012, http://jazztimes.com/articles/58950-dave-douglas-greenleaf-music-label (accessed 27 October 2017).

Whayne, Jeannie M. *A New Plantation South: Land, Labor, and Federal Favor in Twentieth-Century Arkansas.* Charlottesville: University Press of Virginia, 1996.

White, Adam. "A New Universal Emerges as a Global Force: Morris' Team Puts Plan into Action." *Billboard,* 19 December 1998.

White, Adam, and Melinda Newman. "Inside EMI's New Leadership Strategy." *Billboard,* 27 October 2001, 1, 96.

Wilf, Eitan. *School for Cool: The Academic Jazz Program and the Paradox of Institutionalized Creativity.* Chicago: University of Chicago Press, 2014.

"Will Disco Stranglehold Choke Off Black Music?" *Jet,* 10 May 1979, 22, 24.

Wilson, Olly. "The Heterogenous Sound Ideal in African-American Music." In *Signifyin(g), Sanctifyin', and Slam Dunking,* edited by Gena Dagel Caponi, 157–71. Amherst: University of Massachusetts Press, 1999.

Wilson-Smith, Anthony. "Seagram's Shift in Direction." *Macleans,* 16 November 1998, www.thecanadianencyclopedia.ca/en/article/seagrams-shift-in-direction (accessed 27 October 2017).

Wolfe, Patrick. "Settler Colonialism and the Elimination of the Native." *Journal of Genocide Research* 8/4 (December 2006): 387–409.

Wong, Herb. "Terence Blanchard: Joyful Jazz Journeys." *Jazz Educators Journal* 34/2 (September 2001): 36–40, 42, 44–47.

Woods, Clyde. *Development Arrested: The Blues and Plantation Power in the Mississippi Delta.* London: Verso, 1998.

Yanow, Scott. "Retro: Boxing with the Past." *Jazziz,* September 1998, 68–70.

Yarling, John. "Disgusting Funk." *Down Beat,* 10 March 1977, 8.

Zhito, Lee. "M-G-M Buys Verve; Maxin Tops Combo." *Billboard,* 21 November 1960, 2, 22.

Zipp, Samuel. *Manhattan Projects: The Rise and Fall of Urban Renewal in Cold War New York.* New York: Oxford University Press, 2010.

Zukin, Sharon. *Loft Living: Culture and Capital in Urban Change.* New Brunswick, NJ: Rutgers University Press, 1989.

Index